THE
SOUTH CAROLINA
COOK BOOK

REVISED EDITION

Collected and edited by the
South Carolina Extension Homemakers Council
and the Clemson Extension Home Economics staff

UNIVERSITY OF SOUTH CAROLINA PRESS
COLUMBIA, SOUTH CAROLINA

Revised Edition

Copyright © 1953 by the South Carolina Council of Farm Women
Copyright © 1954 by the University of South Carolina Press

First Printing, 1954 (hardcover)
Second Printing, 1969 (hardcover)
Third Printing, 1973 (comb-bound)
Fourth Printing, 1975 (comb-bound)
Fifth Printing, 1977 (paperback)
Sixth Printing, 1982 (paperback)

International Standard Book Number: 0-87249-354-7
Library of Congress Catalog Card Number: 54-4697
Manufactured in the United States of America

CONTENTS

ACKNOWLEDGMENTS

Appreciation is expressed to the committee of the Home Demonstration Department of the South Carolina Extension Service for collecting, checking, and compiling recipes; and for planning and editing the material: Miss Janie McDill, chairman; Miss Sallie A. Pearce, Miss Margaret Martin, Miss Curtys Ballentine, Miss Georgia Taylor, and Miss Annie Rogers, and to the secretarial staff of the department,

To the members of the South Carolina Council of Farm Women for furnishing recipes and to their committee composed of Mrs. Earle Myers, chairman; Mrs. Cosby Newton, Mr. H. G. Wright, Mrs. J. A. Riley for handling the finances,

To South Carolina business firms for funds for the publication of illustrations used in the Cook Book as follows:

Allen Brothers Milling Company, Columbia, South Carolina; Colonial Stores, Inc., Columbia, South Carolina; Greenwood Packing Company, Greenwood, South Carolina; Hollywood Produce Company, Hollywood, South Carolina; South Carolina Frozen Foods Association, Clemson, South Carolina; South Carolina Peach Growers Association, Spartanburg, South Carolina; South Carolina Poultry Improvement Association, Lancaster, South Carolina; South Carolina Turkey Association; to the Atlantic and Pacific Tea Company, District Office Charlotte, North Carolina, for assistance in designing the cover of the Cook Book.

To firms for providing glossy prints for the illustrations used in the Cook Book as follows:

Admiral Corporation, Chicago, Illinois; The Borden Company, New York, New York; Charles B. Knox Gelatine Company, Inc., Johnston, New York; Corn Products Company, New York, New York; Evaporated Milk Association, Chicago, Illinois; General Mills, Minneapolis, Minnesota; Fostoria Glass Company, Moundsville, West Virginia; H. J. Heinz Company, Pittsburgh, Pennsylvania; Kraft Foods Company, Chicago, Illinois; Libby, McNeil and Libby, Chicago, Illinois; National Dairy Council, Chicago, Illinois; National Livestock and Meat Board, Chicago, Illinois; Poultry and Egg National Board, Chicago, Illinois; United States Fish and Wildlife Service, Washington, D. C.; Wheat Flour Institute, Chicago, Illinois; Winthrop College News Service, Rock Hill, South Carolina,

To agencies for educational material used in the Cook Book, as follows:

Alabama Extension Service, Auburn, Alabama; Bureau of Human Nutrition and Home Economics, United States Department of Agriculture, Washington, D. C.; National Home Economics Association, Washington, D. C.

PREFACE TO REVISED EDITION

The University of South Carolina makes this book available to the general public because a large group of South Carolina women have requested it. First printed in 1953, almost the entire supply was immediately bought by members of the South Carolina Council of Farm Women and private subscribers. The few remaining copies served only to invite orders that could not be filled for others who wanted to try these well-tested recipes which utilize local products in traditional style.

South Carolina has been noted for its good food and hospitality for many, many years. Yet, the attempt to find this food or even to discover a dependable recipe has been most discouraging.

Generally, the young people in the public schools and colleges are exposed to foods that grow in other parts of the country. The turnip greens, collards, mustard greens, hominy grits, corn meal, soft wheat flour, sweet potatoes, butter beans—all of which can be had plentifully from the fields and gardens of South Carolina—have not had their well-deserved recognition in the familiar commercial menus and in the cook books which everybody can buy. The abundant seafoods and fresh-water fish have been neglected in the same manner.

Therefore, this revised edition of the South Carolina Cook Book is presented in a new format, with some changes in text and some new recipes, so that the city people of this state and others who are interested in good food may have an opportunity to try out the traditional foods which have been tested and found excellent.

For the most part the recipes in the first edition of the Cook Book have been reprinted from the type in which they were originally set. Members of the Home Demonstration Department of the South Carolina Extension Service selected them from hundreds sent in from the forty-six counties of South Carolina. A specialist with breads gave her attention to that section, an expert with meat concentrated on that part, and so on for each division. Thus, the recipes which usually came out of private homes were given a professional touch before they appeared in book form.

Good food served properly has been one of the most important factors in civilization everywhere and from ancient to modern times has been the subject of thoughtful comment. "Men that have a communion in nothing else, can sympathetically eat together, can still rise into some glow of brotherhood over food and wine," observed Thomas Carlyle in *The French Revolution;* and Samuel Pepys had the same idea when he recorded in his *Diary,* "Strange to see how a good dinner and feasting reconciles everybody."

More recently, the late Charles W. Eliot, who was president of Harvard, noted that "Taking food and drink is a great enjoyment for healthy people, and those who do not enjoy eating seldom have much capacity for enjoyment or usefulness of any sort." There is also the conclusion drawn by philosopher Will Durant: "Cease to feed a man, and soon his reactions will stop. Feed him properly, and he becomes virtuous and patriotic; feed him wrongly, and you can make him an invalid, a criminal, a pessimist, an idiot, a believer in free will. Measure a man's activity from birth to death; it will correspond almost precisely with the energy in the nourishment he has received." Then, there is the psalmist who exhorts the people to praise the Lord "who satisfied thy mouth with good things; so that thy youth is renewed like the eagle's."

—The Publisher.

INTRODUCTION

The People of South Carolina possess a rich heritage in recipes that were handed down by their ancestors from England, Scotland, Ireland, France, and Germany. In addition, typically southern recipes have been developed to use products produced in the state, such as corn meal, grits, sweet potatoes, turnip greens, collards, peaches, melons, fresh water fish, and sea foods. These recipes have helped to make South Carolina well known for its excellent cookery.

The purpose in preparing the cook book was not only to present many of the recipes used in the state but also to provide the principles of cooking which preserve food value and quality of the foods. In spite of the modern homemaker's need to use partially prepared or prepared products, the average person still takes pride in producing his or her home prepared dishes, which retain a personal touch that these recipes permit. The recipes are a combination of dishes from old colonial cookery and dishes from more recent years.

The South Carolina Cook Book was jointly prepared by the members of the South Carolina Extension Homemakers Council (formerly the South Carolina Council of Farm Women) and the Clemson Extension Home Economics staff. Several hundred members of the Extension Homemakers Council contributed their favorite recipes to compose the greater part of the cook book, while the remainder have come from interested persons throughout the state. Thus a variety of recipes are offered to the experienced and the amateur cooks who wish to improve their culinary arts and add variety to their meals. Recipes not ordinarily found in cook books, such as souse meat, hush puppies, red rice, liver pudding, pine bark fish stew, Clemson okra, and sugar pie are included.

Also included is information on weights, measures, substitutions, food values and how to preserve them, guides to meal planning, and table setting and service. The user of this cook book will find it a source for frequent reference.

The cook book committees hope that you make daily use of the cook book in preparing wholesome, nutritious meals for your family. Brides have found a copy of it a welcome wedding gift to be used as a guide in developing their skills in selecting, preparing, and serving balanced meals.

It is hoped that the *South Carolina Cook Book* will become your favorite collection of recipes.

1969

RUBY CRAVEN
State Extension Home Economics Leader

BRIEF HISTORY OF THE SOUTH CAROLINA COUNCIL OF EXTENSION HOMEMAKERS

The Extension Homemakers Council was organized in 1921; however, over the forty-seven years of its existence, the name has been changed from its original name, the South Carolina Council of Farm Women, to the South Carolina Home Demonstration Council, and it now operates under the name of the South Carolina Extension Homemakers Council.

Over the years it has operated in much the same manner, since it has been composed of Extension Homemakers Clubs throughout the state. These clubs are organized into County Councils. The purpose of the State Council is to develop, strengthen, and correlate the work of the county councils in the state in their efforts to assist women in promoting all interests pertaining to higher standards of living in homes and communities. The state council represents the common interests of the county councils in planning cooperative educational work, and in working with extension representatives in determining all statewide policies.

The state council meets annually. Programs are developed to help women keep abreast of state and national affairs.

Extension Homemakers clubs are organized by Extension Home Economists, in natural communities, and hold monthly meetings. Officers are elected to serve three years, and committee chairmen are appointed to help develop the yearly programs of work.

The South Carolina Extension Homemakers Council is affiliated with The National Extension Homemakers Council, The Country Women's Council of U.S.A., The Associated Country Women of the World, and The South Carolina Council for the Common Good.

Members of the council who have served as National or Regional officers are: Mrs. W. T. Humphries, Southern Regional Director, National Extension Homemakers Council; Mrs. Crosby Newton, Southern Regional Director, National Extension Homemakers Council; Mrs. C. D. Sowell, National Legislative Chairman; and Mrs. F. N. Culler, National Citizenship Chairman. Mrs. W. E. Cochran is now serving as Secretary of The Country Women's Council.

Throughout its existence the organization has been assisted by the Extension Service, and much has been accomplished under the splendid leadership of: Miss Lonnie I. Landrum, Miss Harriet Layton, Miss

Juanita Neely, Miss Jane G. Ketchen, Mrs. Sallie Pearce Musser, and our present advisor, Dr. Ruby Craven.

In its forty-seven years, the Council has had fourteen presidents:

* Mrs. Bradley Morrah   Mrs. O. J. Smyrl
* Mrs. L. C. Chappell   Mrs. Gordon Blackwell
 Mrs. E. W. McElmurray   * Mrs. M. H. Lineberger
* Mrs. J. Whitman Smith   Mrs. Irvin Hawthorne
* Mrs. J. L. Williams   Mrs. F. N. Culler
 Mrs. Landrum Sellers   Mrs. W. E. Cochran
 Mrs. C. D. Sowell   Mrs. J. A. Seaber, Sr.

* *Deceased*

Mrs. John A. Seaber
President, South Carolina
Extension Homemakers Council

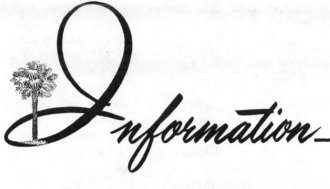

MEASURES—WEIGHTS—SUBSTITUTES

Measures

4 ounces equal ¼ pound

16 ounces equal 1 pound

3 teaspoons equal 1 tablespoon

4 tablespoons equal ¼ cup

8 tablespoons equal ½ cup

16 tablespoons equal 1 cup

2 cups equal 1 pint

4 cups equal 1 quart

Comparing Weights and Measures

Material	Measure	Weight
Butter	1 tablespoon	½ ounce
Butter	2 cups	1 pound
Chocolate	1 square	1 ounce
Cocoa	2 tablespoons	1 ounce
Cornmeal	3 cups	1 pound
Cornstarch	1 cup	4½ ounces
Eggs	1	2 ounces
Medium	8–10	1 pound
Whites	8–10	1 cup
Yolks	12–14	1 cup
Flour (sifted)	1 cup	4 ounces
	4 cups	1 pound
Lard	2 cups	1 pound
Milk (whole)	1 cup	8½ ounces
Molasses (cane)	1 cup	12 ounces
Oats, rolled	1 cup	2¾ ounces
Oil	1 tablespoon	2/5 ounce
Orange juice	1 cup	8 ounces
Peanuts (shelled)	1 cup	5½ ounces

Pecans (shelled)	1 cup	5 2/3 ounces
Raisins	1 cup	5 1/3 ounces
Salt	2 tablespoons	1 ounce
Sugar:		
Confectioner's	1 cup	4½ ounces
Brown	1 cup	5½ ounces
Granulated	1 cup	8 ounces
Gelatin	3 tablespoons	1 ounce

Careful Measuring

All measurements for the recipes in this book are level. You will be more successful in your cooking if you learn always to measure ingredients accurately.

Flour. Flour should always be sifted before measuring. Place the dry measuring cup on a flat surface. Lift flour lightly into the cup to prevent packing. Fill cup to overflowing and level off with a spatula.

Sugar. Sift sugar before measuring if it contains lumps. Use same procedure as for flour.

Brown Sugar. Pack firmly into the measuring cup and level off with a knife or spatula.

Fat—Butter. If you do not have ¼–½ and 1/3 cup size measuring cups, you may quickly measure those amounts of solid fat in a cup measure by partly filling the cup with water. For example, if you want 1/3 cup of fat, fill a cup with water to the 2/3 cup mark. Then add fat until the water level reaches the 1 cup mark.

Liquids. Liquids are measured in standard measuring cup with an extended lip to prevent spilling. Place measure on level surface. Read with the eye on level with markings on measure.

Baking Powder, Salt, Spices. Use standard measuring spoons. Heap ingredients up in the spoon. Level off with a spatula.

Equivalent Substitutions

1 tablespoon flour ....½ tablespoon cornstarch

1 cup cake flour ....⅞ cup hard wheat, all purpose flour

1 cup corn syrup ....1 cup sugar plus ¼ cup liquid, when syrup used replace half of the sugar

1 cup honey ....1 to 1¼ cup sugar plus ¼ cup liquid

1 ounce chocolate ....3–4 tablespoons cocoa plus ½ tablespoon fat

1 cup butter . . . . .1 cup margarine

⅞ to 1 cup hydrogenated fat plus ½ teaspoon salt

⅞ cup lard plus ½ teaspoon salt

⅞ cup rendered fat plus ½ teaspoon salt

1 teaspoon baking powder . .¼ teaspoon soda and ½ teaspoon cream of tartar

The following table gives the sweetening power of different syrups and honey, as compared with refined white sugar:

1 cup honey . . . . .sweetness equal to 1 cup of refined white sugar

1½ cups sorghum syrup . . . .sweetness equal to 1 cup of refined white sugar

1½ cups cane syrup . . . . .sweetness equal to 1 cup of refined white sugar

2 cups corn syrup . . . . .sweetness equal to 1 cup of refined white sugar

DEFINITIONS

Bake. To cook by dry heat; usually done in an oven. When applied to meats it is called roasting.

Barbecue. To roast an animal slowly on a gridiron, or over coals in a specially prepared trench. The animal may be left whole or cut in pieces. While cooking, it is basted with a highly seasoned sauce.

Baste. To moisten meat or other food while cooking to add flavor and to prevent drying of the surface. The liquid is usually melted fat, meat drippings, water, or water and fat.

Beat. To make a mixture smooth or to introduce air by using a brisk, regular motion that lifts the mixture over and over.

Blanch (precook). To pretreat in boiling water or steam. Used to inactivate enzymes and shrink food for canning, freezing, and drying.

Blend. To mix thoroughly two or more ingredients.

Boil. To cook in water or a liquid in which bubbles rise continually and break on the surface. The boiling temperature at sea level is 212 degrees Fahrenheit.

Braise. To brown meat or vegetables in a small amount of fat, then to cook slowly in a covered utensil in a small amount of liquid.

Bread. To coat with bread crumbs alone, or to coat with bread crumbs, then with slightly beaten egg or milk, and again with crumbs.

Broil. To cook by direct heat. Grill.

Candy. (1) When applied to fruit, fruit peel, or ginger, to cook in a heavy syrup until plump and transparent, then drain and dry. Product is also known as crystallized fruit, fruit peel, or ginger. (2) When applied to sweet potatoes and carrots, the term means to cook in sugar or syrup.

Caramelize. To heat sugar or foods containing sugar until a brown color and characteristic flavor develop.

Chop. To cut into pieces with a sharp tool.

Cream. To work one or more foods until soft and creamy, using the hands or a spoon or other implement. Applied to fat and sugar in place of blend.

Cut. (1) To divide food materials with a knife or scissors. (2) To incorporate fat into dry ingredients with the least amount of blending.

Dice. To cut into cubes.

Dredge. To sprinkle or coat with flour or other fine substance.

Fold. To combine by using two motions, cutting vertically through the mixture and turning over and over by sliding the implement across the bottom of the mixing bowl with each turn.

Fricassee. To cook by braising; usually applied to fowl, rabbit or veal cut into pieces.

Fry. To cook in fat; applied especially (1) to cooking in a small amount of fat, also called saute or pan-fry and (2) to cooking in deep fat, also called deep-fat frying.

Glace. To coat with a thin sugar syrup cooked to the crack stage. When used for pies and certain types of bread the mixture may contain thickening but is not cooked to such a concentrated form, or it may be uncooked.

Grill. See Broil.

Grind. To reduce to particles by cutting, crushing, or grinding.

Knead. To manipulate with a pressing motion accomplished by folding and stretching.

Lard. To insert strips of fat into or to place slices of fat on top of uncooked lean meat or fish to give flavor and prevent dryness.

Marinate. To treat with a marinade (an oil-acid mixture which is usually a kind of salad dressing).

Melt. To liquefy by heat.

Mince. To cut or chop into very small pieces.

Mix. To combine ingredients in any way that effects a distribution.

Pan-broil. To cook uncovered on a hot surface, usually a frying pan. The fat is poured off as it accumulates.

Pan-fry. To cook in a small amount of fat. See fry.

Parboil. To boil until partially cooked. The cooking is usually completed by another method.

Parch. To brown by means of dry heat.

Pare. To cut off the outside covering. To peel.

Pasteurize. To treat liquids such as milk and fruit juices with heat from 140 to 180 degrees Fahrenheit.

Peel. To strip off the outside covering.

Poach. To cook in a hot liquid, using precautions to retain shape. The temperature used varies with the food.

Render. To free fat from connective tissue by means of heat.

Roast. To bake; applied to certain foods, such as meats. See bake.

Saute. To brown or cook quickly in a small amount of fat, with frequent turning. See Fry.

Scald. (1) To heat a liquid to just below the boiling point. (2) To dip poultry in moderately hot, not boiling water, to loosen feathers before picking.

Scallop. To bake food, usually cut in pieces, with a sauce or other liquid. The top is commonly covered with crumbs. The food and sauce may be mixed together or arranged in alternate layers in the baking dish, with or without crumbs.

Sear. To brown the surface of meat by a short application of intense heat; used to develop flavor and improve appearance, although shrinkage is increased.

Simmer. To cook in a liquid at a temperature of about 185 degrees. Bubbles form slowly and break below the surface.

Steam. To cook in steam with or without pressure. The steam may be applied directly to the food, as in a steamer or pressure cooker.

Steep. To allow a substance to stand in liquid below the boiling point for the purpose of extracting flavor, color, or other qualities.

Stew. To simmer or boil in a small quantity of liquid. When applied to meat, simmering temperature is used.

Stir. To mix food materials with a circular motion for the purpose of blending or securing a uniform consistency.

Toast. To brown by means of direct heat.

Whip. To beat rapidly to produce expansion, due to incorporation of air. Applied to cream, eggs, and gelatin dishes.

TEMPERATURES AND TIME TABLES

Deep-Fat Frying

Use a deep kettle half filled with fat or oil. Heat and test. The temperature is important because the fat must be hot enough to form a coating on the food instantly but not too hot, for this will cook the outside before the inside is done. (See deep-fat frying temperatures). Fry a small amount of food at a time and, when golden brown, drain on brown paper. Test fat from time to time during the frying process.

Clarifying Fat. Cool fat after using and clarify by cooking in it a few slices of potato. Heat slowly; cook potatoes until slightly brown. Remove potatoes, strain, and cool. Fats may thus be used a number of times.

To Egg and Crumb. Dry bread, roll, sift, and season. Beat eggs until yolks and whites are mixed. Add 1 tablespoonful of milk or water to each egg. Roll food in crumbs, dip into egg, drain, and roll in crumbs again. Put aside until ready to fry.

Deep-Fat Frying

Type of Product	Temperature of Fat Degrees F.	Approx. Time Required to Brown a 1-inch Cube of Bread in the Hot Fat Seconds
Doughnuts		
Fritters		
Oysters, scallops, soft shell crabs	350 to 375	60
Fish		
Croquettes		
Egg plant		
Onions	375 to 385	40
Cauliflower		
French fried potatoes	385 to 395	20

Terms Commonly Used to Describe Oven Temperatures

Term	Temperature Degrees F.
Very slow	250 to 300
Slow	325
Moderate	350 to 375
Moderately hot	400
Hot	425 to 450
Very hot	475 to 500

TIME-TABLE FOR ROASTING

Kind of Roast	Oven Temperature	Internal Temperature	Approximate Min. per Pound
Beef Ribs (Standing)	300° F.		
Rare		140° F.	18–20
Medium		160° F.	22–25
Well-done		170° F.	27–30
Beef Ribs (Rolled)	300° F.	Add 10 min. per lb. to above	
Pork (Fresh)	350° F.		
Loin, 3–4 pounds		185° F.	35
Shoulder		185° F.	30–35
Ham		185° F.	30–35
Butt		185° F.	50–55
Pork (Cured)	300° F.		
Ham, 10–12 pounds		170° F.	25
Half ham		170° F.	30
Large ham		170° F.	20
Tender ham		150° F.	15–20
Lamb	300° F.	180° F.	30–35
Veal	300° F.	170° F.	25–30

BROILING MEATS

Steak 1 inch thick (medium done)	8–10 minutes
Steak 1 inch thick (well done)	12–15 minutes
Steak 2 inches thick	35–40 minutes
Lamb chops ¾ inch thick	10–15 minutes
Lamb chops 1½ to 2 inches thick	25-30 minutes
Pork chops, single	20 minutes
Veal chops, breaded or floured	40–45 minutes
Ham (cured) ½ inch thick	20 minutes
Ham (cured) 1 inch thick	30 minutes

Bacon—Broiled or pan broiled

1. Place strips of bacon in cold pan and place over moderate flame. Turn frequently and drain fat as it develops. Cook until crisp.

2. Place strips of bacon on rack of broiler in moderate oven. Turn bacon and cook until crisp.

Although broiling time varies with weight and thickness of the bird, the table below may help in estimating the cooking time.

Bird	Dressed Weight of Bird, Pounds	Time Minutes Per Pound
Chicken	2	35–45
Turkey	4	60–75
Squab	¾–1	30–40
Guinea	1–1½	35–45
Duckling	2–2½	35–45

ROASTING POULTRY AND FISH

	Pounds	Temperature	Time
Chicken	4–5	325°F.	3½ hrs.
Duck	3½–5	325°F.	2–2½ hrs.
Goose	10–12	325°F.	3½–4 hrs.
Guinea	2–2½	325°F.	2 hrs.
Turkey	6–8	325°F.	3¾–4½ hrs.
	8–10	325°F.	4–4½ hrs.
	10–12	325°F.	4½–5 hrs.
	12–14	325°F.	5–5¼ hrs.
	14–16	325°F.	5¼–6 hrs.
	16–18	325°F.	6–6½ hrs.
	18–20	325°F.	6½–7½ hrs.
	20–24	325°F.	7½–9 hrs.
Fish - whole	4	325–350°F.	40–60 min.
Fish - fillets		325–350°F.	25–30 min.

SUGAR TEMPERATURE TESTS

Temperature	Test	Use
230–234° F.	Spins thread	Syrup
234–240° F.	Soft ball	Fudge, Fondant
240–248° F.	Firm ball	Caramels
250–266° F.	Hard ball	Divinity, Popcorn balls
270–290° F.	Soft crack	Taffies
290–310° F.	Hard crack	Brittle
330– ° F.		Caramelize

QUANTITY AND SERVINGS OF FOOD

Vegetables	Quantity	No. Servings	Approximate Size of Serving
Asparagus	1 lb. 16–20 stalks	3–4	4–5 stalks
Beans (green snap)	1 lb. (2 1/3 to 3 cups cooked)	5	½ cup
Beans Lima (in pod)	1 lb. (2/3 cup shelled)	2	½ cup
Beans Lima (canned)	1 no. 2 can	5	½ cup
Beans Lima (dried)	1 lb. (2 1/3 cups uncooked)	10–12	½ cup
Beans Navy (dried)	1 lb. 2–2 1/3 cups uncooked)	8–10	½ cup
Beets	1 lb. (2 to 3 large beets)	3–4	½ cup
Beets (canned)	1 no. 2 can	4–5	½ cup
Broccoli	1 bunch (1½ to 2½ lbs. raw)	4–6	2 stalks
Brussels Sprouts	1 lb. (1 quart or less)	5–6	½ cup
Cabbage (shredded)	1 lb. (½ small head, 4 cups shredded)	7	½ cup
Cabbage (cooked)	1 lb. (½ small head)	4–5	½ cup
Carrots (raw, shredded)	1 lb. (5–6 medium carrots)	8	½ cup
Carrots (raw, shredded, cooked)	1 lb. (5–6 medium carrots)	5	½ cup
Cauliflower	1 lb. (1½ cups)	2–3	½ cup
Collards	1 lb. leaves	3–4	½ cup
Corn (ears)	12 medium, 3 cups cut	6	½ cup
Egg Plant	1 lb., 4½ cups diced 11 slices, (½ inch)	4–5	½ cup
Greens (spinach, turnip greens, etc.)	1 lb.	3–4	½ cup
Onions	1 lb., 3 large	4	½ cup
Peas (in pod)	1 lb. (1 cup shelled)	2	½ cup
Peas, split, dried	1 lb. about 2 cups, 4 cups cooked	6–8	½ cup
Potatoes, sweet	1 lb., 3 medium	3	1 potato, med.
Potatoes, white	1 lb., 3 medium—2½ cups (mashed)	3	1 potato, med.
Rutabaga	1 lb., 2 2/3 cups diced	4	½ cup
Squash, summer	1 lb. (2 cups cooked)	3–4	½ cup
Tomatoes	1 lb. (2–5 tomatoes) 1 lb. raw—16 slices	3–4 cooked	½ cup
Turnips	1 lb. (3 medium)	3–4	½ cup

Canned Vegetables and Fruits	No. Servings	Approximate Size of Serving
8 ounce can	2	½ cup
No. 2 can	4–5	½ cup
No. 2½ can	6–7	½ cup
No. 3 cylinder (46 oz.)	11–12	½ cup

Frozen		
Family size packages	3–4	½ cup
Juices, concentrated, 6 fluid ounces	6	½ cup

Fruits (Fresh)

For apples, bananas, oranges and pears count on about 3 to a pound
Peaches—about 4 to a pound
Berries—1 quart (3½ cups, whole) 4–5 servings
Cranberries—1 lb. or 1 qt., 16 servings of ⅛ cup
Lemons—1 dozen medium, 3 lbs., 1 pint juice
Oranges—1 dozen medium, 6 lbs. 1 quart juice
Apples—1 lb. 1½ cups apple juice

Fruits (Dried)

	Quantity	No. and Size of Servings
Apples, dried ..	1 pound	3 (½ cup)
Peaches	1 pound (3 cups)	12 (½ cup)
Prunes	1 pound (2½ cups)	8 (½ cup)
Raisins	1 lb. (3 cups) seedless (2½ cups) seeded	

Cereals

Bread	1 pound (12–16 slices)	
Corn Flakes	18–24 cups as purchased	20 (4/5 cup)
Corn meal (as mush)	1 pound (3 cups)	25 (2/3 cup)
Hominy grits	1 pound (2½ cups)	15 (2/3 cup)
Rice	1 pound (2¼ cups)	12 (2/3 cup)
Macaroni	1 pound (4–5 cups)	18 (2/3 cup)
Noodles	1 pound (6–8 cups)	18 (2/3 cup)
Rolled oats	1 pound (5 cups)	12 (2/3 cup)
Spaghetti	1 pound (4–5 cups)	15 (2/3 cup)

Dairy Products

Kind	Quantity and Amount	No. and Size of Servings
Butter	1 pound, 2 cups	48 squares
Cheese, American .	1 pound, 4 cups grated	depends on use
Cheese, Cottage ..	1 pound, 2 cups	depends on use
Cream, coffee	1 pint, 2 cups (32 tablespoons)	25 (for coffee)
Cream, whipping..	1 pint, 2 cups	4 cups whipped, 25 servings
Milk	1 quart, 4 cups	
Milk, condensed ..	1 can (15 ozs.) 1½ cups	= 2½ cups milk plus 8 tablespoons sugar

Kind	Quantity and Amount	No. and Size of Servings
Milk, evaporated ..	1 can (14½ ozs.) 1 2/3 cups	= 3 1/3 cups milk
Dry, whole milk ..	1 pound, 3½ cups	= 3½ quarts milk
Non-fat, dry milk solids	1 pound, 4 cups	= 5 quarts of milk
Ice cream	1 quart, 4 cups	Serves 6–8

Meat, Poultry, Fish

Meat	Amount to Buy Per Serving
Much bone or gristle	1/2 to 1 pound
Medium amounts of bone	1/3 to 1/2 pound
Little bone	1/4 to 1/3 pound
No bone	1/5 to 1/4 pound

Poultry, Dressed Weight

Chicken:

Broiling	1/4 to 1/2 bird
Frying and roasting	3/4 to 1 pound
Stewing	1/3 to 3/4 pound
Ducks	1 to 1 1/4 pounds
Geese	3/4 to 1 pound
Turkeys	2/3 to 3/4 pound

Poultry, Ready to Cook Weight

Chicken:

Broiling	1/4 to 1/2 bird
Frying, roasting	2/3 to 3/4 pound
Stewing	1/4 to 2/3 pound
Ducks	3/4 to 1 pound
Geese	2/3 to 3/4 pound
Turkeys	About 1/2 pound

Fish

Whole or round	1 pound
Dressed, large	1/2 pound
Steaks, fillets	1/4 pound

Meal Planning

Planning meals is a big job. It is a responsible job. What the family eats is vital to family health and important to happiness. If meal planning is your job you have a four-point program:

1. To give enjoyable meals.
2. To keep your family well nourished.
3. To practice thrift when need be.
4. To save time and energy when you can.

To be well fed means more than having enough to eat. It means eating foods at each meal which furnish energy, build and repair the body, and stimulate growth. To supply these needs, there are different types of food materials. These five types of materials are protein, minerals, vitamins, energy givers and water.

Protein

Protein was named from a Greek word meaning "first". Nearly a hundred years ago, it was recognized as the main substance in all the body's muscles. No simple substance could build and renew all the different tissues, and protein has proved to be complex and varied.

Some protein rich foods have all the materials needed for the job. Other good protein foods have only part of these materials and need to be combined with top-rating protein foods. You get the top-rating proteins in foods from animal sources, meat, poultry, fish, eggs, milk, cheese. Some of these protein foods are needed each day; and it is an advantage to include some in each meal.

Next best for protein are peanuts, dry beans and peas. When these are featured in main dishes, try to combine them with the proteins from animal sources.

[12]

Some of the protein may come from cereals, bread, vegetables and fruits. All vegetable proteins need to be supplemented with protein from animal sources.

Minerals

Only small amounts of minerals are needed, but they are very important to good health. Minerals do two major things for us. They act as body builders for teeth, bones, blood, muscles, organs and tissues. Also, they are regulators—keep the heart working properly, and the rest of our muscles, nerves and other tissue doing their job to best advantage. Calcium, iron and iodine are the three most important, and, if we get these, we get the other needed minerals.

1. Calcium

Calcium is one of the chief mineral materials in bones and teeth. About 99 percent of the calcium in the body is used for framework. Small but important, the other 1 percent remains in body fluids, such as the blood. Without this calcium, muscles can't contract and relax and nerves can't carry their messages.

For calcium to be used properly, other substances are needed, too, in right quantities—vitamin D and phosphorus, for example. But vitamin D is the sunshine vitamin and phosphorus is found in foods

2. Iron

One of the essential materials for red blood cells is iron. Without its iron supply, the blood could not carry oxygen from the lungs to each body cell.

When meals are varied, you get some iron from many different foods. Liver is outstanding for iron, and one good reason for eating leafy green vegetables is their iron content.

Some of the other foods that add iron are egg yolks, lean meats, peas and beans of all kinds, dried fruits, molasses, bread and other cereal foods made from the whole grain or enriched.

3. Iodine

Your body must have small but steady amounts of iodine to help the thyroid gland to work properly. The most familiar bad effect of getting too little iodine is a swelling of the thyroid gland, called goiter.

Iodine is found in sea foods and in the water supply and in vegetables, growing in certain sections of the United States. South Carolina produced foods are high in iodine, and, if we get our daily share of these fresh foods grown locally, we should get sufficient iodine in our diet.

Vitamins

Nearly 20 vitamins that are known or believed to be important to human well being have thus far been discovered. When you eat a variety of food you are pretty sure of getting a well-rounded assortment of the vitamins you need, except perhaps vitamin D which is the sunshine vitamin. And you may also be getting other vitamins still undetected in food, but serving you just the same.

The following vitamins are of practical importance in planning family meals:

Vitamin A

Vitamin A is important to the young for growth. And at all ages it is important for normal vision, especially in dim light.

In one way or another, many vitamins help protect the body against infection, and vitamin A's guard duty is to help keep the skin and the linings of nose, mouth, and inner organs in good condition. If these surfaces are weakened, bacteria can invade more easily.

You can get vitamin A from some animal foods. Good sources are liver, egg yolks, butter, whole and skim milk and cream, and cheese from whole milk or cream. Fish-liver oils which children take for vitamin D are rich in vitamin A besides.

Some vitamin A can be stored in the body, so it is to your advantage to eat heartily of foods that provide it. A savings account of vitamin A in your system may be drawn upon, if in any emergency this vitamin is wanting in the diet. One good reason for including a vegetable from the leafy, green, and yellow group every day is to keep well stocked with this vitamin. Margarine, a vegetable fat, is fortified with vitamin A.

The B Vitamin Family

There was once supposed to be just one vitamin B. Then, vitamin B was found to be complex and it has in time been separated into about a dozen vitamins, each with particular duties and importance. Most of them are called by names that tell something about their chemical nature.

Thiamine, riboflavin, and niacin are the most generally known and best understood B's. Getting enough of these in food helps with steady nerves, normal appetite, good digestion, good morale, and healthy skin.

Recently, identified B's are folic acid and vitamin B_{12}, both important for healthy state of the blood.

Few foods contain real wealth of B vitamins, but in a varied diet many foods contribute some and so build an adequate supply.

One way to make sure of raising your B level is to use regularly bread and flour, corn meal and grits that have been made from whole grain or that have been enriched so as to restore important B vitamins.

Getting ample milk in diet is important for B's, too, and for riboflavin in particular.

B vitamins play a part in converting fuel in foods into energy. It follows that any one who eats quantities of starches and sugars also requires more food containing B vitamins.

Vitamin C

The first vitamin separated out from food was vitamin C, now also called ascorbic acid. Tissues throughout the body can't keep in good condition without vitamin C.

When diet is very low in this vitamin, gums are tender and bleed easily, joints swell and hurt, and muscles weaken. In advanced stages, the disease called scurvy results.

Scurvy is rare now in this country. But many people get too little vitamin C for their best state of health.

You need some food rich in vitamin C daily, because the body can't store much of this vitamin.

Good sources of vitamin C include tomatoes and tomato juice, canned or fresh; fresh strawberries, cantaloupes, also raw green vegetables, such as cabbage, green pepper, and green lettuce. The potato includes some vitamin C, especially the sweet potato.

All of the familiar citrus fruits are bountiful sources of vitamin C. Half a glass (4 ounces) of orange or grapefruit juice, fresh or canned, goes far toward meeting a day's needs. The same is true of half a grapefruit, a whole orange, or a couple of tangerines.

Vitamin D

"Sunshine" is vitamin D's nickname, because the sun's rays striking the skin have power to change certain substances in the skin into vitamin D.

A few foods, such as egg yolks, butter, salmon, tuna, and sardines, help out with vitamin D; and some milk, both fresh and evaporated, has vitamin D added. But to supplement sunshine and food, babies and young children usually need to take a special vitamin D preparation or one of the fish-liver oils regularly. These oils from halibut, shark, and cod are the richest natural sources of this vitamin known.

Fuel or Energy-Giving Foods

For the body's energy in work and play, fuel must come from food. The value of foods for this purpose is figured in calories. Main sources are starches and sugars, and fats, but all foods furnish calories—some many, some few, in a given size portion.

If body weight stays about right for your height and build it's a sign that the fuel intake from food matches your needs. The calories are taking care of themselves.

But suppose you are overweight . . . What then?

When the body gets more energy food than it can use, it stores up the excess as fat. Accumulation of too much fat is sometimes termed the most frequent malnutrition problem among adults in this country. To put it more plainly, many adults eat too much.

Up to 35 years, if you can't be just right in weight, it is better to be plump than skinny. Beyond 35, excess fat becomes a greater health liability than thinness. Ills such as high blood pressure and heart and kidney ailments are more common among overweights. Underweights tend to tire readily and may be an easy prey to infections.

Controlling Weight

If you are under 20 years of age, don't try to reduce except under a physician's guidance. This is also advisable if you are a young mother, or have anything wrong with heart or other organs. If you are not in these groups, and need to reduce, take it slowly. A pound or two off a week is plenty.

To reduce calories without starving your body of its other needs:
1. Do not skip meals in order to reduce. It is better to eat less food and eat more often. Remember the total calories eaten per day is the important factor.
2. Avoid high-calorie foods like the fat on meat, cooking fat, salad oil, fried foods, gravies, and rich sauces, nuts, pastries, cakes, cookies, rich desserts, candies, jellies, and jams.
3. Eat small-sized servings of bread or cereal.

4. Don't skimp on fruits and vegetables. Eat a variety—yes, potatoes, too. A medium-sized potato has no more calories than a
big orange or a big apple. But take fruits and vegetables
straight—vegetables without cream sauce or fat; fruit without
sugar and cream.

5. Don't skimp on protein-rich foods, for you need plenty of lean
meat, milk, and eggs.

If you are underweight, you need to turn the tables to put some
fat on your bones. You need three balanced meals, as overweights do.
To these meals, you can freely add the extras shunned by the weight
reducers—such as rich gravies and desserts, salad dressings, and jams.
And you can well take some extra food as between-meal snacks.

Good Meal Planning

A successful meal is one which is nutritionally adequate, skillfully
prepared, carefully served—and enjoyed by the people who eat it.

To accomplish this, plan for a whole day, or for several days
rather than for each separate meal. Visualize your meals as a whole
and strive for nutritional balance with contrast in color, texture and
flavor.

Guide for Planning Balanced Meals— Daily Needs

Leafy, green and yellow vegetables

Plan to use: 1 or more servings daily. This group includes:

All kinds of greens—collards, kale, turnip greens, spinach, and many
others, cultivated and wild; carrots, peas, snap beans, okra, green
asparagus, broccoli, brussels sprouts, green cabbage, green lima beans,
pumpkin, yellow squash, sweet potato.

Tomatoes, raw vegetables, citrus fruits

Plan to use: 1 or more servings daily. This group includes:

Tomatoes, tomato juice, strawberries, cantaloupe, watermelon, and
citrus fruits

or

If eaten raw—cabbage, salad greens, green peppers, and turnips.
If cooked briefly, in very little water—cabbage, collards, turnip greens
and broccoli.

Sweet potatoes, Irish potatoes

Plan to use: 1 or more servings daily.

Other vegetables and fruits

Plan to use: 1 or more servings daily. This group includes:

Beets, cauliflower, egg plant, summer squash, corn, cucumbers, onions, radishes, sauerkraut, cooked cabbage, apples, bananas, peaches, pears, figs, berries, dried fruit—all vegetables and fruits not included in other groups.

Milk, cheese, ice cream

Plan to use: following amounts of milk daily, include milk used for drinking as well as cooking:

Children through teen age: 3 to 4 cups daily.
Adults: 2 to 3 cups.
Pregnant mothers: a little more than 1 quart.
Nursing mothers: 1½ quarts.

On the basis of the calcium they contain, the following may be used as alternates for 1 cup of milk: Cheddar cheese, 1½ ounces; cream cheese, 15 ounces; cottage cheese, 11 ounces; ice cream, 2 to 3 large dips.

Meat, poultry, fish

Plan to use: 1 serving daily, if possible. This group includes:

All lean meats including liver, heart, and other variety meats; poultry; game; fish and sea foods. Count bacon and salt pork in with fats and not under this group.

Eggs

Plan to use: 5 or more eggs a week. Eggs are a source of high-quality protein, iron, vitamin A, riboflavin, vitamin D, and provide very small amounts of calcium and thiamine.

Dry beans and peas, nuts

Plan to use: 1 or more servings a week. This amount includes:

Dry beans of all kinds, dry peas, lentils; soybeans, peanuts, other nuts; peanut butter.

Baked goods, flour, cereals

Plan to use: 1 serving each meal, preferably whole grain or enriched. This group includes:

Flour of meal made from wheat, corn, oats, buckwheat, rye; cooked and ready-to-eat cereals; rice, barley, hominy, macaroni; breads, other baked goods. Be careful not to serve too many foods from this group during the day. Most meals unless carefully planned are likely to contain too much starch.

Fats, oils

Use fat sparingly—it's easy to get too much in the diet. This group includes butter, margarine, salad oil, shortening, bacon, salt pork, lard, suet, drippings. Butter and fortified margarine furnish vitamin A as well as fat content.

Sugar, syrup. preserves, honey

Sugar, syrups, preserves and honey are useful mainly for the calories they provide for energy.

Check your menu plans by this guide. Remember it is easier to prevent nutritional deficiencies than to correct the effects of poor nutrition upon your family's health.

Principles of Table Service

Good Balance. Table utensils and decorations should be arranged in an orderly manner, equally spaced and not crowded. Silverware, napkins, china and glassware should form lengthwise and crosswise lines on the table.

Harmony and Color. The table coverings, napkins, decorations, dinnerware, glassware and food should be chosen with their colors in mind to make sure that they look well together.

Suitability. Select things for the table which are suitable to each other, to the occasion and to the menu.

Distinction. The table can be covered with charm and simplicity by using imagination, originality and a few inexpensive accessories. Every time the table is set a picture is created.

Setting the Table

A well-set table adds much to the enjoyment of a meal. Clean linens, china, silver, glassware, and attractive flower arrangements can do much toward putting a person in the right mood to enjoy a meal.

The way in which a table is to be set depends upon the food to be served. Some rules that apply at all times are:

1. Allow 20 to 24 inches for each person or "cover." The space taken up by the glass, silver, linen, and china for each person is called the cover.
2. The plate is placed in the center of the cover one inch from the edge of the table.
3. Silver is placed on the table in the order in which it is to be used from the outside in toward the plate. All silver is placed one inch from the edge of the table. Butter spreaders, if used, should be placed on the bread and butter plate.
4. Place knives at the right of the plate with cutting edge toward the plate. Spoons are placed at the right of the knife with bowls up.
5. The water glass is placed at the tip of the knife.
6. Place forks to the left of the plate with tines up. It is not necessary to use a salad fork unless the salad is to be served as a separate course in the meal.
7. The bread and butter plate is placed at the tip of the fork. The butter spreader may be placed across the top of the plate, parallel to the edge of the table, or across the side of the plate in line with other silver.
8. Place the salad at the left of the cover near the tip of the fork.
9. Napkins are placed to the left of the fork. Open edges of the napkin are usually placed parallel to the edge of the table so that the open, lower corner is nearest the plate.
10. When cups are used they are placed to the right of the knife.
11. The salt and pepper is placed where they may be easily reached, yet give balance to the table.

COVER

1. Service plate
2. Cup and saucer
3. Glass
4. Napkin
5. Fork
6. Bread and butter plate (if one is used)
7. Salad
8. Knife
9. Spoon

Seating Arrangement

Father, the host, sits at the head of the table. Mother, the hostess, sits opposite him.

The guest, if a man, is seated to the right of the hostess, if a woman, to the right of the host.

The person who waits on the table should be seated nearest the kitchen.

Be seated at the table and rise from the table from the left of the chair.

It is courteous for each man to draw out the chair for the woman who is seated at his left. This courtesy may also be shown by the younger members for any older members of the group.

Serving the Family Meal

1. Have the meal on time.
2. Serve the hot foods hot and the cold foods cold.
3. Fill water glasses three-fourths full and have them on the table before the meal is served.
4. Place, pass and remove all dishes to the left of person served, except beverage, which is placed and removed from the right.
5. If the host and hostess serve the plates, the host serves the main dish and often the vegetables, and the hostess serves the beverage. Vegetables and breads may be placed on the table and passed by other family members. The silver needed for serving is placed to the right of each dish.
6. The first plate served is passed to the right around the table. The person on the host's left gets the first plate. The next person gets the next plate and so on around the table until everyone is served.
7. Pass the dishes of food either to the right or to the left. Passing to the right seems to be preferred, but the important thing to remember is to pass all of them in the same direction.
8. The serving dishes are removed before the individual covers are cleared. The following order is usually preferred: (1) the serving dishes, such as meat platter, vegetable dish, (2) bread plate, (3) salt and peppers on a tray, and (4) individual covers starting with the hostess and leaving only water glasses, silver needed for dessert, and cups and saucers for beverage if desired.

Table Courtesies

1. All be seated at the same time.
2. Unfold napkin below the edge of the table then placed half unfolded across the lap.
3. Do not begin eating until everyone has been served. The hostess begins eating first.
4. When eating soup, dip the spoon away from the body. Sip the soup from the side of the spoon, not the tip.
5. Break bread into small servings. Never butter a whole slice of bread at one time.
6. When the knife or fork is not being used it is placed across the top edge of the plate.
7. Hold the handles of the knife and of the fork lightly in the palm of each hand, the fingers clasped around them. Rest forefingers along the back of the blade of the knife and the handle of the fork.
8. Do not cut all the meat on your plate at one time. Cut bite-size pieces as you go along.
9. After stirring a hot drink, the spoon should be placed on the saucer and not left in the cup. Remove the spoon after stirring an iced drink.
10. Elbows should not rest upon the table or interfere with the person seated nearest you.
11. Eat slowly. Hurried eating causes indigestion.
12. Only forks and spoons are used to carry food to the mouth.
13. Ask for food to be passed, rather than reach across the table or in front of others.
14. Always be thoughtful of others. See that the ones near you are served and that the food near you is passed.
15. Do not discuss the food at the table.
16. When eating be sure to keep your lips closed.
17. Let the conversation at the table be pleasant. Keep up your share of the conversation, but do not monopolize the talk.
18. Do not finger or play with silver or dishes.
19. Fold your napkin at the end of the meal if you will be eating at the same place again. If not, leave it unfolded at the left of the plate.
20. Host or hostess gives signal for leaving table by rising.

ENTERTAINING

Southern Hospitality

Southern hospitality is not a trite saying, tossed carelessly about today, nor does it allude to the days of yesteryear and the plantation houses set in the midst of spacious lawns, surrounded by magnolias, azaleas and camellias and staffed by many servants. "Southern Hospitality" is as real as any welcome—sincerely and generously extended not only by those who live in the big houses but by everyone whether their houses be pretentious or humble. "Southern Hospitality" is traditional rather than a tradition.

You, like every other woman, enjoy entertaining, and mealtime plays a part of real importance when you decide to entertain many or a few of your family or friends.

The ability to entertain with ease and without undue disruption of the regular routine is an art. You, who have a keen appreciation of the meaning of hospitality, will be a successful hostess. You will find simple ways to fit entertaining into your schedule or your scheme of living. A feeling of friendliness and appreciation of people is of first importance.

This section is proposed to help you with your entertaining and suggest the little things that will lend an air of calm that gives the hostess poise that enhances her charm. To attempt elaborateness beyond one's facilities is poor judgment and bad taste.

Invite your friends to your home and have a good time with them. Make them want to come again. To do this you must plan ahead so that you may greet your guests graciously and unhurried. You will plan the food, its preparation and serving.

There are many enjoyable social functions as well as family meals that you will enjoy. You must first determine the number of guests you will have and the facilities available for entertaining them. Then you decide on the way that you will entertain. There are teas, luncheons, breakfasts, dinners, and receptions and some type of food is served at all of them.

Although we dislike to be guided by rules, it is often necessary to have a measuring stick, or rule, by which entertaining may be made easier.

The following are suggested:

1. Attempt only as much as you can do well.

2. Make your food both "good and good for you" and "good to look at."
3. Have your food in keeping with the type of entertaining. Do not serve a heavy meal in the middle of the afternoon for refreshments, and on the other hand do not serve sandwiches for dinner.
4. Consider the likes and dislikes of your guests when planning your menu. Consideration should be given to the age of your guests. Children should have simple foods.
5. Consider your costs—and serve food that is easy to prepare.
6. Hot food should be served hot and cold food cold. Warm your serving dishes for hot food and chill your dishes for cold food.
7. Your linen must be spotless and crisp, your silver and glassware sparkling and your china gleaming.
8. Be happy and make your guests happy. Thoughtfulness of others is the basis for good manners.
9. Be calm, do not rush, make your meal relaxing.
10. You or a member of the family should greet your guests, look after their comfort and make sure that all of the guests are introduced.

In return, you may expect consideration from your guests, perhaps as follows:

1. That they answer invitations promptly.
2. That they be prepared to enter enthusiastically into whatever is planned.
3. That they know when they are expected and leave with as little confusion or commotion as possible.
4. That they express verbally or by note their appreciation for the kindnesses and consideration shown them.

Breakfast

Breakfast is a family meal. It is the hour when they meet to begin the day, and all too often it is the meal that receives least thought and is hurried, when, in truth, it is the one that commands our attention as it can be the occasion that determines the day's success.

If there is a rule or standard for breakfast, it is make it bright and gay. Keep it simple and uncluttered, with everything at hand for quick and easy serving. Simple place mats are quite at home on the breakfast table and used with earthenware or pottery, centered with a bowl of fruit, small plant or flower arrangement, make a setting that will perk up sleepy spirits and be the send-off for the family who go to work or school.

The illustration shown here gives you an idea of the arrangement for the meal that is simple, adequate and appealing.

More and more frequently we are turning to the breakfast hour to entertain guests, and find it an excellent time when the number is small. More elaborate mats and the better china are brought out for this occasion, and you may linger over a second cup of coffee.

Luncheon

Luncheon, being a daylight function, is casual in tone as variable as breakfast, though more elaborate. It is less formal than dinner.

You may use a lunch cloth but not a damask one; luncheon requires a daintier and less formal setting. The decorations are practically the same as for dinner. The luncheon table illustrated here gives an idea of the arrangement and effectiveness of the carefully laid table, set for four, with simple crystal, china and silver.

A typical luncheon menu that may be served with little effort is suggested here.

Cream of tomato soup   Fresh fruit salad
Southern fried chicken   Spanish cream
Buttered asparagus   Tea or coffee

Family Dinner

This gives the hostess an opportunity to show her table at its best—laid with shining damask or fine linen and set with the cherished china, crystal and silver. For all of its inevitable air of elegance and feeling of formality the dinner table reflects the friendliness and hospitality that provide the keynote for gracious entertaining.

Dinners range from the sumptuous to the very light. The serving of dinner has much in common with that of luncheon, though it is more elaborate. The table is covered with damask and has a silence cloth to prevent the cloth from slipping on the polished wood.

In serving the matter of precedence is to be considered. The hostess is no longer served first—this was a legacy from medieval days when the food might be poisoned and now has no reason for existence. Service should begin with the guest on the hostess' right and proceed around the table. It is good practice however to vary this a little and on alternate servings dishes should be passed beginning with the guest on the host's right.

Most of you will be serving with only one maid or possibly with none. Be careful of the menu so that there will be as little confusion as possible.

Buffet Meals

Most of us entertain informally in our homes today, and the buffet meal is one of the most popular innovations that have developed of late. The buffet meal is a time-saving, attractive, "help yourself plan" suitable for family meals or for guests. The guests serve themselves from the dining room table and sit where they choose. An excellent way to make sure that every one will find a seat is to arrange for enough small tables (card tables) covered similar to the dining table. These small tables may be set with the silver and water glasses, a small flower arrangement and peppers and salts.

The buffet table may be covered with a cloth and centered with an arrangement of fruits, flowers or anything you like. If the table is against the wall your centerpiece can be easily and effectively arranged. Special themes may be carried out in the table decorations for such holidays as Christmas, Easter, Thanksgiving and others.

The general arrangement of a buffet setting depends primarily upon the position of the table. It should be placed to allow the easiest service.

It is well to consider certain factors when planning for the buffet meal. Your plans should be made well in advance. It is best to limit the menu to two courses—a main course and a dessert course. One hot dish at least should be in the main course, served possibly from a casserole, platter or some other type of serving dish, a hot vegetable, a bowl of salad, assorted relishes and a plate of hot buttered bread or sandwiches. Your drink would be determined by the season or by the preference of the guests. Arrange the food on the table so that the plates are picked up first, then the food and finally the silver, napkin and beverage. If small tables have not been placed ahead of time, it is wise to have trays available for each guest. It is well to avoid the bread line effect by having a large group line up. The hostess should invite a small group to be served and when they have finished and are seated a new group is invited. This not only saves time but avoids confusion that might lose much of the effectiveness of the lovely table when observed with many guests crowding around.

Teas

There are two types of teas that we may choose from. It may be a very simple occasion for a few guests or it may be a large gathering; it may be most informal or it may be a simple way to serve a large number of guests formally.

Teas offer many possibilities for special appointments. The tea is given to introduce a friend, a guest, a person of prominence, or to extend hospitality to a few friends. The usual hours are from three to five or six.

When food is served the table is the center of interest. A lace or embroidered cloth makes a suitable cover. Flowers are preferred for the centerpiece. Lighted candles lend a pleasant atmosphere if the shades are drawn.

The beverage service for tea is on a tray placed directly in front of the one who pours. The plates are arranged in a small stack at the left and the cups are put near the pourer. At a large tea two persons are asked to pour.

At small teas, each guest upon the invitation of the hostess, goes to the tea table and is served with the beverage. She then helps herself to the other foods, a napkin, and silver. Tea-sized napkins are used. When the guest has finished her tea, she places her used plate and napkin upon some convenient table, or they are removed by the hostess.

At large teas, friends of the hostess usually preside in the dining room. When double service is used, one hostess sits at each end of the table to pour the beverage. Others assist with the serving by seeing that small groups at a time are taken to the tea table.

At a formal tea the cup of tea is brought to the guest. Then cream and sugar and the plates of food are passed by those assisting with the serving. The food never should be placed on the plate for the guest.

Those who assist the hostess should observe the arrangement of the tables and keep this order when they replace the food plates. The table should look attractive and have full service plates at all times.

Placed about the table are glass or silver dishes of candy, nuts and little cakes and the like, with low piles of dishes and napkins.

As guests finish with their tea, a waitress takes their plates, two at a time, to the kitchen.

Refreshments must be simple. No fork or knife should be required. Besides the beverages, serve tiny sandwiches, little cakes, diminutive tarts, creamed-chicken-filled puffs—all finger foods.

Entertaining Your Club

The serving of refreshments is to promote hospitality and to give time out from club activities for friendship and fun. As clubs are organized for study and mutual help, refreshments, when served, should be simple, attractive and low in food value.

When you entertain plan your menu carefully with the thought in mind that this is to be an accessory and not a meal, nor should it be so heavy that it will affect the next meal.

Types of Menu for Club Refreshments:

One of the following:

1. *Light*
   a. Sandwiches
   b. Cookies
   c. Small cakes
       and
       a beverage
2. *Medium*
   One of the following combinations:
   a. Salads with sandwich or other accompaniment
   b. Frozen or other dessert with wafer, cookies or cake
       and
   a beverage

Careful Planning Makes Successful Serving

Some Suggestions Are

1. Have in readiness all china, silver, and linen to be used.
2. Arrange cookies and cakes on plates.
3. Prepare sandwiches and cover with damp cloth in preparation for arranging on plates at the last minute.
4. Have utensils and water ready for preparing beverages.
5. Have chocolate or cocoa syrup made.
6. If refreshments are to be served from a small table, it could be arranged in advance and covered with a clean cloth.

Guide for Determining Number of Services in Common Foods

1 pound of butter will spread about 60 sandwiches.

1 pound loaf of bread will make 13 slices.

4 pound chicken will average about 4 cups of cooked, diced meat, and will serve 12 people.

1 cup cream is doubled when whipped.

1 pound of coffee makes 50 cups medium strong.

1 lemon equals 3 to 4 tablespoons of juice.

1 pound of paper shell pecans equals about 2 cups shelled.

Recipes for Afternoon Refreshments

Sandwiches for Refreshment Plates

The afternoon refreshment sandwich is smaller and daintier than a picnic or lunch sandwich. If the crusts are removed they should be kept, toasted and used in croquettes, stuffings or on scalloped dishes. The bread should be at least 24 hours old and thinly sliced.

Fillings should be soft enough to spread evenly but not moist enough to soak into the bread. If butter is used in the filling, it is not necessary to spread separately. Fillings should be spread to the edge but not run over.

Savory Butter

Stir into thoroughly creamed butter a sufficient amount of one of the following ingredients to produce the desired color and flavor:

Deviled Ham   Catsup
Chicken   Green pepper
Parsley   Cucumber

In order to blend with the butter, the special ingredient must be drained and finely chopped or rubbed to a paste.

Sweet Fillings

a. Cream cheese with strawberry jam.

b. Drained preserved figs and nuts finely chopped and moistened with cream.

c. Peanut butter and grape jelly.

d. Ground raisins and nuts.

e. Honey and peanut butter.

Meat and Meat Substitute Fillings
    a. Cottage cheese and pickle.
    b. Hard cooked egg and green pepper.
    c. Hard cooked egg, pimento, sweet pickle.
    d. Hot whole wheat or plain biscuit with slice of ham, bacon or sausage placed between.

Vegetable Sandwich Fillings
    a. Grated raw carrot, chopped cabbage with ground peanuts.
    b. Wafer thin slices of radishes.
    c. Thin slices of cucumber pickle.
    d. Artichoke relish sandwiches.

REFRESHMENT PLATES

Fall
1. Hot spiced cider or hot tea, small open faced sandwiches, small doughnuts.
2. Iced scuppernong or grape juice, jelly or preserve cookies.
3. Tea, cake, boiled custard with whipped cream, jelly garnish, salted nuts.
4. Cold buttermilk or milk shake, hot gingerbread.

Winter
1. Small slices of fruit cake, salted nuts or mints, coffee.
2. Small whole wheat biscuits, slices of ham, chicken, or small sausages, hot tomato juice.
3. Charlotte russe, coffee.
4. Cinnamon toast strips or nut bread sandwiches, coffee.

Spring
1. Open faced deviled egg sandwiches, carrot strips, radish roses, iced tea.
2. Canned peach or pear salad with cottage cheese, small jelly sandwiches, iced tea or fruit juice.
3. Strawberry shortcake, tea or coffee.
4. Fresh or preserved berry tart, tea or coffee.

Summer
1. Fresh berries with whipped cream, small cookies.
2. Ice cream with fresh fruit—berries, peaches, cantaloupe.
3. Small sandwiches, cookies, iced tomato juice, or iced fruit juice.

4. Fresh chilled fruit—peaches, watermelon, cantaloupe, figs, grapes.

Addition to the Menu

Spiced peaches, pears, figs, watermelon pickle are good additions and can also be used with cheese for a salad.

Cheese balls, potato chips, fresh crisp vegetable sticks, nuts toasted or plain, small candies or mints may be used for color and flavor, and give that additional touch to the refreshment plate.

Appetizers

FRUIT, VEGETABLE AND SEA FOOD APPETIZERS

Fruits and juices, vegetables and sea foods make excellent appetite teasers when served at beginning of a meal. Canned, fresh and frozen fruits are excellent meal openers for they stimulate appetite.

Choose foods which contrast in color, flavor, texture. Chill thoroughly before serving, and cut or dice in attractive mouth size pieces. Select the appetizer according to the meal served. For breakfast only fruits and juices are used. Sea food cocktails from oysters, shrimp, and crab are used only for lunch or dinner.

Fruits

Berries

1. Pick over the berries, place in a colander, pour cold water over them, drain and cap. Serve with cream and sugar if desired.
2. Pick over berries, place in colander, pour cold water over them and drain thoroughly. Arrange berries on a fruit plate around a mound of powdered sugar.

Figs

For breakfast peel, chill, and serve with cream and sugar if desired. Figs may be mixed with other fruits or served chilled for first course of meal. Figs are also good served as a dessert.

Peaches

Select firm, ripe, whole fruit, wash. Serve whole, halves or sliced either with or without sugar for breakfast, as first course for dinner, or as a dessert. Peaches may be served with cream.

Cantaloupe

Cut in half, or, if large cantaloupe, cut in smaller sections. Remove seeds and serve. Excellent for any meal. Serve with salt and pepper if desired. A teaspoon of sugar added to cantaloupe improves flavor of less sweet cantaloupe. Cantaloupe is excellent also sliced, peeled and served along with breakfast meal.

Grapes

Chill, pick over, wash, and serve as first course or ending to an otherwise heavy lunch.

Watermelon

Watermelon is a popular fruit in season. Watermelon balls are good as a first course—a slice of watermelon for dessert is good ending to summer meals.

Melon balls

Cantaloupe or watermelon may be scooped out with ball cutter and served as first course. Lemon or lime slice, sprig of mint give an added touch.

Oranges and Grapefruit

Wash, dry and chill. To serve, cut in halves or remove pulp in sections. First remove seeds. Use sharp knife to loosen sections.

Remove center core with grapefruit corer or scissors. A tablespoon of sugar, honey or grape juice improves grapefruit. To remove sections, peel fruit whole, taking off as much as possible of the white membrane without breaking through to the pulp. Remove pulp in sections by cutting down on either side of dividing membrane. Remove seeds, chill and serve plain or sweetened slightly. Oranges may be peeled, as much of white inner skin removed as possible, and sliced. Arrange slices attractively and serve.

Mixed Chilled Fruits

There are many combinations of fruits—fresh, canned or frozen. Mixed chilled fruits are good for breakfast as first course for meal and as dessert. Some popular combinations are peaches, pears, strawberries; oranges, grapefruit, pineapple; orange sections and melon balls.

Canned Fruit

Select berries, peaches, pears, apples, or plums and chill before serving. Combine or serve separately. Sprinkle with powdered sugar if fruit is too tart.

Fresh Fruit (stewed)

Wash fruit and if necessary pare, quarter, and core. Cook in a small amount of water and sweeten to taste. To retain the shape of the fruit, make a syrup of the sugar and water and cook the fruit in this. The amount of sugar and water to use depends upon the juiciness and the sweetness of the fruit. One cup of water to one-half cup of sugar may be used for most well-ripened fruits. Fresh stewed fruit is excellent to start off a good winter breakfast.

Apple or Pear Sauce

Wash apples or pears and cut into pieces. Cook until soft in a small amount of water. Press through a sieve and add sugar to desired sweetness. A few grains of cinnamon, ground nutmeg, or one tablespoon lemon juice will give additional flavor.

Dried Fruit (stewed)

Wash and place fruit into a saucepan. Cover with boiling water. Soak about one hour. If the fruit is hard and dry, soak it longer. Too much soaking however draws out the flavor. Cook the fruit in the same water in which it was soaked. Cook with lid on. Simmer slowly over low heat until the fruit is tender. Sugar may be added, if desired, just before removing the fruit from heat. Stir until the sugar is dissolved. Dried fruits may be covered with cold water and allowed to soak over night. Cooked dried fruit either plain or with cereal makes a good breakfast fruit.

Baked Fruits

Wash, pare, and core the fruit. Place in a baking dish, sprinkle with sugar, dot with butter, and add a small amount of boiling water. Bake in a hot oven until soft. Baste often with syrup in the dish to prevent dryness. Care should be taken that fruit does not lose its shape. Serve hot or cold with or without sugar and cream.

Juices

Fruit Juices

Have fruit juices chilled and pour over crushed ice and serve. Home canned juices are good served in this way as appetizers—apple and grape are especially popular.

Tomato Juice

Select ripe tomatoes of bright red color. Wash well, remove cores, and cut into small pieces. Simmer until soft. (Do not boil.) Put the softened, hot tomatoes through a fine sieve immediately. Add ½ to 1 teaspoon salt to 1 quart juice. This juice may be served plain or seasoned and served as a cocktail. Juice may be reheated at once and canned.

Miracle Tomato Cocktail

1 quart canned tomatoes	4 tablespoons lemon juice
½ cup diced celery	1 bay leaf
½ cup diced green pepper	1 whole clove
½ small onion, sliced	½ teaspoon Worchestershire sauce

Combine tomatoes, celery, green pepper, onion, bay leaf and clove in saucepan. Cook gently over medium heat, about 30 minutes. Stir occasionally. Force through fine sieve. Add Worchestershire sauce and lemon juice. Cool. Chill thoroughly. Season with additional salt, if desired.   Makes about 3 cups.

Lexington County.

Spicy Cocktail (Good on a cold day)

3 cups tomato juice	3 tablespoons lemon juice
¼ cup orange juice	1 teaspoon salt

1 teaspoon Worchestershire sauce

Serve piping hot.   Marie A. Hamilton, Charleston County.

Sauerkraut Juice Cocktail

Add lemon juice to taste to sauerkraut juice. Serve very cold.

For Fish and Seafood Cocktails, *see* Fish and Sea Foods

Beverages

Beverages consist of milk, water, milk drinks, coffee, tea, and fruit punches. The most important beverage is water. Water has no food value but is just as necessary to life as food. Water aids in body elimination. A person needs to drink 6 to 8 glasses of water each day. This should not be used at meal times to wash down food.

Milk has been called nature's most perfect food because it contains so many food elements. It is especially rich in calcium, a mineral needed for strong bones and teeth; and in vitamins A and B. Research shows that the vitamin A content of milk varies at different seasons of the year. It is much higher when cows are fed on plenty of green feeds. This vitamin helps the body to build up resistance against disease. Milk is rich in riboflavin, too, which is one of the B vitamins. This vitamin promotes a clear healthy skin. Children need to get at least 3 to 4 cups of milk each day in their diet while adults need approximately 2 cups. This amount of milk may be served in hot or cold drinks, soups, custards, sauces and ice cream, or incorporated in other cooked foods.

Fruits and canned juices may be used alone or in combination to make tasty and refreshing drinks. These are excellent served hot or cold when you entertain.

COFFEE

Coffee (Drip)

Place 1 to 2 tablespoons finely ground coffee to each cup of water in the strainer of the coffee pot. Add the boiling water. Cover and allow to filter.

Coffee (Percolated)

Place 1 to 2 tablespoons ground coffee to each cup water in strainer of percolator. Add either hot or cold water. Adjust top. Place over heat and allow to percolate until liquid is amber colored (about 5 minutes after it starts boiling).

Coffee (Boiled)

| 1 cup coffee | 1 cup cold water |
| 1 egg or 3 egg shells | 6 cups boiling water |

Scald the coffee pot. Wash egg, break, and beat slightly. Crush the egg shell. Add half of the cold water to the crushed shell and the coffee. Put into pot and add freshly boiled water. Boil 3 minutes. Add remainder of cold water to clear coffee.

Coffee for 50

1 lb. coffee   6 quarts water

Tie coffee loosely in a flour sack. Place in cold water and let stand overnight or for several hours. Bring to a boil. Remove bag.

After-Dinner Coffee

Use 3 tablespoons coffee to each cup of water. Follow directions for drip, percolated or boiled coffee. Serve in after-dinner coffee cups.

Iced Coffee

Strain hot coffee in glasses filled with ice. Serve with cream and sugar.

TEA

Hot Tea

2 teaspoons tea   2 cups boiling water

Put tea into scalded teapot. Add freshly boiled water, cover and allow to steep 3 minutes. Strain. Serve immediately. Tea balls and tea bags may be used. Remove ball from the teapot after 3 minutes.

Iced Tea

Strain hot tea into glasses partially filled with cracked ice. Serve with sugar and sliced lemon or sprigs of fresh mint. For a clearer product and finer flavor chill as quickly as possible.

Russian Tea

1 teaspoon whole cloves
1 inch stick cinnamon
3 quarts water

Juice of 3 oranges
Juice of 2 lemons
1½ cups sugar

2½ tablespoons tea

Tie spices loosely in bag, and bring to boil in water. Add tea tied loosely in bag and allow to steep 5 minutes. Remove spices and tea and add fruit juices and sugar. Serves 20.

Mrs. J. R. Fairey, Calhoun County.

CHOCOLATE AND COCOA

Chocolate

2 squares chocolate
¼ cup sugar

1 cup water
3 cups milk

pinch of salt

Mix chocolate, sugar and water in double boiler and boil 5 to 10 minutes. Add milk and cook in double boiler 15 to 30 minutes. Beat well before serving.

French Chocolate

2½ squares unsweetened chocolate 2/3 cup sugar
pinch of salt
½ cup cream, whipped
½ cup water
6 cups hot milk

Add chocolate to water and place over low flame. Stir until chocolate is melted and blended. Add sugar and salt and boil 4 minutes, stirring constantly. Cool. Fold into whipped cream. To serve, place 1 rounding tablespoon of chocolate mixture in each serving cup and pour hot milk over it, filling cup. Blend. Serves 8. This is a rich chocolate attractive to serve at the table.

Iced Chocolate

Cool chocolate. Pour over crushed ice, stir well, and sweeten to taste. Serve with whipped cream, if desired.

Chocolate Syrup

4 squares unsweetened chocolate ⅛ teaspoon salt
1¾ cups sugar
1½ cups boiling water

Melt chocolate in a saucepan over boiling water, add sugar and salt, and stir until smooth. While stirring constantly, gradually add boiling water. Boil 5 minutes or until a thin syrup is formed. Cool, place in jar, and keep in refrigerator or cold place. Use 2 or 3 tablespoons syrup to a cup of hot or cold milk.

Chocolate Milk Shake

2 tablespoons finely crushed 2½ tablespoons chocolate syrup
ice
2/3 cup milk

Mix ingredients. Beat with egg beater or put into shaker and shake thoroughly. Strain into glass for serving. A few gratings of nutmeg or a few grains of cinnamon may be sprinkled on top.

Cocoa

1 to 2 tablespoons sugar
⅛ teaspoon salt
3 to 4 tablespoons cocoa
½ cup water
4 cups milk

Combine dry ingredients in the top of double boiler. Stir in water and continue to stir over direct heat until a smooth paste is formed.

Stir in milk, heat over boiling water. Just before serving, beat vigorously with a rotary egg beater to break down the milk solids that may form a skim on top.

Mrs. Millard Jones, Jasper County.

MILK DRINKS

Banana Milk Drink

1 banana
1 cup whole milk

½ teaspoon vanilla
dash of salt

Force banana through a sieve. Mix it with milk, salt and vanilla. Serve over crushed ice.

Milk Punch

¾ cup milk
¼ cup grape juice

1 tablespoon honey
1 egg

Beat egg yolk, add milk, grape juice and honey. Strain egg white through cheesecloth, add to milk, pour over crushed ice and serve.

Spiced Milk Shake

1 quart milk
½ cup sugar
⅛ teaspoon salt

2 eggs
¼ cup cream
1 tablespoon vanilla

½ teaspoon nutmeg

Scald the milk in the top of a double boiler. Beat the eggs in a bowl, add sugar and salt. Add scalded milk and return to the double boiler. Cook over hot water, stirring constantly for 3 minutes. Cool, strain, add cream and flavoring and store in refrigerator until ready for use. When ready to use pour over chipped ice in jar and shake. Pour into chilled glasses and serve.

Strawberry Milk Shake

2½ tablespoons strawberry syrup
   or crushed strawberries

1 cup milk
crushed ice

Mix strawberry syrup and milk well and pour over crushed ice. In strawberry season top with whipped cream and one whole strawberry.

Vanilla Milk Shake

1 teaspoon vanilla   1 teaspoon sugar
2/3 cup milk   2 tablespoons crushed ice

Beat ingredients with egg beater or put into shaker and shake thoroughly. Strain into glass for serving. A few gratings of nutmeg or cinnamon may be sprinkled on top. A spoon of whipped cream added on top helps add to the food value and also the attractiveness of the drink.

High Calorie Eggnog

3 tablespoons lactose   ½ cup milk
3 tablespoons water   2 tablespoons cream
1 egg   ½ teaspoon vanilla

Heat lactose and water to boiling. Cool, beat egg, add lactose syrup, milk, cream and vanilla. Mix thoroughly, chill and serve.

Orange Eggnog

1 egg yolk   1 teaspoon lemon juice
2 teaspoons sugar   1 tablespoon cream
½ cup orange juice   1 egg white

Beat egg yolk until foamy and stir in half the sugar. Add orange juice and lemon juice slowly, and add cream. Beat egg white until stiff, add remaining sugar, and fold into first mixture.

Prune-Ade

½ cup prune juice   1 cup milk
1 teaspoon lemon juice   2 tablespoons sugar
                pinch of salt

Dissolve sugar and salt in juices and add ice. When ready to serve pour in cold milk.

FRUIT DRINKS

Fruit beverages are valuable in the diet. They offer desirable minerals and vitamins. The tang of their acid flavor and their attractive color make them well received by most people.

Combinations of Fruits

Any combination of fruit juices will make a successful drink provided some of the more tart juices, such as those from lemons, sour oranges, limes, or apple cider are present to give the necessary acidity.

Sugar Syrups

Sugar syrup gives a smooth texture and is easily mixed through the whole drink, while sugar has a tendency to sink to the bottom. The amounts of sugar given in the recipes cannot be exact, as the sugar must vary according to the acidity of the fruit and individual taste.

Sugar Syrup

3 cups sugar   3 cups water

Boil sugar and water together for 10 minutes. Pour into clear hot jars and seal. This syrup may be kept on hand and used as needed.

Lemonade (No. 1)

6 lemons   1 to 1½ cups sugar syrup
3 cups water

Squeeze the juice from the fruit. Mix well with the syrup and water. Serve very cold.

Lemonade (No. 2)

6 lemons   ½ to 2/3 cups sugar
4 cups water

Squeeze the juice from the lemons and mix with the water and sugar. See that the sugar is well dissolved. Serve cold.

Limeade

Limeade is made in the same way as lemonade using limes instead of lemons and a little more sweetening. This is even more refreshing than lemonade in the summer.

Orangeade

Make syrup as for lemonade. Sweeten orange juice with syrup and dilute by pouring over crushed ice.

Fruit Juices (Fresh)

Crush berries slightly, add sugar or syrup to taste and let stand over night. Strain through a fine sieve. Pour over crushed ice.

Fruit Juices (Bottled)

Chill juice thoroughly. If juice is concentrated add an equal amount of charged water before serving.

Grapefruit and Ginger Ale

ginger ale   grapefruit juice

Mix 1 part grapefruit juice with 2 parts of ginger ale. Pour over crushed ice. Top with a cherry. Serve.

Albumenized Fruit Juice

1 egg white   ½ cup orange juice

1 teaspoon lemon juice

Beat egg white slightly until foamy. Add fruit juices, mix well, and strain through cheesecloth. Pour over chopped ice. Note: Pineapple, grapefruit, grape or any other fruit juice may replace the orange juice.

Fruit Acid

Sugar (1 pound sugar to each   1¼ ounces tartaric acid
pint of juice)   ¾ quarts water

3 quarts fruit

Dissolve acid in water. Put over mashed fruit. Let stand for 24 hours. Strain and add 1 pound sugar to each pint of juice. Stir constantly until dissolved—bottle. Don't seal tight for several days.

MRS. H. G. WRIGHT, Fairfield County.

Blackberry Acid

To one gallon of blackberries add one quart of boiling water; let stand 6 hours. Pour off and strain. To each quart of juice add one ounce of tartaric acid. To each pint of this juice add one and one-third pounds of sugar. As soon as sugar dissolves, bottle the juice and seal bottles with paraffin.

MRS. LAWRENCE D. NEWTON, Marlboro County.

Mother Walker's Blackberry Nectar

Select sound ripe blackberries, wash and place in stone jar. For every gallon of berries use ¾ quart of good vinegar. Cover top with cheesecloth, let stand three or four days. Stir daily. When ready, strain without crushing berries. Measure, using one pound of sugar for each pint of juice. Boil gently for 5 minutes, put in bottles or jars and seal. When serving, dilute with water and crushed ice. Use less sugar if a tart drink is preferred. This was "Mother Walker's" recipe and has been handed down by friends.

MRS. A. J. HENDRIX, McCormick County.

Scuppernong Nectar

12 pounds fruit   1 cup vinegar
1 cup water

Crush fruit, pour vinegar in and let stand over night. Next morning squeeze out through cheesecloth. To 2 cups juice add 1 cup sugar. Boil 5 minutes. Seal in hot, sterilized jars.

Lexington County.

Unfermented Grape Juice

Pick and wash grapes. Put in a kettle with just enough water to prevent the fruit from burning. Boil until the juice flows. Strain as for jelly. Allow ¼ pound sugar to every quart of juice. Boil 4 minutes, bottle and seal while hot.

MRS. WILLIE HENDERSON, Laurens County.

PUNCH

Strawberry Fruit Punch (with syrup)

1 cup corn syrup   1 cup crushed fresh fruit or juice
1 cup orange juice   1½ cups freshly made strong tea
½ cup lemon juice   1 pint ginger ale or carbonated
                                   water

Mix all ingredients except the ginger ale. Just before serving, add chopped ice and ginger ale. If the punch is too strong, add ice water in small quantities until the punch is of the flavor desired.

Punch

1 large can orange juice   2 pounds sugar
1 large can pineapple juice   1 quart ginger ale
2 small cans lemon juice   1 bottle red cherries
½ gallon weak tea

Mix together tea, sugar and juices, also cherry juice. Just before serving, add ginger ale and stir well. Serves about 20.

MRS. C. C. SISK, McCormick County.

Citrus Fruit Punch

1 large can pineapple juice   ½ dozen lemons
1 dozen oranges   1 quart ginger ale
3 cups sugar

Boil rinds of fruit in three quarts of water 5 minutes, take off, drain and add three cups sugar, cool and add to fruit juice. Add ginger ale just before serving. Makes 4 quarts.

MRS. ANNIE JOSEY, Lee County.

Lime Punch

3 packages lime flavored
   gelatin
1 gallon water

juice of 4 lemons and 4 oranges
1 cup sugar
1 quart ginger ale

Dissolve gelatin in water, cool, add juices of oranges and lemons. Add sugar (to taste) then ginger ale when ready to serve. This will serve about 30 people.

MISS RUBY MAE ROGERS, Darlington County.

Hot Grape Juice Punch

1 pint grape juice
1 pint water
1 teaspoon cloves
½ lemon

½ orange
¼ cup sugar (may not be sweet
   enough for you, so sweeten to
   taste)

Bring sugar and water to boiling point, drop cloves tied in cheese-cloth in water, add grape juice and let simmer long enough for cloves to flavor drink. Add fruit juices and serve hot.

Cranberry Punch

4 cups (1 pound) cranberries
5 cups water

¾ cup sugar
1 teaspoon almond extract

Place cranberries and water in large saucepan. Cover and bring to a boil, remove cover and boil gently about 5 minutes, until all berries have popped open. Strain through cheesecloth removing only clear juice. Add sugar to juice and boil 2 minutes, stirring constantly. Chill thoroughly. Add almond extract. Serve with frozen orange juice cubes.

MRS. EVA S. ADAMS, Spartanburg County.

Oriental Punch
Can be served hot or cold

2 lemons
6 whole cloves
2 cups freshly made hot tea

½ cup sugar
3 cups orange juice
2 cups grape juice

Slice lemons through rind and pulp, add sugar and cloves. Pour cup of hot water over the mixture and let stand for 30 minutes, then heat. Add fruit juices and tea—serve while hot or chill by pouring over crushed ice.

Moonlight Punch

6 cups sugar	4 cups lemon juice
4 cups water	8 quarts ginger ale
1 cup mint leaves	8 quarts ice water

Mix the sugar and 4 cups water and boil three minutes. Add the mint leaves and cool. Add the lemon juice and strain into a punch bowl over a large piece of ice or ice cubes. Add the ice water. Add the ginger ale just before serving. Serves 60.

St. Patrick Punch

1 large can unsweetened pineapple juice	2 cups sugar
	1 quart water
2 large cans orange juice	1 quart ginger ale
2 bottles lemon juice	green cake coloring

Mix and pour over ice. Lime sherbet may be used instead of ice. Serves 30.

MARGARET B. FEWELL, Kershaw County.

Wedding Punch

4 cups sugar	1 cup lemon juice
6 cups boiling water	3 cups pineapple juice
¼ cup tea leaves	6 quarts ginger ale
4 cups orange juice	

Combine sugar and 3 cups of boiling water. Stir until dissolved. Boil 7 minutes, cool. Pour remaining boiling water over tea leaves. Let stand 5 minutes, strain at once. Cool, then dilute with enough water to make one gallon. Combine fruit juices, sugar, syrup and diluted tea. Chill. Shortly before serving, pour over ice in punch bowl and add ginger ale. Lemon or orange slices, cherries or mint may be added if desired.

CORNELIA F. COLLIER, McCormick County.

Punch to Serve 100 to 200

1 dozen bananas	1 dozen oranges
½ gallon tea	2 dozen lemons
1½ dozen bottles orange carbonated drink	1 dozen bottles ginger ale
	1 pint maraschino cherries
1 large can pineapple juice	3 pounds sugar

On night before day to serve punch, add half of sugar to equal measure of boiling water; boil to a syrup. Peel and slice bananas; add the peeling of a few oranges and lemons. Pour boiling syrup over these; cover and let stand until ready to make punch next day. Remove the peeling. Mash bananas through potato ricer or colander.

Make tea and sweeten. Prepare fruit separately (squeeze oranges, lemons, etc.). Do not mix until half an hour before serving. Sweeten to taste and add ice.

Add ginger ale just before serving.

MISS JANE KETCHEN, Winthrop College.

Soups

Some soups can be almost a meal in themselves. Some less nourishing soups are good at the beginning of a meal to pep up the appetite. The kind of soup to be used depends upon the rest of the meal to be served.

Soups may be divided into two classes—those made with meat or meat stock, and those without. For the first, fresh meat or bones, or the bones of cooked meat may be used to make the stock. A ham bone is excellent for making pea or bean soup.

White sauce or vegetable broths to which milk is added are used as bases for soups without meat stock.

GENERAL DIRECTIONS FOR SOUPS USING MEATS

Always use cold water in making soups. The bones are broken and meat cut into small pieces to allow juices to escape more easily. Put pieces into cold water and cook slowly for a long time. Wash, scrape and pare vegetables. Cut them into cubes. Add seasoning and vegetables during last hour of cooking.

Save and use in soups any left-over meat broth, or pot liquor from vegetables. Coarse outer leaves of vegetables can also be used in soups. From our Scottish ancestry we should learn to "let the soup pot and not the brock pail be the receptacle for left overs."

Beef Stock

2 pounds lean meat and bone   2 quarts cold water

Chop meat, crack bones, and soak in water 1 hour. Heat all slowly, simmer 3 hours, strain, remove fat.

Clear Soup or Bouillon

4 pounds meat   6 cloves
3 quarts cold water   12 peppercorns
1 large onion   1 small bay leaf
¾ cup carrots   1 sprig parsley
½ cup turnips   1 tablespoon salt
¼ cup celery   whites of eggs

Chop meat, crack bones and soak in water 1 hour. If a very clear bouillon is desired, omit bones. Heat all slowly, simmer 3 hours, strain, remove fat. Add vegetables and seasonings and cook 3 hours longer; strain, cool, and remove fat. There should be 1½ quarts of stock. To each quart of cold stock add the slightly beaten white and crushed shell of 1 egg. Heat slowly, stirring all the time, boil 2 minutes and simmer 20 minutes. Remove scum and strain through double cheesecloth. Browning part of the meat improves the color and flavor.

White Soup Stock

4 pounds knuckles of veal   ½ onion
   or chicken   ¼ cup celery
3 quarts water   12 peppercorns
              1 tablespoon salt

Follow directions for Clear Soup.

Consomme

Substitute a piece of veal and some fowl for part of the beef in Clear Soup. Consomme has a distinctive flavor due to the cooking together of beef, chicken and veal. Consomme may be varied with types of seasonings used.

Chicken or Turkey Soup

The bony pieces of chicken may be saved for chicken broth. The meat from these pieces may be used in other dishes. Excellent broth can be made from the bones of chicken or turkey which has been broiled, roasted or fricasseed. Place bones in pressure saucepan with a slice of onion, celery and carrot. Add left-over gravy or water. Cook 20 to 30 minutes, strain, season, and cool. If there is too much fat, cool and skim. If pressure saucepan is not available, cook in tightly covered kettle. For seasoning and variety, add diced green pepper, minced parsley, or a tablespoon or two of rice. Milk or cream added also gives food value and variety. A regular cream sauce made with broth is an excellent base for chicken or turkey soups.

Vegetable Soup

Simmer a soup bone in water. To each quart of this meat broth allow:

1 medium-sized onion	1 medium-sized potato
2 small carrots	1 small green pepper
1 turnip	2 stalks celery and leaves

1 cup tomato juice and pulp

Cut all the vegetables about the same size and shape. Cook until tender in the salted meat stock. Season well and serve hot.

Vegetable Soup—(beef stock)

½ cup raw diced carrots	½ cup raw diced potatoes
½ cup raw diced celery	1 quart beef stock
¼ cup raw diced onions	1/3 cup okra
½ cup raw chopped cabbage	1/3 cup corn

2 cups tomatoes

Combine carrots, celery, onion, cabbage, potatoes; barely cover with water and boil for about 15 minutes. Add okra, corn and tomatoes to cooked vegetables and vegetable broth. Use fresh okra and corn if you have it. Beef stock should be good tasting and full flavored. Add to vegetable mixture and let stand at least for 1 hour before serving in order to absorb the vegetable flavors. Salt to taste. Reheat and serve.

Mrs. Marion Bell, Dorchester County.

Vegetable Soup—(milk base)

2 ounces salt pork	1 teaspoon salt
1 small onion, sliced	1 tablespoon sugar
2½ cups corn (No. 2 can)	dash pepper
2 cups diced potatoes	1 quart boiling water
1½ cups tomatoes	1 cup evaporated milk

Cut pork into small pieces and fry slowly to a golden brown in a large saucepan. Add onions and cook slowly without browning for 5 minutes. Add corn, potatoes and tomatoes in alternate layers. Sprinkle with salt, sugar and pepper, then add water and cook slowly until potatoes are tender. Remove from heat and stir milk in slowly.

Florence County.

Vegetable Soup—(ham base)

1 ham bone, or 1 pound ham	3 ears fresh corn, cut from cob
2 pounds okra, cut fine	½ pint butter beans
2 pounds fresh tomatoes or	1 small sprig thyme
1 large can (No. 3 size)	1 tablespoon vinegar

1 tablespoon fat

Put okra into skillet with lard and vinegar. Stir constantly until okra loses its slimy consistency. Put into pot with ham, tomatoes and beans and thyme. Bring to boil and cook slowly until meat is very tender. Add corn and cook 3 minutes. Serve hot with steamed rice. Serves 6.

Effie Almeida, Charleston County.

GENERAL DIRECTIONS FOR CREAM SOUPS

Cook vegetables until they are tender and press through a strainer. Use strained pulp with thin white sauce in the following proportions: One cup of thin white sauce to one-half cup of strained vegetable pulp. If soup is too thick, thin with hot milk or vegetable liquid. Butter or cream may be added if richer soup is desired. Blend white sauce and vegetable pulp well. Season to taste with salt and pepper.

Just a trace of onion is especially good in most vegetable soups. In tomato soup try a bay leaf or a clove. As a garnish and for flavor, too, sprinkle minced parsley on top of potato, carrot, corn, onion, or tomato soup. Minced celery leaves and minced green pepper also add flavor and color. Grated cheese gives added zest and color to many soups. Serve piping hot with toasted biscuit halves, corn bread squares, bread, crackers or croutons.

South Carolina vegetables particularly good for cream soups are Irish potatoes, tomatoes, peas and beans—both fresh and dried, carrots, corn, cabbage, onions, and turnips. Spinach and fresh greens also make a delicious cream soup.

Tips for Cream Soups

Cheese—Add ¾ cup grated cheese to 1 quart of cream of potato or other cream soup just before serving. Stir just long enough to melt cheese.

Grated Carrots—Add ½ to ¾ cup just before removing from heat for color and flavor.

Chopped Parsley—For interest and flavor, sprinkle 1 teaspoon finely chopped parsley over each bowl of cream soup when served.

Paprika—Dash of paprika gives color to an otherwise white soup.

Basic Formula for Cream Soup

½ cup milk
½ cup vegetable juice or
   juice and pulp
1 tablespoon flour
1 tablespoon fat
¼ teaspoon salt
⅛ teaspoon pepper

A medium white sauce is made from milk, fat, flour and seasoning The vegetable juice is heated and added to the sauce, thus diluting the mixture to the consistency of thin white sauce.

Mrs. Millard Jones, Jasper County.

Cream of Tomato Soup

3½ cups fresh or canned
   (No. 2½ can) tomatoes
¼ cup chopped onion
2 tablespoons fat
3 tablespoons flour
½ teaspoon sugar, if desired
3 cups milk
1 teaspoon salt

Cook together the tomatoes and onion—about 20 minutes for fresh tomatoes, 10 for canned. Press through a sieve. Melt the fat; blend in flour and sugar (if used). Gradually add cooled, sieved tomatoes. Cook over low heat, stirring constantly, until thickened. Gradually add tomato mixture to milk, stirring constantly. Heat slowly to serving temperature. Add salt. Serve at once. Serves 6.

Quick Cream of Tomato Soup

Combine 2 cups cooked or canned tomatoes with 3 cups milk. Heat slowly to serving temperature. Add 1 teaspoon salt, a little pepper, and 1 tablespoon fat.

Cream of Potato Soup

2 medium-sized Irish potatoes
1 small onion
water to cover (about 2 cups)
1 tablespoon each melted butter
    and flour, worked together
Top pieces of 1 or 2 stalks
    of celery (depending on
    flavor desired)
2 cups milk

Dice Irish potatoes and cut celery tops in small pieces; cook about 20 minutes, add sliced onions last 5 minutes of cooking (and remove if desired). Add milk, butter and flour. Do not boil, stir with fork, to avoid breaking up of potato cubes.

MRS. W. P. PARKER, Anderson County.

Potato Soup with Cheese

Add about ¾ cup grated cheese to a quart or more of potato soup before ready to serve. Keep the soup hot and stir just long enough to melt the cheese. Do not boil.

Onion Soup

1½ to 2½ cups onion
4 tablespoons butter
6 cups soup stock
salt
¾ cup water
1 tablespoon flour
1 teaspoon Worchestershire sauce
pepper or paprika

Slice onions thin and cook in the water until it is absorbed. Saute the onions until they are light brown, using the four tablespoons of butter, stir in the flour, Worcestershire sauce and soup stock, simmer these ingredients covered for one hour, season. Serve as follows:

Split toasted biscuit or pieces of toast and float on top of soup. Sprinkle with grated cheese. Place the dish under the broiler. Broil the cheese slowly until it is melted and brown. Serve at once.

Mrs. H. G. Wright, Fairfield County.

Quick Turnip Soup

Cook 3 tablespoons of finely chopped onion in 2 tablespoons of fat for a few minutes. Stir in 3 tablespoons of flour. Add 6 cups of heated milk and 2 cups of grated, ground, or finely chopped raw turnips. Season with salt and pepper. Stir well and cook until tender, about 10 minutes.

Peas Porridge Hot

A bowl of bean or split pea soup—piping hot with a slice of lemon and crisp bits of salt pork or bacon sprinkled over the top—is something more than "just bean soup".

Dried Bean or Pea Soup

Soak 1 cup of dried beans or peas over night in a quart of water. In the morning, add another quart of water, ¼ pound of salt pork, an onion, and a few stalks of celery if desired.

Simmer until the beans or peas are tender. Remove the salt pork and rub the rest through a strainer if a smooth soup is wanted. Cut the salt pork into tiny pieces and return to the soup. Add a tablespoon of flour mixed well with a little water to keep the bean pulp from settling to the bottom. Stir, reheat, and season with salt and pepper.

With Meat Left-overs—in place of the salt pork in the recipe above, cook the beans with a ham bone, or add some chopped left-over meat, or a frankfurter cut into thin slices.

Add Roasted Peanuts—finely chopped or ground peanuts are good in bean soup also.

With Tomatoes or Carrots—these add a touch of color and a few more vitamins to bean or pea soup.

For a "Hot" Soup—add a clove of garlic, half a chopped onion, 1 tablespoon oregano, and 2 chili peppers. Strain after cooking. Heat again and serve.

Bean Chowder

1 cup dry beans
1 cup diced carrots
1 cup tomatoes
½ cup shredded green pepper
1 onion, chopped fine

2 teaspoons salt
2 tablespoons uncooked cracked
   wheat or 1 tablespoon flour
2 cups milk
pepper to taste

Soak the beans over night in 1½ quarts of cold water. Cook in a covered pan until the beans begin to soften, then add the vegetables and cook until tender. Add salt and cracked wheat or flour mixed with a little cold water. Stir. Cook about 30 minutes. Add the milk and pepper, heat to boiling, and serve.

Vegetable Chowder

1 cup diced bacon
1 quart sliced okra
4 cups canned tomatoes
1 green pepper, sliced
2 cups cooked, dried lima beans
2 cups water

1/3 cup uncooked rice
2 cups canned corn
1 onion, minced
1 teaspoon salt
¼ teaspoon parsley, minced

Fry bacon until crisp in thrift cooker, on high. Remove bacon. Cook okra in drippings for 5 minutes. Add remaining ingredients. Cook on high until steaming freely, on low for 1 hour. Add the crisp bacon when serving. Serves 6.

MRS. H. G. WRIGHT, Fairfield County.

Cow Peas Soup

2 cups cow peas (field peas)
1 ham bone
2 quarts water

1 chopped onion
2 teaspoons salt or to taste
1 lemon sliced thin

Pepper to taste

Soak cow peas over night. Drain. Add to water and ham bone. Bring to a boil. Add chopped onion and salt, and simmer in covered kettle until beans are soft. Put through a strainer to make smooth. Add pepper to taste and reheat. Serve a slice of lemon in each soup plate. A favorite Low Country plantation soup.

PORTIA SEABROOK, Winthrop College.

Sauces

White sauce serves as one of the main ingredients for cream soups, creamed dishes, souffles, and croquettes. Egg, tomato, mint, hollandaise, drawn butter, lemon butter, and creole sauces are tasty additions to meat, fish, or vegetable dishes. Sauces may also be combined with left-over meats and vegetables for tasty main dishes. A good sauce is often the thing needed to bring out the flavor of canned meat.

White Sauce

General directions for making white sauce:

Melt butter in a saucepan. Add flour and salt, mix well together, making a smooth paste. Add milk slowly to the butter-and-flour mixture, stirring constantly. Cook until thick, stirring to prevent lumping.

Kind	Amt. of Fat	Salt	Flour	Milk	Use
White Sauce I	1 T.	½ t.	1 T.	1 c.	Cream soups
White Sauce II	2 T.	½ t.	2 T.	1 c.	Creamed dishes
White Sauce III	3 T.	½ t.	3 T.	1 c.	Souffles
White Sauce IV	4 T.	½ t.	4 T.	1 c.	Croquettes

T, tablespoon, t, teaspoon, c, cup.

Drawn Butter Sauce
(For Fish)

4 tablespoons butter
2 tablespoons flour
1 cup hot water or fish stock
1 hard cooked egg, chopped

¼ teaspoon salt
Dash of pepper
1 teaspoon lemon juice
2 tablespoons chopped parsley

Melt half the butter, add flour with salt and pepper. Stir to prevent lumping. Continue stirring while adding the hot liquid. Boil 3 minutes. Add remaining butter, the hard cooked egg and chopped parsley just before serving.

Barbecue Sauce

2 cups tomato catsup
1 cup vinegar
4 tablespoons Worcestershire
　sauce
1 tablespoon tabasco sauce

1 tablespoon salt
3 tablespoons prepared mustard
dash red pepper
Juice one lemon
½ lb. butter

Melt butter, add vinegar, then other ingredients, and bring to a boil. Let simmer a few minutes.

Cocktail Sauce

6 tablespoons tomato catsup
4 tablespoons lemon juice

Celery salt and tabasco sauce to
　taste

2 tablespoons horseradish

Shake ingredients of the cocktail sauce in a jar or wide-mouthed bottle until well mixed.

Lemon Butter Sauce
(For Fish)

¼ cup butter
½ teaspoon salt
½ tablespoon finely chopped
　parsley

1 tablespoon lemon juice
⅛ teaspoon pepper

Cream butter, add lemon juice very slowly and stir in other ingredients. Spread over hot fish.

Hollandaise Sauce

½ cup butter
½ tablespoon vinegar or
1 tablespoon lemon juice

2 egg yolks
¼ teaspoon salt
cayenne

Divide butter into thirds. Put 1/3 in a saucepan with acid and egg yolks. Place saucepan over warm water and keep the water well below the boiling point. Stir mixture constantly and as it begins to thicken, add a second third of the butter and, as this thickens, add the last third. When thickened remove from heat and add salt and cayenne. If a thinner sauce is desired, ½ tablespoon of warm water may be stirred into the sauce. Hold over lukewarm water until ready to use. Stir occasionally. Use for fish, broccoli or asparagus.

Mock Hollandaise or Cooked Sour Cream Dressing

1 teaspoon dry mustard
¾ teaspoon salt
1 teaspoon flour
2 teaspoons sugar
cayenne pepper

1 tablespoon salad oil or
  melted butter
4 tablespoons vinegar
½ cup evaporated milk
1 egg beaten

Mix dry ingredients in top of double boiler, gradually blending in salad oil or butter. Add 2 tablespoons of vinegar to egg, mixing well. Then add to salad oil mixture. Cook over hot water, stirring constantly until thick—about 5 minutes. Cool, stir the remaining vinegar into the milk. Beat into the cooked mixture until smooth. Serve on cooked or raw vegetable or combination.

MRS. MARGARET CROSBY, Joynes Hall, Winthrop College.

Egg Sauce

2 hard-cooked eggs
1 tablespoon chopped parsley
2 cups white sauce No. 2

Cut eggs into small pieces, mix with white sauce, and parsley. Serve hot over fish.

Mint Sauce

1 tablespoon finely chopped mint
  leaves
1 tablespoon powdered sugar
½ cup vinegar

Add sugar to vinegar. When dissolved, pour over mint and let stand 30 minutes on back of stove. If vinegar is strong, dilute with water. Serve with lamb.

Creole Sauce

¾ cup finely chopped onions
1 cup finely chopped sweet or
  green peppers
1 minced garlic clove
4 tablespoons butter
2 cups tomatoes
1 teaspoon salt
Dash pepper
Dash paprika

Cook fresh vegetables in fat for 10 minutes or until tender, stirring frequently. Add tomatoes and cook 5 minutes. Season. Serve hot with baked, broiled, and other fish dishes, or with fish cakes. Makes about 2½ cups of sauce.

Tomato Sauce 1
(For Meat Casserole Dishes)

3 tablespoons fat	½ teaspoon sugar
½ teaspoon mixed pickle spice	4 tablespoons flour
1 teaspoon salt	1 cup canned tomatoes

Melt the fat. Add salt, spice, sugar and flour, stirring constantly to make a smooth paste. Add tomatoes. Cook until thickened.

Tomato Sauce 2
(For Meat or Fish)

2 slices bacon, chipped	2 cups canned tomatoes
2 tablespoons flour	1 tablespoon Worcestershire
¼ cup chopped onion	sauce
½ cup chopped celery	½ teaspoon salt
¼ cup chopped green pepper	¼ teaspoon pepper

Lightly brown the bacon. Add flour to meat drippings. Stir to a smooth paste. Add remaining ingredients. Simmer 20 minutes.

Pimento and Cheese Sauce

To 1 cup of white sauce, add 2 pimentoes rubbed through a seive and 1 cup grated cheese.

Cheese Sauce

4 tablespoons fat	2 cups milk
4 tablespoons flour	½ teaspoon salt
2 cups cheese	

Melt the fat, blend in the flour. Stir constantly to prevent lumping. Add cold milk and salt. Heat and stir until thickened. Add the cheese. Stir until it melts. Serve over bread or toast slices, boiled rice, hominy grits, macaroni, or spaghetti, boiled potatoes, cabbage, asparagus, onions, cauliflower, or broccoli.

Sweet-Sour Sauce

½ cup tomato sauce or catsup	2 tablespoons vinegar
1 cup water	2 tablespoons prepared mustard
2 tablespoons brown sugar or molasses	

Baste meat loaf or meat occasionally while baking. Will flavor enough meat to serve six people.

MRS. IRA ROBERTSON, Edgefield County.

Hard Sauce

1/3 cup butter
1 cup powdered sugar

1/3 teaspoon lemon extract or
2/3 teaspoon vanilla

Cream butter and sugar until light and fluffy. Add sugar gradually. Add the flavoring.

Honey Sauce

1 cup honey
1¼ cups grated orange peel

½ cup orange juice
⅛ teaspoon salt

Combine the ingredients and let mixture stand over hot water without cooking for about 30 minutes to blend the flavors.

Lemon Sauce

½ cup sugar
1 cup boiling water
1 tablespoon cornstarch

2 tablespoons butter
1½ teaspoons lemon juice
Few gratings nutmeg

Few grains salt

Mix sugar and cornstarch and add water gradually. Boil 5 minutes, stirring constantly to prevent lumping. Remove from fire. Add butter, lemon juice, and nutmeg.

Strawberry Sauce

1/3 cup butter
2/3 cup strawberries

1 cup sugar
1 egg white

Cream butter and sugar. Fold in stiffly beaten egg white and crushed berries. (Other berries may be used.)

Foamy Sauce

½ cup butter
1 cup powdered sugar

1 egg
1 teaspoon vanilla

Cream butter and sugar. Add well-beaten egg and vanilla. Heat in a double boiler, beating constantly until mixture foams.

Cranberry Mint Sauce

Pick and wash 3 cups cranberries. Put 1¼ cups sugar and 1 cup boiling water in saucepan, bring to boiling point, add cranberries and boil until skins burst. Cool and serve, sprinkled with finely chopped mint.

MRS. ALEX BEVERLY, Marlboro County.

Cereals

Cereals are made from ripened seeds of grains such as wheat, corn, oats, barley and rice. The two staple cereals used in South Carolina are rice and hominy grits, and the two most commonly used cereal products are wheat flour and corn meal.

In the milling of refined cereals the outer coat or husk is taken off and used in animal feeds. Within this outer coat is found most of the grain's mineral and vitamin value. Whole grain cereals have a higher food value than the highly refined cereals.

ENRICHED FLOUR, CORN MEAL, GRITS

The addition of some of the minerals and vitamins lost in the milling process to the milled grain product is known as enriching or fortifying the product. All white flour, corn meal and hominy grits sold in South Carolina are required by law to be enriched. When a farmer takes his own wheat or corn to the mill he should ask for enriched flour or corn meal in exchange.

FOOD VALUE

Cereals are good energy-giving foods. Whole grain and enriched cereals furnish a fair amount of the B Vitamins—niacin, riboflavin and thiamine. Some iron is added through enrichment, also a small amount of calcium is added to enriched corn meal. Cereals furnish about 25% of the protein in our diets. The cereal protein, however, needs to be combined with milk, meat or egg protein to make it a top rating or complete protein.

KIND OF CEREALS

Cereals may be named according to methods of cooking.

Type	Example
1. Flaked	Rolled oats
2. Granular	Cream of wheat, wheatena

Type	Example
3. Cracked	Big hominy, hominy grits, corn meal
4. Paste	Macaroni, spaghetti
5. Whole grain	Rice

The cereal grain is surrounded by a woody substance called cellulose. This is hard to digest and must be softened before it is used for human food. Long slow cooking softens this cellulose. Well-cooked cereal is not lumpy. Each flake or part of the grain keeps its shape and is not broken down into a pasty mass.

GENERAL DIRECTIONS FOR COOKING CEREALS

Pour the cereal into boiling salted water (see table). Stir to prevent lumping. Flaky cereals are stirred with a fork. The granular and cracked cereals may be stirred with a spoon. Cook one to five minutes over direct heat. Then put into a double boiler. Cook for the length of time shown on the chart. In general, long cooking tends to break down the starch grains, thus making the cereal more easily digested.

Table for Cooking Cereal

Kind	Amount of Cereal	Amount of Water	Salt	Time
Flaked	1 cup	3 cups	¾ teaspoon	30 minutes
Granular	1 cup	4 cups	1 teaspoon	20-30 minutes
Cracked	1 cup	4 cups	1 teaspoon	20-30 minutes
Paste	1 cup	10 cups	2½ teaspoons	20-30 minutes
Whole Grain	1 cup	10 cups	2½ teaspoons	20-30 minutes

CORN MEAL

Corn Meal Mush

½ cup enriched corn meal   2½ cups boiling water

¾ teaspoon salt

Sprinkle enriched corn meal, stirring constantly, into rapidly boiling water. Add salt. Cook 30 minutes over direct low heat, or in double boiler 1 hour.

Fried Mush

Prepare enriched corn meal mush. Pour while hot into pan or mold which has been rinsed in cold water. Smooth the surface of mush. Cool until firm. Remove from mold. Cut in ¾ inch slices. Brown in hot fat.

Southern Spoon Bread

4 cups milk

1 cup enriched corn meal

2 tablespoons butter or margarine

1¼ teaspoons salt

4 eggs, well beaten

Mix the milk and enriched corn meal. Scald and cook in top of double boiler until the consistency of thin mush (about 5 minutes). Add the butter and salt. Fold well-beaten eggs slowly into mixture, (whites and yolks may be beaten separately and folded into mixture if desired). Pour into a greased 1½ quart baking dish. Bake in oven at 400 degrees for 45 minutes. Serve at once from pan in which baked with plenty of butter. Serves 4 or 5.

Corn Meal Souffle

2 cups milk

1/3 cup enriched corn meal

1 tablespoon butter

3 tablespoons or more grated cheese

1 teaspoon salt

¼ teaspoon paprika

Few grains cayenne

3 eggs

Scald milk in double boiler. Stir in gradually enriched corn meal, butter and cheese. Cook these ingredients to the consistency of mush. Add salt, paprika, and cayenne. To this mixture add well-beaten egg yolks and cook one minute longer. Cool; fold in stiffly beaten egg whites. Bake in ungreased baking dish in moderate oven 350 degrees for about 30 minutes, or until slightly crusty.

ENRICHED CORN GRITS RECIPES

Grits should be washed as little as possible. While enrichment does not wash out to any great extent, some natural food value is dissolved and floated off in the water. Degerminated or whole enriched corn grits may be used.

Boiled Enriched Grits

1 cup enriched grits   5 cups water
2 teaspoons salt

Add the grits to the salted boiling water. Boil 10 minutes over fire. Then place in top of double boiler and cook one hour. The grits may also be cooked over direct heat, but have to be stirred quite often. Milk and butter added just before removing from the stove improves the flavor. They are good served with country ham, fried chicken, or country fried steak. The gravy is served over the grits.

Fried Enriched Grits

Slice cold cooked grits ¼ inch thick. Dip in beaten egg. Brown in hot fat.

Enriched Grits Souffle

1 cup cooked enriched grits   ¼ teaspoon salt
½ cup hot milk   Dash of paprika
3 eggs, beaten separate

Beat together cold enriched grits and hot milk until smooth. Add salt and paprika. Stir in beaten egg yolks, fold in stiffly beaten egg whites. Cheese may be added if desired. Pour in greased baking dish. Bake in moderate oven (350 degrees) 30 minutes. Serve at once.

Hominy Turnover

1 pint cooked hominy (grits)   1 teaspoon salt
1 cup milk   2 well-beaten eggs
1 tablespoon fat

Mix well together. Turn into a frying pan in which the fat has been melted. Stir until hot throughout. Let it cook until golden brown on the bottom, then fold like an omelet and serve on a hot platter. This is suitable for the main dish at supper or luncheon.

BIG HOMINY

There are several kinds of hominy on the market. The chief differences lies in the fineness to which the different kinds are ground. Lye Hominy may be bought canned or in bulk or may be made at home. Big Hominy is another name for Lye Hominy.

Homemade Hominy or Big Hominy

2 quarts shelled corn 1 pint cold water
2 tablespoons lye 1 gallon boiling water

Put lye into kettle and add cold water; when dissolved, add boiling water and mix thoroughly. Stir in the corn, and bring to boiling point in 15 or 20 minutes, boil 25 to 40 minutes, stirring constantly. If the mixture cooks down so thick that corn begins to stick to kettle, add more boiling water. After boiling 20 minutes, test corn in cold water. If the eyes (or that part of the kernel which has been attached to the ear) fall out when touched, the corn is ready to wash. If the eyes do not come out, boil a few minutes longer and test again.

Remove from stove, fill kettle with cold water and stir thoroughly. Drain off water, repeat 4 or 5 times.

A wooden churn dasher is very good to use in the washing, as it loosens the eyes and one does not need to put the hands in the water. After the lye is washed off, continue working with the corn until eyes are all out. Cover corn with cold water and bring to a boil; drain off and repeat same process 3 or 4 times. After the last boiling, cover corn with cold water, bring to the boiling point and boil 3 or 4 hours. As the corn swells, add more cold water.

The hominy can be started one day and finished the next. On the first day, carry the process through the different washings, then let stand over night in cold water. Next day, drain off water, cover with cold water and boil as mentioned above. However, 2 or 3 boilings will be enough if lye has been properly washed off.

Caution: Don't use anything but an iron kettle and stir with a paddle. When washing the hominy, do not put the hands into the first four wash waters.

Big Hominy

Take 1 quart of corn, cover with hot water and let soak over night. In the morning put corn in a kettle with 1 tablespoon baking soda, cover with hot water and soak until the husks will come off easily. Pour in pan and run through 4 or 5 waters until all the husks are off. Put in kettle and cook until tender.

MRS. RUFUS CAMPBELL, Anderson County.

Hominy and Sausage—(big hominy)

Pile hot buttered hominy in the middle of a platter and arrange baked or fried sausage around the mound of hominy. Some of the brown sausage gravy may be used to season the hominy instead of butter.

Hominy and Bean Cakes

1 cup big hominy
1 cup cooked red kidney beans
½ teaspoon cayenne pepper
½ tablespoon cornstarch (or
   1 tablespoon flour)

½ cup milk
1 tablespoon fat
1 teaspoon salt

Make a white sauce from the last five ingredients by melting the fat, blending it with the cornstarch, salt and pepper, adding the milk, and cooking until thickened. Grind the hominy and beans through a food chopper, mix with white sauce, form into cakes and brown in a little fat. Such cakes may take the place of meat occasionally.

Fried Hominy

Heat 3 tablespoons of butter or bacon fat in a skillet. Add 2 cups cooked big hominy. Pepper and salt. Stir until all grains are covered with fat. Stir occasionally until slightly browned.

Hominy Loaf

(Hominy lacks the bran of the whole grain)

2 cups big hominy
1 cup milk
1 cup soft bread crumbs
2 eggs

1 tablespoon parsley
1 tablespoon green pepper
1 cup grated cheese
1 tablespoon onion juice

1 teaspoon salt

Scald the milk, add bread crumbs, cheese seasonings, beaten eggs and hominy. Turn into a baking dish, place in pan of hot water and bake in moderate oven. Serve with tomato sauce.

Tomato Sauce: Melt 2 tablespoons butter, add 2 tablespoons flour, ½ teaspoon salt, ⅛ teaspoon pepper and blend thoroughly. Cook 1 cup strained tomato with a slice of onion and gradually add to fat and flour. Cook thoroughly.

Hominy and Carrots

2 cups big hominy
2 cups well-seasoned medium
   white sauce or tomato sauce
   season to taste

3 cups carrots diced
2 tablespoons butter
½ cup cheese
1 cup buttered bread crumbs

Cook the carrots. Arrange the hominy and carrots in layers in a baking dish, season each layer. Melt the cheese in the sauce. Add to baking dish mixture, cover with buttered crumbs and bake about 20 minutes. Serves 4–6.

RICE

Rice was first grown in this country in South Carolina. The cultivation of rice in the low country around Charleston is closely woven into the history of the state. A ship from Madagascar, whose captain was John Thurber of New England, sailed into Charleston harbor some time before 1685. He presented a package of Madagascar rice to Dr. Henry Woodward, physician, explorer, and Indian trader, who planted the rice. By 1690 its production had become of considerable importance in the Province. Another variety from the East Indies was sent to South Carolina by Charles DuBois in 1696. These two kinds of rice were raised very successfully for many years, and the first became known as "gold from Madagascar."

Rice Cookery

Rice is most often served along with meat or vegetable dishes. Rice is a dinner or supper dish just as hominy grits is a breakfast or supper dish on most Carolina tables. It is most often served with a meat gravy. Rice lends itself to the making of many excellent dishes in combination with beef, pork, poultry, fish and vegetables.

Rice to reach its peak of perfection should be cooked so that every grain of rice stands apart. To cook rice so that it will be dry and whole grain, it may either be steamed in very small amount of water, allowing grains to absorb all of the moisture, or it may be cooked in large amount of water and drained. If the latter procedure is used, the water drained from the cooked rice should be used in soups, stews, gravies, as most of the mineral and vitamin content will be dissolved in this water.

Steamed Rice

1 cup rice   1¾ cups of water
1 teaspoon salt

Combine ingredients, let come to a boil in heavy pot or top part of double boiler. Cook uncovered until water is absorbed. Fluff up rice with fork so that each grain will stand up separately. Cover, turn heat low. Steam about 40 minutes till rice is dry and fluffy.

If double boiler is used, after the rice absorbs most of the water, fluff up with fork. Place over bottom part of double boiler and steam until dry and fluffy. Serves 4–5.

Boiled Rice

1 cup rice   8 cups hot water
2 tablespoons salt

Bring water with the salt to boil in deep kettle. Meanwhile, wash rice in running water, or in several waters until water is clear. Add rice to boiling water; cook uncovered at gentle boil. Test in 15 minutes. During boiling, lift rice from the bottom if necessary. Do not stir it. When tender, drain in colander. Save rice water for use in soups. Cover, set over hot water 10 minutes or turn rice into shallow pan and place it in warm oven for a few minutes to dry. Serves 6.

MRS. MILLARD JONES, Jasper County.

Parsley Rice

Sprinkle 1 to 2 teaspoons finely chopped parsley over hot rice just before serving. The parsley adds both flavor and color.

(For other rice dishes—see BEEF, PORK, POULTRY, CHEESE and VEGETABLE sections, also desserts using rice.)

Breads

The homemaker today finds an unlimited variety of breads, rolls, and biscuits on the bakery and grocery shelves; some baked, some semi-baked, some in the "mix" stage, and some in the dough stage. Yet, there are times when the homemaker likes to make up a batch of rolls or a loaf of bread in her own kitchen and takes pride in bringing forth a delicious tempting dish far superior to anything that is prepared or pre-cooked from commercial shelves.

Homemade breads are economical, nutritious and have an appeal to sight, palate and appetite. The slogan of our bread-making grandmothers was "To make good bread always be up in the morning early, just at peep of day."

Yet today with our modern equipment and improved ingredients, the housewife does not have to set a sponge the night before, neither does she have to always be up in the morning at the peep of day to watch and work all day to make good bread. Many of our newer recipes can be made in a very short time with all drudgery and kneading eliminated. Good ingredients together with careful measurements and the careful following of instructions all contribute to successful breadmaking.

Breads generally are of two classes: yeast breads and quick breads, depending on the type of leavening or "raising" used. For raised breads yeast is the leavening agent. Yeast is a microscopic plant that when grown under favorable conditions, produces a gas which causes the dough to be light and porous.

On the other hand, quick breads such as biscuit, muffins, waffles, etc., are raised by chemical action that takes place when baking powder is combined with water or sweet milk and soda is combined with sour milk or other acid ingredient. As a result of such chemical combinations a gas is released which causes the dough to expand and rise as in yeast breads.

Because of the difference in chemical changes, yeast doughs are handled and treated in a different manner from quick doughs. The finished breads are also different in texture and flavor.

Both yeast bread and quick bread doughs lend themselves well to many variations. A standard recipe of each may be used as a basis and from these basic recipes many interesting and attractive varieties may be developed.

Yeast Breads

BASIC RECIPE FOR ROLLS

1 cup milk (fresh or evaporated)	1 tablespoon melted fat
1 tablespoon sugar	1 teaspoon salt
1 package granulated yeast	Enough flour to make a very soft dough

Add sugar to milk, heat in double boiler to lukewarm. Add yeast and let stand until yeast is dissolved. Add 2 cups sifted flour and mix slightly; add fat and salt, then add enough flour to make a very soft dough, about the consistency of biscuit dough. Handle just until the dough is smooth; do not knead. Grease top well and let rise until double in bulk. Knead slightly and shape into rolls. Grease well, let rise until double in size, bake rolls at 400°. This dough may be shaped into any type rolls, clover leaf, parker house, or tea rolls, twists, knots, fan-tans or crescent rolls. It also may be made into one standard size loaf of bread. Bake loaf at 350°.

Variations

For cheese rolls. Add ¼ cup grated cheese to dough with the fat. Be sure to use a very sharp cheese, processed cheese does not work well.

Nut bread or nut rolls. Add 1 cup broken nut meats or ½ cup nut meats and ½ cup chopped raisins to dough while mixing.

Whole wheat rolls. Substitute full amount or ½ amount of whole wheat flour for white flour.

Sweet rolls. Use 4 tablespoons fat and 4 tablespoons sugar. One egg well beaten may also be added to dough. The egg adds only to food value, it makes little difference in texture of rolls.

Cinnamon buns. Use sweet dough, roll to ½ inch thickness, brush with melted butter, sprinkle with sugar and cinnamon, roll, cut in 1-inch sections, grease well, let rise, bake at 350°.

Caramel rolls. Use sweet dough, roll ½ inch thickness, brush with melted butter, sprinkle with brown sugar and chopped nuts, roll, cut in 1-inch sections, grease well, let rise, bake at 350°.

Rum rolls. To the sweet dough while mixing add ¼ cup candied orange peel chopped fine and ½ cup currants. After dough has risen knead it slightly, and then roll to ½ inch thickness. Brush it with melted butter, sprinkle with brown sugar, roll, cut in 1-inch sections, then bake and while hot frost with the following mixture:

To ¼ cup butter creamed well add 2 cups powdered sugar and ¼ cup rum. Add more sugar until mixture is stiff enough not to run.

The hot rolls will cause icing to melt and cover roll.

NOTE:

1. This recipe is an original recipe and has been tested many times and used by home demonstration club members in South Carolina. It is easy and quick; rolls can be made, baked and ready to eat easily in two hours.
2. Use all-purpose flour for best results.

3. Make a medium-soft dough that can be easily handled. Knead until smooth and elastic.

4. The sweet dough may be frozen in bulk or made into rolls and frozen. Do not let rolls rise before freezing. The frozen dough should not be kept longer than 2–3 weeks. Rolls frozen after they are baked may be kept 3 months.

MARGARET MARTIN, Extension Food Specialist.

Quick Ice Box Rolls

1 pint sweet milk	1 teaspoon salt
½ cup sugar	½ teaspoon soda
½ cup lard	½ teaspoon baking powder
1 pkg. yeast	½ cup lukewarm water

Enough flour to work into stiff dough

Scald milk, sugar and lard and set aside to cool to lukewarm. Dissolve yeast in ½ cup lukewarm water. Blend this into the first liquid. Then sift flour, salt, soda and baking powder into mixture until of consistency of roll dough. Set aside until it rises to double in bulk, then make out into rolls, cinnamon rolls or coffee cake and

bake, after the bulk is double again. This can also be stored in the refrigerator for several days. Bake at 450 degrees. Yields 4 dozen.

MRS. G. E. LANGLEY, McCormick County.

Kaloches

Dissolve: 1 cake yeast in ¼ cup lukewarm water.

Add: 1 cup flour to 1 cup top milk, gradually, to prevent lumps. Combine these and put in a warm place; let rise, then add:

4 tablespoons sugar	2 beaten eggs
½ cup butter	1 teaspoon salt
1½ cups flour, using enough to mix	

Let rise until double in bulk, then work down. Roll out about ½ inch thick and cut with biscuit cutter, place in an oiled biscuit pan and let rise again. When light, press down in center of each cake, and add any desired fruit mixture.

Filling, mix together:

1 cup chopped cooked prunes	½ cup prune juice
grated rind of 1 lemon	½ cup raisins
½ cup sugar	

Boil together until thick. Cool. Add ½ cup chopped walnuts. Place this mixture in centers of cakes and bake in 325 degree oven about 20 minutes.

MRS. ARTHUR GARRISON, Anderson County.

Parker House Rolls

¼ cup sugar	1 teaspoon salt
1/3 cup lard	1 cup boiling water

When the above mixture is lukewarm after shortening is melted add the following mixture which has set for about 10 minutes.

1 pkg. of yeast	½ cup warm water
½ teaspoon sugar	

Then add:

1 egg	4 cups flour (scant)

Let rise until double in size then make out rolls and let rise, then bake in hot oven. Dough may be covered and placed in refrigerator until ready to use instead of letting rise the first time.

MRS. JOHN BRYAN, Aiken County.

Lila Cox Rolls

1 yeast cake	8½ cups flour
½ cup sugar	¼ cup warm water
1 teaspoon soda	2 teaspoons salt
1 cup warm water	2 cups buttermilk

1 cup lard

Dissolve yeast in ¼ cup warm water. Let stand 10 minutes. Combine sugar, salt, soda, buttermilk and warm water in bowl. Add yeast mixture. Mix well. Sift flour, cut in shortening, add milk mixture to make a soft dough. Place in greased bowl and let stand in ice box over night. Shape into rolls and place in greased pan. Brush with melted butter. Let rise in warm place until doubled in size. Bake 15–20 minutes in oven preheated to 400 degrees. This mixture will last for one week.   Yield 4 dozen.

MRS. HUGH COX, Abbeville County.

Tender Crisp Rolls

1 cup hot water	1 egg well beaten
½ cups granulated sugar	1 cake yeast
1 teaspoon salt	¼ cup lukewarm water
1 tablespoon shortening	4 cups all-purpose flour

Soften yeast with 1 teaspoon sugar in ¼ cup lukewarm water. Combine hot water in large mixing bowl, with the salt, balance of sugar and shortening. When lukewarm, add the yeast mixture and the well-beaten egg. Then add 2 cups of flour and blend well. Add the balance of the flour or as much more as is needed to form a dough that will clear the sides of the mixing bowl. Blend well, grease bowl, return dough. Cover and store in refrigerator for at least 2 hours before using. When ready to use shape into rolls and let rise two hours. Bake in greased baking sheet or in muffin rings at 425 degrees until golden brown, about 12 to 15 minutes.   Yield 12.

THELMA BUTLER, Sumter County.

Rolls

1 cup lard	1 cup boiling water

¼ cup sugar

Cream lard and sugar and add water. Let cool and then add:

2 packages dry yeast dissolved	2 eggs
in 1 cup cold water	1 tablespoon salt

6 cups sifted flour

When first mixture is cool, add yeast and eggs, beaten stiffly. Add flour with salt, through a sifter. Put in refrigerator over night. In the morning, knead till smooth, fill muffin tins cloverleaf style or just plain and let rise for two hours. Bake in hot oven for twenty minutes at 350°.

SALLIE A. PEARCE, Winthrop College.

Refrigerator Rolls

1 quart sweet milk	2 cakes compressed yeast
1 cup mashed potatoes	3½ quarts flour
1 cup sugar	2 teaspoons baking powder
1 cup lard	1 teaspoon soda

1 teaspoon salt

Place milk, potatoes, sugar and lard in large saucepan and heat slowly to boiling point. Cool to lukewarm. Add yeast dissolved in a little of the lukewarm mixture. Sift and measure flour. Sift 3 cups flour with baking powder, soda, and salt. Stir into above with yeast mixture and allow to rise 30 minutes. Knead in remaining flour to make stiff dough. Place in large bowl, cover and store in refrigerator for 24 hours. Shape into rolls and allow to rise 1½ hours. Bake in moderately hot oven for 15 to 20 minutes. This dough can be kept in the refrigerator for a week, kneading down as often as necessary. Yield 8 dozen.

MRS. W. T. WILLIFORD, Anderson County.

Enriched Corn Meal Rolls

1¼ cups enriched flour	1 tablespoon sugar
¼ cup enriched corn meal	2 tablespoons shortening
3 teaspoons baking powder	1 egg
1 teaspoon salt	1/3 cup milk

Mix dry ingredients and cut in the fat. Beat the egg and add to the milk. Combine the liquid with the dry ingredients. Knead slightly, roll out, cut and shape as Parker House Rolls. Bake in hot oven 400-425 degrees for 20 to 25 minutes. Yield 12.

Salt Rising Bread

¼ cup coarse corn meal	1 tablespoon sugar
4 cups milk	5 tablespoons lard
¾ teaspoon salt	10½ cups sifted flour

Scald 1 cup milk and pour over corn meal. Let stand in warm place to ferment, about 24 hours. Heat 3 cups milk, salt, sugar and lard until lukewarm. Stir in 3½ cups flour and then the corn meal mixture. Place bowl containing these ingredients in a pan of lukewarm water for about 2 hours, or until bubbles work up from bottom, then stir in 5 cups of flour and knead in 2½ cups. Place dough in three 5 x 10 inch pans until it has doubled in bulk. Bake in moderate 350-degree oven for about 10 minutes, then increase heat to 425 degrees gradually. Bake 45 to 60 minutes in all. Protect batter from draughts. Do not attempt to bake bread in cold damp weather unless house is heated. Yield 3 loaves.

Mrs. A. C. Sullivan, Abbeville County.

Corn Meal Ice Box Rolls

½ cake yeast
¼ cup lukewarm water
½ cup enriched corn meal
2 cups boiling water
½ tablespoon salt
½ cup melted shortening
¼ cup sugar
1 cup potato water
Enriched flour

Make a sponge of the yeast, ¼ cup water and 1½ tablespoons enriched flour. Cover and allow to stand until light. Sift enriched corn meal slowly into the boiling water, add salt, and stir constantly until thick. Cook in double boiler 30 minutes. Remove from stove, add shortening, sugar and potato water (prepared by boiling ½ cup diced potatoes in 1 cup water). Stir until well blended. Cool. Add the sponge. Add sufficient enriched flour to make a dough stiff enough to knead. Turn onto slightly floured board. Knead until smooth and elastic. Cover with a damp cloth and allow dough to double in bulk. Knead down. Cover closely and place in refrigerator. When ready to use, remove portion of dough. Form into rolls. Place in well-greased pans. Cover and let rise until treble in bulk. Bake in hot oven 450 degrees about 15 minutes. The unused portion of the dough should be worked down, covered closely with waxed paper, and returned to the refrigerator until needed. Yield 36 rolls.

Amadama Bread

½ cup enriched corn meal
2 cups boiling water
2 tablespoons shortening
3 teaspoons salt
2 cakes fresh yeast
½ cup lukewarm water
about 7-8 cups sifted enriched flour
½ cup molasses

Add the enriched corn meal gradually to the boiling water while stirring constantly. Then add the shortening, molasses, and salt, and cool to lukewarm. Soften the yeast cakes in the lukewarm water and stir into mixture. Add enough enriched flour to make a stiff dough and knead well. Place in a greased bowl, cover with a clean cloth, and let rise in a warm place (80 to 85 degrees) until double in bulk. Cut through the dough several times with a knife, or punch down with the fingertips, cover and let rise again for 45 minutes. Toss onto a lightly floured board and knead well, adding more enriched flour if necessary. Shape into 2 loaves and place in 2 greased loaf pans about 10 x 5 x 3. Cover with a cloth, place in a warm place (80 to 85 degrees) and let rise until nearly double in bulk. Bake in a hot oven of 425 degrees for 15 minutes, then reduce heat to a moderately hot oven of 375 degrees and finish baking, allowing about 1 hour in all. Brush the crust with melted fat, then remove and cool on cake rack. Makes 2 loaves. Takes about 5 hours or less to make. Yield 2 loaves.

White Bread—(quick method)

2 cups milk
5 tablespoons sugar
2 packages yeast

2 cups lukewarm water
5 tablespoons shortening, melted
12 cups sifted flour

Scald milk, add sugar, cool to lukewarm. Dissolve yeast in lukewarm water and add to lukewarm milk. Add ½ flour and stir until smooth. Add salt, fat and remaining flour or enough to make easily handled dough. Knead lightly until dough is smooth. Grease dough, cover and let rise until double in size, about 1½ hours. Divide into 4 parts, shape into loaves, place in greased loaf pans, grease top well and let rise about 1 hour or until double in size. Bake in oven 375 degrees. Yield 3 loaves.

BISCUITS

Buttermilk Biscuits

2 cups flour
¼ teaspoon salt
4 teaspoons baking powder

½ teaspoon soda
5 tablespoons shortening
1 cup buttermilk

Sift flour, salt, baking powder, and soda; cut in shortening, until mixture resembles coarse crumbs. Add buttermilk all at once, and stir until dough follows fork around bowl. Turn out and knead ½ minute. Roll ⅜ inch thick; brush with melted fat or salad oil; fold over and cut double biscuits with biscuit cutter. Bake on ungreased cookie sheet in hot oven 450 degrees 12 to 15 minutes. Yield about 24 biscuits.

Mrs. E. E. Hester, Greenville County.

Southern Style Biscuits

2 cups flour, plain   1 teaspoon salt
3 teaspoons baking powder   3 tablespoons cooking oil
              2/3 cups buttermilk

Place flour in deep mixing bowl. Add baking powder and salt and blend well. Add oil and milk, stirring until smooth. Pour onto floured board and knead until manageable. Roll to ½ inch thickness and cut. Preheat oven to 475 degrees and bake. Yield about 24 biscuits.

Mrs. Charles V. Mullins, Cherokee County.

Tea Biscuit

1 cup butter (or ¾ cup   ¾ cup sweet milk
   shortening)   4 cups flour
3 rounded tablespoons sugar   4 teaspoons baking powder
2 eggs   1 teaspoon salt

Cream butter and sugar, add well-beaten eggs, then sweet milk, then dry ingredients well sifted together. Turn out on slightly floured board and roll ¼ inch thick. Cut with biscuit cutter, grease with butter and fold over and press edges together. Grease slightly the top of each biscuit.   Yield 30.

Mrs. Tom Brice, Fairfield County.

Sweet Potato Biscuits

3 cups self-rising flour   ½ cup shortening
¼ cup sugar   2 cups mashed sweet potatoes
              ¼ cup milk

Mix flour, sugar, potatoes, shortening together and add milk. Mix well, roll and cut as regular biscuits. Bake in moderate oven 425 degrees for ten to fifteen minutes. Butter while hot and serve at once.

Mrs. B. H. Willis, Colleton County.

CORN BREAD

Awendaw Corn Bread

1 cup boiled hominy. While hot stir in one tablespoon of butter. Beat 2 eggs very light and stir in hominy. Add ½ pint of milk. Gradually add ¼ pint of corn meal. The batter should be of the consistency of a rich boiled custard. Put into a well-buttered baking dish. Bake with a good heat at the bottom and not much at the top so as to allow it to rise.

MRS. JOSEPH HEYWARD, Berkeley County.

Johns Island Corn Bread

1 cup fat	1¼ cups flour
¼ cup sugar	6 teaspoons baking powder
2 eggs	1 teaspoon salt
1¾ cups corn meal	1¼ cups milk

Cream sugar and fat, add well-beaten eggs. Then add alternately with the milk and the other ingredients which have been sifted together. Bake in greased pan 10 x 14 for 25 minutes at 450 degrees. Cut into squares. Yields 40 pieces.

JULE HILLS, Charleston County.

Corn Dodgers

1 cup meal	½ cup white flour
¾ cup milk	1 egg
2 tablespoons melted	1 tablespoon sugar
shortening	3 teaspoons (heaping)
½ teaspoon salt	baking powder

Sift the dry ingredients. Whip up the egg in a measuring cup. Stir in the milk and pour into the other ingredients. Add the melted shortening and mix thoroughly. Drop by spoonfuls into deep hot fat or vegetable oil. Cook until golden brown. Yield 18-24.

MRS. HAL D. WATSON, Dillon County.

Crackling Cornbread

2 cups sifted meal	1½ cups cracklings (mashed
1 1/3 cups cold water	if preferred)
1 teaspoon salt	

Mix all ingredients, and pour into greased pan. Yield 2 pones.

MRS. W. A. SCOTT, McCormick County.

Corn Sticks

2 cups corn meal	2 eggs
2 cups buttermilk	½ teaspoon salt
4 tablespoons fat	1 teaspoon soda
1 teaspoon baking powder	

Mix dry ingredients, add beaten eggs, slowly add milk, beating thoroughly. Add melted fat last. Grease heated stick mold and bake in moderate oven 350 degrees about 25 minutes. Yield 12 sticks.

MRS. E. C. CHEATHAM, McCormick County.

Corn Meal Hoe Cake

2 cups sifted corn meal	1 teaspoon salt
2 cups cold water	¼ teaspoon soda

Mix dry ingredients and add water. Have bread hoe or iron frying pan well greased and hot enough to fry (not burning hot). Cook on top of stove at moderate temperature. When brown one side, turn over and cook until done. It requires 15 minutes or longer to cook. It is good with butter, fish and vegetables. Yield 8.

MISS EMMIE SHEPPARD, McCormick County.

Corn Muffins

¾ cup flour
4½ teaspoons baking powder
2 tablespoons sugar
1½ teaspoons salt

1½ cups corn meal
1 well-beaten egg
1¼ cups milk
¼ cup melted shortening

Sift all dry ingredients together. Mix egg, milk and shortening. Add to dry ingredients. Mix quickly and pour into 12 greased two inch muffin tins or a greased 8 x 8 x 2 inch baking pan. Bake in hot oven 425 degrees for 20 minutes or until brown. Yield 12.

MRS. JOHN H. BOOZER, Newberry County.

Old Fashioned Southern Egg Bread

2 cups water-ground corn meal
2 raw eggs well beaten together
½ cup melted shortening
  (not butter)

1 level teaspoon salt
3 level tablespoons sugar
3 level teaspoons baking powder
2 cups sweet milk

Sift meal, sugar and salt in bowl. Melt shortening in pan that bread is to be baked in. Add this slowly to meal mixture alternately with the sweet milk. Beat hard for a moment, then add beaten egg and lastly baking powder. Fold this in and pour in greased pan and bake for 20 minutes to half hour. Yield about 12 servings.

MRS. R. W. TISDALE, Beaufort County.

Southern Spoon Bread

1 cup sifted, yellow enriched
  corn meal
1 quart whole milk

3 tablespoons melted butter
1½ teaspoons salt
4 eggs, well beaten

Blend the meal with one cup of milk. Add the remaining milk. Stirring constantly, cook at medium temperature until mixture thickens. Add melted butter, salt. Fold in well-beaten eggs. Pour into a greased pan; bake at 350° for 45 to 50 minutes. Yield 8 servings.

For main dish add 1 cup grated aged cheese just before folding in well-beaten egg whites. Served with asparagus or steamed okra, and broiled tomato halves, this makes a good meal.

ETTA SUE SELLERS, Dillon County.

Corn Pone

2 quarts corn meal
1 teaspoon salt
1 cup buttermilk

3 teaspoons sugar
1 teaspoon soda
3 pints of water

Take one pint of hot water and stir in ½ pint of meal. Cook ½ minute. Add salt and sugar, remove from stove. Pour in 2 pints of cold water, stir in rest of meal. Set in warm place over night, or until pone rises. Take one cup sour milk, 1 teaspoon soda and mix together. Stir in meal mixture. Put in oven and cook 1 hour and 30 minutes at 375 degrees. Yield about 10 servings.

MRS. J. KIRK McCAIN, Lancaster County.

Hush Puppies

2 cups meal
1 tablespoon flour
½ teaspoon soda

1 teaspoon baking powder
1 cup buttermilk
1 teaspoon salt

1 egg

Mix all dry ingredients, add the milk, then the egg last. Drop by tablespoons into hot fat. Yield 20 medium.

MRS. R. W. SHELLHOUSE, Aiken County.

Corn Light Bread

Bring 1 quart water to boil. Wet 2½ cups of meal. Cook mush well. Add 2 cups cold water, 2 cups sweet milk, then 5½ cups meal and 3 cups of flour. Sprinkle meal over top. Let rise over night.

Add:

½ cup buttermilk
1 egg

1 scant teaspoon soda
2 cups sugar and salt to taste

Instead of 2 cups sugar, 1 cup of sugar and 1 cup of sorghum molasses may be used.

Knead, make into loaf. Let rise until double in bulk, bake in moderate oven.

SALLIE A. PEARCE, Winthrop College.

MUFFINS—POPOVERS

Popovers

2 eggs
1 tablespoon shortening
　(melted)

1 cup milk
1 cup flour
1 teaspoon salt

Combine eggs, milk and shortening. Pour into a well made in dry ingredients. Combine, stirring until smooth (rotary egg beater). Pour into greased deep pans, 1/3 to ½ full. Bake in oven 450 degrees for 20 minutes, 325 degrees for 25 minutes. Remove promptly so that the bottom does not steam or soften. Serve hot as bread stuff for creamed mixtures.　Yield 15 small, 8-10 large.

Mrs. Earl Stanley, Jasper County.

Muffins

½ cup liquid
1 cup flour
2 teaspoons baking powder

½ tablespoon fat
¼ teaspoon salt
1 tablespoon sugar

1 egg

Sift dry ingredients together. Combine liquids. Mix liquid into dry ingredients. Stir just enough to dampen dry mixture. Do not beat. Bake at 375 degrees.　Yield 8.

Mrs. Earl Stanley, Jasper County.

Bran Muffins

1 cup all-bran
1 cup milk
1 cup flour
3½ tablespoons baking powder

½ teaspoon salt
1 egg
¼ cup sugar
2 tablespoons melted shortening

Let all-bran soak in the milk for five minutes; mix into it flour, baking powder, salt, sugar. Mix well. Add whole egg and beat mixture until smooth, and add shortening (melted). Grease muffin tins and fill full of the mixture and cook at 400 degrees for 20-25 minutes. Yield 12-14 muffins.

Mrs. Ray P. Hook, Fairfield County.

Berry Muffins

3 cups sifted flour
3 teaspoons baking powder
1/3 cup sugar

4 tablespoons melted shortening
¾ cup milk
1 egg

1 cup cooked or fresh berries

Drain cooked berries. Sift dry ingredients together, combine shortening, milk and egg and add to dry ingredients, stirring just enough to moisten flour mixture. Fold in berries. Bake in greased muffin tins in a moderate oven 400 degrees. Yield 16 muffins.

Mrs. J. P. CHASTAIN, Greenville County.

Popovers

3 eggs
1 cup milk

1 cup flour
3 tablespoons butter

1 teaspoon salt

Beat eggs, add milk, flour, salt, and butter. Do not beat too much. Bake at 425 degrees for 30 minutes. Serve piping hot with butter or jelly. Yield 10-12.

BETTY MANN, Fairfield County.

Sugary Apple Muffins

2¼ cups flour
3½ teaspoons baking powder
½ teaspoon salt
½ teaspoon cinnamon
½ teaspoon nutmeg

½ cup plus 2 tablespoons sugar
1 egg—beaten
1 cup milk
1 cup chopped apples (not too small pieces)

4 tablespoons lard

Sift dry ingredients (save ¼ teaspoon nutmeg and ¼ teaspoon cinnamon and 2 tablespoons sugar for top). Cream lard and ½ cup sugar. Stir in egg, then flour, alternating with milk. Fold in apples. Fill greased muffin tins almost full. Sprinkle with remaining two tablespoons sugar, ¼ teaspoon cinnamon and ¼ teaspoon nutmeg which have been mixed together. Bake at 425 degrees for 20 to 25 minutes. Yield 12.

MARIE A. HAMILTON, Charleston County.

Peanut Muffins

¾ cup enriched corn meal	2 tablespoons sugar
1¼ cups enriched flour	1 cup finely ground peanuts
1 teaspoon salt	1 egg
4 teaspoons baking powder	1¼ cups milk

Mix dry ingredients, add peanuts. Mix milk and beaten egg, add to dry ingredients. Bake in greased muffin tins in moderate oven 350 degrees about 30-40 minutes. Yield 12.

WAFFLES—HOT CAKES

Waffles

2 cups flour	2 teaspoons baking powder
½ teaspoon salt	¼ teaspoon soda
1 cup buttermilk	½ cup melted butter and lard
½ cup cold water	mixed

1 egg

Add salt, soda, and baking powder to beaten egg. Then add milk, flour, water. Last add melted shortening. Yield 6-8 servings.

Mrs. W. E. Senn, Newberry County.

Waffles

1 egg
1 cup milk
3 teaspoons baking powder

4 tablespoons melted shortening
⅛ teaspoon salt
2 tablespoons meal

1 cup flour

Beat egg separately, yolk from white. Add milk to the beaten yolk, then add flour, meal, shortening, salt and baking powder. Fold in stiffly beaten white of egg. Yield 6 servings.

Mrs. D. B. Pridmore, Cherokee County.

Crisp Waffles

2 cups all purpose flour
½ teaspoon soda
½ teaspoon salt
4 teaspoons baking powder

3 eggs
2 cups sweet milk
¼ cup melted butter
1 tablespoon sugar

Sift, then measure flour. Sift again with baking soda, salt, and sugar. Combine milk, well-beaten egg yolks and melted butter. Add dry ingredients to liquid ingredients. Beat until well blended. Fold in stiffly beaten egg whites just before baking. Bake on hot waffle iron 4 to 5 minutes or until done.

Mrs. Kennedy Dowtin, McCormick County.

Hot Cakes

2 cups flour
4 teaspoons baking powder
1 teaspoon salt

2 cups milk
2 tablespoons cooking oil
2 tablespoons honey

2 eggs

Mix ingredients in order given. Grease hot griddle with meat skins. Drop on hot greased griddle and turn when cake bubbles all over. Remove to warm platter and brush with melted butter. Grease griddle each time batter is put in. Yield 20 cakes.

Oscar Sturkey.

CHEESE BREADS

Cheese Straws

1 pound aged cheese
¼ pound butter

2 cups flour
1 teaspoon salt

dash of red pepper

Grate cheese and mix with flour, salt, red pepper and add melted butter and mix thoroughly. Run through cookie press on cookie sheet and bake for 10 minutes. Yield 40.

MRS. DOW BEDENBAUGH, Laurens County.

Cheese Straws

1 cup sifted all purpose flour
½ teaspoon baking powder

1 cup grated cheese
½ cup butter

3 tablespoons cold water

Sift flour and baking powder into a bowl. Cut in cheese and butter with pastry blender. Add water and mix well. Fill a cooky press. Form straws on ungreased cooky sheets, using the star plate. Bake at 400 degrees for 8-10 minutes. Yield 3 dozen.

MRS. W. H. IRBY, Kershaw County.

Cheese Puffs

¼ pound butter
1 cup flour

¼ pound very sharp cheese
pecan halves

Grate cheese. Work in and cream with butter. Work flour into this. Roll out ½ inch thick and cut with cutter 1¼ to 1½ inches in diameter. Bake from 12 to 15 minutes in 450 degree oven. Place ½ pecan on each and brush with powdered sugar. Yield 24 puffs.

MRS. HUNTER NICKLES, Abbeville County.

Cheese Balls

1 cup bread crumbs
1 teaspoon salt

¼ teaspoon cayenne
3 egg whites (beaten stiff)

2 cups grated cheese

Mix. Form into balls and roll in cracker crumbs. Fry in deep fat. Yield 12.

MRS. F. O. BARNES, Lee County.

Cheese Biscuits

½ pound butter
½ pound cheese grated or
  mashed with fork

1 teaspoon salt
2 teaspoons sugar
2 cups sifted flour

Cream butter and cheese, add salt, sugar and flour. Make into a roll. Wrap in waxed paper and let stand several hours in refrigerator. Slice and bake as for ice box cookies. A date may be placed in center of each slice and two sides pulled up to hold date. Makes around 24 biscuits depending on size of cutter.

MRS. A. C. SULLIVAN, Abbeville County.

Cheese Biscuits

2 cups flour
3 teaspoons baking powder
½ teaspoon sugar

4 tablespoons shortening
½ cup grated cheese
⅞ cup milk

1 teaspoon salt

Sift dry ingredients, work in the shortening and cheese, add milk. When well mixed, toss the dough on a floured board and pat to one half inch in thickness. Shape into rounds with a biscuit cutter. Place in a greased baking pan, brush with milk. Bake in a very hot oven, 450 degrees, 12 to 15 minutes. Yield 24.

MRS. ROY MIMS, Sumter County.

Dainty Cheese Biscuits

1 cup butter
2 cups grated cheese (a sharp
  cheese gives better flavor)

1½ cups cake flour (slightly
  more may be needed to
  make a stiff dough)

Mix all ingredients together to make a stiff dough. Roll thin and cut with small biscuit cutter. Press pecan halves in center. May also be cut in other desired shapes. Bake in a hot oven 400 degrees 5 to 8 minutes. Yield 20.

MRS. ROY MIMS, Sumter County.

Cheese Dreams

1 pound flour (plain)
1 pound butter

nuts (halves)
powdered sugar

1 pound sharp cheese

Cream butter and cheese, add sifted flour, roll thin and cut out with a biscuit cutter. Put date stuffed with a pecan half in each pastry. Fold over and pinch together. Bake in a hot oven and while hot sprinkle with powdered sugar. Yield about 30.

Mrs. H. M. McLaurin, Jr., Sumter County.

Cheese Wafers

½ pound butter or margarine
½ pound grated highly flavored cheese
2 cups sifted, plain flour
¼ teaspoon salt
season with red pepper, if desired

Mix butter and cheese thoroughly, blend in flour. Add salt and pepper. Make into a roll, wrap in oil paper, and keep on ice until ready to use. Slice off wafers thick as desired and brown in oven at 350 degrees. Bake 10 to 12 minutes.

Miss Agnes Estes, Cherokee County.

Cheese Rings

½ pound sharp cheese (grated)
¼ pound butter (creamed)
⅛ teaspoon cayenne pepper
1½ cups flour
¼ teaspoon salt

Mix well. Wrap in oil paper and chill over night. Roll dough to ¼ inch thickness and cut with small size doughnut cutter. Bake in oven at 350 degrees until they are slightly brown. These may be cut in ½-inch strips for cheese straws. Yield 18 rings or 30 straws.

Mrs. Killough H. Patrick, Fairfield County.

Cheese Balls

1 cup grated sharp cheese
1 tablespoon flour
Dash pepper
1 egg white stiffly beaten
¼ teaspoon salt

Mix flour, cheese, salt, and pepper. Fold into beaten egg white. Form in balls, or drop by teaspoons full into deep fat (375°F.) and fry till golden brown. Makes 12 balls.

Sallie A. Pearce, Winthrop College.

FRUIT AND NUT BREAD

Old Fashioned Nut Loaf

2 cups cake flour

2 teaspoons baking powder

½ teaspoon salt

2/3 cup butter

3 eggs, unbeaten

¾ to 1 cup nut meats, finely cut

1/3 cup milk

1 teaspoon vanilla

1 cup sugar

Sift flour once, measure, add baking powder and salt, and sift together three times. Cream butter thoroughly, add vanilla and sugar gradually and cream together until light and fluffy. Add eggs, one at a time, beating thoroughly after each addition. Add nuts and blend. Add flour alternately with milk, a small amount at a time. Beat after each addition until smooth. Bake in greased loaf pan in moderate oven 350 degrees 1 hour and fifteen minutes.

MRS. A. L. BAKER, Charleston County.

Apple Nut Bread

Sift together:

2 cups flour

1 teaspoon soda

½ teaspoon salt

Cream:

½ cup shortening

½ cup sugar

1 teaspoon vanilla

    or

1 tablespoon grated orange rind

2 eggs

1½ tablespoons sour milk

½ cup ground nuts

1 cup ground apples, with skin left on

Use electric mixer:

Add ½ of flour mixture to creamed mixture. Add sour milk. Add balance of flour, then nuts, then apples. Bake in shallow pan 350 degrees. Serve with whipped cream on blocks of bread or make sandwiches out of blocks filled with cream cheese.

MRS. E. M. MORGAN, McCormick County.

Date Bread

1 cup nuts

1 cup dates

1 cup white sugar

1 cup boiling water

2½ cups flour

1 egg

1 teaspoon soda

1 teaspoon salt

1 teaspoon baking powder

4 tablespoons butter or lard

Cut dates, add shortening and sugar, pour boiling water over this, let cool. Sift flour with salt, soda and baking powder. Add to the above mixture, put in nuts and add egg last (beaten together). Pour in greased pan with paper in the bottom. Bake in moderate oven.

MRS. W. H. WYLIE, Fairfield County.

Orange Bread

Chop the peel of 4 oranges. Cook 5 minutes with warm water and 1 teaspoon soda. Place in colander, let water run through until it is clear. Add ¾ cup of water and 1 cup sugar. Cook until it thickens like preserves. Let cool. Cream 1 cup sugar with 3 tablespoons of butter. Add 2 well-beaten eggs, 1 cup sweet milk, 3½ cups flour, 3 teaspoons baking powder, 1 cup nuts. Add orange mixture, pour into greased pans and bake 1 hour in moderate oven 375 degrees. Yield 1 loaf.

MRS. W. H. WYLIE, Fairfield County.

Fruit Drop Biscuits

2 cups sifted flour
2½ teaspoons baking powder
2 tablespoons sugar
4 tablespoons butter or other
   shortening

½ teaspoon salt
¾ cup milk (scant)
1 cup apples, pared, cored and
   finely chopped
1½ teaspoons grated orange rind

½ cup raisins finely chopped

Add dry ingredients and milk gradually. Drop from teaspoon on ungreased baking sheet. Bake in hot oven (450 degrees) for 12 minutes. Yield 18.

MRS. W. H. STOKES, SR., Kershaw County.

Orange Marmalade Nut Bread

3 cups pastry flour
3 teaspoons baking powder
½ teaspoon salt
4 tablespoons sugar
1 egg, beaten

2 tablespoons melted shortening
1 cup sweet milk
½ cup walnut meats, chopped
1 teaspoon grated orange peel
½ cup orange marmalade

Sift flour, then measure. Sift together the first four ingredients, (flour, baking powder, salt and sugar). Add remaining ingredients in order given. Pour batter into well-greased pan and let stand for 10 minutes. Bake in moderate oven 350 degrees for 1 hour. Time will depend on size of pan in which bread is baked. Yield 2 loaves.

MRS. E. M. KENNEDY, Fairfield County.

Banana Bread

4 large bananas
2 eggs
1 cup butter
1 cup sugar

4 cups flour
1 cup nuts (pecans or walnuts)
1 teaspoon soda
3 tablespoons water

pinch of salt

Mash bananas, add eggs, cream butter and sugar, then add flour, and nuts. Dissolve soda in water. Add salt. Mix all together. Bake in moderate oven. A baking powder can (large one) is excellent to bake in. Yield 2 small loaves.

MRS. SYBIL F. KOON, Newberry County.

Date and Nut Bread

1 cup dates	1 cup whole wheat flour
1 teaspoon soda	1 egg
1½ cups boiling water	2 cups brown sugar
2 cups all purpose flour	1 teaspoon salt

4 tablespoons melted butter

Pour boiling water over chopped dates and baking soda. Let stand until cool. Sift all purpose flour. Mix with whole wheat flour (½ graham and ½ buckwheat may be used). Beat egg well, combine with sugar, salt and shortening. Alternately add date mixture and flour. Add nuts last. Pour into paper lined, greased loaf pans.   Yield 1 loaf.

MRS. PAUL WHITENER, Oconee County.

Date Bread

2½ cups flour	2 cups finely cut dates
2 teaspoons baking powder	½ cup chopped walnut meats
1 teaspoon soda	1 egg
1 teaspoon salt	2 cups sour milk
1 cup whole wheat flour	3 tablespoons melted shortening

Sift together white flour, baking powder, soda and salt. Stir into this, whole wheat flour, dates and nuts. Beat egg and combine with sour milk. Add this to flour mixture, stirring only until well mixed and then add shortening. Turn into a greased loaf pan and bake 1 hour at 350 degrees.

MRS HUBERT ANDERSON, Abbeville County.

Apricot Bread

Soak for 30 minutes in warm water to cover—one cup dried apricots. Drain and cut apricots with scissors into ¼-inch pieces. Mix together thoroughly:

1 cup sugar	2 tablespoons soft butter or
1 egg	shortening

Stir in:

¼ cup water	½ cup orange juice

2 cups sifted self-rising flour

Blend in the cut apricots. Line bottom of greased loaf pan with paper, grease paper. Pour in batter, let stand 20 minutes. Bake 55 to

65 minutes in moderate oven 350 degrees until wooden pick thrust into center comes out clean. Remove from pan. Take off paper immediately. Let cool on rack.

Brown Bread

2 cups whole wheat flour	1 cup enriched corn meal
¼ teaspoon soda	1 cup seedless raisins
2 teaspoons baking powder	1 cup milk
1 teaspoon salt	1¼ cups sorghum

Sift flour, soda, baking powder and salt together; add enriched meal and raisins. Add milk and molasses; stir until batter is well mixed. Pour into well-greased one pound baking powder cans and steam three hours, or in pressure cooker one hour at 15 pounds. Sour milk may be used instead of sweet; the soda is then increased to ½ teaspoon and only one teaspoon baking powder is used. Yield 2 loaves.

Unleavened Bread

2 cups flour	1 level teaspoon salt
1 heaping tablespoon butter	1 level teaspoon sugar

Mix these four ingredients well.

Add enough fresh sweet milk to make a stiff dough. Beat the dough until it blisters. Roll dough a little thicker than for pie crust. Check off with a knife, but do not cut quite through the dough. Place in a baking tin and bake in a moderate oven until a very light brown.

MRS. E. MEEK DICKSON, York County.

Cheese

Some like it mild—some like it nippy. Some like it cooked—some like it "as is." But any way you take it, cheese is a popular food. A lot of good food value is found in cheese. Its "contents" include protein of the best quality, calcium needed for bones and teeth, and riboflavin of the vitamin B family. Cheese made from whole milk has vitamin A, too.

Cheese is "something to build meals around." An egg-and-cheese combination, macaroni-and-cheese, or any dish with quite a bit of cheese in it belongs in the main-dish class. Like meat, eggs, and fish, cheese has satisfying flavor and staying power. Cheese is one of the most popular meat substitutes.

[98]

Cheese also fits into meal plans in soups, salads, and desserts.

But remember, cheese is a concentrated food and should be used in small amounts, grated or in combination with other foods.

Cheese is a protein food, so must be cooked at a low temperature. Cooked too quickly, cheese gets tough and stringy.

Cheese Sauce

4 tablespoons fat	½ teaspoon salt
4 tablespoons flour	½ pound cheese, shaved thin
2 cups milk	(2 cups)

Melt the fat, blend in the flour. Add cold milk and salt. Heat and stir until thickened. Add the cheese. Stir until it melts. Serve over bread or toast slices, boiled rice, hominy grits, macaroni, or spaghetti—boiled potatoes, cabbage, asparagus, onions, cauliflower, or broccoli.

Scalloped Vegetables

Pour cheese sauce over fresh cooked or left-over vegetables, snap beans, carrots, turnips, peas, corn. Put in a shallow baking dish, cover with bread crumbs, bake until crumbs are brown and the vegetables heated through.

Welsh Rabbit

For an easily made rabbit that will not curdle make a cheese sauce as above and beat lightly until the cheese melts. Add onion and any other seasoning you wish. Beat 1 or 2 eggs well. Pour a little of the sauce into the egg, then pour all back into the sauce. Cook 2 or 3 minutes longer, then serve on toast or crackers.

Tomato Rabbit

2 tablespoons fat	2 tablespoons flour
½ small onion, chopped	1 pint tomatoes
½ green pepper, chopped, if desired	½ pound cheese, shaved thin (2 cups)
½ cup finely cut celery if desired	1 teaspoon salt
	2 eggs well beaten

Melt fat in a heavy skillet. Stir in onion, celery and pepper. Cook a few minutes, stirring frequently. Add the flour, tomatoes, cheese and salt. Stir and cook over low heat until the mixture thickens and the cheese melts. Pour some of this mixture into well-beaten eggs.

Pour all back into the skillet and cook until thickened and creamy. Serve on toast or crackers.

Blushing Bunny

1 can tomato soup
½ cup cream

¼ pound American cheese, grated
salt and pepper

Heat tomatoes and add cheese, cream, salt and pepper. Stir until cheese is well melted. Serve on toast, hot. Serves 6.

REBECCA CLAYTON, Dorchester County.

French Cheese Omelet

4 eggs
½ teaspoon salt
⅛ teaspoon dry mustard

4 tablespoons milk
1 to 2 tablespoons butter
¼ pound cheese

dash pepper

Beat eggs until well blended. Add salt, mustard, pepper and milk and mix well. Heat butter in an 8-inch skillet until moderately hot. Pour egg mixture into skillet. Cook over low heat. An omelet needs to cook evenly to be tender. Tip skillet and lift edge of omelet with spatula so that uncooked mixture runs under cooked portion. When the egg mixture is still moist but almost firm throughout, add the coarsely shredded cheese. Sprinkle it completely over the top of the omelet. When the cheese begins to melt and the bottom of the omelet is golden brown, loosen it gently. Fold it in half and turn out on a hot platter. Serve immediately. Serves 4-5.

MRS. LEVI BOGGS, Pickens County.

Cheese Souffle

¼ cup butter
3 tablespoons flour
1 cup milk
1 cup cheese, grated

3 eggs, separated
½ teaspoon salt
paprika, to taste
1 teaspoon onion juice, if desired

Prepare a cream sauce with butter, flour and milk. Cook this mixture until thick, then add grated cheese and stir until melted. Add 3 egg yolks, salt, paprika and onion juice. Mix carefully and fold in stiffly beaten egg whites. Turn into a buttered baking dish and set it in a pan of water in a moderate stove. Bake until firm. Serves 6.

JANETTE PATRICK, Fairfield County.

Tomato Cheese Souffle

1 cup tomato juice or strained
tomatoes
3 tablespoons butter
3 tablespoons flour
¾ teaspoon salt

generous pinch red pepper
1 cup grated cheese
3 egg yolks beaten
3 stiffly beaten egg whites

Make sauce by melting butter. Remove from heat and stir in flour, then slowly add cup of tomato puree and salt and cook, stirring constantly until thick. Add 1 cup grated cheese to sauce mixture after removing from heat. Fold in 3 stiffly beaten whites, place in buttered dish and bake in a slow oven until a golden brown. Serve immediately. Serves 6.

MRS. A. C. SULLIVAN, Abbeville County.

Cheese Charlotte

Heat 1 cup milk in double boiler and add 2 tablespoons butter blended with 2 tablespoons flour. Cook eight to ten minutes, stirring all the time. Add 1 cup grated cheese, beat well. Then stir in beaten yolks of 4 eggs. Season with salt and pepper. Cool the mixture. Then fold in the stiffly beaten whites and put into a buttered baking dish and bake in oven at 350 degrees for 30 minutes. Serves 6.

MRS. L. Y. WHETSELL, Dorchester County.

Cheese Fondue

1 cup scalded milk
1 cup soft stale bread crumbs
1 cup grated cheese

1 tablespoon butter
½ teaspoon salt
3 eggs

Mix milk, bread crumbs, cheese, butter and salt. Pour over the beaten yolks, fold in beaten whites and bake in a buttered baking dish 20 minutes in a moderate oven.

Cheese Puff

8 slices bread
½ pound cheese grated (2 cups)
3 eggs

2 cups milk
pepper, paprika, mustard
if desired

Fit four bread slices into the bottom of a greased baking dish. Sprinkle with half the cheese and cover with remaining bread. Beat eggs, add milk and seasonings, pour over the bread and cheese mixture, and cover with remaining cheese. Set baking dish in a pan of hot water and bake in a moderate oven for about 40 minutes, or until the custard is set and the bread is puffed up.

Cheese Wheel Dish

1 pound cheese
9 slices bread
3 eggs
1 cup milk
tablespoon butter

Cut bread into triangles. In shallow baking dish place these in pinwheel shape. Cover entire wheel with slices of cheese. Pour over this a mixture of the eggs and milk. Dot with butter. Let stand ½ hour and bake in 300 degree oven for 1 hour, or until lightly browned. Serve immediately. Serves 7-8.

CAROLYN C. BRUNER, Lee County.

Baked Cheese

3 eggs
1 cup bread crumbs
1 pint milk
1 tablespoon butter
⅛ teaspoon pepper
½ teaspoon salt
½ cup grated cheese

Soak the bread crumbs in the milk 15 or 20 minutes. Then stir in the beaten eggs, butter, salt, pepper and cheese. Put in buttered baking dish and bake about 30 minutes, 350 degree oven. Serves 4-5.

Macaroni and Cheese

Put layers of boiled macaroni in buttered baking dish with grated cheese between and on top. Pour over it white sauce No. 2, cover with bread crumbs, and bake until crumbs are brown.

Macaroni Casserole

2½ cups cooked macaroni
½ pound cheese
2½ cups milk
¼ cup butter
1 egg
1 can asparagus tips (green)

Cook macaroni and drain and cool. Place in double boiler, milk, cheese, and butter. Heat until cheese and butter melt. Mix in macaroni and add 1 egg. Put layer of macaroni mixture in casserole, add asparagus tips on top, then pour remaining macaroni mixture over this. Bake in 350 degree oven 30 minutes. Serves 8.

NADINE McARTHUR, Beaufort County.

Cheese Potato Pie

2 quarts peeled and thinly sliced Irish potatoes	2 cups milk
	2 tablespoons butter
1 pound cheese	pepper and salt to taste

2 eggs

Peel and slice potatoes. Cut cheese in small pieces, put potatoes and cheese in layers in baking dish. Stir milk, eggs, butter, salt and pepper and pour over potatoes. Bake until potatoes are tender. Serve as main dish. Serves 8.

MRS. E. C. COLSON, Charleston County.

Cheese and Nut Roast

1 cup grated cheese	1 tablespoon butter
1 cup chopped nuts	juice of ½ lemon
1 cup bread crumbs	¼ teaspoon salt
2 tablespoons chopped onions	⅛ teaspoon pepper

Cook onion in butter and a little water until tender. Mix other ingredients and moisten with water in which the onion has been cooked. Pour into a shallow baking dish and brown in oven.

Nut and Cheese Croquettes

1 cup chopped pecans	1 egg
1 cup cooked rice	1 small onion
½ cup bread crumbs	1 teaspoon salt
¾ cup grated cheese	cayenne

½ cup milk

Combine all ingredients. Make into croquettes and roll in more bread crumbs. If made up ahead of time, put in refrigerator to become firm and they will keep their shape better when fried. Fry in shallow fat, turning frequently so they become uniform golden brown. Can be served plain, with mushroom sauce or with cheese sauce. Serves 8.

MINNIE ROWLAND STOUT, McCormick County.

Toasted Cheese Roll Wrapped in Bacon

Remove crusts from a large loaf of bread. Cut in lengthwise slices 1/3 inch thick, and 6 or 7 inches long. Spread each slice very thick with yellow soft spreading cheese. Roll up the full length of slice like a jelly roll. Wrap each roll with 2 slices of bacon. Toast under broiler, turning frequently so that bread is evenly toasted and bacon well broiled. Delicious served with fruit salad.

MRS. HENRY ESSICK, Richland County.

Cheese Toast

½ to ¾ pound **cheese** thinly sliced (2-3 **cups**)	2 tablespoons water
	2 eggs
1 cup milk	½ teaspoon salt
2 tablespoons flour	1½ teaspoons baking powder

Shave cheese into thin, small pieces. Heat milk in a double boiler, thicken with flour, which has been mixed with water. Cook for 5 minutes. Add this sauce to the beaten eggs. Then add the cheese and salt. Cook slowly until cheese melts and the mixture is creamy. Let it cool. Then add baking powder.

Toast on one side of the bread. Spread cheese mixture thickly on untoasted side—to the very edge. Brown delicately under a low broiler flame or in the oven. Serve hot from the oven. Makes enough for 10 or 12 slices.

Toasted on Crackers

Grate cheese or slice it fine. Spread over crackers. Toast in the oven or under a low broiler flame until the cheese melts. Serve instead of a sweet dessert—or to make soups and salads more substantial.

Cottage Cheese

Take one gallon of sweet skim milk, add three-fourths of a cup sour milk and stir as it is put in. Raise the temperature in hot water to 75 degrees Fahrenheit (barely lukewarm) using a dairy thermometer. Remove from heat and place where it is to remain until set. Add one-eighth of a Junket tablet thoroughly dissolved in four tablespoons of cold water; stir while adding. Cover with cloth and leave from 12 to 16 hours in even temperature, about 75 degrees F. (kitchen temperature). There should be a slight whey on top, and when poured out the curd should cleave sharply. Drain through cotton cloth, not cheesecloth. When whey has been drained out, work one or two teaspoonfuls of salt into the cheese, according to taste. 1½ to 2 pounds of cheese should be obtained from a gallon of milk.

A superior product may be made by adding a starter to the sweet milk which prevents the development of undesirable fermentations and produces a sour milk. Such a starter may be a good real buttermilk, or it may be produced by ripening pasteurized milk with a pure culture of lactic ferment such as used in large creameries.

Sour Cream Cheese

Take 1 cup good sour cream. Whip and add 1 cup cottage cheese and 1 teaspoon salt. Place in glass dish, cover tightly and let stand 24 to 48 hours in refrigerator or cool room. Finely ground pimento— ½ cup—may be molded into the above to improve it for sandwiches.

Cooked Cheese

To the curd from 1 gallon of skim milk add 1 teaspoon soda, 1 teaspoon salt and 1 cup sour cream or butter. Place in top of double boiler and cook until as thick as good cream sauce. Add yellow vegetable color and cook 1 or 2 minutes longer. Pour into greased molds and chill. Use for sandwiches and for seasoning macaroni or similar dishes. This cheese may be cooked down very thick, molded as butter and sliced.

Other recipes for both yellow cheese and cottage cheese may be found under salad, soup, vegetables, and egg dishes.

EGGS EVERY DAY

No wonder we say "a good egg." Eggs have—
Protein in the top class with foods like meat and milk for building
and repairing body tissues.

[106]

Two of the B vitamins—thiamine and riboflavin—plus vitamins A and D to help protect health.

The egg yolk holds a rich store of iron for red blood cells and has phosphorus and other minerals needed for the body.

An egg every day—that's a good rule to follow when eggs are plentiful. Try to give at least five or six eggs a week to children and to pregnant and nursing women—at least four or five to other adults.

When You Store Eggs

Treat a good egg right by storing it under proper conditions. Here are the rules: Clean—covered—cold.

Eggs with clean shells keep best. Wipe off soiled spots with a damp cloth, but don't wash eggs until just before you use them. When eggs are first laid, the shells have a film known as the "bloom" which seals the pores and helps keep out bacteria and odors. Washing removes this protective film.

Store eggs in a covered bowl or pan, away from strong-smelling foods. Without a cover, eggs lose moisture faster and are more likely to absorb odors.

Keep eggs in the refrigerator or other cold place. Stored at room temperature, eggs may lose as much in quality in 3 days as those kept 2 weeks in a good refrigerator. If any of the eggs have cracked shells, use them first.

To keep leftover egg yolks or separated whites until they can be used, place yolks in a dish or cup and add just enough cold water to cover. Put egg whites in a jar or dish and cover tightly. Be sure to keep them cold.

Use Eggs Many Ways

"The egg is the cement that holds the castles of cookery together," once said a famous chef. You may use eggs to thicken a custard or sauce—to leaven, or lighten a souffle or cake—to hold together oil and vinegar in a creamy mayonnaise—you may use egg whites to make cloudy soups clear, or an eggshell with some of the white still clinging to "settle" muddy coffee.

When You Cook Eggs

First and fundamental rule whether you're cooking eggs in water, frying pan, or oven, is to cook them with low to moderate, even heat.

Like all protein foods, eggs cooked at too high a heat get tough and leathery.

Other egg-cooking rules:

To prevent curdling—

When making custards or other dishes that call for hot milk to be added to the egg, mix sugar with the egg and not with the milk. Add hot liquids or mixtures to the beaten egg a little at a time. Don't over-cook.

To beat egg whites—

Let whites stand awhile—they whip up best when they're as warm as room temperature. For a larger foam, add a pinch of salt before beating.

To combine beaten egg whites with other mixtures—

Fold—don't stir—using a light under-and-over motion. And for omelets and souffles fold the heavy mixture into the beaten egg white— not the whites into the other mixture. Don't over-mix or you'll lose some of the air you've beaten into the egg whites.

To make a meringue—

Beat egg whites and salt until the foam forms soft, moist peaks. Add sugar, 1 tablespoon at a time—allowing 2 tablespoons sugar for each egg white—and beat thoroughly each time to dissolve sugar. After all the sugar has been added, beat until meringue piles well.

For a whiter meringue that cuts well and *is flavorful,* add lemon juice before beating.

When you top a pie with meringue, be sure to cool pie filling first—this helps to prevent wateriness.

To help prevent shrinking, spread meringue to edges of pastry so it has something to cling to during baking.

Bake meringue in moderate oven 325 degrees 15 to 20 minutes.

EGGS AS YOU LIKE THEM

Eggs in the Shell

Cover eggs completely with cold water and bring gradually to simmering (just below boiling). Do not let the water boil.

For soft cooked eggs—Simmer 3 to 5 minutes. Break hot into cup for serving; season.

Another way to soft cook eggs is to bring water to boiling, put the eggs in carefully, and take the pan off the stove at once. Cover pan to hold steam, and let the eggs cook in the hot water 5 to 8 minutes. For hard cooked eggs—Simmer 25 to 30 minutes. Serve hot in the shell or plunge eggs into cold water and remove the shells.

Poached Eggs

Break eggs into a saucer and slip into gently boiling, salted water— enough to cover the eggs—in a shallow pan. Bring to simmering, re- move from heat, and cover. Let stand about 5 minutes, or until eggs are as firm as you want them. Remove eggs carefully and serve on toast. Add salt and pepper to taste, and if you like pour a little fat over them. Or serve poached eggs on a bed of seasoned, cooked rice or spinach or other greens.

The egg poacher is a very convenient utensil and can be bought in different sizes to poach from one to eight eggs. Water is placed in bottom part of pan and brought to simmering point. Eggs are slipped gently into each section or egg cup which has been buttered or greased with bacon fat. Eggs are seasoned with salt and pepper, and a small dot of butter placed on each egg. The eggs are covered and placed over low heat until soft or medium poached.

Baked Eggs

Break the eggs into a shallow greased baking dish; add 1 table- spoon of milk for each egg and dot with fat. Season with salt and pepper. Cover and bake in a moderate oven 325 degrees for 20 to 25 minutes, or until as firm as desired.

For variety, omit the milk and sprinkle the eggs with fine, dry bread crumbs, bake uncovered until eggs are set and crumbs are lightly browned. If desired, mix grated cheese with the crumbs.

Scrambled Eggs

For each egg, use 1 tablespoon of milk, and beat them together slightly. Season with salt and pepper. Pour the mixture into a frying pan containing melted fat, and stir constantly over low heat until it thickens. Serve at once.

Or, if preferred, cook the eggs in a double boiler or pan over hot water. Melt a little fat in the pan, pour in the egg mixture, and stir constantly until thickened.

For a "different" flavor or to space out eggs when they're scarce try scrambled eggs—

With bread crumbs—Use 4 eggs, beat slightly with 4 tablespoons milk, season with salt and pepper. Brown 1 cup soft bread crumbs in a little fat in a frying pan. Pour the egg mixture over the crumbs and cook over low heat, stirring constantly, until eggs are thickened. For added flavor, stir chopped onion or green pepper into the egg mixture before cooking.

Or try scrambled eggs with cooked rice, noodles, or cereal in place of the bread crumbs.

With tomatoes—Beat 4 eggs and add 1 cup cooked tomatoes. Season with salt and pepper. Cook as you would plain scrambled eggs. Serve on toast.

Creamed Eggs

¼ cup flour
¼ cup fat, melted
Salt and pepper
2 cups milk
6 hard-cooked eggs, quartered

Blend flour thoroughly with melted fat. Add milk and cook over low heat, stirring constantly until thickened. Add eggs to sauce, season, heat and serve on toast.

If desired, add to the fat 2 teaspoons Worcestershire sauce or grated onion, or ¼ to ½ teaspoon curry powder.

With fish, poultry, meat—Make a thin white sauce by reducing the fat and flour in the above recipe to 2 tablespoons each. Use fewer eggs, if desired, and add 1 to 2 cups flaked cooked fish, chopped cooked meat or poultry.

As an egg sauce for fish—Add 3 finely chopped hard-cooked eggs to the thin white sauce, and serve hot over fried or baked fish.

Omelets Flat—Omelets Fluffy

Flat omelets—fluffy omelets, whichever you like—the ingredients are the same: One or two eggs for each person, 1 tablespoon of milk for each egg, and salt and pepper to taste. To make omelets fluffy beat the egg yolks and whites separately. For a flat omelet, beat all ingredients together.

Plain Omelet

Beat the eggs slightly with 1 tablespoon milk for each egg, season with salt and pepper. Pour into a frying pan containing melted fat and cook over low heat. Lift the egg mixture with a knife, to let the un-cooked part run underneath until the omelet is cooked through. Brown lightly on the bottom, fold or roll the omelet, and turn onto a hot platter.

Fluffy Omelet

Separate the eggs and beat the yolks thoroughly. Add 1 tablespoon milk for each egg. Beat together the egg whites and a little salt until stiff but not dry. Gradually fold in the egg yolk mixture. Pour into a frying pan containing melted fat. Cook over low heat until the omelet is lightly browned on the bottom. Cover and cook until set.

Or when it is lightly browned on the bottom, finish cooking the omelet by baking in a moderate oven 350 degrees 10 to 15 minutes or until browned on top.

Crease through the center, fold over, and roll the omelet onto a hot platter.

Bread Crumb Omelet

4 eggs, separated	½ cup milk
½ teaspoon salt	½ cup soft bread crumbs, firmly
⅛ teaspoon pepper	packed

1 tablespoon fat

Add pepper to yolks, beat slightly. Add crumbs and milk. Add salt to whites and beat until stiff, but not dry. Fold crumbs and yolk mixture into whites. Heat fat moderately hot in a skillet (approx. 9 x 3 inch) pour in omelet mixture. Level surface gently. Place a cover on skillet and cook over sufficiently low heat so that bottom is only slightly browned after 15 minutes of cooking. Cook about 20 to 25 minutes until the surface is dry (touch lightly with finger tip) and knife inserted in center comes out clean. Fold and serve on warm platter. Serve plain or with tomato, mushroom or vegetable sauce. Serves 4.

Many Ways to Serve

Dress up an omelet with a mushroom sauce, tomato, cheese, or Spanish sauce, or top with creamed vegetables or meat.

For a sweet omelet, add jelly or fruit marmalade just before rolling the omelet.

For a tomato omelet, use tomatoes instead of milk for the liquid.

Add potatoes or rice to omelet—this makes a tasty dish and is a good way to space out eggs if they're scarce. Add 1½ cups mashed potatoes or cooked rice to the egg mixture before cooking. Be sure to

beat the potatoes until they are light and smooth before adding them. For fluffy omelet add the potatoes or rice to egg yolk mixture before folding into beaten egg whites.

Add to the egg mixture before it is cooked or sprinkle over the top of the cooked omelet just before folding about 1 cup chopped cooked meat or left-over cooked vegetables, a little grated cheese, or chopped parsley. If you're adding them to a fluffy omelet before cooking, be sure to mix them with the egg yolk mixture before folding into beaten whites.

Puffy Egg Omelet

4 eggs	⅛ tablespoon pepper
½ teaspoon salt	2 tablespoons flour
2 tablespoons water	1 tablespoon butter

Start oven at 300 degrees. Separate eggs. Add salt and water to whites. Beat until standing in peaks. Add pepper and flour to yolks and beat until smooth. Stir smooth yolk mixture into beaten whites gently with spoon or spatula. Melt butter or margarine in large skillet. Spoon mixture into pan carefully and cook over low heat 5 minutes. Place pan in oven and bake 8 to 10 minutes or until puffy. Slide omelet out of pan into hot platter after loosening edges carefully with a knife.

Keep puffy side up and golden side down. Fold in half. Variations: Serve with jelly, mushroom sauce, creole sauce, or other sauces.

Creamed Eggs

3 hard-cooked eggs   1 cup medium white sauce
                         4 slices toast

Cut eggs in quarters, or slice. Make white sauce and combine with eggs. Serve hot on toast.

MEDIUM WHITE SAUCE

1 cup milk, scalded   2 tablespoons butter or butter
2 tablespoons flour   substitute
pepper   ½ teaspoon salt

Melt butter and combine with flour. Add milk slowly, stirring constantly. Cook over hot water or in iron frying pan until thick and smooth. Add salt and few grains of pepper. Use when eggs are plentiful and cheap.

ELLEN FRIDAY, Fairfield County.

Creole Eggs

6 hard-cooked eggs   1 cup canned tomatoes
2 tablespoons butter   1 green pepper
1 medium sized onion   Salt and pepper to taste
                    3 cups cooked rice

Boil rice. Melt butter in saucepan, add chopped onion and green pepper. Cook until tender (not brown). Add strained tomato and season. Cut eggs in eighths. Put pieces into serving dish and pour sauce over them. Serve very hot with rice.

Eggs au Gratin

8 eggs   ½ teaspoon salt
2 cups milk   pepper
4 tablespoons butter   bread crumbs
4 tablespoons flour   4 tablespoons grated cheese

Break eggs into a saucer and slip into a buttered baking dish. Pour in the white sauce made as follows: Melt the butter, blend in the flour, salt and pepper; add the milk and cook 5 minutes, stirring constantly. Cover with bread crumbs and sprinkle with grated cheese.

Cook in a moderate oven until brown on top. Tomato sauce may be used instead of white sauce by using 2 cups of tomato juice instead of milk.

Scalloped Eggs

6 hard-cooked eggs
1 cup medium white sauce
butter or butter substitute
1½ cups bread or cracker crumbs
salt and pepper

Place layer of bread crumbs in well-oiled baking dish. Fill dish with alternate layers of sliced eggs, crumbs and white sauce. Sprinkle with salt and pepper. Dot each layer with butter or butter substitute. Cover with crumbs. Bake in moderate oven 375 degrees until sauce bubbles through crumbs and top is well browned. Serves 6.

ELLEN FRIDAY, Fairfield County.

Stuffed Curried Eggs

6 eggs
¼ teaspoon dry mustard
2 teaspoons vinegar
2 teaspoons Worcestershire
  sauce
3 tablespoons mayonnaise
2 tablespoons butter
2 tablespoons flour
1 teaspoon curry powder
1 teaspoon salt
1 cup milk

Hard boil eggs, cool, cut in half, remove yolks and mash. Add mustard, vinegar, sauce, mayonnaise. Mix well and stuff into egg whites. Place in a shallow baking dish. Melt the butter in saucepan, adding flour, curry powder and salt. Cook 1 minute, and stir in milk slowly. Continue cooking until thick and pour over stuffed eggs. Place in oven at 300 degrees for 20 minutes.

MRS. RAY P. HOOK, Fairfield County.

Eggs Scrambled with Luncheon Meat

¼ cup diced luncheon meat
1 tablespoon fat
4 eggs beaten
¼ cup milk
¼ teaspoon salt
pepper

Lightly brown the diced luncheon meat in fat in a frying pan over moderate heat. Combine eggs, milk, salt and pepper and add to the meat. Cook, stirring constantly until eggs are done. To complete the meal, serve with baked potatoes, carrot and celery sticks and sliced tomatoes or tomato aspic salad. Serve fruit dumplings for dessert. For variety—Salami, canned cured pork loaf, frankfurters or any sliced or canned meat may be combined with eggs in this way for a quick dinner dish. To stretch the eggs when prices are high, add 1 cup soft bread crumbs to the egg mixture before cooking. Instead of luncheon meat, use ¾ cup diced cheese; add it to egg mixture. Garnish with broiled or fried tomatoes or serve with tomato sauce. Substitute diced cooked chicken giblets for luncheon meat and chicken broth for the milk.   Serves 4.

MRS. SAM RILEY, Dorchester County.

Alibi Eggs

3 tablespoons cold water
3 tablespoons tomato sauce
1 tablespoon Worcestershire sauce

1 tablespoon butter
1 tablespoon mayonnaise
1 teaspoon prepared mustard
4–5 eggs

When mixture is boiling, drop in eggs and cook to suit the taste. Use no salt or pepper. Serve on toast or with rice or grits. Do not scramble eggs, they are to be poached in sauce.   Serves 4–5.

MRS. S. L. THOMPSON, Spartanburg County.

Egg Toast

Add ¾ cup milk and ¼ teaspoon salt to 1 or 2 beaten eggs. Mix thoroughly. Dip both sides of bread slices quickly into the egg mixture. Melt a little fat in a frying pan and brown bread on both sides over moderate heat. Makes 10 to 12 slices.

Creole Stuffed Eggs

Hard cook 6 eggs, halve lengthwise, mash yolks and add ½ teaspoon dry mustard, 1 to 2 tablespoons butter or light cream, 2 tablespoons vinegar, ½ teaspoon salt, dash pepper, other seasoning, if desired. Place stuffed eggs on rice in casserole. Make creole sauce as follows: Melt 2 tablespoons butter, add 1 medium sized onion, ½ cup finely chopped celery and cook until onions and celery are tender. Blend in 3 tablespoons flour, then tomatoes; cook, stirring until thickened. Add 1 teaspoon salt, 1 teaspoon sugar, ¼ teaspoon pepper, dash of garlic salt.

Pour hot sauce over casserole of stuffed eggs and rice. Sprinkle top with bread crumbs and bake 10 to 15 minutes or until bubbly. Makes 4 to 6 servings.

JANIE McDILL, Winthrop College.

Meats

All lean meats—beaf, veal, pork, lamb, fish—and variety meats furnish good quality protein needed by the body for growth, maintenance and repair of body tissues. Lean meats are rich in iron and in the B vitamins, niacin, thiamine, and riboflavin.

To many of us, meat is the important food around which we build our meals. The rest of the meal is determined to a large extent by the kind of meat to be served whether we have chicken for dinner or spare ribs. Fresh, frozen, cured and canned meats have much to offer in variety, flavor and ways of preparation.

Know Your Cuts

Cuts differ in tenderness according to part of animal from which they are taken, and to age and fatness of animal. Cuts differ also in the amount of bone and gristle they contain and in the direction the muscles run. All these points have their effect on price, popularity of cut and method of cooking.

It is wise to learn the cuts of meat and how to cook them. Cuts in less demand generally furnish the more economical buys, offer just as good possibilities for attractive dishes and are just as palatable and nutritious.

HOW TO CARE FOR MEAT

Fresh, Cooked, Cured

1. Store fresh meat, uncovered or *loosely* covered, in coldest part of the refrigerator.

2. Store cooked meat, *closely* covered, in the refrigerator.

3. Store cured meat, wrapped, in the refrigerator.

[116]

Frozen

1. Store frozen meat at 0° F. or lower.
2. Defrost frozen meat: (a) in refrigerator; (b) at room temperature; (c) during cooking.
3. Cook meat which has been defrosted as soon as possible.
4. Do not refreeze meat after it has been defrosted.
   Cook frozen and defrosted meat by basic methods

HOW TO COOK MEAT

Basic Methods

Cooking by Dry Heat: 1. Roasting; 2. Broiling; 3. Panbroiling.
Cooking by Moist Heat: 4. Braising; 5. Cooking in liquid.
Cooking with Fat: 6. Panfrying; 7. Deep-fat frying.
Always Cook Meat at Low Temperature

Roasting

1. Season with salt and pepper.
2. Place meat, fat side up, *on rack* in *open* roasting pan.
3. Insert meat thermometer.
4. Do not add water. Do not cover. Do not baste.
5. Roast in slow oven: Beef, Veal, Lamb, Cured Pork, 300° F.; Fresh Pork, 350° F.
6. Roast to desired degree of doneness.

Broiling

1. Set oven regulator for broiling.
2. Place meat two to three inches from heat.
3. Broil until top is brown.
4. Season with salt and pepper.
5. Turn and brown other side.
6. Season and serve at once.

Panbroiling

1. Place meat in heavy frying-pan.
2. Do not add fat or water. Do not cover .
3. Cook slowly, turning occasionally.

4. *Pour off fat as it accumulates.*
5. Brown meat on both sides.
6. Season and serve at once.

Braising

1. Brown meat on all sides in fat in heavy utensil.
2. Season with salt and pepper.
3. Add small amount of liquid.
4. Cover tightly.
5. Cook at low temperature until tender.

Cooking In Liquid
(Stews and Large Cuts)

1. Brown meat, when desirable, on all sides in own fat or hot lard.
2. Season with salt and pepper.
3. Cover with liquid, cover kettle; cook below boiling point until tender.
4. Add vegetables just long enough before serving to be cooked.

Panfrying

1. Brown meat on both sides in small amount of fat.
2. Season with salt and pepper.
3. Do not cover.
4. Cook at moderate temperature until done, turning occasionally.
5. Remove from pan and serve at once.

Deep-Fat Frying

1. Melt enough lard to cover the food to be cooked.
2. Heat lard to 350° to 360° F. before adding food.
3. Maintain temperature of fat at 350° to 360° F. and cook until done.
4. Remove from fat and drain.
5. Serve at once.

Cooking Meat at Low Temperature

Results in: 1. Uniformly cooked meat; 2. Juicier, more tender meat; 3. Fewer and better drippings; 4. Less watching during cooking; 5.

Less work in cleaning; 6. More easily carved meat; 7. More meat to serve and more attractive servings.

For Meat at Its Best: 1. Select it wisely. 2. Care for it properly. 3. Cook it correctly. 4. Serve it attractively.

Beef

Pot Roast Beef

2 pounds beef
¼ cup flour
1 onion

4 tablespoons fat
2 cups water
salt and pepper to taste

Melt fat in pot, salt and pepper beef and rub flour well into all 4 sides, put in pot and brown on all sides. Cut up onion and let brown. Add water and let simmer until tender. Serves 6.

If you like Irish potatoes and carrots cooked with the meat drop them in about 20 minutes before meat is tender.

Mrs. Harry W. Huggins, Williamsburg County.

Pot Roast with Vegetables in Pressure Saucepan

Shoulder or Rump cut—4 to 5 pounds	1 onion
	½ cup water
seasoned flour	6 potatoes
2 tablespoons fat	6 whole carrots, small

Dredge meat with seasoned flour, brown in fat in bottom of saucepan. Place onion on meat, if desired. Add ½ cup water. Cook at 10 pounds pressure for 40 minutes. Reduce pressure immediately. Add potatoes and carrots and cook for about 8 minutes at 10 pounds. Serves 12.

MRS. D. G. BURDEN, SR., Dillon County.

Stuffed Inexpensive Roast

Use 3 pounds shoulder roast. Have bone drawn. Wipe meat and prepare for cooking. Stuff opening with washed uncooked prunes and unpeeled apples. (About 3 apples and 10 prunes). Sew up opening using large needle and heavy cord. The cord will be easily removed when ready to serve. Sprinkle meat with salt (1 tablespoon). Rub meat with 2 tablespoons of shortening. Sprinkle with 2 tablespoons of flour. Have ready roasting pan with 2 tablespoons of melted shortening. Place meat to brown (use medium heat). When brown, turn meat to brown on other side. Add 2 cups of hot water. Cook at low temperature until tender. Place on platter, remove cord and serve. Serves 6.

MRS. PAUL H. ANDERSON, Charleston County.

Beef Short Ribs Creole

3 pounds short ribs beef	2 onions sliced
2 teaspoons salt	1 cup hot water
½ teaspoon pepper	2 cups cooked tomatoes
1 garlic clove (if desired)	1 teaspoon paprika
3 tablespoons fat	¼ teaspoon sugar

Season short ribs with 1 teaspoon salt and pepper, brown with garlic in hot fat, remove garlic. Add onions and water, cover, simmer 2 hours. Add tomatoes, paprika, remaining sugar and salt, simmer 1 hour longer. Remove meat to platter, thicken gravy, pour over meat and serve. If pressure cooker is used, add ingredients to browned meat and cook only 45 minutes. Serves 6.

MRS. E. O. BUTZ, Charleston County.

Swiss Steak

3 pounds round steak
1/3 cup fat
1 bay leaf
1 onion

1 green pepper
Salt and pepper to taste
flour—water (hot)
Cut steak in pieces to serve

Salt, pepper and roll in flour. Put fat in pan, add bay leaf, chopped onion and green pepper, when hot, put in steak, brown nicely. Put in pressure pot, as browned. Add 2 tablespoons flour to fat in pan and brown, add enough hot water to make gravy nice and thick, pour over steak, and cook at 10 pounds pressure for ½ hour.   Serves 6.

MRS. ELIJAH SANDERS, Sumter County.

Swiss Steak

2 pounds of beef cut in slices
  2 inches thick
½ cup flour
salt and pepper

¼ cup fat
½ onion, sliced
½ green pepper, chopped fine
2 cups tomato juice

Pound flour into meat. Heat the fat, and brown meat on both sides. Add onion, green pepper, salt, pepper, and tomatoes. Simmer for 2 hours or until very tender. The steak may be cooked in the oven.

Baked Hash

1½ pints leftover meat chopped
  fine
1 teaspoon salt
½ teaspoon onion juice
1 cup stock or milk

2 tablespoons butter or other
  shortening
2 eggs
½ cup bread crumbs
⅛ teaspoon pepper

1 tablespoon chopped parsley

Combine seasoning with meat. Heat the butter without browning. Add crumbs, stir well, add milk, and cook until thickened. Mix this with the meat. Then add the well-beaten eggs. Place in buttered baking dish and bake uncovered, about 350 degrees, time 40 or 45 minutes. Serves 6. My name for this dish is Blue Monday's Hash.

MRS. JOLA G. POLK, Beaufort County.

Rolled Steak

1 pound round steak 1 inch thick	1 tablespoon chopped parsley
1 cup soft bread crumbs	1 teaspoon salt
1 tablespoon melted butter	Few grains cayenne
¼ cup flour	¼ cup stock or water enough to moisten

Wipe steak and sprinkle with flour. Pound extra flour into steak. Mix other ingredients and spread on steak, keeping mixture 1 inch from edge to prevent squeezing out. Roll the steak, tie securely, and roast. The onion may be omitted or other vegetables added.

Swiss Steak Royal

2 pounds round steak, cut 1 inch thick	½ cup chili sauce or canned tomatoes
¾ cup flour	1 teaspoon dry mustard
2 cups sliced onion	2 teaspoons salt
2 tablespoons fat	¼ teaspoon pepper
1 clove garlic, finely chopped	½ cup water

Pound flour into steak with a meat hammer or edge of heavy saucer. Lightly pan-fry onions in a hot fat in a skillet. Remove from pan. Brown steak on both sides. Cover with onions. Mix remaining ingredients and pour over steak. Cover. Cook over low heat or bake in moderate oven, 350 degrees, about 1½ hours, or until fork tender. Makes 6 servings.

—NANCY CARTER, Director of Home Economics,
Colonial Stores, Atlanta, Georgia.

BEEF STEW

Old Fashioned Beef Stew

2 pounds boneless stew meat	1 large onion, sliced
4 tablespoons fat	1½ cups diced potatoes
4 cups boiling water	3 tablespoons flour
salt and pepper to taste	

Cut beef in small pieces and sear in 2 tablespoons hot fat. Cover with boiling water and let cook until tender. Add potatoes, onions and continue cooking for 20 minutes. To this, add the flour which has been browned in the remaining fat. Season with salt and pepper. **Serves 6–8.**   MRS. H. F. KIRBY, SR., Lee County.

Savory Beef Stew

2 pounds boneless stew beef	2 cans cream tomato soup
2 tablespoons flour	2 cups water
1 teaspoon salt	4 carrots cut in pieces
¼ teaspoon chili powder	8 small onions
⅛ teaspoon black pepper	½ pound green beans, cut in
mashed potatoes	pieces

Wipe meat with damp cloth. Mix flour, salt, chili powder and pepper. Roll meat in this mixture. Brown on both sides in fat. Drain off excess fat. Then add tomato soup, ½ teaspoon salt and the water. Simmer for 1¼ hours, or until tender. Add vegetables and cook for 35 minutes more or until tender. Pour mixture into greased casserole dish. Place mashed potatoes around outside rim. Bake in medium hot oven (375 degrees) if you have heat control on your stove for about 15 minutes or until potatoes are lightly browned. Serves 6–8.

MRS. W. M. BARBER, Greenville County.

Boneless Beef Stew

2 onions	1 pint catsup
5 pounds boneless beef	½ bottle Worcestershire sauce
3 Irish potatoes	pepper and salt to taste
½ bunch carrots	

Cube beef and vegetables. Put in pressure cooker. Cook 20 minutes at 20 pounds pressure. Serves about 15.

MRS. ROY HILL, Calhoun County.

Beef Stew with Vegetables

2 pounds beef stew	2 or 3 onions
3 medium sized Irish potatoes	2 medium size carrots
2/3 cup shortening	

Salt, pepper and flour beef, brown in hot fat. Transfer to saucepan with tight cover. Make pan gravy when meat has browned and pour over meat. Add extra water to allow for cooking. Cook until meat is tender. For last 30 or 40 minutes of cooking add potatoes, onions and carrots. Salt to taste and serve hot. Serves 6–8.

MRS. MARION BELL, Dorchester County.

Mulligatawney Stew

½ cup corn	1 cup cubed and cooked beef
½ cup tomatoes	1 cup beef broth
¼ cup carrots	½ teaspoon salt
¼ cup English peas	pepper to taste
1 small onion	½ teaspoon sugar
½ cup noodles	tablespoon catsup and chili

Cook noodles in beef broth until tender. Add vegetables, cubed beef and seasoning. Cook over slow fire until done. Serves 10.

MRS. J. F. GEIGER, Calhoun County.

Meat and Vegetable Stew

1 pound beef or veal (cut in 1 inch cubes)	¼ teaspoon pepper
4 tablespoons flour	3 tablespoons bacon drippings
3 slices onion	¾ cup diced carrots
	½ cup diced turnips
½ teaspoon salt	

Roll meat in flour and brown in bacon drippings. Cover with water and boil until almost tender. Add vegetables and seasoning and cook until vegetables and meat are tender. Serves 6.

MRS. E. T. McMANUS, Chesterfield County.

Irish Stew

¾ to 1 pound lean lamb, cut in cubes	3 tablespoons fat
salt, pepper, flour	2 potatoes, diced
1 onion, sliced	1 turnip, diced
	4 small carrots, diced
1 tablespoon chopped parsley	

Sprinkle the meat with salt, pepper and flour; brown it with the onion in the fat. Add water to cover. Cover the pan and cook slowly until meat is almost done (about 1½ hours). Add potatoes, carrots and turnip and cook until tender (20 to 30 minutes). Add parsley. Cook over medium flame. Serves 4–6.

MRS. JOAN EDMUNDS, McCormick County.

Brunswick Stew

2 pounds ground beef
1 pound ground lean pork
2 cans tomatoes
1 can corn or 3 ears fresh corn

salt and pepper
3 medium onions
½ can butter beans
3 or more hot peppers

½ pint okra

Cut okra in cubes and brown slightly in bacon fat. Cook for about 20 minutes in a little water. Grind onions and pepper together. Mix tomatoes, corn, onions and pepper, butter beans, and okra and heat them. When hot, add these ingredients to the meat. Be sure to keep stirred or mixture will stick or burn. Add salt and black pepper to taste. Cook down to desired consistency. This will serve 12 to 15.

MRS. R. W. TISDALE, Beaufort County.

MEAT LOAF

Summerville Meat Loaf

2 pounds ground round steak
1 cup suet
4 small onions
½ cup green pepper chopped
2 cups bread crumbs
¾ cup tomato catsup

2 eggs lightly beaten
2 teaspoons salt
¼ cup Worcestershire sauce
¼ cup horse radish
1 teaspoon dry mustard
4 hard-boiled eggs

Chop suet, onions, mix thoroughly with ground steak, crumbs and seasonings. Moisten with slightly beaten eggs. Pack half the mixture in well-greased loaf pan. Place whole, hard-cooked eggs in a line through the center (after having cut a small portion from the ends so the eggs will fit close together) add balance of meat mixture and pat down. Bake 50 minutes at 350 degrees. Serves 6-8.

Summerville, South Carolina.

Meat Loaf

1 pound ground beef
2 eggs
1 cup toasted bread crumbs
1 large onion cut fine
a few celery leaves cut fine

2 teaspoons salt (more if desired)
1 teaspoon pepper
½ teaspoon sage (rubbed)
2 cups tomato juice

Mix all ingredients together and form in a roll and place in a baking dish and pour 2 more cups of tomato juice over the top and cook in a slow oven (300 degrees) until done but not dry.   Serves 6.

MRS. A. D. EIDSON, Lancaster County.

Spicy Meat Loaf

1 pound ground beef	1 cup bread or cracker crumbs
½ pound pork sausage	1 egg
1 cup milk	1 medium onion, chopped
½ cup tomato catsup	1 teaspoon salt

½ teaspoon black pepper

Combine all ingredients. Shape into a loaf in a greased baking dish. Bake in a moderately hot oven (375 degrees) for 35 minutes. Serves 8.

MRS. VICTOR PRIVETTE, Lee County.

Fluffy Meat Loaf

Mix thoroughly:

1 pound ground beef or hamburger	1 egg, beaten
	1½ cups milk
½ pound ground pork	4 tablespoons chopped onions
2 cups bread crumbs	2 teaspoons salt

¼ teaspoon pepper

Pack into greased loaf pan. Bake 1½ hours in moderate oven (350 degrees) or until done.   Serves 7.

MRS. J. D. CAMPBELL, Chesterfield County.

Bacon Meat Loaf

3 cups minced cooked meat	¼ teaspoon pepper
1 small onion	½ cup sifted bread crumbs
3 sprigs parsley	1 tablespoon prepared mustard
2 eggs	1 cup milk

Put meat, onion, and parsley through food chopper. Add beaten eggs and other ingredients. Mix well and put into baking pan lined with strips of bacon. Press down firmly. Bake in a moderate oven 350 degrees, for 45 minutes. Serves 6.

MRS. HENRY ESSICK, Richland County.

Porcupine Balls

Mix well and form into balls:

1 pound ground beef	1 small onion, chopped fine
1 cup rice, raw	1 teaspoon salt
1 egg, slightly beaten	⅛ teaspoon pepper

Put into covered boiler 1 cup water, 1 cup tomato soup. When this comes to a boil, drop in the balls and cook about 1 hour. Serves 8.

MABEL B. McALISTER, Fairfield County.

Porcupine Beef Balls

Mix and shape in rather firm balls:

1 pound ground beef	½ cup washed, uncooked
1 teaspoon salt	rice

Saute in 2 tablespoons butter for 3 minutes:

2 tablespoons green pepper chopped	2 tablespoons chopped onion
½ cup chopped celery	2 cups tomato puree

As the meat balls are shaped, place in greased baking dish. Mix chopped vegetables and puree and pour over meat balls. Bake uncovered so the rice will steam—350 degrees about 1½ hours. During the last 15 minutes the dish may be uncovered so the meat will brown. Garnish with sprigs of parsley and fan-shaped pieces of pickle. Serves 8.

MRS. G. R. CHAPMAN, Kershaw County.

Meat Roll

(Good to Use up Roast)

2 cups flour	½ teaspoon salt
4 tablespoons shortening	4 teaspoons baking powder

¾ cup milk

Mix like biscuit dough—roll out ¼ inch thick. Spread with meat mixture. Roll as for jelly roll. Cut slices 1 inch thick—place in greased pan. Dot with shortening. Bake 450 degrees about 15 minutes. Serve with leftover gravy.

Meat Filling:

chop 1½ cups cooked meat	1 tablespoon minced onion
Moisten with 3 tablespoons gravy	⅛ teaspoon pepper
	¼ teaspoon salt

Other fillings such as ground cooked ham, cooked sausage, creamed chicken, tuna fish, salmon and hard-cooked eggs may be used in above recipe.   Marie A. Hamilton, Charleston County.

Red Rice

½ cup rice
1 cup tomato juice
½ pound ground beef

1 small onion
½ bell pepper
salt and pepper to taste

1 tablespoon butter

Brown ground beef in tablespoon bacon drippings or fat. Cut up onion and bell pepper. Wash rice. Combine all ingredients in a covered casserole. Bake in oven 350 degrees for 1 hour.   Serves 4.

         Mrs. S. L. McFaddin, Williamsburg County.

Spanish Rice

¼ pound bacon
3 onions, sliced
2 green peppers, sliced

2 cups cooked rice
1 teaspoon salt
pepper

3 cups fresh or canned tomatoes

Fry the bacon in a skillet until crisp, remove it from the fat, and break it into small pieces. Cook the onions and green peppers in the fat for 5 minutes, add the tomatoes and simmer for 10 minutes. Stir in the cooked rice carefully so as not to break the grains, add the bits of bacon and when heated through, serve at once.   Serves 8.

         Mrs. Winifred O'Quinn, Colleton County.

Baked Rice and Meat Dish

2 cups cold cooked meat
  (chicken, beef, veal or lamb)
2 cups meat stock
1 cup canned tomatoes

½ cup rice
2 medium sized onions
salt and pepper
2 tablespoons butter

1 tablespoon Worcestershire sauce

Cook meat which has been cut in cubes, stock, tomatoes, 1 of the onions cut fine, Worcestershire sauce and seasonings together for about 10 minutes. Melt butter in frying pan and add onion and uncooked (dry) rice. Allow both to brown slightly and add them to the other mixture. Turn all into buttered casserole and bake for 40 minutes in 350 degree oven.   Serves 8–10.

         Mrs. India A. McLendon, Colleton County.

Casserole of Meat and Rice

¼ pound bacon chopped fine
1 medium sized onion
1 tablespoon minced parsley
3 cups cubed cold roast meat

3 cups seasoned stock
2 peeled tomatoes cut fine
2 sweet green peppers chopped
½ cup well-washed rice

Cook onion with bacon until golden brown. Add meat, cover with stock, add tomatoes, pepper, parsley and simmer for 5 minutes. Then add rice and simmer slowly until rice is tender. This may be cooked in a casserole. Season to taste. Serves 5–6.

MRS. HENRY ESSICK, Richland County.

Dutch Oven Dinner

1½ pounds round steak
6 small carrots
2 stalks celery
3 slices onion
4 tablespoons shortening

2 tablespoons water
4 large potatoes quartered
¾ cup water
⅛ teaspoon pepper
1 teaspoon salt

1 tablespoon flour

Cut steak into 6 individual servings. Rub with salt and pepper. Dredge with flour. Pound slightly as for Swiss steak. On each piece of meat, place a small carrot cut in quarters, and 3 slivers of celery. Wrap steak around vegetables. Fasten with toothpicks. Brown on all sides in shortening. Add the quartered potatoes, onions, and ¾ cup water. Stir in 1 tablespoon flour, which has been blended with 2 tablespoons water. Cover and when boiling turn to low for 1 hour. Remove to heated platter. Serves 6.

MRS. DUFFIE FREEMAN, Newberry County.

Delicious One-Dish Meal

¼ cup chopped celery
1 small green pepper
  (optional)
1 large onion
1 clove garlic
2 tablespoons shortening

1 pound ground meat
1 cup cooked rice
2 teaspoons chili powder
dash of pepper
1 (8 ounce) can tomato sauce
2 teaspoons salt

Brown lightly chopped celery, pepper, onion and garlic in the 2 tablespoons fat. Add the ground meat, brown well and mix thoroughly. Add the cooked rice, chili powder, can of tomato sauce, salt and pepper. Simmer for five minutes, put in a pan 9 x 9 x 2. Make the following corn bread topping:

1 cup enriched flour	1 teaspoon sugar
¾ cup enriched yellow corn meal	1 cup buttermilk
	½ teaspoon soda
2 teaspoons baking powder	2 eggs
1 teaspoon salt	¼ cup melted shortening

Sift flour, corn meal, add baking powder, salt and sugar and resift. Mix ½ teaspoon soda to 1 cup of buttermilk. Add the two eggs well beaten and ¼ cup melted shortening to buttermilk and soda mixture, then add liquid ingredients to the dry ingredients. Stir only until dampened. Put on top of meat mixture and spread evenly. Bake in hot oven 425 degrees for 45 minutes.

MRS. M. H. LAWTON, Beaufort County.

Herb Meat Balls with Spaghetti

2 onions cut very fine	1 pound ground beef
¼ cup oil	2 teaspoons chili powder
1 clove garlic	1 cup celery chopped
2/3 cup green pepper chopped	3 cups tomatoes
1 cup mushrooms (optional)	1 teaspoon salt
2 tablespoons Worchestershire sauce	½ teaspoon basil
	½ box fine spaghetti

salt and pepper to taste

Season meat with salt, pepper and basil, and make into balls about 1 inch in diameter. Brown meat balls in oil. Add onion and garlic and brown slightly. Add celery, green pepper, tomatoes. Add spaghetti broken in pieces, carefully push down so tomatoes are over spaghetti. Cover, bring to steaming point and simmer for 45 minutes. Serve and sprinkle with chopped parsley and grated Romano cheese.

MRS. S. W. MAYSON, Aiken County.

Spaghetti Sauce with Ground Meat
(A Whole Dinner)

1 package spaghetti	1 bell pepper, chopped fine
1½ pounds ground beef	6 small spring onions, chopped fine with tops
½ pound ground pork	
1 tablespoon salt	2 tablespoons cooking fat
1 tablespoon pepper	1 No. 2 can tomatoes or 1 pint tomatoes
1 can tomato paste	

Brown onions and bell pepper in hot fat. In skillet add seasoned meat. Cook until half done about 20 minutes. Add tomatoes and tomato paste. Cook very slowly for about 30 minutes more. Have spaghetti cooked very tender as directed on package and serve by forming a nest of spaghetti on plate with ground meat sauce in center.

LUCY K. HARTER, Abbeville County.

Dunbar Macaroni

1 cup macaroni
¼ pound butter (or margarine)
1 small can tomatoes
1/3 lb. sharp cheese

1 tablespoon Worcestershire sauce
½ pound good stew meat, beef, chicken or pork

Cook macaroni until tender. Stew tomatoes until water is cooked out. Melt butter and brown; then mix in tomatoes, Worcestershire sauce, salt and pepper. Cook meat until tender (save the stock). Cut meat in small pieces. Combine tomatoes with macaroni, stock and meat. Cool mixture and add cheese. Sprinkle top with grated cheese and bread crumbs. Put in oven and bake at 400 degrees for 15 minutes. Serves 6.

MRS. J. D. RUFF, Newberry County.

Chop Suey

1 bunch celery
2 cans bean sprouts
1 can mushrooms
1 cup chestnuts (if available)
1 teaspoon molasses

1 large onion
1 pound pork
1 pound beef
½ bottle soy sauce
¼ bottle Chinese sauce

Meat must be lean, no fat. Cut in 1-inch cubes and sear in heavy pan, place in large size cooker, cut celery crosswise in ½-inch pieces, chop onion and add to meat. Open all cans and add contents. Add sauces, cook three or four hours; the longer the better. Boil chestnuts, peel and add the last hour of cooking. Serve on fluffy rice with Chinese noodles, add soy sauce to individual taste. Do not salt, the salt is contained in soy sauce. Do cook slowly. Serves 6.

J. D. THOMPSON, Greenwood County.

Pork

Pork is perhaps South Carolina's most popular meat. The plantation smokehouses of yesteryear have given way to the modern refrigeration and curing plants of today scattered throughout the state. Cured hams, shoulder roasts, spare ribs, bacon, sausage, liver pudding, hog's head cheese, and the traditional hog jowl for hopping john for New Year's day all play an important part in South Carolina meals. And rightly so, for who can deny that a pork roast with sweet potatoes, turnip greens, artichoke relish and corn bread is good eating?

Cooking Pork

Rule 1:

Pork should be thoroughly cooked. Cook pork well done, brown and crusty on the outside, and juicy, white and tender on the inside. If fresh pork has pink color, it is underdone.

Rule 2:

Like other meats, pork should be cooked at low to moderate temperature, 300°–350° F. Long, slow cooking improves flavor and prevents shrinkage.

Roasting

Any part of pork may be roasted. The choice roasts are ribs, loins, and shoulder. Fresh hams and leg of pork are good roasted or braised.

Pork Roast

Wipe a 4 to 5 pound roast with damp cloth. Cut off surplus fat. Season with salt and pepper. Place roast fat side up in roasting pan with rack. Place in oven preheated 325°. You do not need to flour the roast. Do not add any water. Cook 30 to 35 minutes per pound, or until meat thermometer registers 185° F. Make gravy from drippings.

Potatoes may be peeled and placed around the roast last hour of cooking or steamed until half done then placed around roast 30 to 45 minutes before taking roast from oven. Basting once or twice helps to season and also brown potatoes. Apples and pears may be cut in halves or quarters and broiled around the pork in place of potatoes, or apple sauce may be served with roast.

MRS. O. A. TRAUTMAN, Calhoun County.

Backbone

Cut in convenient sizes. Backbone and spare ribs may be seasoned with salt and pepper, dredge with flour and brown in small amount of hot fat. Add 1 to 1½ cups of hot water, bake in 325° oven until tender.

Ribs may be dredged with flour when half done in place of at the beginning and cooked uncovered. This gives crusty outside. A pod of red pepper added to meat during cooking adds flavor.

Make gravy of meat broth and serve with rice, dumplings or sweet potatoes.

Backbone Pilau

Season backbones with salt and black pepper. Boil until tender, then remove from the pot. Add rice to the stock and after it is cooked, return meat to the pot and steam slowly, about 1 hour. Pork ribs, chicken or any leftover turkey or chicken or other meat may be substituted for the backbones.

MRS. FOSTER SPEER, McCormick County.

Spareribs and Sauerkraut

2 sides spareribs	1 medium onion
salt, pepper	1 large can sauerkraut
2 stalks celery	1 teaspoon caraway seeds

Have spareribs cut into serving pieces. Sprinkle with salt and pepper and place in a deep pan or Dutch oven. Add 2 cups hot water, sliced celery and sliced onion. Simmer, covered, for 1½ hours. Lift out spareribs, place sauerkraut in botton of pan, mix in caraway seeds and a little sugar, place ribs over kraut, cover pan and continue cooking for 30 minutes. (Ribs may be browned before cooking in water, if desired.)

Spareribs and Sauerkraut with Dumplings

2 pounds spareribs	1½ cups all-purpose flour
1 pint jar or No. 2½ can	1 teaspoon salt
sauerkraut	1/3 cup shortening
½ cup warm water	

Cut 2 pounds spareribs into serving size portions. Put into heavy stewing pan, add water, salt to taste, cover, simmer until tender. Remove to platter. Save liquid, add sauerkraut and more water if needed. Sift flour, measure and resift with salt. Mix shortening into flour with finger tips or fork until fat-flour mixture is mealy. Add water little at a time until mixture can be put on bread board to be made into dumplings. Roll pastry out until thin, cut and drop in hot liquid where sauerkraut was added. After dumplings are added to liquid and sauerkraut, put spare ribs back into pot, simmer 15 minutes. Serves 5.

MRS. JOHN D. CORNWELL, Berkeley County.

BARBECUE

Oven Barbecued Spareribs

2 pounds spareribs	1 onion sliced

salt and pepper

Sauce:

½ cup tomato catsup	½ tablespoon salt
½ cup water	½ tablespoon paprika
1 tablespoon vinegar	¼ teaspoon black pepper

¼ teaspoon chili powder

Place ribs in roaster with sliced onion on ribs and pour sauce over top. Bake at 350° for nearly 2 hours with cover on.

Remove cover and cook for ½ or ¾ hour. I always double the amount of sauce. Baste continuously. Serves 4.

MRS. G. E. BAMBERG, Bamberg County.

Spareribs with Bar-B-Cue Sauce

2 pounds spareribs	¼ cup catsup
1 teaspoon salt	1 teaspoon Worcestershire
¼ teaspoon pepper	sauce
½ teaspoon paprika	⅛ teaspoon chili powder
1 tablespoon shortening	¼ teaspoon celery seed
1 large onion, sliced	¼ cup vinegar

Cut ribs into serving pieces. Season with salt, pepper, and paprika. Heat pressure cooker and add fat. Brown ribs on both sides. Add onion. Combine catsup, vinegar, Worcestershire sauce, chili powder and celery seed; pour over meat in cooker. Place top on cooker. Allow steam to flow from vent pipe to release all air from cooker. Place indicator weight on vent pipe and cook 15 minutes at 10 pounds. Let steam return to down position. Serves 6.

MISS MARY SUE LAGROON, McCormick County.

Barbecued Spareribs

Cut 2 pounds ribs into serving portions. Broil 20 minutes on each side to brown. Then place the ribs in a shallow baking pan and cover with sauce. Bake in slow oven (325° F.) for 1 hour. Baste frequently with a sauce.

To make sauce, cook 1 chopped onion in 2 tablespoons of melted butter or margarine until clear. Add 1 teaspoon of pepper, 1 table-spoon sugar, 2 teaspoons dry mustard, 2 teaspoons paprika, 2 table-spoons Worcestershire sauce, ½ teaspoon tobasco sauce, ½ cup catsup, ¼ cup water, ¼ cup vinegar and 1 teaspoon salt. Bring to a boil and simmer about 30 minutes.

Barbecued spareribs should be cooked slowly so that the sauce cooks into the meat. This sauce is "hot" and tangy. It may be kept in a covered jar in the refrigerator and used as needed. This recipe makes about 1 pint of sauce.

MRS. HAL SMITH, Pickens County.

How to Barbecue a Pig

One 80 pound pig

Dress the pig, whole. Place pig, with skin side up, on a rack over a small bed of hot coals (just enough to keep grease dropping). Cook 10 hours in this position, never letting coals get too hot. Turn pig over and cook 1 hour to brown the skin. While browning the skin side of the pig, pour a little of the barbecue sauce on top. When the skin side is brown, take pig off the fire, place on a table and remove all bones. Grind meat through a course food chopper. Then mix remaining barbecue sauce thoroughly with ground meat. Mixture may be re-heated before serving. Serves 80.

(NOTE: Many excellent barbecue cooks prefer not to grind meat in food chopper but prefer to cut it up in small pieces and season with sauce.)

Barbecue Sauce

3 ounces salt	2 (14 ounce) bottles tomato
2½ ounces red pepper	catsup
1¼ ounces black pepper	½ pint vinegar
4 lemons (juice)	1 pint tomato juice

MR. R. E. MOODY, Dillon County.

Oven Bar-B-Cue

1 (10–12) pound pork shoulder	3 tablespoons chili powder
1 (14 ounce) bottle catsup	½ tablespoon red pepper
¾ cup salt	2 tablespoons Worcestershire
1 cup vinegar (add more if	sauce
meat is old)	½ tablespoon black pepper

Saw off end of bone, wash and place in roaster. Slice criss-cross on meat side. Cover with water. Roast until tender at 325° F. Remove all bones and cut up after which add the above ingredients which have been brought to boiling.   Serves 20 to 24 people.

MRS. GUY GRANTHAM, Dillon County.

Barbecue Sauce—(for beef, veal, chicken or pork)

½ cup butter	1 onion, finely chopped
¼ cup vinegar	2 teaspoons salt
3 teaspoons paprika	1½ teaspoons Worcestershire
1 clove garlic (optional)	sauce
2 cups tomatoes, sieved	¼ teaspoon tobasco sauce
1 tablespoon sugar	½ pod red pepper

1 tablespoon black pepper

Mix ingredients and simmer about 15 minutes. Remove clove garlic and red pepper pod. Makes enough sauce for about 5 pounds of meat. Potatoes roasted in the ashes, a tossed salad and iced tea or hot coffee with the barbecue will make a tasty meal.

Pork Chops with Barbecue Sauce

6 pork chops	flour

barbecue sauce

Wipe the pork chops with a damp cloth and dust with flour. Sear on both sides until browned, then place 1 tablespoon sauce on each chop. Reduce heat, cover and cook slowly 5 to 8 minutes. Turn chops and place 1 tablespoon of sauce on other side. Cover and cook slowly until tender, about 40 minutes. Serve with sauce.   Serves 6.

Barbecue Sauce

4 tablespoons minced onion	1 teaspoon salt
1 cup tomato puree	1 teaspoon paprika
¾ cup water	1 teaspoon chili powder
3 tablespoons vinegar	½ teaspoon pepper
2 tablespoons Worcestershire sauce	½ teaspoon cinnamon
	dash ground cloves

Combine all ingredients in order listed. Heat to boiling and use as desired.

MRS. RAY REESE, Aiken County.

Pork Chops Supreme

6 pork chops (½ to ¾ inch thick)	2 cups No. 2 can tomato juice
6 tablespoons rice	1 tablespoon fat
1 onion	1 tomato
	1 green pepper

Season pork chops with salt and pepper and brown in fat. Place 1 tablespoon rice on each pork chop and add a slice of tomato, onion and pepper to each. Cover mixture with tomato juice, adding water if necessary. If desired, 1 teaspoon salt and ½ teaspoon pepper may be added to mixture. Cover and bring to a boil, reduce heat and simmer until done (45 minutes—1 hour). Remove cover and broil until top browns. Serves 6.

OTTIE TUCKER, Abbeville County.

Dinner in a Skillet

6 pork chops	1 No. 2 can or 2½ cups tomatoes
2 tablespoons chopped onion	1/3 cup rice
1 green pepper, sliced in rings	¼ teaspoon pepper
1 teaspoon salt	

Brown chops in hot fat. Add onion, green pepper and tomatoes. Sprinkle rice around chops. Season with salt and pepper. Cover, cook over low heat until chops are tender, about 1 hour. Remove chops and arrange on warm platter. Fill center with rice mixture. Serves 6.

MRS. M. L. KNIGHT, Greenville County.

Baked Pork Chops and Dressing

10 slices bread

1 teaspoon poultry seasoning

5 pork chops

½ large onion

1 teaspoon bacon fat

1 egg

1 teaspoon salt

Moisten bread with water. Add eggs, onion, salt, pepper and poultry seasoning and mix. Put chops in deep pan, add salt and pepper and cover with dressing. Put water in pan to half cover chops, baste occasionally. Cook 1 hour in medium oven. Serves 5.

MRS. ODELL BURGESS, Anderson County.

HAM

Roast Fresh Ham

Wipe the ham with a damp cloth, and leave the rind on. The ham will cook more quickly and shrink less when the rind is not removed. Sprinkle the surface of the meat with salt and pepper and rub with flour. Place the ham, rind side up, on a rack in an open roasting pan, without water. Make a small incision through the rind with a sharp knife or steel skewer, cut short gashes around it with scissors, and insert a roast-meat thermometer through the opening so that its bulb reaches the center of the fleshiest portion of the ham.

Place the pan containing ham in oven preheated to 325° and continue baking until roast meat thermometer registers desired temperature for type of ham baked. Between 26 and 30 minutes per pound will probably be required for cooking. Do not add water and do not cover the meat during roasting.

When the ham is done; remove from the oven and carefully take off the rind. To remove the rind easily, break through it on the fleshy side of the hock, then turn the ham over, and lift the rind off in one piece. With a sharp knife score the fat covering in squares. Stick long-stemmed cloves into the intersections and sprinkle brown sugar over the fat surface. Return to a moderately hot oven (375°F.) to brown over the top. Serve hot or cold.

Boiled Ham

Place ham in covered type roaster, cover with boiling water. Have heat low enough to simmer but not boil. Cover and cook 25 minutes per pound for ham above 12 pounds, approximately 30 minutes per pound for 10-12 pound ham, and for smaller cut hams 35 minutes per pound.

Allow ham to cool in water in which cooked. Remove, pull off skin. For variety of flavor, ½ cup vinegar or apple cider, or small onion, celery, and bay leaf may be added.

Baked Cured Ham

A good country-cured ham is moist, not dried out with too much salt, of excellent flavor and texture. The method for curing hams given in "Pork for Carolina Farmers", Clemson Bulletin, Number 77, produces hams of superior quality. Home-cured hams, if very salty, need to be soaked over night, and are tender and juicier if boiled until tender and then baked long enough to glaze. Tenderized or pre-cooked commercial hams need no soaking since these hams have been partially pre-cooked. These hams should be placed on rack in roasting pan, baked without water at 325°F. until tender or until thermometer registers 182°F.

To Glaze

Cut off outside skin, place on rack in roasting pan fat side up. Spread with one of the following mixtures: brown sugar moistened with vinegar or fruit juices, mustard mixed with brown sugar and fine bread crumbs, honey and fruit juices.

Score ham by marking in squares using sharp knife and stick whole cloves in each square. Baste with mixture several times during baking and bake at 325°F. for about 30 minutes until brown.

Baked Ham

Place skin side up on rack in shallow, uncovered roasting pan (broiler pan is excellent roasting pan for ham). Place in oven (350°F.) and cook 15 to 30 minutes per pound. Remove from oven about ½ hour before ham is done. Peel off rind and score fat in ¾-inch squares. Spread with favorite coating and return to oven about ½ hour until glazed.

Spread prepared mustard thinly over scored surface and sprinkle with brown sugar. Insert whole clove in center of each scored section. Baste with honey, maple syrup, fruit juice or brown syrup.

Mrs. Pete Busbee, Aiken County.

Stuffed Ham

Take 6- or 8-pound ham with leg end cut off, split open, cut bone out, mix 1 pound of sausage meat, all lean, seasoned well with onion, salt, black pepper, poultry seasoning, and a little piece of garlic cut fine. Put it in where bone was cut out, close up tight, wrap with small twine well, put in oven. Bake with temperature 325°F. Time 45 minutes to the pound. When about done, place sliced pineapple on ham. Stick toothpick in to hold in place. Serves 16–20.

Mrs. J. P. Harter, Beaufort County.

Mother's Glorified Ham

6 or 8 slices cured ham   1 cup self-rising flour
1 cup lard or cooking oil

Rinse sliced ham in warm water, dredge in flour. Then fry over medium heat or until nicely browned. Result: tender, juicy and most delicious fried ham. Serves 4–6.

Mrs. R. R. Gibson, Bamberg County.

Baked Slice of Ham with Milk

Melt about 2 tablespoons of brown sugar in a frying pan. Place a slice of ham about 1½ inches thick in the pan and brown it on both sides. Pour 1 cup of sweet milk around it and bake it in a slow oven at 300°F. for about 30 minutes. Remove the ham, thicken the gravy, and serve. Serves 2.

Billie Dove K. Brady, Newberry County.

Baked Ham with Broiled Peaches

1 slice ham 1 inch thick   ¼ cup brown sugar
canned or spiced peaches   6 cloves

Place ham in baking dish, pour on 1 cup pickled peach syrup, sprinkle with brown sugar, stick with cloves. Bake at 300°F. until ham is tender. Arrange peach halves around ham and bake until

peaches are slightly browned, basting frequently with syrup. Canned peaches may be used and spices and vinegar added.

JANIE McDILL, Winthrop College, Rock Hill, S. C.

Ham and Scalloped Potato Casserole

1 thick slice ham   1½ cups thin white sauce
4 cups sliced raw potatoes   salt and pepper

Cut slice of ham 1½ inches thick and flour lightly. Fry each side until it begins to brown, put in baking dish, cover with white sauce and bake 300°F., for ½ hour. Turn and bake ½ hour longer. Cut pared potatoes into medium thick slices, boil until almost tender and drain. Arrange in the casserole, lay the slice of ham on top, and bake 25 minutes. Serves 4–5.   MRS. HENRY ESSICK, Richland County.

Ham Souffle

2 tablespoons butter   1 cup toasted bread crumbs
2 tablespoons flour   2½ cups ground cooked ham,
2 cups milk   smoked or cured ham is
3 eggs   more desirable
salt and pepper to taste

After ingredients are blended, turn into a greased baking dish and bake (300°F.) for 1 hour. Serves 6–8.

MRS. J. M. ROOF, Calhoun County.

Ham Loaf

3 cups minced ham	½ teaspoon pepper
1 small onion	½ cup sifted bread crumbs
3 sprigs parsley	1 tablespoon prepared mustard
2 eggs	1 cup milk or tomato juice

Put ham, onion and parsley through food chopper. Add beaten egg and other ingredients. Pack into well-greased loaf pan and bake 40 minutes in a moderate oven (350°F.). Serve hot or cold. Serves 6.

MRS. HENRY ESSICK, Richland County.

Thanksgiving Meat Loaf

3 eggs	1½ cups fine bread crumbs
½ cup milk	1 small onion
½ teaspoon salt	3 pounds fresh ground pork
½ teaspoon pepper	2 pounds ground ham
2 cups tomatoes	

Beat eggs, add milk, salt, pepper, minced onion, bread crumbs, pork, ham and more milk if necessary. Shape into large loaf, cover with tomatoes. Cook uncovered at 275°F. for 2½ hours. Serves 15 to 20.

MRS. I. A. MOODY, Darlington County.

Ham Rolls

1½ cups ground ham	1 tablespoon minced green
1 tablespoon minced onion	pepper
1 cup milk	1 tablespoon catsup

Combine ham with onion and pepper. Moisten with milk and catsup. Roll biscuit dough about 1 inch thick. Spread with ham. Roll as for jelly roll. Cut into slices. Place cut side down on greased baking sheet. Bake in hot oven (425°F.). Serves 8.

MRS. J. D. CAMPBELL, Chesterfield County,
MRS. LEX WATTS, Chesterfield County.

Pork Sausage

50 pounds meat (¾ lean and· ¼ fat)	1 pound salt
	3 ounces black pepper
¼ ounce cayenne pepper	2 ounces powdered sage

The trimming from the hams, shoulders and bacon should be made into sausage. Three-fourths lean and ¼ fat is about the right proportion. Use care to keep out all skin and gristle. If more sausage is wanted than can be provided from the trimmings, meat from the top of shoulder or meat from the loin may be used for this purpose. Cut meat into small pieces to be easily fed into the sausage cutter. Mix the seasoning before sifting it over the meat and mix thoroughly to make certain it is evenly distributed. Grind through medium plate of the grinder and, if a finer-ground sausage is desired, regrind by putting through the grinder the second time.

This formula will make rather hot sausage, and, if desired, the cayenne pepper may be reduced in amount. The sage also may be reduced, if desired.

Although sausage is commonly stuffed in animal casings, it may be stuffed in muslin sacks 2 inches wide and 12 inches long. The muslin-filled casings may be coated with melted paraffin, and when so treated the sausage contained in them will keep better than in ordinary casings.

MRS. W. K. NELSON, SR., Calhoun County.

Sausage

To 12 pounds of meat use:

4 tablespoons salt	1 tablespoon red pepper
2 tablespoons black pepper	3 tablespoons sage

Mix the seasonings together and sprinkle them over the meat before it is ground. Mix the meat and the seasoning until a fairly good distribution is secured. A second grinding improves the texture, and assists in the distribution of the seasoning. For larger quantities of sausage the following formula is recommended:

To 100 pounds of meat use:

1¾ pounds salt	2 to 4 ounces black pepper
2 to 4 ounces ground sage	1 ounce red pepper

If desired, one ounce of ground cloves, one ounce of ground nutmeg, and 12 ounces of sugar may be added.

"Pork for Carolina Farmers," Clemson Bulletin No. 77.

Italian Skillet Sausages

1 pound sausage meat	2 tablespoons minced onion
2 cups cooked rice	1½ cups cooked tomatoes

½ cup chili sauce

Fry the onion and sausage together until brown and crumbly. Add rice, tomatoes and chili. Cover and cook over low heat for 30 minutes. Do not uncover until 30 minutes are over. This can also be done in a casserole in the oven. Serves 8.

MRS. LOUISE VICKERS, Beaufort County.

Apple Sausage Loaf—(one-dish meal)

1 pound bulk pork sausage	1 1/3 cups bread crumbs
1/3 cup evaporated milk	8 small sweet potatoes, cooked
1/3 cup canned apple sauce	⅛ teaspoon salt

Mix ingredients together and shape into a loaf. Put into a greased, shallow baking pan and bake in the oven at 350°F. for one hour. Arrange sweet potatoes around loaf. Spoon the fat in the pan over the potatoes. Sprinkle the salt over potatoes. Bake 20 minutes longer until loaf is brown. Serves 4.

MRS. CHESTER MOODY, Dillon County.

One-Dish Meal

Boil cabbage 12 minutes, drain and season. Fry sausage, remove from iron skillet, drain off fat, add sliced boiled Irish potatoes, salt, and pepper to skillet and let cook slowly until potatoes have formed a golden crust. Place cabbage, sausages and potatoes on platter and serve hot.

MRS. DOROTHY P. HARRIS.

A Meat Vegetable Pie

½ pound pork sausage	2 pounds backbone or other
4 boiled eggs (chopped)	meat or chicken

4 tablespoons butter

Cook sausage and other meat until done. Take meat from bones. Make any ordinary pie pastry. Roll out bottom crust for baking dish. Then place a layer of meat and sausage, eggs, two green peppers, chopped, 1 cup carrots, 1 cup corn, 1 cup tomatoes, ½ cup celery, 1 onion if desired. Any vegetables can be used. When you have filled your dish with alternate layers of vegetables and meats, put butter on top. Pour part of meat broth in pie dish. Cover with top pie crust. Bake in a moderately hot oven until thoroughly brown. Take out of oven, pour remaining broth over top of pie if it seems dry or brush with butter if there is plenty of broth in pie. Serve hot.

Mrs. PERRY RICHARDSON, Richland County.

HOG'S HEAD AND FEET

Scrapple

1 pound pork	2/3 cup corn meal
2 pig's feet	pepper
1 quart water	small onion
2 teaspoons salt	sage

Cook pork in boiling salted water. Cover and cook at simmering temperature until meat can be easily taken off bones. Remove meat from broth and cut in small pieces or grind. Strain broth into top part of double boiler. Add corn meal to broth and cook over direct heat five minutes. Stir constantly to prevent lumping. Add meat, chopped onion and season to taste. Cook over boiling water about one hour. Pack into small loaf pan rinsed with cold water. Serve cold or slice and pan fry until brown.

Scrapple with Wheat Meal

In making scrapple use the same kind of meat, and some lean beef if desired, and cook and chop as for head cheese. Return the chopped meat with the liquid to the fire, season and bring to a boil. Stir in a cup of wheat flour, enough corn meal until a consistency of corn meal mush is reached. Cook for ten more minutes, stirring constantly to prevent burning, pour into shallow pans to cool and solidify.

Grandmother's Souse Meat

Split a hog's head, take out the eyes and brains; clean the ears thoroughly, dash hot water over all parts and scrape clean. Do this until the water is clean, then put in pot or kettle large enough that it will be covered in water. Boil until all flesh leaves the bones. Remove from boiling water with a skimmer; let stay in a colander for 3 hours to drain well. Then put in bowl, remove all bones, run through a sausage grinder. Season with 1½ tablespoons salt, 1 tablespoon pepper, 1½ cups vinegar. Press into flat dish or bowl and keep in refrigerator.

MRS. T. H. YOUNG, SR., Kershaw County.

Hog's Head Cheese

1 hog's head	2 tablespoons sage
1 set feet	½ teaspoon black pepper

1 teaspoon home-grown red pepper

Scrape and wash well the head and feet, removing hair and eyes from head, and hoofs and hair from feet. Cook in salted water until meat is soft and tender. Keep meat well covered with water while cooking. When done, remove all bones and with hands work the meat to very fine pieces. Do not grind. Add seasoning and more salt if needed. Mix well. Skim fat from 2 cups of broth and add to mixture. Pack in pan and let cool until firm enough to slice.

MRS. W. W. HOWLE, Darlington County.

Hog's Head Cheese

1 hog's head	2 quarts of water
2 medium-sized onions	salt and pepper to taste

1 tablespoon vinegar

Clean and wash hog's head thoroughly. Put in pot with two quarts of water, bring to a boil and simmer until meat drops from bones. Pick out the meat and cut into very small bits, or grind coarsely. Chop onions and cook 5 minutes. Combine all ingredients, using the water left in the pot also. Pour into loaf pan and cool until set. Slice and serve with greens and rice. Serves 6.

MRS. J. W. ALMEIDA, Charleston County.

Boiled Pig's Feet

6 pig's feet	1½ tablespoons salt

Scrape feet, wash thoroughly and tie each separately in a piece of cheesecloth. Cover with boiling water and add salt. Heat to boiling, reduce heat and simmer 6 hours. Cool in the water. When cold, drain but do not remove cloth. Chill. Use for frying, broiling or pickling. Serves 6.

MRS. ROB KNIGHT, Dorchester County.

Hamburgers, Hot Dogs and Frankfurters

Meat and Potato Burgers

¾ pound ground beef
¾ cup ground or coarsely grated raw potato (white)
2 tablespoons chopped green pepper
¼ cup ground or grated onion
1 teaspoon salt
drippings or other fat
1 cup tomato juice or sieved tomatoes
1 tablespoon flour

Mix all ingredients except fat, tomato juice and flour. Form into 4 or 5 flat cakes. Brown the cakes on both sides in fat in frying pan. Add tomato juice, cover and simmer slowly until done, about 25 minutes. Remove cakes and keep hot. Mix flour with a little water and stir slowly into tomato juice in which the cakes simmered. Cook slowly, stirring constantly until thickened. Pour sauce over cakes.

Mrs. Sam Riley, Dorchester County.

Hamburger as U. S. Marines Like It

1 pound ground meat
½ cup evaporated milk
1½ tablespoons fat

1 teaspoon curry powder
1 cup beef stock
3 tablespoons flour

Make a sauce of the fat, flour, evaporated milk, beef stock and curry. Braise the meat, in a little of the fat, and cook until brown and crumbly. Add to sauce, and simmer a short while to blend. A bouillon cube, or consomme may be used instead of beef stock.

MRS. LOUISE VICKERS, Beaufort County.

Toasted Hamburger

1 pound ground beef
1/3 cup chili sauce
1½ teaspoons prepared
   mustard
1½ teaspoons horse radish
1 pinch pepper

1 teaspoon minced onion (or
   a little more)
1½ teaspoons Worcestershire
   sauce
1 teaspoon salt
8 buns

Add all ingredients to meat and put on half bun, pat it well, then put butter on top and pat it again. Put in oven and cook 6 minutes at 300 degrees; then put other half of bun over top and put back in oven and brown. Serves 8.   MRS. L. M. ROGERS, Dillon County.

Hamburger Barbecue

1 pound ground beef
¾ cup diced onions
2 tablespoons fat
1 (10½ ounce) can condensed
   chicken gumbo soup

2 to 3 tablespoons catsup
¼ cup water
⅛ teaspoon pepper
¼ teaspoon salt
2 tablespoons mustard

Brown onions in fat. Add beef and brown. Add remainder of the ingredients. Use any seasoning (garlic, etc.). Cover and simmer for 30 minutes, stirring occasionally. Split and toast buns on both sides. Put hamburger mixture on them. Serve with a salad and a drink.

MRS. S. B. VASSEY, Cherokee County

American Chili

2 pounds hamburger meat
4 tablespoons butter
4 medium onions
2 cups tomato juice

4 celery stalks, chopped
garlic to taste
1 teaspoon red pepper
1 teaspoon chili powder

Melt butter in pan, add hamburger, onion and cook until nicely browned. Put in pot, add tomato juice, celery, salt and pepper. Simmer 1½ hours. Add chili powder and let simmer for about 15 minutes. Serve hot. Very good over weiners.

MRS. JIM HENDERSON, McCormick County.

Good Spaghetti Sauce

4 medium chopped onions
2 tablespoons chopped parsley
4 cloves garlic (if desired)
½ cup butter
1 pint tomatoes
1 pint tomato sauce
1 pound ground beef

3 tablespoons Worcestershire sauce
¼ pound pork
chili sauce
salt and pepper
1 tablespoon sugar
½ pound cheese, grated

Cook parsley, onions, and garlic in hot fat until soft—add tomatoes, butter, tomato sauce and Worcestershire sauce. Cook slowly. Brown meat in bacon grease. Mix and cook 3 hours slowly. Add grated cheese ½ hour before serving. Serves about 8.

MARIE A. HAMILTON, Charleston County.

Barbecued Frankfurters

1½ pounds frankfurters
1 medium onion, chopped
2 tablespoons butter or
  margarine
2 tablespoons vinegar
2 tablespoons brown sugar
2 tablespoons lemon juice

1 cup catsup
2 tablespoons Worcestershire sauce
½ tablespoon mustard
½ cup water
salt
red pepper

Brown onion in butter. Add all ingredients, excepting frankfurters, and simmer for 30 minutes. Arrange frankfurters in shallow pan. Pour sauce over them. Bake in moderate oven for 30 minutes, uncovered.

MRS. JOHN K. TAYLOR, Laurens County.

Sauce for Hot Dogs

1 pound ground beef
1 teaspoon salt

1 cup tomato juice
1 teaspoon chili powder

Cook beef until tender. Add salt and tomato juice and bring to boil, add chili powder and remove from heat. Serve on buns with weiners.

MRS. HOMER LONG, Newberry County.

Hot Dog Relish

4 cups ground onions
1 medium head cabbage
  (4 cups ground)
10 green tomatoes
  (4 cups ground)
12 green peppers
6 sweet red peppers

½ cup salt
6 cups sugar
2 tablespoons mustard seed
1 tablespoon celery seed
1½ teaspoons turmeric
4 cups cider vinegar
2 cups water

Grind vegetables, using coarse blade. Sprinkle with ½ cup salt; let stand over night. Rinse and drain. Combine remaining ingredients; pour over vegetable mixture. Heat to boiling. Simmer 3 minutes. If it needs a little thickening, add a little cornstarch mixed with water and add to the above, stirring until thickened. Seal in sterilized jars, add wax. This is wonderful on hot dogs or to use with meats.

MRS. M. H. LAWTON, Beaufort County.

Chili

2 pounds ground beef
2 tablespoons butter or
  other shortening
2 cups tomatoes or canned
  tomatoes

1 large onion
1 tablespoon chili powder
salt and pepper to taste
1 cup water
3 tablespoons flour

Melt butter or shortening, add ground beef and onions (chopped). Brown thoroughly, stirring constantly; add tomatoes and let simmer. Add chili powder, salt and pepper. Mix flour in water and add to thicken. Cook until done.

MRS. SAM McCOWN, Anderson County.

Beef Curry Sauce

1 large coconut
3 large onions
3 tablespoons butter
2 cloves garlic

3 pieces ginger root
1 tablespoon flour
¾ tablespoon curry powder
¼ teaspoon crushed red pepper

Pierce eye of coconut and strain the milk through a fine strainer into an enamel or glass saucepan. Crack shell and remove the meat. Pare off the thin brown skin from the coconut meat and put meat through food chopper, using finest blade.

Add chopped coconut meat to coconut milk and just barely cover with cold water. Bring this to a boil and let it boil 10 minutes. Take off the stove and strain through a muslin cloth. Now you have 2 to 3 cups of coconut cream. Save the coconut meat.

Slice onions and fry very slowly in butter until pale gold. Pound together the garlic cloves and ginger root until they are well bruised (this helps the oils to escape into your sauce). Combine with flour, curry powder and red pepper. Then stir in enough warm water to make a thick paste. Stir this paste into the coconut cream, add onions and put back on the stove to simmer gently ½ hour. Do not let it boil because curry should never be boiled. Strain the sauce before combining with the meat.

Allow ½ pound meat per person. Cut beef, veal or lamb up into 1-inch cubes and dust lightly with flour mixed with curry powder (not too much). Brown the meat in butter, then cover with water. Add a bay leaf, a piece of ginger root, a split garlic clove and simmer until you can pierce the meat easily with a fork.

When meat is done, add to the curry sauce. Then strain the meat broth. Use this broth to extend the curry sauce. You may add a dash of hot sauce, too. Set mixture aside to cool, then store in refrigerator at least 24 hours.

With curry serve fluffy rice and the following condiments: Chopped peanuts, eggs, bacon, fresh coconut meat, and onions; also, chutney and pineapple pickle.

Method of serving: A generous serving of rice, on top of the curry, then dabs of each of the condiments, finally a good squeeze of lemon.

MATTIE LEE COOLEY, Fairfield County.

Sausage Spoonbread

1 pound pork sausage meat	2 teaspoons salt
2 cups canned tomatoes	¾ cup yellow cornmeal
2 teaspoons chopped onions	1 cup milk

3 eggs

Boil together tomatoes, onions and salt. Stir in cornmeal slowly. Stir and cook until thick. Stir in milk. Keep hot. Pan-fry crumbled sausage meat until uniformly cooked and brown. Drain off fat. Save. Beat eggs thoroughly. Combine with cornmeal mixture, sausage and ¼ cup sausage fat. Pour into a 1¼-quart casserole or deep cake pan. Bake in moderate oven (375°F.) about 45 minutes. To serve, spoon onto hot plates. Serve with a tart jelly.

JANIE McDILL, Winthrop College.

Variety Meats

Such meats as liver, heart, kidneys, tongue, tripe, brains and sweet-breads may well be called variety meats. They each have a distinctive flavor and are "good to eat" as well as "good for you."

These organs or variety meats are rich sources of nutrients needed by the body. Although they vary in food value, they are like other meats—good protein foods. They are higher in iron content than most other cuts of meat. The liver, heart, kidney, and brains are especially valuable for their iron content. Kidney and liver are especially good sources of the two vitamins, riboflavin and niacin. Liver contains more thiamine than any of the other muscle meats except lean pork. Vitamin A is also found in quantity in liver.

GENERAL METHODS OF PREPARATION

Liver. In preparation, scalding is not necessary for any kind of liver. If liver is to be ground, it should be dropped into hot water and simmered for a few minutes. This makes grinding much easier. Beef and pork liver are especially adapted to braising methods, while lamb and veal liver may be successfully broiled.

Kidneys. The kidney should be washed and split through the center. The tubes should be removed before cooking. Marinating kidneys in a well-seasoned French dressing may improve the flavor.

Tongue. Tongue should be simmered in water until tender. After it is cooked this way it may be reheated, either whole or sliced, in a spicy sauce or served cold.

Brains. Since brains are very tender, they are easier to handle when pre-cooked, and most recipes call for pre-cooking. To pre-cook the brains, wash and simmer for 20 minutes in water to which 1 tablespoon of vinegar and 1 teaspoon of salt have been added for each quart of water used.

Sweetbreads. Sweetbreads have long been regarded a delicacy and are favorite party fare. They are often creamed with chicken or veal, but are equally good when served alone. Sweetbreads are pre-cooked if they are to be creamed or made into a salad. To pre-cook, they are washed and simmered for 20 minutes in water to which 1 teaspoon of salt and 1 tablespoon of vinegar and seasoning have been added for each quart of water used. Any membrane can be removed after pre-cooking.

BEEF LIVER

Broiled Liver

1½ pounds beef liver cut in   salt
   slices ¼ inch thick   pepper

butter

Wipe the slices of liver with a damp cloth. Place the liver on a greased baking sheet. Place in oven 2 inches below the flame. Cook from 8 to 10 minutes, turning frequently. When done, it will have lost its red color. To serve, sprinkle with salt and pepper and spread with melted butter. Serve while hot.

Creamed Liver and Ham on Toast

1 pound liver   1½ cups cream or rich milk
1 pound slice of ham   2 tablespoons chopped parsley

Wipe the liver and remove the skin. Grease a moderately hot skillet with a small piece of fat. Add the ham and cook slowly, turning frequently. When tender, remove the ham from the pan and grind it. Cook the liver slowly in the ham drippings until tender. Cut into small pieces, add the ground ham, the chopped parsley and the cream or rich milk, and stir until well mixed. Serve on hot toast.

Chopped Liver Spread

½ pound liver   pepper
water   3 tablespoons melted butter
2 medium onions   salad greens
6 hard-cooked eggs   salt

Simmer liver in water until tender. Drain. Chop in chopping bowl or put through food chopper with fine knife. Chop onions and 5 hard-cooked eggs. Combine all with salt and pepper to season and melted butter to make a thick paste. Pack into mold and chill thoroughly. Turn onto chilled platter and garnish, with sliced hard-cooked egg and greens. Serve as a luncheon meat or spread on toast or crackers or make into sandwiches.

Homemade Liverwurst

1 cup cooked liver   ¼ teaspoon sage
1 cup cooked pork   ⅛ teaspoon pepper
2 tablespoons grated onion   ½ teaspoon salt

Grind meat in a food chopper. Mix well with onion and spices. Keep in cool place. When ready to make sandwiches, mix with salad dressing to make a paste that can be spread.

Liver and Bacon

½ pound sliced bacon	pepper
1 pound sliced liver	flour
salt	parsley

Cook the bacon slowly in a skillet. As soon as it is delicately browned and crisp, drain on paper and keep warm. Wipe the liver. Sprinkle the pieces of liver with salt and pepper, dip in flour, and cook in the bacon fat at moderate heat until the liver is lightly browned. Serve surrounded by the crisp bacon on a hot platter and garnish with parsley.

Liver Loaf

1½ pounds liver	1¼ teaspoons pepper
2 slices bacon	1 cup cracker crumbs
1 medium onion	1½ cups liquid
2 eggs	½ cup catsup
	1 teaspoon salt

Cover liver with water and cook slowly 5 minutes. Reserve liquid. Grind liver in food chopper with bacon and onion. Add all other ingredients except the catsup. Tomato juice, milk, or liquid in which the liver was cooked may be used for moisture. Mix thoroughly. Pour the catsup into a well-greased loaf pan. Pack meat mixture over catsup. Bake in a moderate oven (350 degrees) for 1 hour.

Liver and Rice Loaf

½ cup rice	1 cup chopped celery
4 cups boiling water	¼ cup chopped parsley
1 pound sliced liver	2 tablespoons flour
2 tablespoons fat	1 cup tomatoes
1 small onion, chopped fine	2 teaspoons salt

Cook the rice in boiling water until tender, do not drain, but let the rice absorb the water so as to form a sticky mass which will act as a binder for the loaf. Wipe the liver with a damp cloth. Sprinkle the liver with salt and flour, and cook in the fat for about 3 minutes. Remove the liver, and grind or chop very fine. Cook the onion, celery, and parsley in the drippings for a few minutes, add the flour and tomatoes, and stir briskly until thickened. Then mix all the ingredients until thoroughly blended. Form into a loaf. Bake for about 30 minutes in a modern oven (350 degrees).

Liver Rolls

1 pound liver	salt
2/3 pound pork sausage	pepper

½ cup water

Have liver sliced ¼-inch thick. Trim away coarse membrane and cut into pieces about 3 x 3 inches. Shape sausage into small rolls and wrap each with a slice of liver. Fasten with a wooden pick. Place in a baking dish, season, and add water. Bake covered for 45 minutes in a moderate oven (350 degrees). Remove cover last 15 minutes to brown.

Scalloped Liver and Potatoes

1 pound liver, sliced thin	2 tablespoons bacon fat
salt	1 quart thinly sliced potatoes
pepper	1 small onion, minced
flour	1½ cups milk

Salt and flour the liver. Brown lightly in the bacon fat. Place a layer of the raw potatoes in a greased baking dish, sprinkle with salt and pepper, add some of the liver and onion, and continue until all are used. The top layer should be potatoes. Pour on the milk, cover and bake for 1 hour in a moderate oven, 350 degrees, or until the potatoes are tender. When almost done, remove the cover and allow the potatoes to brown on top.

Scalloped Liver and Rice

1 cup rice	4 slices of bacon
½ pound liver, sliced	1½ teaspoons salt
1 onion, sliced	3 tablespoons bacon fat
½ cup rice water	few drops tabasco

Cook rice in 2 quarts of lightly boiling salted water until it is soft. Drain the rice in a colander, cover it with a clean towel, and place over hot water to steam and become flaky. Save some of the rice water. In the meantime, fry the bacon until crisp, remove it and brown the onion in the fat. Salt and lightly flour the liver and cook it slowly in the bacon fat, after the onions are done. Cook the liver over low heat until the red color disappears, turning it frequently. Cut up liver and bacon, mix with the onions, and add salt to taste and a few drops of tabasco. Mix the bacon fat with the rice and make a layer of the rice in a greased baking dish. Add the liver mixture and continue until all the ingredients are used. Pour the rice water around the sides of the dish, cover and place in the oven until thoroughly heated. Serve at once.

Liver Dumplings

½ pound liver
½ pound suet
1 or 2 eggs
salt
¼ teaspoon baking powder

1 teaspoon black pepper
1 teaspoon sweet basil—
  powdered
3 cups flour
1 small onion

Cook liver until done. Then grate. Cut suet very fine or grate on coarse part of grater. Mix all together and use enough water to make a stiff dough. Then drop by spoonfuls into boiling beef broth. Cook slowly for ½ to ¾ of an hour. Will scorch easily. Do not take cover off boiler until dumplings have cooked a while.

MRS. W. B. SHEALY, Newberry County.

Liver Knepp—(liver dumplings)

Put 1½ pounds liver through meat chopper. Fry a large, diced onion in butter with a few bread crumbs, to which add 2 beaten eggs. Mix ingredients with 2 tablespons of flour and add to the ground liver. Drop from a tablespoon into rich soup or broth and boil for 20 minutes. Serves 6.   MRS. H. C. BYRD, Lancaster County.

Liver Nips

6 cups beef stock
2 tomatoes (add to stock and
  cook 15 minutes)
1 cup chopped or ground
  raw liver
1 egg
flour

1 cup chopped or ground
  suet
medium-sized onion
1 teaspoon salt
1 teaspoon baking powder
1 teaspoon sweet basil
1 cup sweet milk

Mix all ingredients together and add flour to make a medium-stiff batter. Put batter into boiling stock in very small amounts with a teaspoon. Let boil about 30 minutes.

Lexington County.

Pork Liver Hash—(Williamsburg style)

6 pounds pork	1 small onion
2 pounds liver	salt, red and black pepper

Place meat in pot, use parts of head, 2 feet, also scraps from ribs and backbone. Cook liver separate, add salt, boil until tender. Cook, drain and take out all bones. Chop or grind meat, add liver, onion, pepper, put back in pot, boil down low, stirring to keep from sticking. Serve hot or pack in dish to congeal, slice cold. Especially good for storing in freezer. Nice for church suppers or barbecue suppers. Serves 15.

MRS. S. A. GUERRY, Williamsburg County.

Macaroni and Liver

A good way to get your family to eat liver if they do not care for it "as is".

1 8-ounce box elbow macaroni	1½ cups medium white sauce,
2 or 3 large slices liver	well seasoned
1 tablespoon chopped onions	¼ pound sharp cheese
2 tablespoons butter	

Cook the macaroni in plenty of salted boiling water until tender, but not mushy. Drain, rinse with cold water, and immediately add and mix in the butter, so that the macaroni does not get dry. Saute the liver until done, cool, and put through the food chopper. Combine the macaroni, liver, onion and white sauce. Place in well-greased casserole and grate the cheese over the top. Bake in 350-degree oven until the cheese is bubbly and brown in about 20 minutes. Serve with tossed green salad for a 900 calorie meal.

MRS. G. O. WALLACE, McCormick County.

Liver Pudding

1 pound liver	1 big onion
½ hog head	salt, pepper (both red and black) and sage to suit taste

Cook liver and hog head until real tender. Cut meat off bone and grind with liver and onion. Mix with seasoning. Stuff in sausage casings or press into pan to cool. This is good with grits for breakfast or supper.

MRS. STROM CULBREATH, McCormick County.

Liver Scrapple

Boil one hog liver until tender. Remove from broth, mash fine and return to broth. Add two cups sifted meal, salt, pepper, and small onion or sage if desired. Press, slice and serve cold or cooked in oven to brown or broil.

Liver Pudding

Haslet from medium size pork   salt to taste
1 tablespoon black pepper   2 medium-sized onions
2 tablespoons sage   1 tablespoon ground red pepper
2 to 3 cups corn meal

Trim and wash the haslet (liver, lights, and heart) cook until tender, grind in food chopper, grind onion and cracklings along with haslet. Add other seasoning and mix. Add meal to stock in which haslet was boiled. Mix haslet to stock and meal, bring to boil, then let simmer for 15 minutes, stirring constantly to keep from sticking. Pour in covered glass bowl and place in refrigerator. If you like—stuff casings loosely with pudding. Tie ends together with cord. Place in boiling water and cook from 2 to 3 minutes.

Mrs. Worth Rogers, Marion County.

Pressed Liver

2 pounds pork liver   salt
1 pound lean pork   pepper
poultry seasoning   ¼ cup quick cream of wheat
1½ cups broth

Cook pork liver and pork together until very tender. Use enough water to have about 1½ cups broth. Mash liver very fine and either mash pork or run it through food chopper. Cook cream of wheat in broth. Pour on finely divided liver and pork in large mixing bowl. Add seasoning, salt and pepper to suit taste. Put in glass loaf-shaped dish. Cover with waxed paper and keep in refrigerator. May be sliced and served either hot or cold.

Mrs. E. H. Ballentine, Anderson County.

BRAINS

Breaded—Creamed—in Croquettes—Scrambled with Eggs—in Salad

Wash brains, soak in cold water (with or without salt) for half an hour, then remove blood vessels and membrane. Brains to be served are easier to handle if precooked. To do this cover the brains with slightly salted cold water and simmer for about 15 minutes. Cool in the broth.

Breaded. Drain the cooked and cooled brains and separate into fairly large pieces. Dip them into a beaten egg, diluted with 1 tablespoon of water, sprinkle with salt and pepper, then roll in finely sifted bread crumbs, and fry slowly in fat. Serve hot. Tomato sauce is good with breaded brains.

Creamed. Drain the cooked and cooled brains. Cut into fairly small pieces, sprinkle lightly with salt and flour, brown delicately in fat, then remove the browned pieces from the pan. To make sauce blend 2 to 3 tablespoons of flour with the drippings in the pan, stir in 1 to 2 cups of liquid—the liquor in which the brains were precooked and milk or cream or broth—and cook until smooth. Serve the brains and sauce on toast or in party shells or with waffles. If desired, add chopped parsley or paprika.

In Croquettes. Cook 1½ pounds of brains as described and cool them in the broth. Drain the brains and cut into small pieces; sprinkle with salt, pepper, and flour; brown lightly in fat and remove from the frying pan. To get all the good flavor rinse the pan with ½ cup of the broth in which the brains were cooked. Make a very thick sauce with 3 tablespoons of fat, 5 tablespoons of flour, 1 cup of milk, and the broth used to rinse the frying pan. Let the sauce stand until cold, then add the brains, and ¾ cup sifted dry bread crumbs. Season the mixture to taste with salt and pepper, and if desired add chopped parsley, and paprika. Mold the mixture into croquette shapes or flat cakes, dip in beaten egg and crumbs and fry in either shallow or deep fat, or bake, as described under Beef or Veal Croquettes.

Brains Scrambled with Eggs

1 lb. brains	½ cup milk
Water	¾ teaspoon salt
6 eggs	¼ teaspoon pepper
Vinegar	3 tablespoons bacon drippings

Wash brains and simmer 20 minutes in water to which 1 teaspoon salt and 1 tablespoon vinegar have been added for each quart of water used. Drain. Beat eggs; add milk, salt and pepper. Brown brains in hot bacon drippings. Add egg mixture and cook slowly, stirring constantly.

HEART

Braised Stuffed Heart

Select 1 beef heart, or 2 or 3 calf hearts. Wash and slit the heart, remove gristle and blood vessels. For the stuffing, chop an onion and a stalk of celery and cook in 2 tablespoons of fat, add 2 or 3 cups of soft bread crumbs, and season to taste with salt and pepper. Thyme goes well with heart—add a pinch to the stuffing.

Fill heart with the stuffing; sew up the slit. Brown the heart on all sides in fat; place it in a baking dish or casserole; add ½ cup of water, cover closely, and cook until tender in a very moderate oven (about 300 degrees). A beef heart will require about 4 hours. A calf or a hog heart will cook tender in much shorter time—about 1½ hours. Make gravy of the drippings.

Stuffed Baked Heart en Casserole

1 lb. heart (beef, pork, or lamb)	1½ onions chopped
¼ cup bread crumbs	3 medium potatoes, diced
	2 cups tomatoes
2–3 turnips, cubed	

Remove the veins and arteries from the heart. Wash it and then simmer it for one hour; then drain and stuff with bread crumbs and 2 teaspoons of the chopped onion. Rub with salt and pepper and dredge with flour. Brown it, and then place in a baking dish, add the stock in which the heart was cooked to half the depth of the meat. Cover and bake slowly for 2 hours or until tender. Add the vegetables one-half hour before meat is done. This serves four or five persons.

Beef Heart and Lung

Beef heart and lung go well together in stew, loaf, and pickle. To prepare heart and lung wash thoroughly, then remove gristle and the larger blood vessels. Simmer in water to cover. A beef heart and an equal weight of beef lung will probably require 4 to 5 hours to cook tender. If possible let the cooked meat cool in the broth.

In stew with onion gravy. Make onion gravy as follows: Cook a finely chopped onion for a few minutes in 1 tablespoon fat. Then stir in 3 tablespoons flour. Add gradually 2 cups of the broth in which the heart and lung were cooked. Dilute the broth with water if the flavor is strong. To the onion gravy add 3 pints of diced cooked heart and lung and heat the mixture thoroughly. Season to taste with salt and pepper, and if desired add also several peppercorns, about ¼ teaspoon thyme, and a dash of red pepper. Serve piping hot.

KIDNEYS

Broiled Kidneys

Select calf or lamb kidneys for broiling. Wash kidneys, remove the outer membrane, split through the center and cut out the fat, blood vessels, and connective tissue. When ready to cook, dip the kidneys in melted fat, lay the pieces in a shallow pan, and broil for 10 to 20 minutes, turning for even cooking. Sprinkle broiled kidneys with salt and pepper, and serve on toast on a hot platter. If desired, garnish with parsley and thin slices of lemon.

Kidney Loaf

1 lb. kidney	1 minced green pepper
1 cup milk	1½ teaspoon salt
8 slices bread	¼ teaspoon pepper
¼ cup bacon drippings	3 tablespoons grated onion
2 eggs	½ teaspoon powdered sugar

Wash the kidney and grind in food chopper, pour milk over bread and soak. Combine all ingredients and mix thoroughly. Pack firmly in loaf pan. Bake in moderate oven (350 degrees) for 1½ hours.

Kidney Rolls

1 lb. kidney	Bread dressing
Water	½ lb. sliced bacon

Remove all fat from kidneys. Split in half and remove the tubes. Cut kidney into 1-inch cubes. Cover with water and simmer until tender. Drain. Cover kidney with ¼-inch coating of bread dressing and wrap with a slice of bacon. Fasten each with wooden pick. Place in baking pan and bake in a moderate oven, 350 degrees, for 30 minutes or until bacon is crisp and brown.

Kidney Stew

Wash and skin a beef kidney. Cut out the fat, blood vessels, and connective tissue. Cover with cold water, heat slowly to boiling, discard the water, and repeat the process until there is no strong odor. Then add about 1 quart of fresh water and simmer the kidney until tender. Remove the kidney and cut into small pieces. Cook diced potatoes and a small onion in the broth, if the flavor is mild. If it has a strong flavor, cook the vegetables in water instead. Pour off the liquid and measure it. To each cup, allow about ½ tablespoon of flour for thickening. Blend the flour with an equal quantity of fat and add the liquid gradually with constant stirring over low heat. To this sauce add the potatoes, onion and kidney. Season to taste with salt, pepper, and if desired, chopped parsley and lemon juice.

OTHER VARIETY MEATS

Breaded Sweetbreads

½ lb. sweetbreads	1 beaten egg
1 quart water	2 tablespoons drippings
1 teaspoon salt	1 teaspoon salt
1 tablespoon vinegar	⅛ teaspoon pepper

Wash sweetbreads and simmer 20 minutes in water to which salt and vinegar have been added. Drain and detach any membrane. Roll in egg diluted with 1 tablespoon water. Then roll in bread crumbs. Brown in hot drippings. Season.

Creamed Sweetbreads

Cut the cooked lobes of the sweetbreads into small pieces. Sprinkle with salt and flour, brown lightly in fat, and remove the browned pieces from pan. To make sauce, blend 2 tablespoons of flour with the drippings in the pan, stir in 1 cup of liquid—the liquor in which the sweetbreads were cooked and milk or cream, or both—and cook until smooth. Serve the sauce over the sweetbreads, on toast, or in patty shells.

Tongue

Fresh. Wash a fresh beef tongue and place in hot water to cover. Add an onion, a sprig of parsley, a bay- leaf, several peppercorns or cloves and salt. Cook slowly until tongue is tender—2½ to 3 hours.

Skin tongue, slice, serve hot; or, cool skinned tongue in the liquid and serve cold.

Smoked. Soak tongue over night in cold water. Drain, cover with fresh cold water. Bring to boiling point and discard water. Cover with hot water, cook slowly 2½ to 3 hours.

Smoked Beef Tongue

1 smoked beef tongue   10 chopped cooked mushrooms
1 cup Spanish sauce

Scrub tongue and let stand overnight in cold water and simmer for 4 hours until tender. Drain, place in cold water 2 or 3 minutes. Remove skin and roots and place in hot water for a few minutes. Drain, place in serving dish. Pour mushrooms or sauce over tongue.

MRS. ROB KNIGHT, Dorchester County.

Braised Tongue with Vegetable Gravy

1 fresh tongue   ¾ cup diced celery
water   3 tablespoons flour
2 tablespoons salt   1½ cups liquid in which
½ cup diced onions   tongue was cooked
1 cup diced carrots   ¼ teaspoon pepper

Wash tongue and cover with water. Add salt. Cover and simmer until tender, allowing 1 hour per pound. Trim and remove skin. Slice tongue and place in pan with diced onions, carrots and celery. Make a smooth paste of flour and small amount of water, gradually adding liquid and seasonings. Pour sauce over tongue and vegetables. Simmer for 1 hour.

Tripe

If tripe isn't bought already cleaned, wash well through several boiling waters, then put it in cold water and let stand overnight. Then stew with onions. Take 2 pounds of tripe and 2 onions and simmer in salted water for 3 hours. Drain, then chop the cooked onions very fine, place them in hot milk and season with salt, pepper and butter. Pour this over tripe and serve at once. Serves 6.

MRS. ROB KNIGHT, Dorchester County

Tripe

Drain water from can of tripe and cut in pieces. Make a batter of egg and flour. Dip tripe in batter and brown in deep fat.

Mrs. P. A. Salvo, Dorchester County.

Poultry

The rules of modern poultry cooking are few and easy to follow.

RULE 1: Cook at moderate heat so the meat will be juicy, tender, and evenly done to the bone. It holds for birds of all ages and kinds from the spring chicken to the old hen sent to market when she ceases to pay her way in eggs. Turkeys—young toms and hens, and the older heavier birds—ducks, geese, guineas, even the succulent squab, have most food value and greatest appeal on the plate when cooked at moderate heat.

Intense heat hardens and toughens the protein of poultry as of any other meat, shrinks the muscle, and drives out juice. With moderate heat the cooking times are longer, but there is actually more meat to serve, with more juice and flavor retained.

RULE 2: Vary the cooking method according to the age and fatness of the bird. For young, tender, well-fatted birds broiling, frying and open-pan roasting are best. For young birds that are very lean and for full-grown birds past their prime for roasting but not yet in the stewing class, braising in a covered roaster or a casserole makes them tender and savory. The very old birds need long, slow cooking in water or steam to make them tender all through. Then they may be fricasseed, creamed, curried, or made the base for many a dish, hot or cold.

These two general principles—cooking at moderate temperature and cooking according to the age and fatness of the bird—hold for fresh, chilled, and frozen poultry.

Poultry is a very perishable food that must be kept cold when raw and quickly chilled after cooking if it is not to be eaten at once.

CHICKEN

Broiled Chicken

For broiling select plump young chicken, not over 2½ pounds dressed weight. The smaller sized broilers are often split down the back only, and broiled whole. Larger birds are split down both back and breastbone, so that each half makes a serving.

Broiled chicken is easier to manage on the plate if the joints are broken and the wing tips removed. Or with practice and a sharp knife broilers can be boned completely.

Before cooking wipe the chicken as dry as possible. Then coat with melted fat, sprinkle with salt and pepper, and if desired dust lightly with flour.

Start the cooking with the chicken skin side down on the rack of the broiler or in a roasting pan several inches from the source of heat. Keep the heat very moderate for even cooking.

Turn the chicken several times as it browns, and baste frequently with the pan drippings or with other melted fat.

A 2-pound chicken (dressed weight) will probably need from 30 to 45 minutes when broiled at moderate heat, in order to be thoroughly done to the bone. The slow, even cooking keeps the juices in the meat while the outside takes on a delicate brown.

Serve broiled chicken hot off the grid, with the pan drippings or melted fat poured over it. Garnish with toast points and a sprig of parsley or cress.

If chicken is getting too brown under broiler before cooking through to the bone, aluminum foil may be placed lightly over chicken until tender.

Fried Chicken—(shallow fat)

For pan frying in shallow fat, disjoint and cut up plump young chickens into serving portions.

Before cooking, wipe the chicken as dry as possible, season with salt and pepper, and roll in flour. Or dip in egg beaten with a tablespoon of water and coat with very fine dry bread crumbs or corn meal.

Have ready a thick skillet or chicken fryer with a half inch or more of fat heated to frying temperature, but not to the smoking point. Fat should be fresh and free from any foreign odor or flavor.

Put the thickest pieces of chicken in the skillet first. Leave space for the fat to come up around each piece; do not crowd.

Cover, cook at moderate heat, and turn when brown. The thickest pieces of a 3-pound chicken (dressed weight) need from 20 to 25 minutes if fried entirely on the top of the stove.

Many cooks prefer to finish fried chicken in a moderate oven (300° F.), particularly when cooking several birds and skillet space is limited. Shift the well-browned pieces to a pan with a rack to let the fat drain through, cover, and let the cooking continue until no pink remains near the bone. Serve with cream gravy made with the pan drippings.

Cream Gravy

To every 2 tablespoons of fat in the skillet allow 2 tablespoons of flour, brown for a few minutes, stir constantly, add 1½ cups of milk, or part milk and part water, and cook until thickened. Season to taste and serve hot.

Fried Chicken—(deep fat)

Chicken for frying in deep fat is generally cut into quarters and dipped in thin batter (1 egg, ¾ cup milk, 1 cup sifted flour, ½ teaspoon salt).

Or, if preferred, use an egg-and-crumb coating.

Have the deep kettle of hot fat ready—any fat suitable for deep frying, heated to 350° F., and enough of it to cover the chicken without overflowing the kettle. A deep-fat thermometer clipped to the side of the kettle is a great help in getting the fat to the right temperature.

Lower the chicken, piece by piece, carefully into the hot fat but do not overcrowd the kettle. The temperature of the fat will immediately drop below 350° F. Regulate the heat so as to fry the chicken at 300° to 325° F.

In 10 to 15 minutes, with the fat this temperature, the quarters of a 2½-pound chicken (dressed weight) should be done . . . crisp and golden brown, ready to drain on absorbent paper, and serve on a hot platter . . . with or without corn fritters or other garnish.

Instead of keeping the chicken in the fat until thoroughly done, many cooks like to take out the pieces as they brown, drain them on absorbent paper, and finish in a moderate oven (300° F.).

Fried Chicken

2 (2 pound) fryers, cut up	1½ teaspoons salt
½ cup flour	¼ teaspoon pepper
1 tablespoon cayenne pepper	shortening

Place mixture of flour, salt and pepper in paper bag and toss pieces of chicken in bag until well coated. Melt enough shortening to a depth of ½ inch in heavy skillet on high. Place chicken in skillet, skin side down, and brown. Turn unbrowned side down (it will brown during remaining cooking time). Cover. Cook 30 to 35 minutes at low temperature or until tender. Remove cover for last 5 minutes, allowing chicken to become crisp on outside. Serves 4–5.

MRS. ALLEN PALMER, Abbeville County.

Fried Chicken

1 fryer salted to taste	1 cup thin cream
2 eggs	½ cup flour

Whip eggs slightly and add cream. Dip seasoned chicken in mixture then roll in flour. Fry in deep fat till medium brown.

VOX CLUB, Florence County.

Oven Fried Chicken

3 to 3½ pound frying chicken	½ teaspoon salt
½ cup flour	½ cup fat

Wash, dry and disjoint chicken. Dredge with seasoned flour. Place in shallow baking dish. Pour melted fat over each piece of chicken. Cook in a 375° oven for 1½ hours. Serves 8.

MRS. STROM CULBREATH, McCormick County.

ROASTING

Selecting the Bird

Select a young, plump, well-fattened bird. For each person to be served allow ¾ to 1 pound in the dressed weight of chicken, guinea, or turkey (that is, picked but not drawn and including head and feet). A 15 pound turkey makes about 20 generous servings. When selecting a fat duck or goose, allow from 1 to 1½ pounds (dressed weight) per person.

Preparing the Bird for the Oven

Pull out the pin feathers. Singe off the hairs over a flame quickly so as not to darken or scorch the skin. Cut off the head and feet. Scrub the bird with a wet cloth and a little corn meal. Rinse thoroughly and wipe the bird dry. Cut off the oil sac on the top of the tail. Save the giblets to stew for the gravy.

When drawing turkeys, chickens, or guineas, make the cut crosswise of the body no longer than necessary; and leave a band of skin and flesh under the tail so that the legs can be securely tucked in after the bird is stuffed. The legs of ducks and geese are too short to tuck in, so make the cut for drawing them lengthwise of the body.

Stuffing and Trussing

When ready to roast the bird, sprinkle the inside with salt, and fill the body cavity with stuffing, but do not pack. Stuffing swells as it cooks so give it plenty of room to expand.

Put the stuffing in hot and cook the bird at once, otherwise it should not be stuffed until ready to cook.

To hold in the stuffing at the tail, slip the heel of a loaf of bread into the opening. Then tuck the legs under the band of skin, and put in a few stitches with soft white twine to help hold the legs in place, or tie the legs close to the body.

Next stuff the loose skin at the base of the neck, again putting the stuffing in without packing it tight. Fold the neck skin toward the back across the breast for it will leave marks on the surface.

Then rub the stuffed, trussed bird all over with butter or other fat, sprinkle with salt, and if desired dust lightly with flour.

The Bird in the Oven

Place the stuffed and trussed young bird breast down on a rack in a shallow, not a deep, pan. Do not add water and do not cover. Keep the oven temperature moderate to slow according to the dressed weight of the bird.

Start roasting the bird with the back up and breast down, if you use a V-shaped rack. Keeping the back up most of the time allows the thighs to cook thoroughly without cooking the meat away from the breastbone.

Every half hour, turn small- or medium-sized birds and baste with pan drippings or with melted butter or other fat. Turning every hour is sufficient for very large birds when the oven is slow—250° F.

To keep from breaking the skin in turning, lift the bird at the head and foot, with clean folded cloths to protect the hands. To test for "doneness," run a steel skewer or cooking fork carefully into the thickest part of the breast and into the thigh next to the breast. If the meat is tender and the juice does not show a red tinge, the bird is ready for the carver's knife.

Giblet Gravy

Simmer the giblets (liver, gizzard, and heart) and the neck in a quart of water for about an hour, or until tender. Drain the giblets, chop them fine, and save the broth.

Skim off excess fat from the drippings in the roaster. Leave about ½ cup, and stir in 6 tablespoons of flour. Then gradually add the cool broth and enough more cold water to make a thin, smooth gravy. Cook for 5 minutes, stirring constantly, and add the chopped giblets. Season to taste with salt and pepper. Add chopped parsley, if desired.

Pot Roast Chicken

3 pounds roasting chicken
make bread stuffing
2 teaspoons salt
¼ teaspoon pepper

4 tablespoons flour
½ cup fat
12 small onions peeled
½ cup boiling water

6 medium potatoes peeled

Clean, stuff and tie chicken. Season and flour lightly. Brown chicken in fat. Brown onions around chicken and add water. Cover and cook until tender, putting potatoes in pot during the last cooking hour. Serves 6.

CENTER CLUB, Florence County.

Cornbread Stuffing—(5-pound chicken)

6 tablespoons butter or other fat

¾ cup chopped celery

¼ cup chopped parsley

1 small onion, chopped

1 quart cornbread crumbs

¼ to ½ teaspoon thyme

½ to 1 teaspoon salt

pepper to taste

In the melted fat cook the celery, parsley, and onion for a few minutes. Add to the cornbread crumbs and dry seasonings and stir all together.   Serves 6.

Cornbread stuffing is particularly good with a braised fowl, and it is frequently desirable to make extra stuffing—baked outside the bird. To make extra stuffing, double the above recipe, fill the bird, then to the remainder of the stuffing add an egg, and moisten with broth. Drop by spoonfuls into a greased pan, brown in a hot oven and serve immediately with the fowl. Doubled the recipe serves 12.

Bread Stuffing

6 cups corn bread

2 cups biscuit or day old bread

½ medium-sized onion chopped fine

1 teaspoon salt

¼ teaspoon pepper

½ cup chopped celery

½ cup melted butter or margarine

3 eggs beaten

sage to taste—preferably home grown

enough broth and sweet milk to make mixture moist

Combine all ingredients, allow at least 1 cup dressing for 1 pound meat.   Serves 12.

MRS. HERBERT BLANCHARD, Spartanburg County.

BRAISING

Braised Fowl With Cornbread Stuffing

Prepare and draw a fowl as if for roasting, and tuck the legs into the band or under the tail.

Place the bird up on a rack in a large kettle to steam partly done. Pour in boiling water up to the rack, not over the bird. Cover the kettle, and let the water boil gently. Add more boiling water from time to time.

After about 1½ to 2 hours, remove the bird from the kettle and stuff.

To make cornbread stuffing for a 5-pound bird, cook about 1 cup of mixed chopped celery, parsley, and onion for a few minutes in 6 tablespoons of butter or other fat, and add 1 quart of cornbread crumbs. Season to taste with salt and pepper, and from ¼ to ½ teaspoon of thyme. If more is desired to bake separately, double this recipe.

After the bird is stuffed, brush with fat, sprinkle with salt, and with flour also if desired. Place the bird on a rack in a roaster, add about 1 cup of the broth and cover the roaster. Cook in a moderate oven (350° F.) from 1½ to 2 hours or until the bird is tender. Occasionally turn the bird for even cooking.

To the extra stuffing, add an egg and moisten with broth. Drop by spoonfuls into a greased pan, brown in a hot oven, and serve these crusty patty cakes with the braised bird and gravy made from the broth and pan drippings.

To braise other birds that are past their prime for roasting, follow the same general method as for a fowl. A 10- to 14-pound turkey will probably need from 2 to 3 hours of steaming, followed by 3 to 4 hours in a covered roaster, with the oven temperature about 325° F.

STEWING AND STEAMING

For stewing or steaming, prepare an old bird as for roasting.

To stew, place the bird on a rack in a kettle, half fill with water, partly cover, and simmer until the bird is tender. Simmer, do not boil.

To steam, follow the same general method except keep the bird breast up all the time, and add water only to the level of the rack. As it boils away add more to keep a good circulation of steam around the bird all the time. A fowl may need 3 to 4 hours to cook tender— an old turkey, 5 to 7 hours or longer.

Or, to cut down cooking time, steam an old bird under pressure, according to directions that come with the cooker.

Cool a stewed or steamed bird in the broth, breast down, in a cold place. The cold place is important because warm broth spoils easily.

Creamed Chicken with Hard-Cooked Eggs

2 cups cooked chicken
  removed from bones
  diced or cut in strips

2 cups white sauce
½ teaspoon salt
1 dash celery salt (optional)

4 hard-cooked eggs

Heat chicken in medium white sauce. This should be heated over simmer heat on an electric range, or a very low flame on any other type range. 1 cup cooked vegetables, such as peas, celery, carrots, may be substituted for 1 cup of the chicken. Shortly before removing from range, add the eggs which have been cut in halves lengthwise, and then cut in quarters crosswise. Serves 6.

MRS. B. B. PRICE, Jasper County.

Chicken a la King

2 cups chicken (cut up)
1 tablespoon grated onion
1 cup chicken stock
1/3 cup chopped green pepper
2 tablespoons chopped pimento

1 10½-ounce can condensed
  mushroom soup
3 tablespoons butter
3 tablespoons cooking sherry
1 egg yolk

Combine chicken, onion, chicken stock, green pepper and pimento. Simmer 10 minutes. Heat mushroom soup, butter and sherry in double boiler—add a little hot mixture; heat thoroughly. Serve on hot toast or in pastry cups. Serves 6.

MRS. GEORGE JENKINS, Charleston County.

Baked Creamed Chicken

1 large hen
2 cans mushrooms
1 pint milk
¼ cup flour
salt, red pepper, nutmeg,

parsley (chopped)
1 small onion grated
¼ cup flour
1 pint chicken stock
½ cup chicken fat

Boil chicken in salted water until tender. Shred chicken fine with finger. Set aside liquor the chicken has been boiled in, and skim off the rich yellow fat. Make a rich thick sauce as follows:

To ½ of chicken fat (about ¼ cup) add ¼ cup flour. Add 1 pint of milk and 1 pint chicken broth and cook until thick, stirring constantly. Season to taste with salt, red pepper, nutmeg, and chopped parsley.

Season *high*! Let sauce cool before using. Butter rectangular shallow casserole or baking pan, and line with bread crumbs. Put in layer of chicken, mushrooms, onion, and cream sauce. Then add another layer of each ingredient with a layer of bread crumbs over top. Bake in moderate oven 20 or 30 minutes, or until golden brown on top. Temperature 350° F.   Serves 8.

The original recipe, which came from Kentucky, called for only the breasts of 2 chickens, but for economy, I have used all of one chicken and found it almost as good.

MRS. NED DARGAN, Darlington County.

Chicken Pie

Boil chicken until tender. Remove from broth. With a fork make a stiff dough of 3 cups sifted flour and 1 tablespoon salt, using *boiling water*. Put in broth and boil about 3 minutes. Be sure that the broth covers pastry.

Spread ½ the pastry on the bottom of a casserole. Add a layer of chicken and a layer of pastry. Season with salt, pepper and a little milk. Cover with a pie crust and bake in moderate oven until nicely brown.   Serves 6.

MRS. E. A. GRAY, Darlington County.

Dixie Chicken Pie

1 (3 pound) chicken
2 cups cold water
1½ teaspoons salt
¼ teaspoon pepper

biscuit dough
½ cup shortening (butter is
preferable)

Cut chicken in small pieces, place in saucepan. Cover closely and simmer until tender, adding salt and pepper when chicken is done. Prepare biscuit dough. Roll half of it out thinly and use to line baking dish. Place a few pieces of chicken in lined baking dish, lay over it thin strips of dough and dot with butter. Continue in this way until chicken is all used. Place strips of dough lattice-fashion over the top. Bake 25 minutes in moderate oven. Serve hot. Top layer of dough may be brushed over with egg wash, if desired. Egg wash is yolk of 1 egg, ½ cup sweet cream.   Serves 6–8.

MRS. THELMA SMITH, Anderson County.

Chicken Cream Pie

2 cups flour
2 teaspoons baking powder
1 teaspoon salt
1 egg yolk

2/3 cup shortening
½ cup hot water
3 teaspoons lemon juice
1 stewed fryer, boned

Mix and sift the flour, baking powder and salt. Melt the shortening in the hot water, add lemon juice and egg. Add this slowly to the dry ingredients and mix well. Line the sides of a baking dish with dough (it is soft and works better chilled), patting it out with the fingers. Fill the dish with boned chicken which has been cut in small pieces, and cover with a thin white sauce made with broth or rich sweet milk. Pat out the remainder of the pastry dough to fit the top of the baking dish. Cut small slits in the pastry to allow the steam to escape. Place in a hot oven about 425° F. and bake about 25 minutes. For individual service, bake in custard cups or ramekins. Serves 6–8.

MATTIE LEE COOLEY, Fairfield County.

Chicken Pie

2 pounds chicken
1 cup milk

3 tablespoons butter
1 cup chicken stock

Cook chicken until it falls off bone. Cut it up into small pieces and mix it with milk, chicken stock and butter. Add salt and pepper to taste. Bake crust and then put 1 layer of crust and 1 of mixture. Add uncooked crust on top and bake in oven at 425°. Serves 6–8.

MRS. R. W. SHELLHOUSE, Aiken County.

Chicken and Dumplings

1 chicken
3 tablespoons flour

salt and pepper
1 teaspoon salt

1 cup milk

Clean and cut up chicken, place it in a pot and nearly cover with water. Cover the pot and simmer gently. An old fowl will require at least 3 or 4 hours of slow cooking, but a year-old chicken should be done in 1½ hours. Remove the cover during the last half hour of cooking to reduce the gravy about 1½ pints when done.

Three-fourths of an hour before time to serve, make dumplings. When the dumplings are ready to serve, add salt and pepper to the chicken and make the gravy by adding to the liquor in the kettle

3 tablespoons of flour stirred to a paste in 1 cup of milk. Skim out the chicken, lay it on a platter, place the dumplings on the top and pour over the gravy. Serves 6–8.

Dumplings

2 cups flour 1 teaspoon salt
4 teaspoons baking powder 2 tablespoons fat
1 cup milk

Sift together dry ingredients. Cut in fat, add the milk. Drop by spoonfuls on top of the stew, cover tightly and cook slowly for 12 minutes. Do not uncover until they have steamed 12 minutes.

MRS. PAUL STROMAN, Orangeburg County.

Chicken and Dumplings

Cut chicken in serving pieces and stew until tender, seasoning with salt and pepper. Add 2 hard-cooked eggs cut in pieces and dumpling batter made as follows:

2 cups sifted flour 1 tablespoon shortening
4 teaspoons baking powder 1 cup milk
1 teaspoon salt

Sift flour, salt and baking powder together, cut in softened shortening and add milk. Drop by tablespoonfuls into chicken stew. Cook few minutes longer until dumplings are done. Serve hot. Serves 6–8.

MRS. M. H. SMITH, Berkeley County.

Chicken Noodle Pie

1 hen boiled and cut as for 1 large tablespoon butter
salad 1 package medium egg noodles
1½ quarts chicken broth 2 hard-boiled eggs, cut fine
1 cup sweet milk

Bring broth to boil, add milk and let come to boil, add noodles, broken up, and cook on low heat for 20 minutes after begins to boil. Season with salt and pepper. Add butter. Mix cut chicken, eggs and noodle mixture. Put in large oblong pyrex dish and cover just the top of pie with cut out raw biscuits made by using 2 cups of self rising flour, ½ cup shortening and 2/3 cup sweet milk. Roll out biscuits ¼ inch thick and cut in round or square shape. Brush top of biscuits with top milk before baking. Makes them brown better. Bake at 400°

until biscuits are brown. When done, spoon broth over biscuits and serve hot. Serves 9.

Mrs. F. Newton Dantzler, Orangeburg County

Chicken Bog

1 dressed hen (4 to 5 pounds)　　4 cups chicken stock
4 cups rice　　2 tablespoons salt
4 cups boiling water　　2 teaspoons black pepper

Cut up chicken, cook until tender in enough water to cover chicken. Remove chicken from stock and measure 4 cups chicken stock and 4 cups water and let come to boil. Add 4 cups of rice and the chicken which has cooked tender. Season with salt and pepper, let come to another boil. Stir well once. Cook at low temperature until done (approximately 30 minutes). Serves 12–15.

Mrs. Campbell Lane, Marion County.

Chicken Pilau—(whole meal)

5-pound hen dressed　　2 tablespoons salt
5 cups rice (cooked)　　2 tablespoons black pepper
1 dozen boiled eggs　　5 cups boiling water

Cut hen into serving pieces. Boil at moderate temperature until very tender. Cut very fine and season with salt and pepper. Simmer a few minutes. Have rice cooked in water until done. Keep rice and chicken at serving temperature. Peel and cut hard-boiled eggs very fine. Combine the cooked warm rice and minced chicken—the hard boiled eggs in alternate layers in a large container—pour the chicken broth over all and keep very warm until served. Serve with cucumber pickles, fresh vegetable salad, bread and any drink you may desire.

Lucy K. Harter, Allendale, S. C.

Chicken Pilau

salt and boil together until tender, 1 hen and 6 or 8 slices of fat side or juicy brown meat　　4 cups rice to 5 cups liquid stock
4 or 5 hard-boiled eggs
pepper to taste

Salt and cook chicken. When chicken is thoroughly done and meat is dropping from the bones, remove bones from chicken. Add rice which has been rubbed, washed and soaked in cold water to the liquid in which the chicken has been boiled. Add pepper and add hard-cooked eggs cut fine. Cook rice tender and dry. Don't stir. Cook in a thick pot and cook on slow heat after rice has been added. Serves 12.

This recipe was clipped from a Lake City, S. C., newspaper during World War I and has been used constantly since.

GASKIN CLUB, Florence County.

Mum Rosie's Rice Pie

5 cups rice	sage, if desired
1 fat hen	salt and pepper
2 cups milk	¼ pound butter
8 eggs	

Steam rice until done. Unjoint hen and boil until tender, being sure to leave 1 cup liquor. Melt butter in hot liquor, and add the milk, salt, pepper, sage and 6 eggs. Mix thoroughly.

Now, in deep pan place alternate layers of rice and chicken until supply is completely used. Be sure to leave enough rice to make a top layer. Pour milk and egg mixture over all. Let soak a few minutes.

Beat the remaining eggs and smooth over the top layer of rice with a big spoon. Dot with ¼ pound of butter and bake in a 300° oven for 1 hour or until nicely browned. Serve hot.

A salad added and you have a meal for 12.

CAROLYN C. BRUNER, Lee County.

Rice Cooked in Broth

2 cups chicken, pork or beef broth	1 cup uncooked rice

To 2 scant cups of boiling broth add 1 cup of uncooked rice—boil rapidly until nearly dry and tender, then pull to back of stove or remove to very low heat to steam or dry out so that grains stand apart. Serves 6.

We children called this rice "greasy rice" but it was not really greasy. It had a delicious meat flavor and was served with sliced chicken, pork or beef. Oftentimes I now place the rice in the boiler over a kettle of boiling water to steam and dry out.

MRS. A. C. SULLIVAN, Abbeville County.

Chicken Curry with Rice

1 pound mushrooms	¼ teaspoon pepper
2 tablespoons salad oil	1½ teaspoons curry powder
1/3 cup diced apples	¾ cup top milk
3 tablespoons margarine	¾ cup chicken broth
3 tablespoons flour	¼ cup raw rice
⅜ teaspoon salt	3 cups diced cooked chicken

Saute mushrooms in fat. Remove. Cook minced onion and apples in butter or margarine until tender. Add flour, salt, pepper, and curry powder and blend. Add top milk and chicken broth. Cook until thick. Cover and cook for 10 minutes. Add mushrooms and chicken. Heat well. Serve with cooked rice and the following on top.   Serves 8.

1 cup chopped bacon	chopped celery
3 hard-boiled eggs (yolks and whites chopped separately)	coconut grated
	chutney
2 green peppers chopped	ground parched peanuts

American Chicken Chop Suey

2 cups cold cooked chicken chopped	1 teaspoon salt
1 cup celery	½ teaspoon pepper
1½ cups boiled rice (cooked in 2 quarts boiling water)	1 tablespoon butter or fat
	2 tablespoons flour
	1½ cups chicken stock

Dice chicken and celery and steam until tender. Mix them with rice, salt, and pepper. Melt butter and make into a smooth paste with the flour. Add stock slowly, stirring constantly. Bring to a boil, continue stirring. Add the chicken and rice mixture and heat thoroughly. Serves 6.

MRS. ELIZABETH STEEDLY.

Chicken-Mushroom-Spaghetti

1 hen	2 cans cream of mushroom soup
2 (8 ounce) packages spaghetti	1 dozen hard-cooked eggs
1 cup butter	

Dress hen as for baking—Cover with water and boil until well done. Chop medium fine (by hand). Place ½ the broth in smaller saucepan and keep hot to use as needed. Place chopped chicken, butter, chopped eggs, mushroom soup in heavy bottomed saucepan and season to taste. Bring to boil. Add spaghetti broken in 4- to 5-inch lengths. Cover and cook on medium heat until spaghetti is tender, stirring from bottom occasionally with ladle. Add hot broth as needed to keep juicy.

Ideal for buffet meals when you never know whether 10 or 20! Serve with tossed salad, pickle, hot rolls, butter and preserves for complete meal. For variations add 2 cans drained garden peas or 2 small pimentos.

For grange or church suppers double for 25. Use eight hens for 100. For summer meals instead of tossed salad, serve with sliced tomatoes, and sweet pepper rings.   Serves 10.

MRS. GRAHAM HAWKINS, Greenwood County.

Chicken-Spaghetti Casserole

In 4 tablespoons melted butter, cook ½ cup minced onion and ½ cup minced green pepper until tender. Add 4 tablespoons flour and stir well, then add ¼ teaspoon pepper, 1½ teaspoons salt, 1½ cups chicken stock and 1½ cups tomato juice and cook until smooth and thick. Add 2 tablespoons prepared mustard and stir well. Combine 3 cups diced chicken and 3 cups thin cooked spaghetti and put in a greased casserole. Add broth mixture and sprinkle with ¾ cup grated cheese. Bake in 350° oven 30 minutes.   Serves 6.

Hungarian Chicken

Cut 1 grown chicken (rooster, even, can be tenderized) as for frying. Place on rack over vegetables and steam in pressure cooker. Beans are fine for the vegetable. Make sauce of flour and water thickened, plus diced onions, carrots and celery. Place steamed chicken in baking dish and cover with the vegetable sauce. Bake at 350° until nicely browned.   Serves 8.

MRS. ETHEL STURKEY, McCormick County.

This recipe was given us by Mr. Furst who operated a Jewish restaurant in Augusta. It was the way his mother prepared chicken in Hungary.

Chicken en Casserole with Tomato Sauce

2 chickens (2½ pounds each)	1 onion, chopped
1 can tomatoes (or 4 fresh tomatoes)	3 or 4 tablespoons butter
	1 wine glass white dry wine
salt and pepper to taste	

Braise the chicken in a casserole with butter until well browned. In a separate pan brown the chopped onion in butter and put into the casserole with chicken. Put into casserole the rest of the ingredients and simmer until cooked. Take the chicken out and strain the sauce which if still watery, should be boiled down to a thick consistency. Now replace the chicken in the sauce and keep hot until served.   Serves 15.

LILLIAN WATSON, Marion County.

Casserole Fowl with Vegetables

4- or 5-pound fowl
salt and pepper
2 tablespoons butter or other
    fat
1 bunch celery

1 onion
1 green pepper
1 cup hot water
1 cup milk
1½ tablespoons flour

Cut the fowl, season with salt and pepper, dust with flour, and brown in the fat. Remove the browned pieces to a casserole.

Pour the chopped vegetables into the frying pan and let them absorb the browned fat. Then transfer them to the casserole, add a cup of hot water, and cover.

Cook in a slow oven (275° F.) for 3 hours, or longer if the fowl is very tough. Add more water from time to time if necessary.

Just before serving, remove the pieces of fowl, and add the blended milk and flour. Cook for 10 minutes longer, season to taste, and pour the vegetable sauce over the fowl, or replace it in the sauce and serve from the casserole.

Smothered Chicken

Smothering is a good way to cook a lean young chicken. A small bird may be cooked whole, or a larger one disjointed as for frying.

Sprinkle with salt, pepper, and flour. Brown the chicken in fat, then cover the pan and finish the cooking in a very moderate oven (300° F.). When the chicken is tender, remove from the pan.

Make gravy with the drippings. A three to four pound chicken will probably require 1½ to 2 hours to cook.

JANIE McDILL, Winthrop College.

Red Chicken Stew

Cook a 5-pound chicken until very tender. Remove the chicken and allow to cool. To the chicken stock add the following to make sauce:

1 bottle tomato catsup
2 tablespoons prepared mustard
1 tablespoon Worcestershire sauce

4 to 6 hard-boiled eggs which have been cut up
1 medium onion, chopped fine
salt, pepper and hot sauce to taste

While this sauce is cooking, cut up the chicken into bite size pieces. Add to sauce and heat through and serve. This is good for family meals. May be cooked in quantity for large groups such as church suppers, etc. Served on rice, it goes a long way. Serves 12.

Mrs. Roy Mims, Sumter County.

McKagin Stew

1 large fat hen
½ stick butter
¼ pound bacon

2 very large onions
1 large bottle catsup
6 boiled eggs

Cook, chicken, pull off bones. Put stock back on stove, chop bacon in small bits and cook until thoroughly dried out. Take bacon out and combine with chicken. Put onions in grease and cook until done, but not brown. Add onions to chicken and bacon. Add catsup, salt, pepper, and flour to thicken stock. Add chopped eggs and bacon, chicken, onions just before serving. Serve hot. Serves 10-12.

Mrs. J. Whitman Smith, Lee County.

Hen Mulligan—(a quantity recipe)

20 medium-sized fat hens and broth
4 gallons sweet milk
salt and pepper to taste

2 large onions (more if desired)
1 to 2 pounds butter
potatoes

Cook hens until meat falls from bones. Remove all bones and see that meat is well cut up. Dice onions and potatoes. Put in meat, broth, and butter. Bring milk to boil and stir in other mixture. Serve piping hot. This amount serves 200 easily.

This is a delicious stew-like mixture that has often been served at hot suppers at some of our southern schools. It was prepared by my home economics classes and served to around 200 people at a banquet. It was well liked.

Mrs. A. CARLISLE SULLIVAN, Abbeville County.

Chicken Stew

1 large grown chicken (steam in small amount of water until meat drops from bones)	¼ lb. butter
	1½ bottles tomato catsup
	2 tablespoons Worcestershire
4 slices breakfast bacon	sauce
2 medium sized onions	Salt and pepper to taste

Chip up bacon and onion together and fry until onion is tender. Add to the chicken that has been cooked until it begins to leave the bones. Add butter, catsup, Worcestershire sauce, salt and pepper to taste and let simmer for about 1 hour. Remove large bones from stew and serve on rice. This also makes a nice supper dish when served with a beverage and a green salad.

LAURA CONNER, Winthrop College.

Pressed Chicken with Vegetables

1 chicken, cut up fine	1 cup nuts
2 cups green peas	4 tablespoons chopped pickle
2 cups celery	3 tablespoons gelatin
1 cup mayonnaise	

Dissolve 3 tablespoonsful of gelatin in 6 tablespoonsful of water (warm) or chicken stock. Add 1 cup of mayonnaise and then mixed ingredients given above. Congeal in large pan or individual molds. Serves 12.   Mrs. J. WHITMAN SMITH, Lee County.

Pressed Chicken—(plain)

1 (5 or 6 pound) chicken	mayonnaise, as needed
8 to 10 eggs	lemon juice to taste
1 cup warm stock	red pepper
3 tablespoons plain gelatin	salt
pimento	

Boil chicken until meat falls off the bones. Pick to pieces and grind. Boil eggs and grind. Dissolve gelatin in cup of warm stock. Mix chicken and eggs, and season with lemon juice, salt, pepper and mayonnaise. Add pimento for color. Pack tightly in mold or tall glass overnight. Slice and serve on lettuce. This is nice for parties.   Serves 10–12.

Mrs. GRAY HARRIS, Laurens County.

Ruth's Chicken Loaf

1 hen, cooked and cut into medium-sized pieces

small size loaf of bread, pulled apart in pieces

3 tablespoons Worcestershire sauce

1 cup thick white sauce

3 raw eggs

salt and pepper to taste

Mix and put into greased loaf pan. Set in pan of hot water in oven. Bake about 45 minutes at 375° F. or 400° F. Gravy: Melt 1 stick of butter (or use some of the fat from the broth of chicken). Brown flour (about 1 tablespoon or 1½ tablespoons flour) very brown in butter. Add 1 cup chicken broth and can of mushrooms if desired. Pour over loaf and serve. This can be mixed the day before, if desired, and placed in refrigerator, then baked at the last moment. Serves 8.

MARIE A. HAMILTON, Charleston County.

Barbecued Chicken

1 2½-pound fryer cut up

1 medium-sized onion, chopped fine

2 tablespoons butter

2 tablespoons vinegar

4 tablespoons lemon juice (or additional vinegar may be substituted)

2 tablespoons brown sugar

⅛ teaspoon cayenne pepper

⅛ teaspoon black pepper

1 teaspoon salt

1 cup tomato catsup

3 tablespoons Worcestershire sauce

½ tablespoon ground mustard

1 cup water

½ cup chopped celery

Roast chicken in oven for 45 minutes. Then add all the ingredients which have been mixed together to the chicken and roast 45 more minutes. Set oven at 350°. Serves 4–6.

MRS. H. W. LANGLEY, Kershaw County.

Barbecued Chicken—(easy to fix)

1/3 cup butter

1 tablespoon sugar

1 teaspoon salt

few grains cayenne

¼ teaspoon tabasco sauce

¼ cup vinegar

2 tablespoons flour

2/3 cup water

1½ tablespoons lemon juice

2 tablespoons Worcestershire sauce

1 cup green pepper

1 clove garlic

Prepare 3-pound chicken as for frying, salt, pepper and dip in flour, brown in heavy frying pan in hot fat. Drain off excess fat. Melt butter and add flour until smooth, chop pepper, slice garlic thinly, add all ingredients to butter, pour over browned chicken. Place in oven at 350°, cook for an hour or until chicken is thoroughly done, and sauce has thickened.   Serves 4–6.

STELLA THOMPSON, Greenwood County.

Barbecued Chicken

One 2- to 3-pound plump chicken, dressed ready to cook. Disjoint and brown in 1/3 cup of fat. Meanwhile make sauce of following:

1 cup catsup	¼ cup lemon juice
2 tablespoons brown sugar	3 tablespoons Worcestershire
½ tablespoon prepared mustard	sauce
½ cup chopped celery	1 cup water
1 medium onion, chopped	2 teaspoons salt
2 tablespoons vinegar	¼ teaspoon tabasco

Combine and simmer for 10 minutes. Place browned pieces of chicken in baking pan and pour sauce over it. Put into medium oven (325°) and bake uncovered for hour, basting frequently. Test drumstick for doneness and if pink meat shows, bake 15 minutes more. Serves 4–6.

MRS. TALCIE J. HOWELL, Lee County.

Mrs. Howell won first prize in the National Chicken Contest in Dover, Delaware, in 1950. Mrs. Howell says that the recipe was given to her by her grandmother many years ago.

TURKEYS—DUCKS—SQUAB

Broiled Squab, Duckling, or Young Turkey

Plump squabs, ducklings, or fat young turkeys are broiled like chicken. The same rules hold: moderate heat . . . start skin side down . . . turn when brown . . . baste with melted fat . . . cook slowly until thoroughly done . . . serve at once, hot and juicy.

The time for broiling differs of course with the weight of the bird. A squab from ¾ to 1 pound (dressed weight) will probably need from 30 to 40 minutes . . . a 2½-pound duckling, 35 to 45 minutes . . . a 3½-pound young turkey, 45 to 60 minutes.

Roast Turkey

1. Brush skin of bird thoroughly with cooking fat.

2. Place bird, breast up, on rack at least ½ inch high in a shallow open pan. If a meat thermometer is used, insert it so that the bulb rests in the center of the inside thigh muscle adjoining the body cavity. If a V-rack is used, place turkey breast down.

3. Take a piece of aluminum foil 4 or 5 inches longer that the turkey. Lay it over the bird. Pinch the foil at the drumstick and breast ends, pressing it lightly at those ends to anchor it. Leave the cap loose over the top and at the sides. Or, the turkey may be covered with fat-moistened cheesecloth, large enough to cover the top and drape down on all sides. Do not wrap bird in the cloth. Aluminum foil or cloth helps in uniform browning.

4. Place in preheated slow oven (325°F.). Do not sear. Do not add water. Do not cover. When the turkey is about 2/3 done, according to the timetable, cut the cord on the band of skin holding the drumstick ends to the tail, to release the legs. This permits the heat to reach the inside thigh to assure thorough cooking.

5. If the cheesecloth dries during cooking, moisten with drippings in the bottom of the pan.

6. About 20 minutes before the turkey is done, according to the approximate total time prescribed in the timetable, or (if meat thermometer registers 190°F.) apply these physical tests for doneness:

a. Press fleshy part of the drumstick between the fingers, protected with paper or cloth. Meat should feel very soft.

b. Move the drumstick up and down, the drumstick should move readily or twist out of the joint.

7. When the turkey is done remove from oven. Keep turkey hot while preparing gravy with drippings in the roasting pan.

Roast Duck with Apple Stuffing

Rub duck inside and out with salt. Mix together the following:

3 cups whole wheat bread   3 cups diced apples
1 tablespoon onion   1 teaspoon poultry seasoning

Moisten with hot water. Brush duck outside and inside with melted butter. Stuff lightly and bake in shallow pan 30 minutes per pound at 325°. Serves 9.

MRS. E. T. GULLEDGE, Sumter County.

Duck Dressing

2 cups cold biscuits (bread   1 small diced onion
    crumbs)   salt and pepper to taste
4 eggs   1 cup broth (water duck was
¼ pound butter   boiled in)
1 teaspoon baking powder

MRS. J. J. MAYSON, Edgefield County.

Quail or Dove Pie

Always skin a quail and pick a dove. Boil bird until tender. Remove meat from bones. Make up pie crust (using lard); take one-half the amount of dough, roll out and cut into tiny strips. Into a greased pan place meat, strips of dough, 2 hard-boiled eggs (diced), 1 cup whole milk, butter to taste. Top with remainder pie crust. Bake in moderate oven 45 minutes to 1 hour. If more liquid is needed use water bird has been boiled in.

MRS. JANELLE WINN, Edgefield County.

Baked Stuffed Squab

6 squabs
6 slices bread
3 large onions
½ teaspoon black pepper

½ teaspoon salt
2 tablespoons vinegar
3 tablespoons broth or water
½ teaspoon sage

Draw squabs for roasting. Crumble bread, add vinegar and water. Chop onion fine and add along with pepper, salt, and sage. Mix well. Stuff squab with this dressing.

Place in pan for baking in 325°-350° oven. Brown well. Add two cups of water, put cover on pan and bake an hour and a quarter longer.

GRADY JOHNSON, Ocean Drive, S. C.

Smothered Squabs

6 squabs
1 cup chopped onions
1/3 teaspoon salt
⅛ teaspoon black pepper

2 cups water
2 tablespoons flour
6 tablespoons bacon grease or butter

2 teaspoons Worcestershire sauce

Split squabs down back. Wipe inside and out with damp cloth. Brown both sides in bacon grease or butter. Remove squabs from pan. Sprinkle flour in grease and brown. Replace squabs, add water and onions. Sprinkle with salt, pepper and sauce. Cover and steam over low heat for 50 minutes or until tender.

Serve hot with asparagus tips and boiled potatoes sprinkled with parsley. Use other vegetables if preferred.

GRADY JOHNSON, Ocean Drive, S. C.

Fish - Shell Fish

Fish and shellfish provide high quality protein, vitamin A and B complex, and some of the minerals. Deep-sea fish furnish iodine necessary for healthy functioning of the thyroid gland, but lake fish contain little iodine. Bones of canned fish are soft and should be eaten since they are a good source of calcium. Other minerals found in fish are copper, iron, phosphorus, and magnesium, all necessary for good health.

So include fish in your diet because:

Fish are always in season.

There is a great variety of fish.

They are easily digested.

They contain many food materials needed for the body.

FISH

Fresh Fish

If a fish is fresh—

Gills are bright red.

Eyes are bright, clear, bulging.

Flesh is elastic and firm. (Finger impressions should not remain.)

Scales cling to the skin.

Odor is fresh and fishy, not tainted or sour.

Fish spoil quickly. They need quick handling. When fish are caught do not bruise or expose them to the sun. If ice is not available, remove entrails and sprinkle the cavity with salt. At home, keep fish directly on ice or in the coldest part of the refrigerator.

Tips for Cooking

Fish are delicately flavored. Cooking, seasoning, and sauces should bring out this flavor, not overpower it. The tender protein food needs but little cooking; long cooking toughens it.

To get the best flavor, juiciness, and tenderness cook fish at a moderate temperature (350 to 375 degrees). This means baking at a moderate temperature or simmering, rather than boiling. When fish flesh separates from the bone, it is done. At this stage the flesh is still moist, tender and the natural flavor is at its best.

Fish are sometimes classified as lean and fat. Fat fish need little if any additional fat. When cooking, lean fish may be spread with French dressing, basted with melted fat, or may be overlaid with strips of bacon during baking. Allow 1/3 to ½ pound of fish per person.

Baked Fish

Clean the fish. Sprinkle inside with salt and pepper. Fill with stuffing. Fasten edges with skewers, round tooth picks, or tie or sew

with wrapping thread. Brush outside with salad oil or melted butter. Place on a well-greased, shallow baking pan. Cut gashes crosswise in upper side of fish. Place strips of bacon in these slits. Bake at 375 degrees 12 to 15 minutes for each pound. For the stuffing use:

2 cups soft bread crumbs	1 tablespoon minced onion
2 teaspoons lemon juice	1 teaspoon salt
¼ cup chopped parsley	⅛ teaspoon pepper

¼ cup butter

Combine and use for stuffing fish or fish fillets. About 2 cups of stuffing are enough for a 3 to 4 pound fish or 6 fish fillets.

Broiled Fish

Clean, wash, and dry fish. Oil a heated broiler pan. Brush fish with oil. Place fish on broiler pan about 2 inches below flame. Cook until skin is covered with dark brown bubbles. Turn only once. Baste with French dressing or melted butter several times. Broil at 500 degrees 6-8 minutes, depending on thickness of fish.

Deep Fat Fried Fish

Use a deep kettle and a frying basket. Cut fish into serving pieces. Sprinkle both sides with salt and pepper. Dip fish into mixture of egg and water. Then roll pieces in flour, cornmeal, or bread or cracker crumbs. Fry in hot fat. Drain fried fish on absorbent paper.

Baked Cream Fish Fillets

2 pounds fish fillets, fresh or
    frozen
¼ teaspoon salt
few grains pepper
¼ teaspoon paprika
juice of 1 lemon

2 tablespoons flour
2 tablespoons butter
½ cup buttered bread crumbs
1 tablespoon minced parsley
1 tablespoon dry mustard
1 cup top milk

salt and pepper

Cut fillets in serving pieces. Place in greased, shallow baking dish; sprinkle with salt, pepper, paprika and lemon juice. Make a white sauce of butter, flour seasonings and milk. Pour over the fillets.

Sprinkle with crumbs and parsley. Bake in moderate oven 350 degrees for 35 minutes. Serves 6.

Mrs. ROBERT C. WASSON, Laurens County.

Fish Pie

1 cup flaked cooked fish (or 1 pound raw fish)

1 cup water in which fish has been boiled

2 tablespoons flour

1 cup milk

2 tablespoons butter

1 egg

1 tablespoon Worcestershire sauce

salt and pepper to taste

Make a cream sauce of flour, butter, milk and liquor in which fish has been boiled. Add fish, beat thoroughly, add Worcestershire sauce, and beaten egg. Put in baking dish and cook in a moderate oven (350 degrees) for about 15 minutes. Sprinkle with buttered bread crumbs on top before baking, if desired. Serves 4.

Salmon Fish Stew with Potatoes

4 medium Irish potatoes

1 medium onion

1 quart canned or fresh tomatoes

1 teaspoon salt

dash black pepper

4 slices bacon

2 tablespoons butter

1 tall can pink salmon

½ cup tomato catsup

Cube potatoes and onion, cook in 1 cup of water until tender. Add tomatoes, cook 10 minutes. Add salmon, bacon, butter and seasoning. Cook slowly 10 minutes longer. Serve hot. Serves about 10.

Mrs. J. F. GEIGER, Calhoun County.

Salmon Stew

½ cup butter or substitute

4 tablespoons chopped onions

1 can salmon

1 small bottle tomato catsup

½ teaspoon Worcestershire sauce

salt and pepper

Brown lightly the onions in melted butter. Add salmon, catsup, Worcestershire sauce, salt and pepper to taste. Add 2 cups boiling water and mix well, breaking salmon up fine. Continue cooking gently for about 10 minutes. Serve hot with rice.

Mrs. ARNOLD LOCKLEAR, Marlboro County.

Salmon Loaf

2 cups canned salmon	salt and pepper
3 tablespoons fat	2 tablespoons minced parsley
3 tablespoons flour	2 cups bread cubes
1 cup milk and salmon liquid	1 egg, beaten

Drain canned salmon, saving the liquid. Make sauce: Blend fat and flour together. Add enough milk to the salmon liquid to make 1 cup, and stir slowly into the fat and flour. Cook until thickened, stirring constantly. Add seasonings. Mix the sauce with the other ingredients. Form into loaf. Bake in uncovered pan in a moderate oven (350 degrees) about half an hour, or until brown.

Salmon Croquettes

2 cups salmon	dash of paprika
1 cup bread crumbs	dash of pepper
1 tablespoon parsley	1 cup No. 4 white sauce
1 tablespoon lemon juice	

Mix ingredients. Shape and roll in flour, beaten egg, and bread crumbs. Fry in deep fat (shapes are easier made if mixture is allowed to chill).

SHELL FISH

Oyster Cocktail

3 to 6 oysters

Wash in cold water, drain, and chill. Arrange in glasses. Pour cocktail sauce over the oysters. Serves 1.

Cocktail Sauce:

2 tablespoons tomato catsup
½ tablespoon lemon juice
¼ teaspoon salt

3 to 4 drops tabasco sauce
½ teaspoon horse-radish
¼ teaspoon Worcestershire sauce

Combine ingredients. Can also be used with crab meat and shrimp.

Oyster Stew

1 quart oysters
4 cups scalded milk

½ tablespoon salt
⅛ teaspoon pepper

¼ cup butter

Pick over oysters, reserve liquor, and heat it to boiling point. Strain, add oysters, and cook until oysters are plump and edges begin to curl. Add hot milk, butter, salt and pepper.

Fried Oysters

3 dozen large oysters
1 cup fine cracker crumbs
   or cornmeal

salt and pepper
cooking fat or oil
2 eggs well beaten

Drain oysters, season with pepper and salt, dip in the beaten egg, then in the dry crumbs or meal. Fry in a single layer in a frying pan, or heat deep fat until it begins to smoke, place a single layer of oysters in an oiled fry basket and cook to a golden brown.

Scalloped Oysters

1 pint oysters
¾ teaspoon salt
⅛ teaspoon pepper

3 cups buttered crumbs or
   crackers
2 tablespoons butter

Remove bits of shell from oysters. Put crumbs in bottom of buttered baking dish. Add a layer of oysters then a layer of crumbs and dot over with butter. Use oyster liquid for moisture. Bake 20 to 30 minutes in a moderate oven.

Oysters on Half Shell

Serve oysters on deep halves of the shell, allowing 6 to each person, arrange on plates on crushed ice, with ¼ of a lemon in center of each plate. (Serve with cocktail sauce.)

Oysters Broiled on Toast

Allow one slice bread for each person. To each slice of bread allow 6 to 8 good sized oysters. Butter the bread and place oysters on each slice, 6 to 8 to each slice. Sprinkle with salt and pepper, dot thickly with butter, and place under broiler to brown. Cook slowly. Serve hot. A grand dish for supper, cooked in a hurry.

MRS. R. W. TISDALE, Beaufort County.

Oyster Sauce

1 pint oysters
2 tablespoons oleo or butter
2 tablespoons flour

1 tablespoon Worcestershire
   sauce
salt and pepper to taste

Brown flour in oleo; add oyster juice and water to equal ½ cup liquid. Add oysters, etc. Cook until oysters frill. Serve over rice or grits.   Serves 3-4.   MRS. A. W. BAILEY, Beaufort County.

Oyster Pie

1 pint oysters
½ cup milk
2 tablespoons butter

1 cup oysterettes or saltine-type crackers
salt and pepper to taste

Into a baking dish from which they are to be served put a layer of oysters, salt, pepper and bits of butter then a layer of crushed crackers (not too fine). Repeat layers. Pour milk over all and dot with butter. Bake in a moderate oven hot through, approximately 30 minutes. Serve immediately.

Plain Boiled Shrimp

Place green shrimp in boiling water, salted, and cook approximately 10 minutes. Remove from water and peel by breaking the under shell and opening from front to back. This will allow the meat to be removed in one piece. Remove the dark sand vein from the center back of each shrimp. Chill. Use plain boiled shrimp for cocktails, or salads.

French Fried Shrimp

1½ pounds shrimp
2 beaten eggs
juice of 2 lemons

sifted cracker crumbs, flour, or meal
cooking oil or fat

salt and pepper

Peel shrimp, wash, and remove sand vein. Place in a bowl with lemon juice, salt and pepper, and allow to stand for 15 minutes. Dip shrimp into the beaten egg and then roll in crumbs. Place a single layer into a well-oiled frying basket and cook to golden brown.

Shrimp Omelet

1 cup finely chopped shrimp
or cup of shrimp cut up
(boiled or peeled)

2 raw eggs, beaten together
1 level tablespoon butter
little salt and pepper

1 tablespoon hot water

Beat eggs together until light, add salt, pepper and water. Have frying pan hot and grease with a little butter, about the size of a walnut. Pour in egg mixture and let cook slowly. When omelet looks as if set, drop in the shrimp and butter. Fold over with spatula and allow to cook on the other side. Serve hot.

Mrs. R. W. Tisdale, Beaufort County.

Shrimp Creole

½ pound cooked shrimp meat
2 tablespoons melted butter
1 cup chopped onions
1 cup chopped green pepper

½ chopped garlic clove
⅛ teaspoon paprika
1 pint stewed tomatoes
salt and pepper

Brown the onion, green pepper, and garlic in the butter. Let simmer until pepper is tender. Add tomato and seasoning. Boil 5 minutes. Add shrimp and boil 10 minutes longer. Serve on bed of rice.

Shrimp a la Newburg

1 pint shrimp
3 tablespoons butter
½ teaspoon salt
few grains cayenne

1 teaspoon lemon juice
1 teaspoon flour
½ cup cream
2 egg yolks

2 tablespoons sherry wine

Cook boiled and picked shrimp 3 minutes in 2 tablespoons butter. Add salt, cayenne and lemon juice and cook 1 minute. Remove shrimp and put remaining butter in pan, add flour and cream; when thickened, add yolks of eggs (slightly beaten) shrimp and wine.

MRS. ANSEL PRICE, Charleston County.

Shrimp Cocktail

Cocktail Sauce:

To ¾ cup catsup add 1½ tablespoons lemon juice, 1 tablespoon Worcestershire sauce, 1 tablespoon prepared horse radish, few drops tabasco sauce, ½ teaspoon salt, chill thoroughly. For each serving, place lettuce in cocktail glasses, allow 6 shrimp for 1 serving. Place shrimp on lettuce and pour 1 to 2 tablespoons cocktail sauce over each serving.   RAYMOND B. NICHOLS, Newberry County.

Shrimp Salad

To cooked, cooled shrimp add chopped, hard-cooked eggs, celery, cut fine, and mayonnaise or salad dressing. Serve on crisp lettuce.

Shrimp and Oyster Delight

1 pound fresh shrimp	½ green pepper (diced)
2 dozen large oysters	½ cup chopped pimento
1 cup flaked cooked crab meat	2 tablespoons butter
6 mushrooms (or 1 small can)	2 cups thin cream sauce
salt and pepper to taste	

Thin Cream Sauce:

1 tablespoon butter	1 cup milk (light cream)
½ teaspoon salt	1 tablespoon flour

dash pepper

Prepare shrimp, boil, remove shell and black vein along the back. Heat oysters in their liquor until the edges curl. Saute mushrooms and pepper in butter for about 5 minutes. Add crab meat, cream sauce and pimento. Heat thoroughly. Serve on toast. Serves 10.

MRS. LILLIAN M. ROBINSON, Beaufort County.

Shrimp Paste

1 cup ground boiled shrimp   ¼ cup creamed butter

Season with red pepper, salt, mace, nutmeg or Worcestershire sauce. Tomato catsup may be added if desired. This can be molded, rolled into balls or spread on thin slices of bread or crackers or to stuff celery. Serve with tart vegetables or fruit salad.

Shrimp Pie

3 cups picked and boiled shrimp	1 cup milk
3 or 4 slices bread (slightly toasted)	1 tablespoon butter
	2 hard-boiled eggs
1 medium-sized bell pepper	2 tablespoons sherry wine

salt and pepper

Put a layer of shrimp in baking dish, then a layer of crumbled bread, then a little bell pepper diced very small, a layer of sliced hard-boiled egg; sprinkle with salt and pepper. Continue layers until all shrimp are used up. Add milk until ingredients are moistened but not soupy. Add sherry. Top with dry bread crumbs. Bake at 350 degrees until lightly brown.

MRS. ANSEL PRICE, Charleston County.

Shrimp Stew—Potatoes

¼ pound smoked bacon (cubed)	2 medium potatoes
	3 pounds shrimp
2 medium onions	boil and pick shells from shrimp

Over low heat, fry out bacon cubes, add onions chopped fine, saute until light brown. Add potatoes, cubed, cook slowly until tender, add peeled shrimp, salt and pepper to taste and cook slowly for 15 minutes. Serve with steamed rice. Serves 6.

MRS. EFFIE ALMEIDA, Charleston County.

She Crab Soup

1 dozen she crabs	black pepper and salt
2 cups milk	½ teaspoon Worcestershire
½ cup cream	sauce
1 teaspoon butter	1 teaspoon flour
1 small onion	1 tablespoon sherry

Cook the crabs until tender—about 20 minutes in boiling, salted water. Pick the meat from the shells and put the crab meat with the crab eggs into a double boiler. Add the butter, onion and a little black pepper. Let simmer for 5 minutes. Heat the milk and add to the mixture. Stir together and add the cream and the Worcestershire sauce. Thicken with the flour, add the sherry and salt to taste. Cook over a low flame for a few minutes.   Serves 6.

Mrs. Marie A. Hamilton, Charleston County.

Crab Soup

1½ pounds crab meat	grated rind 1 lemon
2 tablespoons butter	1 quart rich milk
1 tablespoon flour	2 hard-boiled eggs
1 tablespoon Worcestershire	salt
sauce	½ cup sherry

Mash eggs through strainer, blend with the butter and flour and grated rind. Add to scalded milk, and cook in the top of double boiler. When thick, add crab meat, and simmer 5 minutes. Add sherry just before serving.

Mrs. Louise Vickers, Beaufort County.

Crab Casserole

1 pound can crab claw meat	*To Taste:*
small box soda crackers or	Worcestershire sauce
oysterettes, ½ of which are	salt
crumbled into crab and egg	pepper
4 hard-boiled eggs	

Stir in mayonnaise to make very moist and bake in hot oven in casserole until brown.

Mrs. W. D. Gregorie, Charleston County.

Deviled Crab

¼ cup butter
2 tablespoons flour
½ cup milk
2 cups crab meat, flaked (or canned)
yolks of 3 hard-cooked eggs mashed

½ teaspoon salt
½ teaspoon paprika
¼ teaspoon pepper
½ teaspoon prepared mustard
1 tablespoon chopped parsley
1 tablespoon lemon juice
2/3 cup buttered crumbs

Melt butter in a saucepan, blend in flour. Add milk gradually, and cook over low heat, stirring constantly, until sauce boils and thickens. Fold in remaining ingredients except buttered crumbs, and mix until well blended but do not mash. Turn mixture into a greased 6-cup casserole, or into individual casseroles or cleaned crab shells. Sprinkle with buttered crumbs (2 tablespoons of butter) and bake in a moderately hot oven (400 degrees) for 5 to 10 minutes or until crumbs are temptingly brown and mixture is heated through. Serve at once directly from casserole. Serves 4.

THELMA BOLLINGER, Newberry County.

Deviled Crab with Onion and Bell Pepper

3 cups crab meat
1 cup cracker meal
2 tablespoons each of minced red and green pepper

1 small onion grated
1 cup sea food cocktail sauce
1 egg
2 teaspoons salt

½ teaspoon pepper

Combine all ingredients and fill crab shells. Bake at 400 degrees until golden brown. This makes 1 dozen medium servings.

PROSPECT CLUB, Florence County.

Deviled Crab—(St. Helena Delight)

1½ cups fresh crab meat
  (or 1 can claw crab meat)
1 tablespoon flour
½ teaspoon Worcestershire
  sauce
1 tablespoon butter
salt and red pepper to taste

1 teaspoon grated onion
½ cup fine bread crumbs
  buttered
1 tablespoon red and green
  pepper chopped
1 teaspoon lemon juice
1 egg yolk

½ teaspoon mustard

Melt butter; stir in flour; add milk and cook until it thickens. Add slightly beaten egg yolk and crab meat shredded, add seasonings. Cook 3 minutes. Stir in onion and lemon juice and red and green peppers. Fill crab or scallop shells with mixture. Sprinkle bread crumbs. Bake in hot oven until top is brown. Serves 4.

MRS. SIDNEY BATES, Beaufort County.

Deviled Crab with Cheese

4 tablespoons butter or
  margarine
2 tablespoons flour
1 tablespoon chopped parsley,
  optional
2 teaspoons lemon juice
1 teaspoon Worcestershire
  sauce

1 teaspoon prepared mustard
2 tablespoons catsup
1 teaspoon salt
few drops hot sauce
1 cup milk
2 cups crab meat
1 egg, beaten
½ cup buttered bread crumbs

4 tablespoons grated cheese

Melt fat in double boiler, add flour and mix well. Stir until smooth. Add milk slowly—then all other ingredients. Fill crab backs with mixture. Sprinkle with grated cheese and bread crumbs. Bake in hot oven 400 degrees for 10 minutes. Serves 6.

MRS. A. E. JURY, Charleston County.

Baked Sea Food Casserole

1 cup shrimp (boiled and
  peeled)
1 cup crab meat
1 large green pepper
1 small onion

1 cup celery
1 cup mayonnaise
½ teaspoon salt
1 teaspoon Worcestershire
  sauce

pepper

Combine crab meat and shrimp with vegetables which have been
chopped very fine. Add mayonnaise. Add salt, pepper and Worcestershire; mix well. Cover with buttered crumbs. Bake in moderate oven
30 minutes at 350 degrees.

MRS. ANSEL PRICE, Charleston County.

Clam Chowder

1 quart clams
4 cups potatoes diced
1 ½-inch cube fat salt pork

1 onion
1 tablespoon salt
4 tablespoons butter

1 quart scalded milk

Remove soft part of clams. Chop hard parts. Reserve clam water,
heat and strain it. Cut pork into small pieces, fry out with onion
minced. Parboil potatoes 5 minutes, drain and put into saucepan;
add chopped clams, sprinkle with salt and pepper and dredge with
flour; add remaining potatoes, sprinkle with salt and pepper and
dredge with flour; add 2½ cups boiling water; cook 10 minutes. Add
milk, soft parts of clams and butter. Boil 3 minutes. Reheat clam
water, thicken with one tablespoon flour and 1 of butter and add
the remainder of the butter just before serving.

MRS. A. H. LUCAS, Charleston County.

FISH STEWS

Pine Bark Fish Stew

Sauce to be incorporated in recipe for stew:

6 pints tomatoes (fresh or
  canned)
2 tablespoons salt
4 tablespoons sugar
1 tablespoon whole allspice

1 tablespoon whole cloves
1 tablespoon whole black
  pepper
⅛ teaspoon cayenne pepper or
  two small red peppers

1 tablespoon stick cinnamon

Put tomatoes through a sieve; tie whole spices in cheesecloth and cook all ingredients until sauce measures about 3 cups.

Recipe for Stew:

Fry ¼ pound bacon, add 12 tablespoons chopped onions and fry until brown. Take 5 pounds of fish, pour over 2½ cups hot water. Add fried bacon and onions, 3 cups tomato sauce (recipe above), 2 tablespoons Worcestershire sauce, ¼ pound butter, 2 tablespoons salt, 1 tablespoon black pepper. Cook all together 20 minutes. Serve on rice or cornbread.   Serves 25-30.

The story is that a party of hunters and fishermen, cooking their meal over a fire of burning pine bark, served the stew on sheets of dry pine bark.

Catfish Stew

½ pound bacon	1½ pints water
1½ pounds onions	2/3 bottle tomato catsup
2 small cans (10½ ounce) of	2 pounds catfish
condensed tomato soup	salt and pepper

Slice and fry ½ pound bacon until crisp. Remove from pan. Add 1½ pounds onions to bacon fat and fry until medium brown. Add soup and water and bring to a boil. Add catfish and let cook for 15 to 20 minutes. Add salt and pepper to taste. Add catsup and stir lightly. Remove from fire. Serve hot with rice, crackers, or light bread. Serves 6.

SAM A. TRULUCK, Sumter County.

Catfish Stew—(cush stew)

4 catfish	1½ cups water
½ cup fat	3 eggs
1 cup cream and milk	1 onion
2 Irish potatoes	salt and pepper to taste

Put the fat in pot; salt and flour fish. Then put fish in the fat and brown on both sides. To the brown mixture add water, sliced potatoes and onions and cook until fish leaves bone. Stir often to prevent burning. Beat eggs and add milk and cream and pepper, then pour this into fish mixture and stir until all is well blended. Serve hot.

MRS. H. W. MURDAUGH, Colleton County.

Catfish Stew with Boiled Eggs

4 pounds dressed catfish　　　½ dozen chopped boiled eggs
1½ pounds chopped onions　　1 cup evaporated milk
1½ pounds smoked side meat　½ stick butter
　　cut in ½-inch cubes　　　　salt and pepper to taste

Boil catfish in large container along with onions until fish leaves the bones adding water as needed, just enough to cover fish. Cook bacon done and pour off grease and add to mixture. Boil about 1½ hours then add eggs, butter and boil 10 minutes. Take off fire and add milk. Stir when pouring in milk. Put back on fire and let simmer until hot.　Serves 6-8.

"BUTCH" JOHNSTON, Dorchester County.

Red Horse Bread

1 cup cornmeal　　　　　　　¼ cup self-rising flour
　　　　　　　　3 eggs

Mix cornmeal, flour, eggs and enough water to make stiff enough to hold shape when dropped in hot grease. Fry until golden brown. Add just a little baking powder or soda to make fluff up if necessary. This is prepared to be eaten especially with fish.

"BUTCH" JOHNSTON, Dorchester County.

Catfish Stew with Potatoes

½ pound sliced bacon　　　　1 cup hot water
4 pounds catfish　　　　　　1 can condensed tomato soup
3 pounds Irish potatoes　　　4 tablespoons butter
2 pounds onions　　　　　　hot sauce
　　　　　salt and pepper

Fry bacon in pot until brown. Take up meat and to the grease, add in layers the catfish, diced potatoes and diced onions using about 2 layers of each. Add hot water, cover and cook for 1½ hours, without stirring. Then add tomato soup, butter, hot sauce, salt and pepper to taste. Serve hot.

MARVIN STROM, Aiken County.

Fish Stew with Potatoes

1 cup bacon fat
4 Irish potatoes (large)
4 onions (large)

1 can tomato soup
2 bottles tomato catsup
6 pounds dressed fish

salt and pepper to taste

Mix bacon fat, potatoes and onions together and cook until potatoes fall in pieces. Then add soup, catsup, salt and pepper. Cook until this comes to a hard boil. Then add fish and cook 20 minutes on medium heat. Stir often to keep from sticking. Serves 15.

R. E. Moody, Dillon County.

Fish Stew

8 pounds fish
1 pound fat back
2 pounds onions
2 cans tomato paste
2 cans tomato soup

2 quarts water (more if needed)
1 bottle catsup
2 tablespoons black pepper
2 teaspoons red pepper
8 tablespoons salt

⅛ pound butter

Dice fat back and fry in large heavy soup kettle. Add onions and fry until brown. Add remaining ingredients, except butter and fish, and stir to keep from sticking. Bring to boil and add fish. Cook for 30 minutes after fish are added. Add butter about 5 minutes before fish are done.

E. L. Helms, Darlington County.

Game

O'POSSUM, VENISON, RABBIT

Barbecued Rabbit

Stretch rabbit full length in long baking pan. Put a very little water in bottom of pan to keep rabbit from sticking and place in hot oven. After rabbit has been in oven ten minutes, rub well with butter, and reduce heat to a low degree.

Make a basting of:

1 teaspoon salt	1 teaspoon dry mustard
1 teaspoon black pepper	1 teaspoon paprika
1 teaspoon sugar	1 teaspoon flour

1 cup vinegar

Baste rabbit with this several times during the cooking. Bake 1½ to 2 hours. When done, most of moisture should be cooked out of pan.

MRS. CHARLES MAULDIN, Greenwood County.

Steamed Rabbit

This is a good recipe for a mature rabbit.

Cut the rabbit into serving pieces, flour well, add salt and pepper and fry quickly to a rich brown in hot fat. Place in a roaster or pan with a tight fitting cover, add a cup of water, cover tightly and place in oven to steam about two hours. (If desired, add a slice of onion, a slice of lemon, a bay leaf, a very little thyme, when it is put in oven to steam.)

MRS. CHARLES MAULDIN, Greenwood County.

Rabbit in Tomato Sauce

1 large rabbit	1 large onion chopped fine
2 tablespoons fat	2 teaspoons salt
1½ cups tomato pulp and juice	pepper

3 cups water

Dip the pieces of rabbit in flour and brown in fat in a deep iron skillet. Add the chopped onion and tomato juice with the seasonings and the boiling water. Cover and let simmer on top of stove or in the oven for 1 hour. The tomato sauce cooks down and gives a very good flavor to the rabbit. A little more thickening may be needed just before serving.

Rabbit Salad

Follow any good chicken salad recipe and substitute cooked rabbit cut in cubes for the chicken.

Roasted Opossum

1 opossum   1 pod red pepper
salt and pepper to taste

Parboil opossum until tender, changing the stock two or three times according to age to get out some of the wild taste. Boil a piece of red pepper with it. Place in roaster, add small amount of water in bottom of roaster. Sprinkle opossum with flour and baste with fat if necessary. Usually fat is sufficient. Cook to a light brown, surrounded by steamed sweet potatoes in a moderate oven 325° to 350°.

Mrs. Effie Thomas, Colleton County.

Flavor of Venison

It should not be necessary to make any attempt to conceal the flavor of venison. The characteristic flavor seems to be concentrated in the fat and if strong, trimming away excess fat will help. However, venison is a rather dry meat and is improved by addition of suet, butter or other fat when using dry heat methods—roasting, broiling, and frying. The standard methods of meat cooking for beef and lamb are most successful for venison. The use of bacon, vegetables and fruit juices is suggested to impart a different flavor. Spices such as bay leaf, thyme, garlic, savory and the like may be added to suit your taste.

Venison Roast

6 pounds venison

In a skillet fry 3 medium pieces of salt pork. In the rendered fat brown the roast on all sides. Place meat in covered roaster and salt. To the frying fat add:

2 cups chopped celery   1 cup catsup
2 cups chopped onion   some hot sauce
½ cup vinegar   2 teaspoons Worcestershire
½ cup sugar   sauce
1 cup water

Cover meat with mixture and cook at 350 degrees, baste occasionally. Cook for about four hours. Taste gravy to determine if any more seasoning is desired. The gravy is excellent served on rice.

Mrs. Guy E. Seagle, Sumter County.

Roast Venison

Lard venison plentifully with fat salt pork or bacon drippings. Rub with well seasoned flour. Roast in a 300 degree oven. Cook covered until almost finished. Roast 25 minutes per pound if rare meat is desired; 30 minutes per pound for medium roast. Serve with sauce in the pan or make a delicious brown roast gravy in the same manner as used for roast beef. Sour cream is excellent for use in making gravy. Brown 1 tablespoon flour in meat pan, add sour cream and simmer to rich brown consistency. Season to taste.

Venison Barbecue

1 cup catsup
1 tablespoon barbecue sauce
1 tablespoon salt
¼ cup vinegar
1 tablespoon butter

⅛ teaspoon cinnamon
3 slices lemon
1 onion, sliced thin
⅛ teaspoon allspice
3 pounds venison

Sear 3 pounds venison in frying pan, mix other ingredients in saucepan and bring to a boil, stirring to avoid burning. Simmer 10 minutes. Cover venison with sauce and roast in moderate oven for 2 hours, turning occasionally.

MRS. JESSE D. PADGETT, Colleton County.

Martha's Venison Soup

1 saddle of venison
2 quarts of cold water (approx.)
1 tablespoon salt or to taste
¼ cup small crisp-fried pieces of bacon

4 tablespoons flour
2 bay leaves
1 teaspoon whole cloves or allspice
Pepper to taste

¼ cup of wine—sherry or port

For Stock

Place saddle of venison in large soup pot, add enough cold water to cover, and bring to a boil uncovered. Remove scum, add salt, and boil gently, covered, until meat is tender.

To Finish Soup

Remove meat from bone and cut into small pieces. Return meat and the crisp-fried bacon to the stock, reserving a cup of stock for the thickening. Brown flour in saucepan and add flour to cup of stock reserved for this purpose. Beat until smooth. Pour thickening gradually into soup, stirring soup as you pour for smoothness. Cook 15 minutes. Pepper to taste. Add wine last, before serving.

MARY RUTLEDGE STROMAN, Charleston County.

Vegetables

Out of the good earth come many vegetables—the yellow and white potato, crimson beets, orange carrots, turnips—white and yellow and purple topped—red and white radishes, green spring onions, dry winter onions—brown, red, and silver skinned.

Even the fruit, flowers, stems, seeds, and leaves of vegetables are eaten—tomatoes—red and ripe—purple egg plant, yellow squash, cool green cucumbers, asparagus, broccoli, okra, beans and peas—green and dried—yellow corn, and the deeper and lighter green leaves as collards, turnip greens, mustard, kale, spinach, parsley, cabbage, and lettuce.

Vegetables from under the ground, the flower, stem, leaves, seed pod and fruit, all bring vitamins, minerals, starches, and sugars to help supply the body needs. The wealth of color, food value, and good flavor of vegetables give beauty, zest and variety to meals every day.

Here in South Carolina an abundance of these vegetables can be grown the year round. It is easy for us to plan and have vegetables in our meals if we follow the recommended planting and conservation guides for South Carolina. But whether you grow your own vegetables or buy them fresh from the grocery store, use vegetables—fresh, canned, frozen, or stored—every day.

Vegetables Every Day

Each one of us needs four or five servings of vegetables every day. Here is how to choose your daily vegetables:

1 serving green or yellow vegetables;

1 serving tomatoes, raw cabbage or other raw greens;

1 serving potatoes, sweet or Irish;

2 servings of other vegetables or fruits.

THE GREENS

Fresh—Crisp—Clean

Use green vegetables fresh—the fresher the better. Vitamins disappear as vegetables wilt and wait.

If you must hold them for a day or so, keep green vegetables cool, damp, and lightly covered. Pile loosely to prevent crushing.

Wash quickly, never soak, and lift from water to free from sand and grit.

To crisp up salad greens after washing, wrap in a clean cloth or put in a covered dish and let stand for a little while in a cold place.

Save for the soup kettle leaves and stems too coarse to use "as is."

Some Cooked—Some Raw

Cooked vegetables are at their best when they are as much like the fresh vegetable as possible. They should be cooked only long enough to be tender but not long enough to be mushy. Avoid over-cooking. For vegetables at their best—(1) use soon after harvesting, (2) cook in shortest time possible, (3) cook in least amount of water possible, (4) save liquids from cooked or canned vegetables for soups and gravies, (5) cook vegetables whole or in large pieces when you can, or cook them with skins on to save food value.

Remember the greener the leaf, pod, and stem, the richer the Vitamin A value. You can store Vitamin A in your body for months ahead. When green vegetables are plentiful, build your Vitamin A bank for the future.

More Vitamins from Your Vegetables

Vegetables that are good sources of vitamin C: tomatoes, raw cabbage, green peppers, raw turnips, and the deeper greens used raw.

If you observe the rules for cooking vegetables, a fair amount of vitamin C can be had from cooked greens.

Remember that water, air, heat, and the cook are the four enemies of vitamins and minerals. Control these enemies. Here's how to conserve not only vitamin C but the other precious vitamins and minerals, too.

Vitamin and Mineral Enemy	What Enemy Does	How to Control Enemy
Water	Soaks out vitamins B and C and some minerals when food is cooked or allowed to stand in much water.	1. Do not let vegetables stand in water for a long time. 2. Cook in small amount of water. 3. Save and serve any water that is left. 4. Do not throw away liquid from canned foods.
Air	Too much air destroys vitamins A and C.	1. Use vegetables soon after gathering. 2. Do not cut or peel long before using. 3. Cook in pan with lid on. 4. Stir as little as possible. 5. Keep prepared vegetables cold in refrigerator in covered dish until ready to cook or eat.

Vitamin and Mineral Enemy	*What Enemy Does*	*How to Control Enemy*
Heat	Heat destroys s o m e vitamins, especially B and C.	1. Cook in as short time as possible. 2. Do not keep hot for long periods.
The Cook	Throws away or destroys minerals a n d vitamins. Spoils t h e flavor a n d looks of vegetables.	1. Cook vegetables in skins when possible, or peel very thinly. 2. Do not add soda. It d e s t r o y s vitamins. 3. Too much c o o k i n g ruins looks, flavor, and destroys vitamins. 4. Don't throw away cooking water, save it and serve it.

Methods of Cooking Vegetables

The Greens: Cook greens without cover to keep that fresh green color. All vegetables contain milk acids which escape with the steam. If vegetables are cooked with the cover on the pan this tends to hold in acids which act upon color pigment causing a change from original green to a brownish green. If lid is left off, or if cooking time is very short with lid on, the acid does not have time to affect the color. For vegetables that require long cooking, lid may be so placed as to allow steam to escape or lid may be left off for approximately five minutes and then placed on to shorten length of time.

The White and Yellow Vegetables: White and yellow vegetables may turn dark when over-cooked. Yellow vegetables have a tendency to burn easily because of sugar content. Don't over-cook.

Red Vegetables: The red color in beets and cabbage may turn a a dark bluish color if water is alkaline, or their color may bleed if too much water is used. Cook whole beets in skins to save color.

Strong Flavored Vegetables: Strong flavored vegetables such as cabbage, turnips, broccoli, cauliflower, and brussels sprouts should be cooked quickly and only until tender. Long cooking brings out unpleasant flavors and odors.

For whole vegetables or those cut in large pieces use moderate amount of boiling water in uncovered pan; the plant acids are diluted and allowed to escape with steam. Remember, however, with the larger amount of water, food value will escape into the steam, and vegetable water should be used. A smaller amount of water can be used if cover is placed on pan half-way through cooking period.

Cabbage, turnips, and cauliflower may be cut in smaller pieces and cooked in smaller amount of water. The vegetables then cook so quickly that no strong flavor develops.

Baking—Vegetables such as potatoes, tomatoes, and squash bake excellently because they contain enough water to form steam and keep moist. Other vegetables may be baked in casserole.

Steaming—Vegetables may be steamed whole for best value, or for quick cooking, cut and only enough water added to prevent sticking.

Boiling—Cooking vegetables whole or in skins saves food value and flavor. See directions above for amount of water and whether to cover or leave uncovered while cooking.

Panning is a quick and easy top-of-stove method and is thrifty of food values. Vegetables are cooked in own juices with just enough fat to season. Use heavy pan, allow about two tablespoons fat for each quart of vegetables, melt fat, add vegetables, cover to keep in steam, stir occasionally. Cook slowly until tender, season and serve.

Frying is least desirable method of cooking vegetables. When fried, vegetables such as potatoes should be crisp and not greasy.

Methods of Serving Vegetables

RAW.   Vegetables should be served raw often because they contain more food value than vegetables served in any other way. Serve them as a relish or in salads.

AU GRATIN.   Alternate layers of cooked vegetable and white sauce. Add cheese to sauce or sprinkle cheese on each layer of sauce.

BUTTERED.   One to 1½ tablespoons butter for 2 cups of cooked vegetable or about 1 tablespoon butter for ½ cup (individual serving).

BRAISED WITH MEAT.   Vegetables may be cooked for their entire cooking time with the meat or they may be parboiled and added to the meat to complete the cooking.

CREAMED.   Use ¼ to ½ cup of medium-white sauce to 1 cup of cooked vegetable.

SOUPS.   Use ½ to 1 cup of vegetable to 1 cup of thin white sauce.

GLAZED.   Add cooked or parboiled vegetables to a mixture of brown or white sugar and butter, and cook until the syrup is partially absorbed and the vegetables are coated with a brown glaze.

MASHED.   Add 1 tablespoon butter for 1 cup of mashed vegetable.

ASPARAGUS

How to Clean

Careful but gentle cleaning is needed to remove grains of sand bedded under scales at blossom end. Wash under running water and, if necessary, remove scales. Cut stalk with knife to determine tenderness. Cut off any woody part.

To cook fresh asparagus:

1. Whole:

    Tie asparagus in bunches, five or six stalks to the bunch. Stand upright in deep saucepan in boiling salted water with tips left out of the water. Cook until stems are tender. Season with butter or serve with sauce. A little lemon juice adds to flavor. Cheese either grated over hot asparagus or added to sauce also gives flavor and variety.

2. Cut up Stalks:

    Cut stalk ends and cook until tender in rapidly boiling salted water. When tender add heads. It is easy to over-cook asparagus. It should be tender but fresh and green in color and hold its shape without breaking. Serve with butter or cream sauce.

French Fried Asparagus

1 can asparagus tips	2 tablespoons asparagus liquor
salt and pepper	dry cracker crumbs

1 egg

Drain asparagus and season with salt and pepper. Beat egg slightly and combine with asparagus liquor. Dip asparagus in egg then in crumbs, chill. Fry in deep lard until golden brown. Serve immediately.

MRS. WARE CARNS.

Baked Asparagus

1 layer asparagus	1 layer hard-cooked eggs, sliced
1 layer cheese, grated	1 layer crushed potato chips

Repeat the above and cover with white sauce and bake in moderate oven until hot. Serve piping hot.

MRS. J. M. McCABE, Calhoun County.

Peas and Asparagus Casserole

1 No. 2 can asparagus	1½ cups grated cheese
1 No. 2 can peas	½ cup top milk

bread crumbs

Put asparagus and peas in buttered baking dish. Heat milk and grated cheese in top of double boiler until cheese is melted. Pour milk and cheese mixture over asparagus and peas, cover with bread crumbs, grated fine, and brown in slow oven. Serves 8-10.

MISS MINNIE TALBERT, McCormick County.

Asparagus and Garden Pea Casserole

1 can asparagus	4 hard-cooked eggs
1 can garden peas	1 cup medium-white sauce

½ cup grated cheese

Alternate layers of vegetables, eggs and sauce, in which grated cheese has been melted. Dot with butter and salt to taste. Top with bread or cracker crumbs. Heat in oven. Serves 6.

MRS. O'DELL BRYANT, Dillon County.

Asparagus Mold

2 cups white asparagus, cut up   1 cup almonds, cut fairly
1 cup medium-white sauce   small
3 eggs, lightly beaten   ½ cup grated cheese

Make white sauce and melt the cheese in it. Add the beaten eggs
and asparagus and nuts in that order. Line the mold with waxed paper
and butter it well. Place mold in a pan containing water and cook
in slow oven 350 degrees for about 40 minutes, or until firm. It is
well to cover with waxed paper for at least part of cooking time.
Serves 10.

                    MRS. R. E. SHANNON, JR., Fairfield County.

Asparagus Pie

1 can green asparagus (No. 2)   ½ cup chopped nuts (almonds
1 can cream of mushroom soup   or pecans)
4 tablespoons grated cheese   8 olives, sliced (optional)
               salt and pepper to taste

Arrange in layers in shallow baking dish. Top with bread crumbs
and butter. Brown in 425-degree oven. Serve hot. Serves 6.

                    MRS. J. K. LEE, Kershaw County.

GENERAL METHOD OF COOKING GREEN SNAP BEANS

Wash beans—cut or break off the blossom end and, if beans are
not the stringless variety, be sure that no string is left around the
outer edge of beans.

Cut or have whole—whole beans keep more of their food value
Drop beans into small amount of boiling salted water. Cooking time
should be short or beans will be mushy and will lose color. If ham
hock or lean bacon is used, serve slices on top of beans.

Sweet-Sour Green Beans

A little vinegar and sweetened cream or evaporated milk added
to cooked green beans gives that different flavor that your family will
enjoy as a change.

Creole String Beans

1 quart canned or frozen beans	1 teaspoon dried mixed herbs
1 onion	6 strips bacon (cut in 1-inch
2 cups canned tomatoes	pieces)

Chop beans and cook in salt water until tender, add remaining ingredients and simmer for 20 to 25 minutes and serve while hot. Serves 6.

MRS. ALEX BEVERLY, Marlboro County.

DRIED BEANS

Baked Beans

Soak over night 1 pound small pea beans. Use the same liquid that the beans are soaked in, as that contains food value, add to them 1 teaspoon powdered mustard, ¼ pound salt pork, 1 whole onion and ¼ cup molasses and salt. Put into a beanpot or heavy cooking pan and cook for 4 to 5 hours in a slow oven or on back of your stove, adding a little water if necessary. Serve with frankfurters or broiled sausages, pepper relish and brown bread.

MRS. HAMPTON COBB, Greenwood County.

Variations of Baked Beans

Place 1 pound of fat back or salt pork in bottom of bean pot. Then add 1 quart of navy or great Northern beans and the water in which they are soaked over night. Add 4 tablespoons molasses and 1 tablespoon salt. Do not stir. Place in slow oven (200 degrees to 250 degrees) 12 to 14 hours, adding water as needed to keep beans moist. Cook without stirring. Serves 12.

MRS. RAYMOND B. NICHOLS, Newberry County.

Another variation—Simmer 1 cup beans, soaked over night in water to cover, until tender. Mix together ½ cup catsup, dash of black pepper, 1 tablespoon brown sugar. Add alternate layers of beans and catsup mixture. Place bacon strips on top (approximately ¼ pound bacon) and bake at 350 degrees until bacon is brown and beans thoroughly hot. Serves 8.

MRS. L. W. KING and MRS. HARRY CHAMPY, Calhoun County.

Lima Beans in Tomato Sauce

1 cup dry lima beans	1 cup canned tomatoes
3 cups water	½ cup chopped onions
¾ teaspoon salt	4 slices bacon

Wash beans, add water, boil 2 minutes—soak 1 hour. Add ½ teaspoon salt. Boil gently 45 minutes. Put onions and beans in a greased baking dish. Add tomatoes and rest of salt. Arrange bacon strips on top. Bak₋ 350 degrees 45 minutes to 1 hour. Serves 4.

MRS. RUTH G. HALTIWANGER, Calhoun County.

Lima One-Plate Luncheon

Cook together in as little water as possible, 1 tart apple diced and one finely chopped onion. Add 1½ cups of white sauce, add ½ tablespoon curry powder to cooked apple mixture and 2 cups cooked dried limas. Select even sized beets—cook until tender (scoop out centers), pepper cups may also be used. Sprinkle lightly with salt. Fill centers with lima mixture and set in oven in a covered dish to heat through. If peppers are used, cook until peppers are tender. Garnish with parsley.

MATTIE LEE COOLEY, Fairfield County.

BEETS

Cut tops from beets leaving about 1 inch of stem. Wash thoroughly, removing any small roots. Cook with skin on since beets are easily peeled by holding under cold water and rubbing gently. Cook in enough water to cover. Beets may be served with melted butter or prepared in a number of ways.

Pickled or Spiced Beets

Cooked beets may be sliced or small whole beets used and plain vinegar poured over them. Vinegar to which a small amount of sugar, two or three cloves, and a small stick of cinnamon has been added, then brought to a boil and strained gives a spicy taste to the beets.

Harvard Beets

3 cups cooked, diced beets	½ teaspoon salt
½ cup sugar	2 tablespoons butter or
2 tablespoons all-purpose flour	margarine
½ cup vinegar	¼ cup water

Mix the sugar and flour; add water and vinegar. Cook on medium heat until thick, about 10 minutes. Add salt, butter or margarine, then diced beets. Cover. Continue cooking about 10 minutes. Serves 4-5.

Mrs. B. B. Price, Jasper County.

Yale Beets

2 cups whole small beets

2 tablespoons flour

3 tablespoons sugar

¼ teaspoon salt

2 tablespoons butter

¼ cup cold water

1 cup orange juice

2 tablespoons lemon juice

Place beets in greased casserole. Mix flour, salt and sugar together. Combine with butter, water, orange and lemon juice and cook until thick, about 5 minutes. Stir occasionally. Pour over beets and bake in oven 30 minutes. Serves 4-6.

Mrs. O. S. Long, Calhoun County.

Dutch Style Beets

6 cooked or canned beets

2 tablespoons butter

1 tablespoon flour

2 teaspoons minced onion

1 cup boiling water

1 tablespoon sugar

2 tablespoons vinegar

¼ teaspoon salt

Melt butter, add flour and minced onion, and blend. Add water, cook until thick. Add seasonings, then beat, add beets, cut in thick slices and heat. Serves 4-6.

Lexington County.

Vegetables in Beet Cups

Cook medium beets until tender, peel. Cut a slice from the root end of each. Scoop out centers. Fill cavities with buttered peas and carrots. Brush beet cup with melted butter. Sprinkle with grated cheese. Brown in moderate oven 375 degrees. Serve at once. Serve 1 beet to each person.

Mrs. R. H. Tilley, Anderson County.

BROCCOLI

Cut off tough parts of stalk and coarse leaves. If stalks are large, may be cut in strips. Cook in boiling, salted water in an uncovered vessel. Broccoli is very easily over-cooked, and over-cooking develops a strong flavor and destroys the fresh green color. Broccoli should be tender and hold its shape, not soft and mushy. Serve with melted butter, white sauce, or cheese sauce. Lemon juice or vinegar may be added to butter before serving over the broccoli.

CABBAGE

Take off old or wilted leaves. Wash cabbage and look for worm infestation. Cut in halves or quarters, and cut out core. Cook in boiling, salted water in uncovered vessel. Drain and serve with butter, bacon fat or cream sauce. Don't over-cook. It takes only 8 to 12 minutes for cabbage and the length of time makes a difference in its flavor, texture and looks.

Five-Minute Cabbage

Heat 3 cups of milk, add 2 quarts of shredded cabbage and simmer for about 2 minutes. Mix 3 tablespoons of flour with 3 tablespoons of melted fat. Add to this blended flour and fat a little of the hot milk. Stir into the cabbage and cook for 3 or 4 minutes stirring all the while. Season to taste with salt and pepper and serve at once.

Steamed Cabbage

3 strips bacon	1½ pounds cabbage
½ teaspoon salt	dash of pepper
½ teaspoon sugar	1 cup water

Fry grease out of bacon. Wash and chop cabbage and pour into hot grease. Add water, cook 10 minutes uncovered. Add salt, sugar, pepper, and cook 10 more minutes. Serve hot. Serves 6.

MRS. E. S. McLIN, Allendale County.

Creamed Cabbage

Shred a head of cabbage with one medium-sized onion. Boil rapidly in salted water until tender. Drain. Add enough milk or cream to cover. Sprinkle generously with flour. Season with pepper and butter (if milk is used instead of cream). Add very carefully, so as not to curdle the sauce, one tablespoon of vinegar—this may be omitted but it *makes* this creamed cabbage.

MATTIE LEE COOLEY, Fairfield County.

Fried Cabbage

Cut fine one average-size cabbage, drain well, do not add any water. Add one teaspoon salt, one-half teaspoon sugar, four tablespoons fat meat grease that has been fried out of good meat. Cook twenty minutes.

MRS. TALLIE BONEY, Richland County.

Red Cabbage

1 small head of red cabbage	1 teaspoon salt
1 tablespoon pork fat or	6 whole cloves
other shortening	3 tablespoons vinegar
1 large apple, diced	4 allspice or ¼ teaspoon ground
1 small onion, minced	1 bay leaf
2 tablespoons sugar	

Cut cabbage as for coleslaw; put in frying pan or pot with enough water to cover bottom of pan. Add fat and other ingredients. Cook only until tender. Keep pan covered, adding more water if necessary. Serves 6-8.

MRS. J. A. BELL, Kershaw County.

Cabbage Casserole

4 cups chopped or shredded	2 teaspoons brown sugar
cabbage	2 teaspoons salt
4 cups apples	½ teaspoon pepper
½ teaspoon vinegar	½ pound sausage

Spread the shredded cabbage on bottom of pan or dish. Two cups of apples cooked but unpeeled on top of cabbage. Season with sugar, salt, and pepper on top of this as given in recipe. Repeat other ingredients as given above. Put sausage in small cakes on top of dish and bake in a 350-degree oven for 45 minutes.

DORA TALBERT, McCormick County.

Quick Cabbage Kraut

Quarter and wash cabbage, then chop or shred. Pack firmly into clean hot jars. Do not pack too tight. To each quart add one teaspoon salt. Insert a silver knife or set jars in hot water to prevent breakage. Add boiling water to cover cabbage. Remove knife and seal tight using rubber rings and screw caps. Caps will probably bulge which usually means spoilage but kraut ferments and will cause a bulge in the caps; therefore, do not disturb the caps nor throw out the jars. It usually takes five to six weeks for kraut to become ready for use.

MRS. IRA ROBERTSON, Edgefield County.

COLLARDS

Boiled Collards

Collards have a better flavor after several frosts. In preparing a collard for cooking use all the outer leaves that are good. Wash them carefully. Boil a quarter of a pound of good side bacon, or fat back until it is thoroughly done. A ham bone may be used which gives added flavor. Then, add the collard leaves which have been torn apart, rather than cut, because you will want to chop them after cooking.

The cooking time will depend on the method used. If cooked in a pressure saucepan the time will be about 10 minutes at 5 pounds pressure. If open kettle is used it will be easy to test the collards by tasting, but will take about 20 to 30 minutes rapid boiling. Delicious served with pepper relish and baked sweet potatoes.

MRS. HOYT CLARK, Chesterfield County.

Panned or Fried Collards

1 quart collards   2 or 3 tablespoons drippings
salt to taste

Heat drippings in heavy pot or frying pan. Add collards and salt. Cover and cook slowly until collards are tender. Stir often to prevent sticking. Variety: Before frost has fallen to "sweeten" collards, use ½ quart shredded cabbage when collards are nearly done. Allow 10 to 15 minutes for cabbage to cook. Add 1 or 2 tablespoons drippings, according to taste. Serves 6.

MRS. HASTING WOODWARD, Aiken County.

Collard Kraut

Wash collards, cut medium fine. To 5 gallons of collards use 1 cup salt. Place about a gallon of cut collards in jar and sprinkle over with 2 tablespoons salt. Then add another layer of collards and more salt until jar is full. Cover top with larger uncut collards (leaves). Place weights to keep down; add water until it comes to the top of jar.

Mrs. J. J. Mayson, Edgefield County.

CARROTS

Buttered Carrots

Wash. Cook with skins on for best results but be careful not to break while slipping skins gently off or carrots may be scraped. Drop whole carrots into rapidly boiling salted water—if very large, carrots may be cut in halves or thirds. Cook only until tender. Season with butter, light cream or cream sauce.

Panned Carrots With Apples

Slice carrots thin, place in frying pan with a little melted fat. Cover and cook slowly until almost tender. Add apple rings sliced with skins on, sprinkle with salt and brown sugar. Brown well.

Carrot or Squash Ring with Peas

2 tablespoons butter	2 cups hot-mashed carrots
4 tablespoons flour	1 cup soft bread crumbs
¾ cup milk	1 teaspoon salt
4 eggs, separated	1 can peas

lump sugar

Melt butter in top of double boiler; add flour, and blend. Add milk and slightly beaten egg yolks and cook until thickened. Add carrots, crumbs and salt; blend. Fold in stiffly beaten egg whites and turn into a well-greased ring mold. Bake in moderate oven (350 degrees) for 30 minutes, or until firm. Heat liquor from peas with the lump of sugar, until liquor has evaporated two thirds. Add peas and heat. Turn carrot ring out on serving dish. Fill center of ring with peas. Squash may be used in place of carrots.

Mrs. W. H. Wylie, Fairfield County.

CORN

Corn on the Cob

Select young tender ears; remove husks, silk and bad spots. Wash corn and inner husks. Make a bed of the inner husks in the bottom of vegetable pan. Place corn on bed in layers sprinkling each layer with salt; cover. Place over medium heat until cover is hot to touch, about 5 minutes. Reduce heat to low; cook 10 to 15 minutes. Serve hot with butter. Serve one small or ½ large ear to each person.

Mrs. R. C. Rodgers, Williamsburg County.

Stewed Corn

1 dozen ears tender corn   2 or 3 tablespoons drippings
salt to taste

Cut corn from cob and scrape cob. Put ingredients in saucepan and add about ½ cup water to cook. Cook slowly until corn boils 10 to 15 minutes. Butter may be used instead of drippings. Black pepper may be used also. Serves 6 to 8 depending on the maturity of the corn.

Mrs. Hastings Woodward, Aiken County.

Fried Sweet Corn

4 ears corn   2 tablespoons butter
½ cup rich milk

Cut corn from cob. Saute in butter for 7 minutes, add rich milk and serve as soon as hot. Season with salt and pepper. Serves 5.

Mrs. W. Madison Wade, Charleston County.

Corn Souffle

1 tablespoon butter   ⅛ teaspoon pepper
1 tablespoon flour   2 cups fresh corn pulp
½ cup milk   yolks of 2 eggs, well beaten
1 teaspoon salt   whites of 2 eggs, stiffly beaten

Melt butter, add flour and seasonings, mix well, add milk and cook until thick. Add corn pulp, cool, add egg yolks and mix well. Fold in whites. Bake in a greased casserole set in pan of hot water in moderate oven 375 degrees for 40 minutes. Serves 6.

Mrs. R. Cosby Newton, Marlboro County.

Corn Pudding

2 cups milk or thin cream
2 cups corn
2 tablespoons melted butter

3 eggs, well beaten
1 tablespoon sugar
1 tablespoon salt

¼ teaspoon pepper

Add milk, corn, butter, sugar, and seasonings to eggs. Turn into greased casserole and bake in moderate oven (350 degrees) for about 45 minutes or until pudding is set. One tablespoon minced onion or ¼ cup chopped green pepper, pimento, ½ cup cheese, or ½ minced ham, or chopped mushrooms may be added for variety if desired. Serves 6.

MRS. S. B. EUBANKS, Chesterfield County.
MRS. D. M. EVANS, Clarendon County.
MRS. LUTHER WILLIAMS, Horry County.

Corn and Wiener Pie

1 can whole kernel corn
2 eggs, well beaten

1 tablespoon butter
salt and pepper to taste

4–6 wieners

Mix together, add enough milk after pouring into pyrex dish to cover corn mixture. Then put 4–6 wieners on top of mixture and let bake about 30 minutes, at about 300 degrees. Serves 4–6. This is my own original idea of corn pie and usually is very good.

MRS. WATTIE TUTEN, Hampton County.

Barbecued Green Beans and Corn

1 medium onion
2 tablespoons salad oil
½ teaspoon Worcestershire sauce
¼ cup catsup

1 No. 2 can (or 2½ cups cooked) green beans
1½ cups cooked or canned whole kernel corn

Mince onion; brown in salad oil. Add Worcestershire sauce and catsup. Drain beans; combine with corn and sauce. Heat. Serves 4–6.

MRS. ALBERT S. CAVE, Beaufort County.

EGG PLANT

Fried Egg Plant

Wash egg plant, cut into slices about ¼-inch thick; or leave tender outer peeling on. Sprinkle with salt and pepper. Dredge with flour and brown slowly in butter or melted fat until crisp and brown. Slices may be dipped in flour, egg and crumbs and fried in deep fat.

Baked Egg Plant (In Casserole)

1 egg plant (1 to 1½ pounds)	⅛ teaspoon salt or to taste
⅛ pound cheese (or more if desired)	½ cup bread crumbs, cracker crumbs, or bran flakes
1 egg (beaten)	1 tablespoon butter

Peel egg plant and slice thin, boil in very little water until tender. Drain off any excess liquid, mash, add egg, cheese, cut small (saving some to layer top), salt and pepper to taste, and crumbs, mix well. Put in buttered baking dish, cover with layer of cheese in thin strips, some cracker or bread crumbs, and melted butter. Bake in 450 degree oven 15 to 20 minutes or until brown.

Mrs. John A. Seaber, Richland County.

Baked Egg Plant

3 cups egg plant (cooked and mashed)
1 tablespoon butter
2 eggs (beaten lightly)
1 cup milk
½ teaspoon salt
⅛ teaspoon pepper
1 cup cheese, grated
Cut Fine:
1 tablespoon bell pepper
1 tablespoon onion

Mix all ingredients. Put in baking dish. Top with bread crumbs. Bake about 15 minutes in 350 degree oven.

Mrs. Ansel Price, Charleston County.

Stuffed Egg Plant

For a large egg plant:
2 medium-sized tomatoes
1 medium onion
1 stalk celery
¼ green pepper
2 tablespoons bread crumbs
1 tablespoon chopped parsley
salt and pepper to taste
cayenne

Cut egg plant in half and scoop out pulp, leaving wall about inch thick. Cut up pulp and parboil until tender. Drain. Add tomatoes, peeled and chopped fine, seasonings, and other ingredients. Simmer until well blended and tender, and then add bread crumbs. Fill shell with this mixture. Sprinkle with more bread crumbs and dot generously with butter. Bake in oven at 375 degrees until thoroughly hot and delicately browned. Serve in shell.

Sudie M. Rowland, McCormick County.

Egg Plant Pie

Cook egg plant in water until tender. Remove and take off skin. To 1 large plant use 2 eggs, beat in. Salt and pepper to taste. Put a layer of this in the bottom of a baking dish, then a layer of cheese and a layer of bread crumbs. Repeat. Dot the top with butter, put in a hot oven and bake at 375 degrees, until brown.

MRS. A. D. EIDSON, Lancaster County.

Creole Egg Plant

2 small egg plants	1 green pepper
1 cup tomatoes	1 egg
2 small onions	1 tablespoon bacon drippings
1 cup grated cheese	½ cup bread crumbs
2 teaspoons baking powder	salt and pepper to taste

Peel and slice egg plant. Leave in salt water 1 hour, then cook until tender. Drain, mash. Add egg, tomato, salt, cheese, onion, pepper (cut in fine pieces). Add baking powder, bacon drippings. Mix well, put in greased baking dish, sprinkle with bread crumbs and bake about 40 minutes in 350-degree oven. Serves 6.

MRS. C. D. WRIGHT, Lee County.

GREENS, TURNIP GREENS, TENDER GREENS, MUSTARD, ETC.

Boiled Greens

Remove crushed yellow leaves and roots. Wash in several waters until free from sand or grit. Cook in boiling salted water. Use only enough water to prevent sticking, and with spinach only the water that clings to the leaves. Cook with lid on. Cook only until tender, drain. (Save pot liquor for soups.) Season with bacon fat or butter. For a different flavor, add chopped parsley or chives just before serving.

Greens with Bacon

1 pound mixed tender greens   ¼ pound streak fat–streak lean

Put meat on in about 2 cups water and let come to boil while washing greens. Look over greens carefully and wash in 3 or more (warm) waters. Lift greens from water each time. Put in with meat and bring to a full boil, then cook at low temperature until tender but not mushy.

Take up in serving dish and drain off any excess pot liquor. Save liquor for soups. Add extra salt if not salty enough. Greens may

be cut with two knives for ease in serving. Slice bacon and serve with greens. Individual may like to add a few drops of vinegar from pickled hot green peppers.   Serves 5–6.

Mrs. Guy Hunsucker, Marlboro County.

Turnip Greens and Corn Dumplings

1 cup corn meal	¼ teaspoon soda
1 teaspoon salt	1/3 cup sour milk
	½ cup cold water

Just before turnip greens finish cooking, make corn dumplings. Roll into balls and drop on top of greens and cook 15 minutes. Take out dumplings, separate from greens then pour water that the greens were cooked in over dumplings.

Mrs. Juanita Johnson, Chesterfield County.

Panned Vegetables

Use cabbage, kale, collards, spinach, okra, or summer squash. Finely shred cabbage, kale, collards, or spinach. Slice okra or summer squash thin.

For four servings use 2 quarts spinach; 1 quart cabbage, kale, or collards; 3 cups okra or summer squash. Measure vegetable after cutting.

Heat 2 tablespoons table fat or drippings in a heavy frying pan. Add vegetable and sprinkle with salt. Cover pan to hold in steam. Cook over low heat; stir once in a while to keep from sticking.

Cabbage will be done in 5 to 10 minutes; other vegetables take longer.

Wilted Greens

First cousin to panned vegetables is the old fashioned way of wilting garden lettuce and other greens.

To every 2 quarts of the greens, measured after they are looked over and washed, allow one-fourth cup meat drippings, one-half cup vinegar, and if desired a small onion chopped. Cook the onion in the fat until it turns yellow. Add the vinegar, and when it is heated add the greens. Cover and cook until wilted. Season with salt and pepper and serve hot. Or let cool and serve as a salad.

OKRA

Select young, tender pods not more than 2½ inches in length. Okra may be tested with knife and, if easily cut, will be tender when cooked. Okra matures rapidly on the stalk and care is needed in the selection of okra for a good product. Wash okra pods, cut off stem end to tender part of okra but do not cut into the pod. Okra should be cooked only until tender and pods hold their shape when served.

Buttered Okra

Drop well-washed tender pods in small amount of boiling salted water. Cover and cook tender. Season with salt, pepper and butter or margarine.

MRS. H. G. WRIGHT, Fairfield County.

Fried Okra

Cut okra in slices, season with salt and pepper, roll in flour or meal. Fry in small amount of fat until crisp and brown. Drain on brown paper.

Stewed Okra and Tomatoes

2 tablespoons bacon drippings or other fat	2 cups cooked or canned tomatoes
1 small onion, chopped	½ teaspoon salt
2 cups sliced okra	pepper

Melt fat in frying pan. Brown onion and okra slightly, stirring as it cooks. Add tomatoes and salt. Cook over moderate heat until vegetables are tender and mixture is thick—about 20 minutes. Stir occasionally to prevent sticking. Season with pepper and more salt, if needed. Four servings. For variety: Add 3 tablespoons rice with the tomatoes. Cook until rice is tender—20–30 minutes. Add a little water if needed.

Okra and Tomato Pilau

2 cups rice (washed)	1 can (quart) tomatoes
1 quart okra (cut up)	5 slices bacon
salt and pepper	

Fry bacon, add tomatoes and okra. Bring to boil, add rice, salt and pepper. Put in steamer and cook for about 1½ hours.

ANNA GUILDS GRIMBALL, Charleston County.

ONIONS

There is no vegetable that can be used in more ways than the onion. It is not only good as a vegetable, in an escalloped main dish for luncheon or supper, but it is also used in many meat and vegetable dishes. When the food budget is limited, it adds flavor and variety to otherwise flavorless and uninteresting meals.

Onions

Peel and cook in large amount of boiling salted water in an uncovered vessel. (Cook until tender—and no longer.) Season with butter or serve with milk or white sauce. Garnish with parsley.

Spring Onions on Toast

If you have an abundance of spring onions, allow 6 or 7 finger-size ones to each serving. Cook, green tops and all, until tender in lightly salted boiling water, about 20 minutes if onions are young and fresh. Season with melted fat and serve on toast.

French Fried Onions

3 large onions	1/3 cup milk
½ cup flour	¼ teaspoon salt

Slice onions ¼-inch thick, separate into rings, dip in milk, then combined flour and salt. Fry in deep fat until onions are brown and crisp.

Mrs. D. E. Tallon, Lee County.

Scalloped Onions and Tomatoes

2 cups tomatoes, canned or fresh	½ teaspoon salt
	⅛ teaspoon pepper
2 medium-sized onions	½ cup bread crumbs

Cut alternate layers of tomatoes and sliced onions in baking dish. Add seasoning, sprinkle with buttered bread crumbs and bake in moderate oven 375 degrees about 30 minutes. Top with crumbs and bake until crumbs are brown.

Onion Casserole

9 large onions	½ cup chopped ham
1 slice bacon	½ cup tomato puree
1 tablespoon fine chopped green pepper, if desired	½ cup grated cheese
	salt and pepper

Garlic if desired

Rub the sides of a baking dish lightly with a bruised clove of garlic, and grease the bottom of the dish. Arrange peeled onions in the dish, sprinkle lightly with salt and pepper, add fine cut bacon, the green pepper, ham and tomato puree. Cover and bake until the onions are tender. Remove the cover, sprinkle with cheese, and bake in a moderate oven about 30–40 minutes.

PEPPERS

Peppers—Sweet

Green peppers may be used raw and one medium pepper furnishes amount of Vitamin C needed for diet for one day. They can be picked from garden until October or until frost falls.

Green pepper because of its tangy hot flavor can be used as seasoning in stews, meat dishes, cabbage slaws and vegetable salads and sandwiches.

Stuffed Green Peppers

Wash and cut peppers in half lengthwise, remove seed and parboil fifteen minutes. Dip in cold water, fill with equal parts chopped, cooked, chicken or veal and bread crumbs, moistened with chicken broth and seasoned with onion juice, salt and pepper. Cover with buttered bread crumbs, place in well-buttered pans and bake in hot oven 425 degrees for ten minutes, or until crumbs are brown.

Well-seasoned uncooked ground beef, tomato pulp and cooked rice, seasoned with salt and a bit of onion may also be used. Top with bread crumbs and cook at 350 degrees for approximately 40 minutes.

PEAS

Fresh Garden Peas

New green peas coming in early May are as welcome as the fresh spring.

Buttered Fresh Peas

Shell, pick over and discard peas too immature or too old, also any bits of pod or leaf. Drop into a small amount of boiling, salted water, cook only until tender. Season with butter and serve. A small amount of thin cream may be served over the peas. Another South Carolina seasoning is streak-of-lean and a streak-of-fat bacon pre-cooked until almost tender in boiling water. Add the peas and continue to cook until peas are tender and meat cooked. Slice bacon and serve with peas. For older peas, cream sauce is used.

Peas, Crowder Green

Shell and remove any faulty peas. Wash. Boil a piece of side bacon or ham hock. Add one pint of shelled peas to just enough of the boiling, salted liquid and meat to cover peas. Simmer gently until tender.

Dried Cow Peas—Black-Eyed Peas Crowder Peas

Some variety of peas is produced on most farms and is a staple food in most homes. However, they might well be used more extensively in most homes. They are a wholesome nutritious food, with a pleasing flavor from which many palatable and wholesome dishes may be made.

Dried peas are classified as a protein food because of their high protein content. The protein in peas, however, needs to be supplemented with milk, meat and egg protein to be a complete protein. Peas combine well with meats, rice and other vegetables to form main dish meals.

The green peas in the pod are prepared for table just as snap beans would be prepared and green shelled peas are used as green lima beans are now.

Hoppin' John

On New Year's Day all will have to have green collards for dinner and "Hoppin' John." Tradition says collards will bring you greenbacks and "Hoppin' John" small change the year round—if they are eaten on New Year's Day. Mrs. M. B. Hutchinson, Abbeville County, uses the recipe given by her kinsman Irvin S. Cobb in 1900:

"To make 'Hoppin' John,' you take some leftover cold boiled rice that has been boiled in an iron pot and every grain standing out like popcorn. Mix your rice with cold boiled Crowder peas—only, upcountry about fifty miles they'd be called black-eyed peas or in some sections whippoorwill peas. Stir these together and fry with sweet butter in a hot skillet. And don't bet you won't pass your plate back for a second helping!"

Dried Peas with Rice and Tomatoes

¾ cup rice	½ teaspoon salt
1 cup dried peas	⅛ teaspoon pepper
3 medium-sized onions	1 cup tomatoes

Soak peas overnight in two quarts of water. Cook until tender in the water in which they were soaked. Add cooked rice. Then add sliced onions, tomatoes and seasoning. Pour into a baking pan or casserole and cook 30 minutes.

MATTIE LEE COOLEY, Fairfield County.

Mock Sausage

1 cup mashed field peas	1 teaspoon sage
⅛ teaspoon red pepper	1 teaspoon flour
⅛ teaspoon black pepper	little onion, if desired

Cook peas and mash them fine, add pepper, sage, flour and onion. Fry in deep fat as you would sausage.

MRS. GORDON SNOW, Spartanburg County.

POTATOES

One serving of Irish or sweet potatoes each day is a good rule to follow. The two are not of the same family but have several characteristics in common. They both furnish bulk, energy growing carbohydrates and a good amount of vitamins A and C. The sweet potato has more vitamin A and C value than the white potato. Both are too much alike in value and texture to be served at the same meal. For balance and variety let sweet potatoes alternate with white potatoes in meal planning.

Another way in which the white potato and sweet potato are alike is in general methods of cooking. Get the good from both white and sweet potatoes.

Best way to get most food value from potatoes is to cook them in their jackets. And of the two ways of cooking potatoes in jackets, boiling conserves more vitamins than baking. So start with potatoes "boiled in their jackets" whether you're serving them parsleyed, mashed, creamed, hash-browned, or in salad.

When raw potatoes are called for as in scallop or soup, keep the peelings thin. Peel potatoes just before you cook them—don't let them soak. If you must peel them ahead of time, put them in salted water.

Best way to serve all potatoes is quick-cooked and steaming hot, for the longer they stand exposed to the air, the more vitamin C they lose. But if you have left-overs, save them to start a good dish for another meal. And be sure to keep them covered and in a cold place until you're ready to use them.

The Perfect Baked Potato

Wash and dry potatoes of uniform size. Bake in a hot oven (425 degrees) 40 to 60 minutes or until tender. If you want the skin to be soft, rub a little fat on the potato before baking.

Cut crisscross gashes in the skin of the baked potato on one side. Then pinch the potato so that some of the soft inside pops up through the opening. Drop in meat drippings, bits of crisp-cooked salt pork, or table fat. Save fuel by baking potatoes when you oven-cook other food. If a moderate oven is called for, allow a little extra time for the potatoes to bake.

Stuffed: For an extra special, cut large baked potatoes in half lengthwise. Scoop out the inside. Mash, add fat and seasonings. Stir in hot milk and beat until fluffy and smooth. Stuff back into potato shells, brush top with melted fat, and brown in a hot oven. For a main dish, add chopped left-over cooked meat or grated cheese.

Boiled in Jackets

First of all, scrub the potatoes, then drop them into a kettle of boiling water—enough to cover them. Cook covered until tender; drain at once so the potatoes won't get waterlogged.

Peel and season with butter, meat drippings, or gravy, salt and pepper to taste. Or eat skins and all if they are small new potatoes.

Irish or White Potatoes

Potatoes can be used in many different ways and are one of the vegetables most often abused. For good mashed or baked potatoes use a mealy, flaky variety of potato; for salads, creaming and the like, use firm, waxy kinds that hold their shape.

New Potatoes

The skins of new potatoes scrape or flake off easily when rubbed. Scrape, drop in boiling, salted water, just enough to cover. Boil until tender, careful not to over-cook. Drain, using water in soup or thin white sauce to use over potatoes. Season with butter and chopped parsley. Serve hot.

IRISH POTATOES

Fluffy Mashed Potatoes

6 medium-sized potatoes, peel   1/3 cup warm milk
and boil until tender, drain   1 tablespoon melted butter
salt as desired

Add warm milk and melted butter to boiled potatoes a little at a time. Season salt and pepper and beat 3 to 4 minutes at high speed using mixer. Serves 5 to 6.

MRS. E. C. CHEATHAM, McCormick County.

Mashed Potatoes

6 potatoes (medium size)   1 teaspoon salt
3 tablespoons butter   ½ cup milk or part cream

Cook potatoes uncovered in boiling water until soft. Drain well and partially cover (permitting steam to escape). This will make them dry and mealy. Mash potatoes and remaining ingredients and beat with fork or mixer until creamy. This may be covered with buttered crumbs or milk and grated cheese and browned. Serves 5 to 6.

MRS. ZELLE SIMPSON, Chesterfield County.

Baked Irish Potato Puffs

6 potatoes   ½ teaspoon pepper
1 teaspoon salt   2 tablespoons butter
1 tablespoon caraway seed   ½ cup milk
2 egg yolks

Bring to a boil 2 quarts water and add potatoes, salt, caraway seed. Cook until tender, peel, put through potato ricer. Add butter to milk, heat almost to boiling point, then add to potatoes and beat to a fluffy consistency. Add egg yolks, beat well. Then dip out equal parts on oiled baking sheet, making a hollow in center. Fill with onion sauce. Bake until lightly browned. Serves 8 to 10.

Onion Sauce

12 onions   1 cup white sauce

Cook onions, put through coarse sieve and blend with white sauce. Fill centers of potato puffs and sprinkle with paprika.

MRS. DAVIS POOLE, Lee County.

Fried Country Style Potatoes

Peel and slice thin, enough raw potatoes to make 1 quart. Put in a frying pan with 2 tablespoons of melted fat or meat drippings. Cover closely. Cook over medium heat 10 to 15 minutes or until browned on the bottom. Turn and brown on the other side. If desired, brown a little chopped onion in the fat before adding the potatoes.

Roast Potatoes

Peel medium-sized potatoes and place around meat in roasting pan during the last hour or hour and a half of cooking the meat. Turn and baste potatoes occasionally with meat drippings.

Potatoes au Gratin

1½ pounds potatoes	1 cup cheese
2 or 3 tablespoons butter	1½ teaspoons salt
2 tablespoons flour	¼ teaspoon pepper
1 cup milk	

Wash, pare and slice potatoes. Boil a few minutes in a little water until tender. Put into a greased baking dish, sprinkling each layer very lightly with flour, salt and pepper. Pour hot milk (which has the butter melted in it) over the potatoes. Just before taking from oven, sprinkle cheese over top and bake until brown. Serves 6.

MRS. H. C. OAKES, Anderson County.

Scalloped Potatoes with Egg and Cheese

2¼ cups potatoes, boiled	½ tablespoon salt
1 cup white sauce	4 eggs, cooked hard
1¼ cups cheese	¼ cup bread crumbs
1 teaspoon butter	

Peel boiled potatoes and slice thin. Grate cheese. Make medium white sauce. Cool. Add cheese and seasonings. Slice hard-cooked eggs crosswise. Grease one baking pan. Put layer of potatoes into pan, then sliced eggs and then cheese sauce until pan is filled. Have potatoes on top. Cover with buttered bread crumbs. Bake in hot oven at 425 degrees for 15 to 20 minutes or until crumbs are browned. Serves 6.

MRS. J. P. LaGROON, McCormick County.

Potato Dumplings and Sauerkraut

8 medium-sized potatoes	6 or more cups flour
1 tablespoon salt	1 can sauerkraut
2 eggs, beaten	15 small onions

pork roast

Cook potatoes until done. Cool and grind through food chopper. Add 1 tablespoon salt, 2 beaten eggs, and mix together until smooth. Add flour and knead to make a stiff dough, enough to work and handle without sticking. Make a long roll. Cut in about 1-inch width pieces. Put in kettle of boiling water and cook for about 20 minutes. When done, take out of water. Cut 15 small onions in pieces. Put 1 cup roast drippings in skillet and fry onions in this until done. Salt and pepper to taste. Heat sauerkraut. This is how it is served: 1 layer of dumplings cut in small pieces, over this put a large helping of sauerkraut, and the onions over this. With a piece of pork roast, this is a dish for any man.   Serves 6 to 8.

MRS. ARTHUR GARRISON, Anderson County.

SWEET POTATOES

The sweet potato is a South Carolina favorite and rightly so, for it's a prize package of food values. If you grow your own, use the early crop of sweet potatoes and store the later varieties. They keep better. Use Clemson Agricultural Extension Bulletin for methods of storage. Sort and handle sweet potatoes with care—they are easily bruised.

In the Jacket's Best

Most of the recipes call for sweet potatoes cooked first in their jackets. The thin skin of the cooked sweet potato is easy to remove and takes with it less of the goodness underneath. Besides, when the protective brown jacket is gone, some sweetness is dissolved in the cooking water.

If, for a special dish, you do peel first, peel thin just before you use the sweet potatoes. If you must peel ahead of time, put the pared sweet potatoes in salted water to keep them from darkening.

Cook sweet potatoes quickly. Serve piping hot so there's little chance for air to rob their good store of vitamin C.

When there are left-overs, cover the dish of peeled potatoes or leave on their jackets and place in the refrigerator or other cold place. Then they are ready to cook again to make their second appearance.

Baked

"Bake 'em and butter 'em"—that's tops as far as sweet potatoes are concerned. Bake according to general directions for baking potatoes. Make crisscross cut, pinch to pop up the juicy yellow inside. Place generous serving of butter on top and serve piping hot.

Boiled or Steamed Potato in the Jacket

Sweet potatoes are good steamed until tender in pressure saucepan. Dry out in oven and serve as you would baked potatoes.

If boiled in ordinary vessel, be sure to drop in boiling water. Cook until tender and drain at once to prevent taking up too much water and soaking out the minerals, vitamins and natural sweetness. Peel and serve hot with butter or meat drippings.

Roast Sweet Potatoes

Place peeled raw sweet potatoes around meat in roasting pan during the last hour or hour and a half of cooking the meat. Time will depend on size of sweet potatoes and whether you cover them with a lid. Turn them and baste occasionally with meat drippings.

French Fried Sweet Potatoes

Wash, peel and slice sweet potatoes as you would shoestring Irish potatoes. Fry brown in deep fat. Place on brown paper and sprinkle with sugar.

Mrs. A. C. Sullivan, Abbeville County.

Whole Candied Yams

10 potatoes the size of an egg   ¼ pound butter
2 cups sugar   1 teaspoon vanilla
2 cups water   ½ teaspoon salt

Select and wash potatoes, put in pot, cover with water, cook until skin will slip, drain off hot water, cover with cold water and peel. Put the sugar, water, butter, vanilla, and salt on stove, cook until thick as syrup. Drop in peeled potatoes. Cook until syrup is thick. Turn potatoes once while cooking.

Thelma T. Butler, Sumter County.

Sliced Candied Potatoes

3 good-sized-sweet potatoes, thinly sliced. Add 1½ cups sugar, stirring in 2 tablespoons flour before you pour over potatoes. Add 4 tablespoons of butter, dash of salt, 1 teaspoon lemon flavoring, or any flavor you like. Add hot water enough to cook until tender. Put in oven, bake ½ hour. Serves 6.

MRS. T. MANLEY HUDSON, Greenville County.

Gingered Candied Sweet Potatoes

In a skillet make a syrup of 1 cup brown sugar, 1 cup white sugar, ¼ cup slivered crystalized ginger, 3 tablespoons butter, ½ cup pineapple juice. Put layers of sliced, baked sweet potatoes with this syrup in between layers in a glass baking dish and bake in moderate oven, basting with the syrup occasionally until the top layer of potatoes is browned. Any surplus syrup may be saved for future use.

MRS. E. G. LAWTON, Berkeley County.

Candied Sweet Potatoes and Apples

6 medium sweet potatoes	½ tablespoon nutmeg or
6 medium apples	cinnamon
6 tablespoons butter	1 lemon
1 cup brown sugar	1 cup hot water
1 cup white sugar	2 tablespoons flour

Parboil potatoes until tender. Peel and slice. Peel, core and slice raw apples crosswise. Arrange in buttered baking dish with alternate layers of potatoes and apples. Sprinkle over each layer butter, sugar and thin slices of lemon. Add thickening made of 2 tablespoons flour in 1/3 cup cold water. Pour on 1 cup hot water and bake in slow oven until apples on top layer are brown and syrup is thick. Serves 6.

MRS. CLYDE GIBSON, Charleston County.

Sweet Potato Balls (Fried)

6 medium potatoes (sweet)	2 cups corn flakes
2 eggs	1 box marshmallows
1 teaspoon vanilla	

Cook potatoes in their jackets in boiling, salted water. As soon as potatoes are tender, peel them. When cool, mash, add vanilla. Pat potatoes in round balls and place a marshmallow in each. Roll balls in beaten egg, then in crushed corn flakes. Fry in deep fat. Very pretty served around a pork roast.

Mrs. H. D. McCoy, Lee County.

Sweet Potato Balls (Baked)

2 cups mashed potatoes
½ cup sugar
6 marshmallows
1 egg white
1 cup corn flakes

Make a ball of potatoes with marshmallows in center, dip in egg white. Roll in corn flakes. Bake in moderate hot oven 450 degrees from 5 to 10 minutes. Serves 6.

Mrs. Jannie Miley, Colleton County.

Sweet Potato Nut Puffs

2 medium sweet potatoes
½ cup sugar
1 tablespoon butter
1 cup chopped pecans
1 egg
cracker meal

Mash potatoes while hot (either boiled or baked). Add butter, sugar and nut meats. Mix thoroughly. Shape in small balls. Dip into beaten egg, then roll in cracker meal. Fry in fat 365 degrees until brown. Yield 12 puffs.

Mrs. Milton Anderson, Darlington County.

Sweet Potato Souffle

1 cup milk
2 cups cooked mashed potatoes
2 tablespoons butter
2 tablespoons sugar
½ teaspoon salt
2 eggs
1 teaspoon nutmeg
¼ cup raisins
¼ cup broken nut meats

Scald milk. Add butter, sugar and salt. Stir until butter is melted, then add to sweet potatoes. Stir until smooth. Beat yolks and whites of eggs separately. Stir yolks into potato mixture, then add nutmeg, raisins and nuts. Fold in stiffly beaten whites and pour into buttered casserole. Bake in moderate oven (350 degrees) for about 25 minutes, or until set. If desired and obtainable, arrange 5 marshmallows over the top.

Mrs. R. Cosby Newton, Marlboro County.

Sweet Potato Orange Casserole

6 medium sweet potatoes	¼ cup white sugar
2 small oranges	½ cup finely chopped nuts
4 tablespoons butter or	¼ teaspoon nutmeg
margarine	¼ teaspoon salt
¼ cup brown sugar	14 marshmallows

Drop scrubbed potatoes in boiling salted water. Cook until tender or can be pierced with fork. Peel, mash and beat hard until fluffy and smooth. Before you start mixing the ingredients, start your oven, setting it at 350 degrees or moderate. Also grease an 8-inch casserole. Grate rind from the oranges and melt butter or margarine. Mix the latter into the potatoes, then the rind. Next add the white and brown sugar, nuts, nutmeg and salt. Stir hard until everything is thoroughly mixed. Put potato mixture in casserole, arrange orange sections in ring in center and marshmallows around edge or anyway you desire.

MRS. J. K. LEE, Kershaw County.

Spiced Sweet Potatoes and Carrots

1 large or 2 medium-sized	1 cup sweet cream
potatoes	2 small carrots
½ cup brown sugar	⅛ teaspoon nutmeg

Peel and slice potatoes and carrots. Place carrots in bottom of a 2-quart saucepan, sprinkle with part of sugar. Then place sliced potatoes on top of carrots and sprinkle with remaining sugar. Pour over this 1 cup of sweet cream. Cook over medium heat 45 minutes or until done. Remove from stove, sprinkle with nutmeg and cover. This serves 6.

MRS. P. B. DEMPSEY, Bamberg County.

SQUASH

Buttered Squash

Wash and scrub yellow summer squash. Drop into small amount of boiling salted water. Cook until tender and serve whole with butter. Young tender onions steamed whole with squash make a good combination. Squash may be mashed, seasoned with onions, and lightly browned in butter or bacon.

Baked Stuffed Squash

8 or 10 small yellow crookneck
squash
1 medium large onion, chopped
fine
2 eggs

3 tablespoons butter or
margarine
bread crumbs
1 teaspoon salt
¼ teaspoon pepper

Scrub and boil whole squash in salted water about 10 minutes or until almost tender. Drain and cut off the necks, scoop out centers of squash leaving a shell about ¼ inch thick. Put butter in frying pan and cook the onion until it is just clear, not brown. Mash squash pulp and necks, add the onion, beaten eggs, and salt and pepper to taste, a tablespoon of sugar may be added if desired. Fill the shells with mixture, sprinkle with grated bread crumbs and put a dot of butter on each. Place squash in shallow pan with a little water and bake in a moderate oven (350 degrees) for 25-30 minutes.　Serves 8-10.

MRS. ROBERT DAVIS, Hampton County.

Squash Souffle

3 cups cooked mashed squash
1 tablespoon minced onion
1 teaspoon salt

3 eggs, beaten
1 cup cooked peas
⅛ teaspoon pepper

3 tablespoons melted butter

Pour into buttered ring mold and place in 9-inch square pan with ½ cup water. Bake for 1 hour, 350 degrees—fill center of mold with buttered steamed peas before serving.　Serves 6.

MRS. E. T. GULLEDGE, Sumter County.

Squash en Casserole

Cook summer yellow squash until tender, drain all water off, mash. Grease casserole with butter. Arrange layer of squash in casserole, add layer of cracker crumbs over this, add layer of grated yellow cheese. Fill casserole using 2 layers of each. Add sweet milk to moisten, dot with butter, salt and pepper to season, as arrangement is placed in casserole. Bake in moderate oven 350 degrees until delicate brown.

MRS. R. COSBY NEWTON, Marlboro County.

Summer Squash Fritters

1½ cups cooked summer squash   ½ cup sifted flour
1 egg, well beaten   ½ teaspoon pepper
1 teaspoon baking powder

Scrape squash (white, green or yellow). Cut in inch pieces, steam until tender, wash, add squash to well-beaten egg and combine with sifted dry ingredients. Drop by spoonfuls onto hot greased skillet and saute in melted butter until golden brown.   Serves 4.

Mrs. R. Cosby Newton, Marlboro County.

TOMATOES

Tomato time is any time. They may be served the year around fresh from your garden or your pantry shelf. Remember, your canning budget says: 20 to 25 quarts for each person in your family. Tomatoes add that special note of bright color, tempting flavor, and vitamin value to your meals. Use one serving of tomatoes, raw greens, or citrus fruit daily for your vitamin C.

Tomato Tips

Sort and use ripest tomatoes first. Keep the rest spread out where it's cool—the refrigerator is a good place. Peel and cut tomatoes quickly, just before you are ready to cook them or serve raw in salad. If you must prepare tomatoes ahead of time, be sure to keep them covered in a cold place until you use them.

To peel tomatoes:

Stroke the skin with the back of a knife until loosened, or dip in hot water 1 to 2 minutes, then quickly into cold water or run tip of fork into tomato and rotate over a flame until the skin wrinkles slightly.

When the Frost Is on Tomatoes

Green tomatoes, caught by the first light frost, can be brought indoors. "Mature Greens"—those about to turn color and often with a white spot around the blossom end—will ripen at cool room temperature (55 to 70 degrees) in either sunlight or shade. Spread them out in the cellar, or woodshed, or on the porch if not too cold. Or line them up on the window sill if the room is not too warm. Immature green tomatoes won't ripen and are likely to rot if kept too long. It's best to pickle or cook them soon after picking.

Stewed Tomatoes

Remove stem ends and quarter 6 medium-sized ripe or green tomatoes (peel ripe tomatoes if preferred). Add 1 tablespoon minced onion for flavor, if desired. Cover and cook until tender—10 to 20 minutes for ripe tomatoes, 20 to 35 minutes for green. Season with 1 teaspoon salt; a little pepper; sugar, if desired—½ teaspoon for ripe tomatoes, 1 tablespoon for green; and 1 tablespoon fat. For variety, add ½ cup soft bread crumbs before serving or top with toasted bread cubes. Six servings. Season canned tomatoes in the same way as fresh ripe, and heat (if onion is added cook until onion is tender).

With Onions or Celery

Cook together half as much sliced onion or chopped celery as ripe tomatoes. Season as above. Cook covered until onion or celery is tender, about 20 minutes. This is an excellent way to use the outer stalks of celery that are less desirable for eating raw.

Fried Tomatoes

Sliced 6 medium-sized ripe or green tomatoes about ½-inch thick. Dip in mixture of ¼ cup fine, dry bread crumbs or flour, ½ teaspoon salt, and a little pepper. Cook in a small amount of fat until brown on both sides. If desired, dip tomatoes in beaten egg, then in flour or bread crumbs before cooking. Serves 6.

Scalloped Tomatoes

3½ cups fresh or canned No. 2½ can tomatoes
¼ cup minced onion
2 tablespoons minced green pepper, if desired
1 teaspoon salt
pepper
sugar if desired—½ teaspoon for ripe or canned tomatoes, 1 tablespoon for green
2 cups soft bread crumbs
2 tablespoons fat

Combine tomatoes (ripe or green), onion, green pepper, salt, pepper, and sugar if used. Place in a baking dish alternate layers of tomatoes and bread crumbs, ending with bread crumbs. (For a thinner mixture, omit 1 cup of the crumbs). Dot with fat. Bake in a moderate oven (375 degrees) 20 to 30 minutes for ripe tomatoes, 30 to 45 minutes for green. If desired, sprinkle ½ cup grated cheese over the top for the last 10 to 15 minutes of baking. Serves 6.

For Variety, Combine Ripe Tomatoes with Other Vegetables

Reduce tomatoes in above recipe to 2½ cups and add 2½ cups cooked whole kernel corn; or 3 cups shredded cabbage; or 1 medium-sized eggplant, pared and cut in ½-inch pieces; or 4 cups sliced crookneck squash; or 4 medium-sized onions, sliced or quartered, in place of the minced onion. Combine as for scalloped tomatoes. Cover and bake until vegetables are tender; with corn, 20 to 30 minutes; with onions, about 1 hour; with cabbage, eggplant or squash, the scallop will need to bake 45 to 50 minutes.

Broiled Tomatoes

Wash 6 medium-sized tomatoes, ripe or green, and remove stem ends. Cut tomatoes in two and place cut side up in shallow pan or on broiling pan. Brush with melted fat and sprinkle with salt and pepper. Place under direct heat with top of tomatoes about 3 inches below tip of flame or broiler unit. Broil until tender—10 to 15 minutes for ripe tomatoes, 15 to 25 minutes for green. If desired, sprinkle with fine bread crumbs or grated cheese for the last few minutes of broiling. Serves 6.

Add Tomatoes to Meat Stand-bys

Add 1 cup fresh or canned tomatoes to your favorite recipe for a 1½-pound meat loaf that calls for about 1 cup of soft bread crumbs as a binder. For extra flavor and moistness in ground meat patties, add ¾ cup fresh or canned tomatoes to 1 pound ground beef. Add ½ cup uncooked, quick-cooking oats as the binder. Season. This combination has a "different" flavor and helps stretch the 1 pound of meat to serve 6.

Pour 2½ cups fresh or canned (No. 2 can) tomatoes over a pot roast the last hour of cooking. It makes a delicious gravy, especially if a clove of garlic and a little thyme are cooked with the meat.

Tomatoes are a "must" for Spanish steak. Pour 2½ cups fresh or canned (No. 2 can) tomatoes over the browned meat and add chopped onion and green pepper. Season with salt and pepper. Cook until tender.

Stuffed Tomatoes with Corn

6 medium tomatoes	¼ cup minced onion
1 cup corn	½ teaspoon salt
½ cup crumbs	2 tablespoons butter
¼ cup minced celery	buttered crumbs

First, remove stem from the tomato and remove the pulp with a spoon, being careful not to break skin. Drain. Second, mix tomato pulp with the other ingredients. Stuff the tomato cases. Third, sprinkle with the buttered crumbs and bake. Bake in oven 45 minutes, temperature 350 degrees. Serves 6.

MRS. MANLEY McCLURE, Anderson County.

Tomato Surprise

Cook slowly 5 minutes:

3 tablespoons finely cut onions in 2 tablespoons hot fat

Blend in:

¼ cup flour	few grains pepper
	1 teaspoon salt

Stir in:

2¼ cups canned tomatoes

Boil slowly 5 minutes, stirring constantly. Heat to boiling ½ cup milk. Remove tomatoes and milk from heat. Stir tomatoes into hot milk. Do not heat after combining. Serve on toast with 8 slices browned bacon.

NOTE: If you use fresh tomatoes, use 2¾ cups cut up, and cook 10 minutes.

MRS. INEZ DUNN, Anderson County.

Tomato Pilau

2 pounds fresh or 1 No. 3 can tomatoes	¼ pound smoked bacon, cubed
2 cups whole rice	2 medium onions
	salt and pepper to taste

If using fresh tomatoes, scald and remove skins. Strain through a colander. Over low heat fry out bacon cubes. Add solid portion of tomatoes and cook slowly until dry, stirring all the while. Add liquid from tomatoes, and onion. Cook until well blended. Add rice, washed well. Stir into tomato mixture, cover tightly and steam until grains split open. There should be 3 cups tomato mixture for 2 cups rice. Serve with roast and gravy.   Serves 6.

EFFIE ALMEIDA, Charleston County.

TURNIPS

Lowly Turnips Made Tasty

There's nothing glamorous about the turnip, but it is a thrifty dish and it does have character. A good source of vitamins and minerals, it is an economical vegetable. Seldom is the turnip cooked in any way, but boiled or mashed. It can be made into a good many different kinds of dishes, such as croquettes, salads, or stuffed with a vegetable or cheese filling.

MRS. W. M. REDMOND, Lexington County.

Turnips and Greens

Cook tiny turnips and their greens together in water until tender (about 30 minutes). Drain. Season with salt, bacon fat.

Turnips in Bechamel Sauce

Dice three cupfuls of turnips and cook until tender. Meanwhile, fry a small onion chopped fine, one tiny carrot also chopped, in a tablespoon of fat, until a pale golden tint; then stir in one and one-half tablespoons of flour and cook until the mixture bubbles. Now pour one and one-half cupfuls of white stock or milk and stir until thick and creamy. Season with one and one-fourth teaspoonfuls of salt, one-eighth teaspoonful of pepper, one-eighth teaspoonful of paprika, and a few grains of cayenne pepper, and pour over the turnips. Reheat and serve sprinkled with chopped parsley.   Serves 4.

Turnips O'Brien

Chop cooked turnips and season with salt and pepper. Add chopped green or sweet red pepper. Melt 2 tablespoons of fat in a frying pan and spread a thin layer of the vegetable in the pan. Heat slowly, serve hot.

Mashed Rutabagas and Potatoes

Cook equal portions of rutabaga and potato together. Drain. Mash and season with salt and pepper. Serve hot.

Salads

Salad making offers a real adventure—not a new adventure, however, for the salad is not a modern dish. Lettuce was used by early Greeks, Romans and Persians. Cabbage was held in high regard by the Greeks and Romans before the Christian Era. In 1597, Gerard, the English botanist, writes "Lettuce Maketh a pleasant Salad, being eaten raw with vinegar, oil and a little salt." The young leaves of spinach were used in a salad in Queen Elizabeth's day. The wild dandelion was used in England as a salad green over a century ago, and the French ate the stalks and tender leaves of the plant with bread and butter.

Despite the fact that the salad is of ancient origin, it only came into its own in comparatively recent years. Today it enjoys a very important and prominent place in every-day meals, in formal dinners, at the bridge party or afternoon tea, and at the outdoor supper or community picnic.

Salad Making a Real Adventure

Why? Because a really good salad must have taste appeal, interesting texture, perfect seasoning and skillful preparation. It must also have eye appeal, color contrast, and artistic service.

An Every-Day Adventure

The salad knows no season. The almost limitless ways to combine mineral- and vitamin-rich vegetables and fruits fresh from the garden or orchard, canned, frozen or stored; as well as most meats, poultry, fish and sea food make salad preparation easy, fun and a real adventure—an every-day adventure.

A salad should appear on the menu at least once a day—not only does it give color and texture, but is rich in vitamins, minerals and bulk—all necessary for growth and health.

When and What to Serve

As an appetizer—at the beginning of the meal a tangy combination of one or two foods—fruit sections, a crisp raw vegetable, small-jellied molds of fish, sea food, vegetables or fruits stimulate the appetite and get the meal off to a grand start.

With the main course—a salad gives color and flavor pick up to hot or cold meats and cooked vegetable dishes. For ingredients try a spoonful of something crisp in a lettuce cup, raw vegetable chips, wedges of lettuce, a tart vegetable or fruit combination or jellied mold that lends a spot of color. Dressings should have snap—and servings should be small.

Salads are the popular addition to the out-door meal when the family gets together at home or in a nearby state park. The community barbecue, fish fry or chicken bog calls for a crisp salad or cole slaw made on the spot just before the meal is served.

As the Main Course

A hearty, well-balanced salad in meal size proportions may be used in place of the hot main dish and should provide comparable food value. Use meat, poultry, fish, eggs, cheese, cooked starchy vegetables, crisp raw vegetables, fruits cooked and uncooked, mixed lightly or molded in many combinations with a variety of dressings both for blending and as a topping.

Because the salad is easy to prepare and easy to serve, it is a popular main course for buffet meals and bridge luncheons as well as family meals on a hot summer day.

As Separate Course between the Main Course and Dessert

The salad should give a taste and texture break between main course and dessert. Make sure textures are crisp.

As a Dessert Course

A dressed up sweet or savory salad makes a light ending to the meal or it may be scheduled for party service. Use cheese, meats, fruits—either fresh, cooked, molded in plain or fruit gelatin, or frozen. Vary the dressing to suit the salad—sweet fruit French, tangy French or velvety boiled dressing with whipped cream added are excellent dressings for dessert salad.

Where to Serve

There seems to be no rule as to where a salad shall be placed on the table. It fits in where there is room. It may be served on its own plate at the right or left of the cover. If there is a bread and butter plate at the left, the salad may go to the right. If there are two or more beverages at the right, it goes to the left. It may be placed on the same plate as the main course, particularly if the meal is a light one. It has become more and more the custom to serve the salad in a large bowl and allow each person to help himself.

Salad Secrets

1. Plan the salad to fit into the meal for flavor, color, texture and food value.
2. Salads should be kept cold, crisp and dry.

3. Cut or break ingredients into distinct pieces—mashed or shredded too finely they make the salad uninviting.

4. Do not combine too many ingredients—3 or 4 are usually enough in one salad.

5. No salad should be colorless, but don't overdo it, and keep in mind color combinations.

6. Combine crisp ingredients with soft ones.

7. Use sweet fruits with sour, mild vegetables with highly flavored ones.

8. Add dressing just before serving to tossed green salads and fruit salads. For freshness and crispness, make just before serving.

9. Some foods are better marinated (allowed to stand in oil dressing) for one hour before serving. Such foods are fish, meat, and certain vegetables which do not wilt easily.

10. Some fruits like apples, peaches, pears have a tendency to turn dark. A little lemon juice or clear French dressing will prevent this.

11. Toss with a fork when adding dressing. A spoon leaves the texture too heavy.

12. Drain vegetables in a sieve—canned fruits on a paper towel.

13. Selection of dressing should be suggested by flavor of salad. Distinction in salad making comes from serving the right dressing with the salad.

14. In making molded salads, give them plenty of time to stiffen, and in very warm weather, remember that gelatin in frozen salads does not take the heat gracefully for any length of time out of the refrigerator.

15. And, above all, remember that salads should be simple and good to eat, not made to resemble candlesticks and butterflies. Nor is it good taste to have them all beribboned even for special occasions.

Salad Tips

1. To separate head-lettuce leaves, cut out core with a sharp knife. Run cold water into opening.

2. Wash greens free from excess moisture. Separate leaves and roll in a towel or place in a flour sack. Place in the refrigerator so leaves will become crisp.

3. To remove fruit sections, pare grapefruit or orange just under membrane. Cut down one side of section inside of membrane to center. Turn knife and lift sections scraping from membrane.

4. For scored cucumber s l i c e s, draw fork lengthwise from end to end. Make thin slices.

5. For celery pinwheels, separate celery stalks. Fill with cheese. Put together, tie, chill, slice.

6. For celery curls, cut celery sticks about 4 inches long. Slice thinly to within 1 inch of end. Place in ice water to curl.

7. For radish roses, cut down side close to skin in several places. Place in ice water to open.

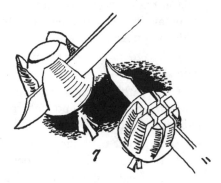

8. For carrot curls, slice carrots lengthwise into very thin strips. Arrange into desired shapes. Secure with toothpicks or rubber bands. Place in ice water to crisp.

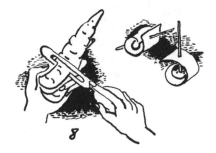

The Relish Tray

For variety, serve a combination of vegetable strips, strips of carrots, celery, turnips may be crisped by dropping in cold water and then putting into refrigerator or cool place in covered dish. If allowed to stand in water vitamins are lost. Green and red bell pepper may be cut into strips and served with other relishes. Cucumbers may be cooled, then cut into strips. Several piles of these strips served crisp and cold in a relish dish make a very appetizing and attractive accompaniment to any meal. Radishes with some of the green left on, left whole or made into roses taste good and look well on relish tray.

Cabbage Combination

Cabbage is one of our cheapest vegetables—can be grown in mountain or coastal areas—combines well with other vegetables and adds crispness and freshness to a meal.

Cabbage is the cole slaw green and there is no one recipe for cole slaw.

Chop rather than shred cabbage. Cooked salad dressing, sweet or sour cream dressing and hot vinegar dressings are much better with cabbage than oil dressings. Oil tends to make the cabbage slick.

Some good cabbage combinations:
1. Cabbage, onion, tomatoes, green pepper.
2. Red cabbage, white cabbage, green pepper, onion.
3. Cabbage, carrot, peanut.
4. Cabbage, raw beet.
5. Cabbage, cucumber, radish.
6. Cabbage, spinach or other tender greens.
7. Red cabbage, lettuce, watercress.
8. Cabbage, celery, turnip.
9. Cabbage, apple, raisins.
10. Cabbage, pepper, cottage cheese.

Tossed Salads

Men like to adventure with a tossed salad, and whether it's for the family, the outdoor supper or the community fish stew or barbecue, many men excel in this art.

The combination possibilities are many. A clever cook will think of dozens of ways to combine fresh vegetables in season. The vegetable garden should be so planned that salad greens can be had for the picking the year round. Lettuce in a cold frame, young tender greens as endive, escarole, parsley, green and red pepper, radishes, chives and onions, tender greens, spinach, carrots, and turnips make delightful salads.

Go adventuring with salads and your whole family will like it.

Cooked Vegetable Salads

Many cooked vegetables such as peas, green beans, carrots, asparagus, beets, dried peas and beans may be used in salads. Always combine some raw vegetables with the cooked for crispness and interest.

Some good combinations are:

1. Cold green beans (1 cup), small onion cut fine, ½ dozen thinly sliced radishes.
2. Cooked asparagus, green pepper rings.
3. A mixture of cooked vegetables served on chopped cabbage, shredded lettuce or endive.
4. Cooked vegetables may be added to a tossed salad.

A good way to use left-overs but be sure the cooked vegetables still have life in them and are not over-cooked.

Chopped Cabbage Toss

2 cups crisp chopped cabbage
¼ to ½ cup chopped parsley
  (optional)
1 medium onion, sliced

3 tablespoons sugar
1 teaspoon salt
3 tablespoons vinegar
2 tablespoons salad oil

Mix sugar, salt, vinegar and salad oil together, stirring until sugar and salt are dissolved. Mix together, lightly, cabbage, parsley and onion. Pour the vinegar mixture over cabbage and toss lightly. Serves 4.

MRS. ROBERT L. FELKEL, Calhoun County.

Cabbage, Radish Salad

2 cups thinly sliced cabbage
1 cup thinly sliced unpeeled
  radish (red ones preferred)

1 medium-sized bell pepper
2 heaping tablespoons salad
  dressing

1 tablespoon prepared mustard

Prepare cabbage, radishes and pepper and mix, add mustard and salad dressing and mix again. Small onion may be added. Serves 6.

Mrs. E. C. Colson, Charleston County.

Cabbage, Carrot Salad

½ head cabbage, sliced
3 medium-sized raw carrots
   shredded

1 No. 2 can shredded pineapple
   and lettuce
   salad dressing

Mix sliced cabbage with shredded pineapple and mayonnaise. Place individual servings on lettuce leaf and sprinkle shredded carrots over salad. Serves 8-10.

Mrs. W. K. Nelson, Sr., Calhoun County.

Cole Slaw

1 quart finely chopped cabbage
1 teaspoon sugar
¾ teaspoon salt

1 tablespoon onion
2 tablespoons red, sweet pepper
   or pimento

2 tablespoons chopped green pepper

Mix with French dressing, boiled sour cream dressing or mayonnaise. Serves 6.

Hot Slaw

3 cups chopped cabbage   1 tablespoon sugar
3 tablespoons vinegar   1 teaspoon celery seed
2 tablespoons water   1 teaspoon salt
                   2 tablespoons butter

Mix ingredients, heat gradually to boiling point, remove from stove. Serve hot. One large apple peeled and grated, added just before taking up, adds a delightful touch.

Mixed Green Salad

Combine two or more of the many varieties of salad greens such as different kinds of lettuce, watercress, sprigs of parsley, young, tender spinach leaves, young turnip greens, kale, young mustard leaves, cabbage or other greens.

With this salad to start with, you can add any one of a number of things—sliced cucumber, tomato, or green pepper, sliced radishes, slivers of raw carrot or mild onion, or chopped hard-cooked egg. Toss whatever you have chosen in with the greens and set in a refrigerator to chill.

When you are ready to serve the salad, shake French dressing well and pour it over the salad until the leaves glisten. With a salad fork and spoon, lightly turn the salad over and over so that all of it is well seasoned with the dressing.

Green Tossed Salad

½ head lettuce   ½ teaspoon prepared mustard
1 medium cucumber   salt to taste
2 medium onions or 1 dozen   3 ripe tomatoes
   small green onions   1 green pepper
½ cup chopped pickled   1 tablespoon vinegar
   cucumbers   2 tablespoons mayonnaise
                    pickles

Cut into small pieces the peeled tomatoes, cucumbers, pepper, and pickles. Peel onions and slice in rings. Break lettuce in small pieces (do not cut). Add vinegar, mustard, and mayonnaise, and toss together. Sprinkle with salt. Serve at once. Delicious with meats. Serves 6.

MRS. ROY HOUGH, Lancaster County.

Fresh Green Salad Bowl

Rub a wooden bowl with clove of garlic, put salad bowl in refrigerator to chill. Tear lettuce apart and put in strainer to drain. Add watercress, cucumbers sliced and not peeled, chopped onion, radishes sliced and celery. Also cooked peas or raw spinach may be added. Sprinkle with salt, mustard, paprika, sugar, black pepper and any other seasoning desired. Pour olive oil over the greens, toss lightly, add only a few drops of vinegar. This salad depends on the person mixing it. Season to taste.

MRS. E. T. GULLEDGE, Sumter County.

Green Bean Salad

2½ cups or 1 No. 2 can green beans cooked or canned
1 small onion, chopped fine

½ head lettuce, coarsely chopped
creamy, French dressing
½ pound tomatoes, diced

Boil beans, drain and save liquid for soup or sauces. Toss beans, onions, tomatoes and lettuce together lightly. Chill and serve with mayonnaise or salad dressing or creamy French dressing. Serves 6-8. Note: Bean Salad combinations:

celery   beets
carrots   spinach
cauliflower buds   bell pepper
radishes   potatoes
                  cucumbers

MRS. J. P. LaGROON, McCormick County.

Green Pepper Salad

3 medium-sized green peppers   ¼ pound pecan meats
½ pound cream cheese   1 sour pickle (sweet pickles
3 hard-boiled eggs   may be used)

Wash peppers. Cut off tops and cut out centers. Cream the cheese. Put eggs, nut meats and pickle through food chopper. Combine with cheese and add enough salad dressing to make thick paste, about 1/3 cupful. Blend well and fill peppers with mixture. Allow to chill in refrigerator over night. Slice thinly crosswise and serve several slices on a lettuce leaf. Garnish with mayonnaise. When used as a Christmas salad pimento may be added. Serves 6.

MRS. ELIZABETH GULLEDGE, Marlboro County.

English Pea Salad

2½ cups peas or 1 large can   2 eggs
   English peas   1 medium-sized potato
1 medium-sized tomato   2 tablespoons mayonnaise
  (half ripe)   1 teaspoon salt

Cut potatoes in small squares and cook 20 minutes. Drain liquid from peas, cut the tomatoes and boiled eggs. Mix peas, tomatoes, eggs, and potatoes lightly together adding salt and mayonnaise. Serve on platter or flat dish with lettuce. If desired you may add a small amount of fresh celery, 1 small green bell pepper, and 1 small white onion. Serves 6.

MRS. GEORGE HALL, McCormick County.

Wilted Lettuce

Pour hot vinegar, bacon fat, salt and sugar over shredded lettuce. Garnish with slices of hard-cooked eggs.

Potato Salad

4 medium Irish potatoes	2 green peppers
1 teaspoon salt	½ cup chopped onion
4 hard-cooked eggs	1 cup chopped celery
1 cup chopped pickle	1 cup salad dressing

½ cup chopped pimento

Cut potatoes in rather large squares. Boil until tender, about 20 minutes. Drain and cool. Mix all ingredients together and add the salad dressing. Be careful not to over-cook or mash the potatoes while mixing. Serves 10-12.

Mrs. Bennie Spell, Bamberg County.

Mother Essick's Potato Salad
(Serve Hot Or Cold)

6 medium-sized potatoes	1¼ cups mayonnaise
6 hard-boiled eggs	salt to taste
1 medium-sized onion	1½ tablespoons celery seed
4 slices bacon cubed—	¼ cup vinegar
1/3 pound	¼ cup hot water

¼ cup sugar

Peel potatoes and eggs while hot, cube potatoes, slice eggs, chop onion, add celery seed, salt and mayonnaise, blend. Fry bacon crisp, remove from heat; then add vinegar, hot water, sugar, to drippings. Return to fire and simmer gently until sugar dissolves. Add potato mixture and heat through. A great favorite with the men. Serves 6-8.

Mrs. Henry Essick, Richland County.

Mashed Potato Salad

6 medium Irish potatoes	½ cup finely chopped celery
½ stick butter	2 hard-boiled eggs,
½ cup thin cream	finely chopped
1 medium-sized onion,	2 tablespoons catsup
finely chopped	1 tablespoon mayonnaise

Peel potatoes, cut into small pieces. Boil in salted water until tender. Drain and mash. Add butter and milk. Blend well. Add celery, onion, eggs, catsup and mayonnaise. Mix. Chill before serving. Sprinkle with paprika and chopped olives or garnish with green pepper rings. French dressing may be substituted for catsup and mayonnaise. Serves 6-8.

Mrs. J. C. Bishop, Beaufort County.

Hot German Potato Salad

Prepare about 2 cups diced Irish potatoes and boil tender. Drain and add 1 chopped onion, salt and set aside. Fry out 3 or 4 pieces bacon very crisp, crush and sprinkle over potatoes. Add 2 tablespoons flour to 3 or 4 tablespoons of fat, salt and pepper and ¼ cup vinegar and ¾ cup of milk to make thin sauce. Pour over potatoes and serve while hot. Serves 4.

MRS. HAMPTON COBB, Greenwood County.

Tomato Salad

2 medium-sized tomatoes   1 large bell pepper
  (half ripe)   3 tablespoons mayonnaise
1 small head of lettuce   1 teaspoon salt

Dice tomatoes and bell pepper. Cut lettuce in small pieces and then combine with tomatoes and pepper, adding salt and mayonnaise. Serve immediately. Serves 6.

MRS. GEORGE HALL, McCormick County.

Tomato Salad

2 cups ripe tomatoes   2 sweet peppers
1 small onion   ½ cup white vinegar
salt to taste

Peel tomatoes, remove seed and cut into cubes. Add chopped onions, pepper and vinegar. Salt to taste. Let set in refrigerator for an hour. Serves 4.

MRS. WILLOCK MIXON, Jasper County.

Stuffed Tomato

6 medium-sized tomatoes   1 tablespoon chopped green
½ cup chopped celery   pepper
½ cup chopped cucumber   2 hard-cooked eggs, chopped
1 tablespoon chopped onion   salt

mayonnaise

Plunge medium-sized tomatoes into boiling water and peel. Remove slice from top of each, and take out seeds and some of pulp. Sprinkle inside with salt, invert and let stand ½ hour. Chop pulp in medium-sized sections, add other ingredients—fill tomato cups. Serve on lettuce.

Tomato Mexican Salad

4 medium tomatoes, diced
1 medium onion, diced
1 medium bell pepper, diced

1 medium green hot pepper
¼ cup vinegar
salt and pepper to taste

Mix above ingredients and serve with string beans or black-eyed peas. Serves 6.

MRS. H. G. WRIGHT, Fairfield County.

Creole Salad

1 cup elbow macaroni (cooked and cooled)
1 small onion (cut fine)

few stuffed olives, cut in pieces
2 medium-sized tomatoes, peeled and chopped

Combine all together with any good mayonnaise or salad dressing. Serves 6.

MRS. M. H. SMITH, Berkeley County.

Tomato Soup Salad

1 can tomato soup
2 packages cream cheese
1 cup mayonnaise

2 envelopes gelatin
½ cup each of bell pepper, onions and celery

Soak gelatin in ½ cup water. Bring soup to boil, add cream cheese and dissolve thoroughly in soup. Nuts may be added. Cool. Add mayonnaise and bell pepper, onion and celery. Mold. Serves 12

MRS. R. P. BLAND, Sumter County,
MISS MYRTLE NESBITT, Greenville County,
MRS. MARIE A. HAMILTON, Charleston County.

VEGETABLE GELATIN SALADS

Tomato Aspic with Cream Cheese

2 cakes cream cheese
1 can tomato soup
1 cup chopped celery
1 large bottle stuffed olives (sliced)

¼ teaspoon Worcestershire sauce
¼ teaspoon black pepper
2 tablespoons tarragon vinegar
2 tablespoons gelatin

Dissolve gelatin in ¼ cup cold water. Heat soup to boiling point, add cream cheese and stir until dissolved. Add gelatin and let stand

until begins to congeal. Add other ingredients and pour in wet individual molds. Let stand in refrigerator over night. One cup finely
chopped nuts may be added. Serves 8.

Mrs. J. R. Fairey, Calhoun County.

Tomato Aspic

2 tablespoons (2 envelopes)   3 whole cloves
   unflavored gelatin   1 small onion, sliced
1/3 cup cold water   dash of salt
3 cups tomato juice   ½ teaspoon Worcestershire
1 bay leaf   sauce

Soften gelatin in cold water. Combine tomato juice, bay leaf,
cloves, onion, salt and Worcestershire sauce. Heat to boiling. Simmer
5 minutes. Strain. Add softened gelatin, stirring until gelatin dissolves.
Pour into oiled dish. Chill until firm. Unmold. Garnish. Serves 6.

Molded Vegetable Salad

1 quart mixed vegetable juice   1 box plain gelatin

Heat half the juice and add to gelatin that has been dissolved in
1 cup of cold water. Add remaining juice and following ingredients:

4 hard-boiled eggs   2 cups cabbage grated fine
2 cups chopped celery   ¼ cup green pepper, cut fine
2 small bottles olives   2 tablespoons vinegar
2 tablespoons onion juice   1 teaspoon salt

Pour in mold and chill.   Serves 20.

Mrs. Hal D. Watson, Dillon County.

Molded Salad

2 level tablespoons gelatin   ½ cup mild vinegar
½ cup cold water   2 tablespoons lemon juice
2 cups boiling water   ½ cup sugar
                  1 teaspoon salt

Soak gelatin in cold water about 5 minutes and dissolve in boiling
water. Add sugar, vinegar, lemon juice and salt. Set aside in a cool
place and when it begins to congeal, add the following combination:

   1 cup shredded cabbage, 1 cup grated raw carrot,
   1 cup finely cut celery.

Rinse molds in cold water and fill with the mixture. Allow salad to congeal in cold place. To serve, unmold on lettuce and garnish with mayonnaise.

Miss Mattie Lee Cooley, Fairfield County.

Vegetable and Cheese Salad

1½ pounds sharp cheese, grated
1½ envelopes plain gelatin
¾ cup cold water
1 cup sweet milk
6 to 8 tablespoons mayonnaise
dash of Worcestershire sauce

1 small bottle chopped olives
1 small grated onion
1 small bell pepper chopped fine
1 cup almonds or pecans,
    chopped fine
dash of tabasco

Dissolve gelatin in water. Cream cheese with milk. Add mayonnaise, olives, onion, bell pepper, almonds or pecans, tabasco and Worcestershire sauce. Add gelatin last and mold. Chill and serve. Serves at least 20.

Mrs. B. F. Hardy, Jr., Dillon County.

Egg Salad (Congealed)

1 tablespoon unflavored gelatin
¼ cup cold water
1½ cups boiling water
2 tablespoons lemon juice
1 teaspoon salt
6 hard-cooked eggs, sliced

½ cup chopped celery
2 tablespoons chopped green
pepper
2 tablespoons chopped pickle
or pickle relish
1 tablespoon chopped pimento

1 tablespoon grated onion

Soften the gelatin in the cold water. Add boiling water, lemon juice and salt. When the gelatin begins to stiffen, add the other ingredients. Pour into a mold that has been rinsed with cold water, and chill until firm. Serve with salad dressing on lettuce or other salad greens.

Egg Salad

Cut 6 hard-cooked eggs in halves crosswise. Remove yolks and mash. Add enough French dressing to moisten. Refill whites. Arrange on bed of lettuce. Serve with French dressing or mayonnaise. (Chopped pickles may also be added to the egg yolks.)

Egg and Tomato Salad

Cut 4 deep, intersecting slits across bottom of large tomato. Place cut side up on lettuce leaf. Insert slices of egg into each slit. Serve with mayonnaise.

CHICKEN SALADS

Molded Chicken Salad

3 teaspoons gelatin
2 tablespoons cold water
½ cup hot water
⅛ cup vinegar
1 teaspoon salt

⅛ teaspoon pepper
2 teaspoons sugar
1 cup cooked diced chicken
½ cup diced celery
2 tablespoons pimentos

½ cup mayonnaise

Soak gelatin in cold water, dissolve in hot water; cool, combine with remaining ingredients. Pour into mold, chill and serve sliced on lettuce, topped with mayonnaise. Serves 4.

MRS. GEORGE W. STACK, Anderson County.

Chicken Salad

1 hen, baked until very tender,
chopped
1 apple, chopped

1 bunch celery, chopped
8 hard-boiled eggs, chopped
1 pint salad dressing

Home cooked dressing as follows:

1 cup vinegar
butter size of walnut
1 teaspoon dry mustard
dash red pepper

2 tablespoons sugar
2 eggs
salt and pepper to taste
nut meats, if desired

Bring vinegar, sugar and butter to a boil. Pour over the well-beaten eggs. Add mustard, salt, pepper, and dash of red pepper; then put this back on the stove and cook slowly, stirring constantly, until mixture thickens. When cool, add most of this cooked dressing to the above ingredients and season well with salt and pepper. Nuts may be added, if desired. Serves 12–15.

MRS. BEN C. WORKMAN, Laurens County.

Mayonnaised Chicken

1 hen (4 or 5 pounds) boiled
and diced
1 can midget peas
2 cups celery, diced

4 hard-boiled eggs, chopped
2 tablespoons India relish
1 cup nuts
2 packages gelatin, softened in
½ cup hot chicken stock

Add ½ pint salad dressing to gelatin mixture, then stir in dry ingredients. Put in refrigerator to congeal. Serves 10.

MRS. W. NORRIS LIGHTSEY.

Meat Salad

2 cups cubed cooked meat
1 cup diced celery
1 teaspoon salt

3 chopped hard-cooked eggs
3 chopped pickles
mayonnaise to moisten

Combine ingredients. Moisten with mayonnaise. Toss lightly with two forks. (Note: This is a basic recipe which can be used for most meat or meat substitute salads. Canned or left-over cooked meats may be used for salads.)

FRUIT SALADS
General Suggestions

1. Use fruit raw whenever possible.
2. All cut fruit should be well drained.
3. If fruit is tart, some of the juice may be used in the dressing.
4. Skins of apples should be used unless they are very tough or disfigured.
5. If apples, peaches, pears or bananas are sliced or diced immediately into a sour fruit juice, they will not turn dark. A little lemon juice adds to flavor and prevents discoloration. Apples may be cut into salted water (use 1 tablespoon salt to a cup of water). Allow to stand one minute before draining.
6. Rubbing wooden bowl with mint leaves gives a fruit salad a refreshing flavor.

Some Good Combinations of South Carolina Fruits

1. Peaches, pears—fresh or frozen—strawberries or red raspberries.
2. Watermelon—mint and tart fruit salad dressing.

3. Canteloupe–grapes–peaches.
4. Spiced or pickled peaches, cottage cheese.
5. Apples–red or green–pecans, celery.

Fruit and Cheese Salad

6 tablespoons cream or cottage
  cheese
6 halves canned peaches or pears
  or pineapple

lettuce
mayonnaise

Arrange pear halves or pineapple on lettuce leaves. Fill centers
with cheese and top with mayonnaise. Peaches may be used in the
same way. (For variety, add chopped nut meats to the cheese.) American cheese may be used in the place of cream cheese. In that case, the
fruit centers are filled with mayonnaise and the cheese over the top.
Garnish with a cherry.

Marshmallow Fruit Salad

2 apples
2 oranges

2 bananas
4 marshmallows

salad dressing

Wash and dice apples with peeling on. Peel oranges dicing them,
taking out all tough fibers. Peel bananas and dice, also dice marshmallows. Toss all these together and add enough whipped salad
dressing to this to make it stick together. Line a bowl with lettuce
leaves and toss in. Serves 6–8.

Mrs. O. A. Troutman, Sr., Calhoun County.

Peanut Fruit Salad

½ head lettuce
2 apples

mayonnaise
1 banana

½ cup salted peanuts

Chop lettuce into bite-sized pieces. Chop up apples and bananas.
Add finely chopped peanuts. Add mayonnaise and toss until well
mixed.

Mrs. J. C. Bishop, Beaufort County.

Frosty Peach Salad

12 canned peach halves
1 tablespoon milk
salad green for garnish
mayonnaise or fruit salad dress-
    ing

2-3 ounce package cream cheese
salt
finely chopped water cress

Drain peaches thoroughly. Frost outside of peaches with cream cheese whipped with milk and salted to taste. Secure two halves together with toothpicks to form a whole peach. Arrange on garnished salad plates and sprinkle generously with water cress. Serve with mayonnaise or fruit salad dressing. Serves 6.

LILLIAN WATSON, Marion County.

Pineapple and Carrot Salad

2 cups grated carrots
½ cup drained crushed pineapple

6 marshmallows
1 tablespoon salad dressing

Cut marshmallows in pieces, add other ingredients, toss. If salad is made beforehand put a few drops of lemon juice on carrots to keep from turning dark. Serves 4.

MRS. BILL McCLARY, Williamsburg County.

Frozen Apple-Carrot Salad

3 cups apple sauce   ½ cup grated cheese
1 cup grated carrots   1 tablespoon mayonnaise

Add sugar to taste and mix above ingredients. Place in ice trays and freeze. Slice and serve on lettuce. Use a dressing of equal parts mayonnaise and whipped cream with nuts added.

Mrs. Mary S. Steele., Chesterfield County.

Angel Salad

2 tablespoons water   20 marshmallows
2 well-beaten eggs   2 tablespoons vinegar
1 tablespoon butter   1 tablespoon sugar
1 small can diced or chunk   ½ pint whipped cream
   pineapple   1 cup chopped pecans

Heat water and vinegar, add well-beaten eggs to mixture in a double boiler. Add 1 heaping tablespoon sugar and 1 tablespoon butter and cook until thick. Remove from stove and when cool, add ½ pint whipped cream, chopped marshmallows, pecans and pineapple. Put into ice box to set. Serve on lettuce with dressing as salad or alone for dessert.

Mrs. A. Carlisle Sullivan, Abbeville County.

Cooked Dressing Fruit Salad

Dressing:
3 egg yolks   1/3 cup vinegar
1/3 cup sugar   pinch salt

Beat eggs, add sugar, vinegar and salt. Cook in double boiler until thick. When cold, add 1 cup whipped cream.

Chip into this dressing:

6 medium apples   ½ pound white grapes
4 slices pineapple   6 marshmallows
2 bananas   2 oranges
               I cup nuts

Mix thoroughly. Serves 12.

Minnie Talbert, McCormick County.

Cranberry Relish (Raw)

1 lb. (1 bag) cranberries   2 apples
2 oranges   2 cups sugar

Wash and pick berries. Remove core and seeds from apples. Remove seeds and center from oranges. Put fruit, peel and all, through food chopper using medium knife. Save all juice. Add sugar, mix well. Will keep for weeks in covered jar in refrigerator.

Cranberry Salad

1 quart cranberries   2 oranges
3 cups sugar   2 cups nuts
1 large can pineapple   2 packages lemon gelatin

Grind cranberries and cook with sugar until stiff. Cut pineapple and oranges into small pieces; drain juice from fruit and add water to make 1½ pints. Boil juice and water and pour over gelatin, stirring well. Let cool and mix ingredients. When congealed, serve on lettuce.

MRS. T. F. McTEER, Lee County.

Cream Salad

2 eggs   2 teaspoons vinegar
2 teaspoons water   pinch salt

Cook this together in a double boiler until of a firm consistency. In mixing, add vinegar last.

1 pint whipping cream   ½ pound marshmallows, diced
1 No. 3 can pineapple, diced and   ¼ pound almonds, diced
     drained

Whip cream stiff and add the above mixture, then add cooled egg mixture to this and blend well. Cover in refrigerator and let stand 12 hours before serving.

MISS MYRTLE NESBITT, Greenville County.

Pineapple Cream Cheese Salad

2 packages lime gelatin   1 cup nuts (broken in pieces)
2 packages cream cheese (3   1 cup crushed pineapple
     ounce)

Dissolve gelatin and let chill. Add cream cheese and chill again (work cream cheese with milk until thin). Then add pineapple and nuts. Put in trays and congeal. Cut into blocks and serve on lettuce. Serves 12–15.

MRS. OSCAR J. HATCHELL, Dillon County.

Yum Yum Salad

2 cups crushed pineapple
1 scant cup sugar
juice of one lemon
2 tablespoons plain gelatin

½ cup cold water
1 cup grated cheese
½ pint cream, whipped
½ cup sliced, stuffed olives

½ cup chopped nuts

Soak gelatin in cold water for 10 minutes. Heat two cups of crushed pineapple, add sugar and lemon juice. Add soaked gelatin to hot mixture. When cool and beginning to set, add cheese, whipped cream, olives and nuts. Place in refrigerator to finish congealing. Makes enough for about 15 servings.

MRS. J. E. COTTINGHAM, Dillon County.

Heavenly Delight Congealed Salad

1 cup cream
1 cup mayonnaise
1 cup chopped nuts

1 bottle cherries
1 can pineapple
2 packages gelatin (plain)

Dissolve gelatin in ¼ cup juice from pineapple and cherries. Boil the remainder of juice and combine with dissolved gelatin. Let congeal slowly. Then add fruit. Let stand until firm and serve on lettuce. Serves 6.   MRS. MALDON SHIRLEY, Lee County.

Raspberry Tang Salad

1 package raspberry gelatin
1 package cream cheese
¼ cup salad dressing or
    mayonnaise

1 cup whipped cream
1 cup crushed pineapple
1 banana, diced
¼ cup shredded coconut

½ cup nut meats

Prepare gelatin as directed and add all the remaining ingredients and congeal.   MRS. JOE POOLE, Laurens County.

Lemon Dessert or Salad

1 package lemon gelatin
½ cup mayonnaise or
    ½ cup cream, whipped

1 No. 2 can crushed pineapple
½ cup nuts

Measure juice from pineapple, add water to make 2 cups. Bring to boil and pour over gelatin. Cool. Whip when hard enough. Add mayonnaise, if served as salad or cream if for dessert, then pineapple and nuts. Line bottom of pan with crushed graham cracker crumbs. Pour in mixture and let stand for 12 hours. If served as salad, serve in lettuce leaf, and top with mayonnaise. Delicious served with cheese straws and coffee.

MISS MYRTLE NESBITT, Greenville County.

White or Club Salad

1 box plain gelatin (4 envelopes)
½ pound blanched almonds or pecans
2 large cans crushed pineapple with juice
1 large can white cherries (seeded)
1 pint boiling water
1 quart mayonnaise
¾ cup sugar
1 teaspoon salt

1 quart whipping cream

Soak gelatin in some of the pineapple juice for 5 minutes. Add 1 pint boiling water. (Use juice from cherries and pineapple with enough water added to make 1 pint). Add the sugar and put in cool place. Whip cream stiff and put on ice. Cut almonds in small pieces and seed white cherries. As soon as gelatin begins to congeal, add in the following order, this is important: whipped cream, mayonnaise, cherries, pineapple, nuts and salt. Pour into flat pans and when stiff cut into squares. Serves 24.

MRS. BROOKS USHER, Marlboro County.

Lime Gelatin and Pineapple Salad

1 package lime gelatin
1 cup nuts
1 cup pineapple juice or water
1 cup celery cut fine
1 cup pineapple
1 cup mayonnaise

1 cup whipping cream

Dissolve gelatin in hot pineapple juice. When mixture begins to thicken, add the cream which has been whipped, and other ingredients. Mold and serve on lettuce. Serves 12–14.

MRS. HUGH M. KOLB, Newberry County.

Cabbage and Apple Salad

1 package lemon gelatin
4 teaspoons vinegar
2 cups hot water
½ teaspoon salt
½ cup shredded cabbage
1 cup diced red apples

¼ cup chopped walnut meats

Dissolve gelatin in hot water, chill until slightly thickened. Combine cabbage, vinegar and salt. Let stand 20 minutes. Fold seasoned cabbage, apples and nuts into gelatin. Turn into individual molds. Chill until firm. Unmold on crisp lettuce. Garnish with dressing.   Serves 6.

MRS. KITTY CARSON, Calhoun County.

Strawberry Salad

1 cup crushed strawberries   2 tablespoons mayonnaise
1 tablespoon gelatin   ½ cup cold water
1 cup whipped cream

Soak gelatin in cold water. Sweeten berries to taste. Dissolve soaked gelatin over hot water. Cool slightly. Add berries, whip cream mixed with mayonnaise. Nuts may be added. Put in mold and cool. Serves 6.

MARIE A. HAMILTON, Charleston County.

Congealed Evaporated Milk Fruit Salad

2 packages cherry gelatin   1 small jar cherries
1 can crushed pineapple   1 tall can evaporated milk
1 tablespoon mayonnaise

Soften gelatin with one cup of cold water. Boil juice from pineapple and cherries, then add it to the gelatin and dissolve well. Whip chilled milk and fold into gelatin. Add chopped cherries and pineapple and stir in mayonnaise. Set in refrigerator until ready to serve.

MRS. D. B. PRIDMORE, Cherokee County.

FROZEN SALADS

Cooked Frozen Salad

2 eggs, beaten   2 teaspoons vinegar
2 teaspoons sugar

Cook in double boiler until custard consistency. Add 14 marshmallows, beat until melted. Set aside to cool. Whip 1 small can milk, add 1 No. 2 can fruit cocktail, and 1 banana diced. Fold this into egg mixture and put in tray of refrigerator to freeze.   Serves 6–8.

MRS. V. S. GOODYEAR, Lee County.

Fruit Cocktail Frozen Salad

1 pint cream	1 tablespoon mustard
¼ teaspoon salt	1 cup chopped nuts
2 tablespoons sugar	1 package marshmallows
½ cup mayonnaise	1 can fruit cocktail

Whip cream, add salt, sugar, mayonnaise and mustard. Into this, put the chopped nuts, fruit and marshmallows cut into 4 pieces. Let stand in refrigerator for 2 hours. Then take out and stir—then freeze. Serves about 12.

MRS. GRACE HOLLEY, Kershaw County.

Mixed Frozen Fruit Salad with Cream Dressing

Soak for 5 minutes 1 tablespoon gelatin in ¼ cup cold water. Dissolve over boiling water. Combine the following:

1 cup diced pineapple	1 cup diced pears or apricots
1 cup diced peaches	3 tablespoons lemon juice
1 cup diced bananas	½ cup sugar

Add dissolved gelatin to above ingredients and chill. As mixture begins to congeal, fold in 1 cup mayonnaise and 1 cup whipped cream. Turn into refrigerator tray, place in freezer and freeze. Cut into squares and serve on lettuce cups with a cream salad dressing.

MRS. E. T. GULLEDGE, Sumter County.

Pineapple-Cherry Frozen Salad

2 cakes cream cheese	12 to 15 marshmallows
1 small bottle cherries	¼ teaspoon salt
1 small can crushed pineapple	1 tablespoon sugar
juice of 1 lemon	½ pint cream, whipped

Heat marshmallows and cherries. Add pineapple juice, lemon juice, and salt. Let stand until marshmallows are soft enough to mix. Cream the cream cheese, add whipped cream and gradually add all other ingredients. Blend well and put in tray to freeze. Slice and serve on lettuce. Serves 8–10.

MRS. W. E. SENN, Newberry County.

SALAD DRESSINGS

Cooked Salad Dressing

2 eggs	½ teaspoon salt
3 tablespoons vinegar	½ teaspoon sugar
1/3 cup milk	½ teaspoon mustard
1 tablespoon table fat	dash of paprika

⅛ teaspoon celery seed

Beat the eggs and vinegar together until smooth. Add the other ingredients. Cook over hot water (stirring constantly) until the mixture is as thick as heavy cream. Makes ¾ cup. If you have 3 or 4 egg yolks left from other cooking, use them in place of whole eggs.

French Dressing

¼ teaspoon salt	1 tablespoon vinegar or lemon
⅛ teaspoon pepper	juice

3 tablespoons salad oil

Mix the ingredients and beat until well blended. Other seasonings may be added as desired—mustard, paprika, cayenne, garlic, onion juice or vinegar, tomato catsup, Worcestershire sauce.

Variations of French Dressing: French Dressing plus any of the following:

(1) ½ teaspoon minced parsley
(2) ½ tablespoon chopped pepper
(3) 1 tablespoon catsup
(4) 2 tablespoons minced egg
(5) 2 tablespoons grated cheese
(6) 2 tablespoons chopped celery
(7) 2 tablespoons chopped pickle
(8) horseradish

Mayonnaise Dressing

1 egg yolk	2 tablespoons vinegar or lemon
½ teaspoon mustard	juice
½ teaspoon pepper	1 pint salad oil
dash cayenne	¼ teaspoon salt

Beat together until well mixed the egg yolk, mustard, pepper, cayenne, and vinegar. Add the oil very slowly at first, beating after each addition. When the mixture begins to thicken the oil can then be added in larger quantities. Add oil until the dressing is stiff. Add salt at the end. (Note: The quantities of vinegar and oil may be varied according to taste and thickness of dressing desired.)

Cold Marinade

2 tablespoons salad oil   4 tablespoons lemon juice
salt and pepper to taste

Mix and season to taste. Use to marinate meats and vegetables before combining with the dressing for a salad.

Thousand Island Dressing

To 1 cup of mayonnaise add 2 tablespoons chopped olives, 2 tablespoons chopped pickles, 1 tablespoon grated onion, 1 chopped hard-cooked egg and 1 tablespoon finely chopped parsley.

Sour Cream Dressing

1 cup thick sour cream   1 teaspoon sugar
juice of ½ lemon   2 teaspoons vinegar
¾ teaspoon salt

Whip the cream and add the other ingredients.

Cole Slaw Dressing

1½ teaspoons salt   1 tablespoon butter
⅛ teaspoon pepper   2 eggs
1 teaspoon sugar   2 tablespoons cream
2 tablespoons vinegar

Mix dry ingredients, add vinegar and melted butter. Pour slowly into beaten eggs, stirring constantly. Cook over hot water until thickened. Add cream and pour over 3 cups finely chopped cabbage.

Vegetable Salad Dressing

3 tablespoons prepared mustard 1½ tablespoons mayonnaise
3 tablespoons sugar   3 tablespoons vinegar
½ teaspoon celery seed

Mix in order listed. Blend well and serve over green salad or slaw. Especially delicious over sliced lettuce. Sufficient for 8–10 servings.

MRS. W. P. RUFF, Fairfield County.

Thousand Island Dressing

1 cup salad oil mayonnaise
1/3 cup chili sauce
1/3 cup whipped cream
1 hard-boiled egg, chopped fine

2 tablespoons chopped sweet
pickle or chow chow
1 chopped pimento
1 tablespoon chives or ½ tablespoon grated onion

Combine the ingredients in order given and serve at once. Delicious with plain green salad or with egg, chicken, ham or asparagus, or on wedges of lettuce.

MRS. J. A. BELL, Kershaw County.

Blue Cheese Dressing

½ cup evaporated milk—chilled then whipped.

Fold in 2 cups mayonnaise, then add 5-6 ounces finely crumbled blue or roquefort cheese. Season with garlic salt or lemon juice. Will keep in refrigerator for 2 weeks.

Cream Salad Dressing

1 cup thick cream, sweet or sour
2 tablespoons lemon juice
2 tablespoons vinegar
1 to 2 tablespoons sugar

1 teaspoon salt
¼ teaspoon paprika
1 teaspoon prepared mustard or
few grains dried mustard

Beat the cream with an egg beater until smooth, thick and light. Mix other ingredients together and gradually add to the cream, beating all the time.

Variation of Cream Dressing: Omit vinegar and mustard and add ½ cup tomato catsup and 2 tablespoons oil. This dressing is suitable for fish salad.

Desserts

The whole meal should be considered when planning the dessert. If the meal is light, then a substantial dessert should be served; if the meal is heavy a light dessert adds the right note on which to complete the meal.

This classification of desserts should help you in choosing the dessert you need:

Light

fruit—fresh   fruit cocktails
fruit—canned   fruit juices
fruit—dried   fruit ices or sherbets
fruit whips   junkets

Medium

custards	cornstarch puddings
souffles	sponge cakes
tapioca	gelatin with milk and cream
	cheese and jam

Heavy

pastry desserts	suet puddings
rich shortcakes	dessert with whipped cream
rich cake desserts	fillings or topping
	ice cream and parfaits

The dessert should be more than just a sweet. Sugar gives only energy. Desserts made from fruit, milk, and eggs furnish vitamins and minerals as well as energy. Try to use these in planning your dessert. In serving the dessert regardless of what it may be, it should be served daintily and look attractive. A baked apple can be a welcome dessert if served properly but can also be a disappointment if it is not served in an attractive way.

Ambrosia

6 large oranges   1 cup grated fresh coconut
1 small can shredded pineapple

Remove sections from oranges and cut in thirds. Combine with coconut and pineapple. May be topped with whipped cream for a special occasion.

Charlotte Russe

¼ tablespoon plain gelatin   1½ teaspoons vanilla or wine
¼ cup cold water   flavoring
1/3 cup scalded milk   1/3 cup powdered sugar
1 cup cream   6 lady fingers, or sponge or
                                                             plain cake

Soak gelatin in cold water, dissolve in the scalded milk, add sugar and flavoring. Beat until fluffy. Fold in the whipped cream. Pour into a mold which has been rinsed in cold water. Chill. When set and ready to serve, turn on serving dish. Garnish with lady fingers and whipped cream.

Heavenly Hash

1 can sliced pineapple   ½ pound nuts (pecans)
½ pound marshmallows   1 bottle cherries
1 pint cream (whipped)

Cut marshmallows and let stand in pineapple juice about 30 minutes. Then cut pineapple and add with nuts and cherries. Mix together and last add whipping cream sweetened, and beat thoroughly together.

Mrs. H. E. Lindsey, McCormick County.

Orange Charlotte

1 1/3 tablespoons plain gelatin	3 egg whites
1/3 cup cold water	2 cups cream
1/3 cup boiling water	juice of 1 lemon
1 cup sugar	1 cup orange juice
1 cup orange pulp	

Soften gelatin in cold water. Add boiling water, then sugar, fruit and juice. When it begins to set, beat until light, and fold in beaten whites and cream. Serve with whipped cream. If too rich, cream may be omitted from the gelatin, and served on top.

Mrs. H. O. Long, Newberry County.

Pineapple Charlotte Russe

1 pint cream	2 tablespoons gelatin
2 egg whites	1 can pineapple (drain off
1 cup sugar	juice of medium-sized can)
2 cups sweet milk	

Dissolve gelatin in ½ cup milk. Bring 1½ cups milk to boiling point. Mix hot milk with dissolved gelatin. Let cool. Whip cream and whites of eggs, then add milk and gelatin, whipping constantly. Then add sugar and pineapple. Rinse ring mold with cold water. Pour mixture into mold. Store in refrigerator until congealed. I vary this—sometimes I use orange pulp, same amount as pineapple.

Mrs. Killough H. Patrick, Fairfield County.

Peach Mousse

2 cups fresh sliced peaches	3 or 4 drops almond extract
2/3 cup sugar	2 cups cream (whipped)

Cover peaches with sugar and let stand 1 hour. Mash or rub peaches through a sieve. Fold in whipped cream. Chill in refrigerator.

Mrs. J. H. Propst, Aiken County.

Baked Apples

Select large, good-quality baking apples. Wash and remove core. Place in deep baking pan. In center of each apple place 1 to 2 tablespoons brown or granulated sugar and ½ teaspoon butter. Pour 1 cup water around apples and bake covered in moderate oven (375 degrees) about 45 minutes or until tender. Apple centers may be filled with chopped dates, raisins, mincemeat, or cranberries. If baked uncovered, baste several times during baking.

Baked Apple Dumplings

Use recipe for pastry. Roll thin and cut into 6-inch squares. In center of each place 4 quarters of medium-sized apples. Sprinkle with a mixture of ¾ cup sugar, ½ teaspoon nutmeg, and ⅛ teaspoon salt. Dot with butter. Fold opposite corners together, pinching the edges so they will stick together. Bake 20 minutes in a hot oven. Serve with cream or sauce.

Apple Crisp

5 apples	¼ cup butter
1 teaspoon cinnamon	1 cup sugar
1 teaspoon lemon juice	¼ cup flour

¼ teaspoon nutmeg

Slice peeled apples into buttered baking dish. Sprinkle with the spices and lemon juice. Work together the sugar, flour, and butter until crumbly. Spread over the apples. Bake uncovered for 45 minutes in a moderate oven (375 degrees) or until apples are tender. Serve cold with whipped cream or hot with plain cream. If mixture becomes dry while cooking, add a small amount of water.

Variations: Use apple sauce. Bake for 15-20 minutes or until brown. *Peach Crisp*—use canned peaches instead of apple sauce.

Apple Pan Dowdy

4 large tart apples, sliced thin	¼ cup melted butter
¼ cup brown sugar	½ cup white sugar
1 cup cake flour	1 egg
1 teaspoon baking powder	¼ cup sweet milk
⅛ teaspoon salt	1 lemon rind, grated

1 teaspoon lemon juice

Place the apples sliced in a greased heavy pan. Sprinkle the brown sugar evenly on them. Stir the white sugar into the melted shortening, add unbeaten egg and stir well. Sift dry ingredients and add alternately with milk. Fold in lemon rind and juice. Pour this batter over the apple slices and bake in 350-degree oven for 30 minutes, or until batter is done. Serve warm with plain whipped cream. If red apples are not pared before slicing, this adds a pleasant touch of color.

MRS. G. O. WALLACE, McCormick County.

Apple Brown Betty

1/3 cup sugar
½ teaspoon cinnamon
¼ teaspoon salt

2 cups fine, dry crumbs
4 tart apples, pared and diced
3 tablespoons melted table fat

Mix sugar, cinnamon, salt. Put layer of crumbs in greased baking dish. Cover with layer of apples. Sprinkle with sugar mixture. Continue until all ingredients are used. Have layer of crumbs on top. Pour melted fat over crumbs. Cover dish. Bake at 375 degrees (moderate oven) 40 minutes. Remove cover the last 10 minutes to brown the top. Serves 4.

Glazed Magic Apples

4 to 12 tart apples
2 cups sugar
2 cups water

Flavoring which may be used:
Few drops mint extract and green coloring, or ¼ cup red cinnamon candies

Wash, pare, and core the apples. Place in a covered saucepan with the water and cook until tender, but not soft, when tested with a fork. Remove apples. Add sugar to the liquid and bring to a boil, cooking until the sugar is thoroughly dissolved. Add flavoring to the syrup and vegetable coloring if it is being used. Return apples to the syrup and cook until clear and translucent. Remove apples from syrup and cool.

Variations:

Rosy apples: Do not peel or add additional flavoring.

Mint apples: Use mint flavoring and green color.

Cinnamon apples: Use red cinnamon candies for flavoring and color.

Uses for Magic Apples:

These variations may be served as a salad, dessert, or as a garnish for meats or desserts.

German Applejack

1 egg	few drops of water
½ cup flour (self-rising)	1/3 cup sugar

2 medium apples

Grease a small pyrex baking dish. Peel apples, quarter and cut in small chips into the baking dish. In separate bowl, break the egg and add sugar. Stir a few minutes until sugar is dissolved. Add the sifted flour and combine well, then add a few drops of water to make the dough just soft enough so it will drop off your spoon easily, but slowly. Spread the dough over apples and top it with a few dots of butter, then sprinkle cinnamon lightly over it. Bake in a 375-400-degree oven until top and sides are nicely browned. This dish serves 4. Time to prepare dish is 10 minutes. This dish is very tasty and economical. It is wonderful for lunch boxes, since it is equally as good warm or cold.

MRS. JOHN A. PRINCE, Abbeville County.

Pineapple Crisp

2 large cooking apples, pared and diced	3 tablespoons butter or margarine
1 cup drained, canned crushed pineapple	½ cup brown sugar, firmly packed
⅛ teaspoon nutmeg	6 tablespoons flour

Heat oven to 375 degrees. Combine apples and pineapple in 1 quart casserole. Sprinkle with nutmeg. Combine sugar, flour and add butter. Cut in until crumbly. Sprinkle over fruit. Bake at 375 degrees 35 to 40 minutes or until lightly browned. Serve with whipped cream, light cream or ice cream. Serves 6.

MRS. W. E. LUPO, Dillon County.

Baked Custard

2 cups milk	¼ cup sugar
2 eggs	dash salt

vanilla or nutmeg

Beat eggs with sugar and salt. Add cold milk and flavoring. Pour into custard cups. Bake in pan of hot water in moderate oven 325 degrees, until mixture does not adhere to knife, about 30 to 40 minutes. Serve warm or chill and serve. Serves 6.

Variations: Caramel Custard—Caramelize the sugar, use vanilla flavoring. To caramelize sugar, place in a heavy pan to melt over low heat. Stir constantly until it becomes a light brown syrup. Add to scalded milk gradually, being careful that milk does not boil over because of the high temperature of the sugar. As soon as sugar is melted in milk, proceed as in Baked Custard. *Coconut*—Put 1 teaspoon shredded coconut in each cup before pouring custard mix into cup.

MRS. A. A. CLELAND, Newberry County.

Boiled Custard

1 pint sweet milk	¼ cup sugar
2 eggs	½ teaspoon vanilla

Heat milk in top of double boiler. Beat eggs and add sugar. Pour a small portion of milk into egg mixture. Add more gradually, stirring constantly. Heat mixture in top boiler, stirring constantly until it will coat the spoon. Remove from heat. Add flavoring. Let get very cold before serving.

Spanish Cream

Make custard as for Boiled Custard. Soften 2 tablespoons of plain gelatin in ½ cup cold water. Add softened gelatin to hot custard mixture. Mold, chill. Serve with whipped cream or fruit sauce.

Chocolate Custard

1½ cups sugar	pinch of salt
2 tablespoons cocoa	3 egg yolks
3 tablespoons flour	3 cups sweet milk

butter size of an egg

Mix all dry ingredients and add egg yolks. When mixed well, add ½ cup hot water, then pour into hot milk and stir until thick, then add vanilla.

MRS. FLEET MCCLAIN, Anderson County.

Raisin-Nut Supreme Custard

½ cup butter	1 cup raisins
1 cup white sugar	1 cup walnuts or pecans
4 eggs (whole)	1 teaspoonful vanilla

Cream butter and sugar. Break eggs one at a time and beat after each one is added, then add raisins, nuts and vanilla. Make crust and pour above mixture in it. Bake for 10 minutes at 450 degrees, then 30 minutes at 325 degrees. Serves 6.

MRS. L. M. ROGERS, Dillon County.

Spanish Cream

Make custard as for Boiled Custard, but separate eggs and add only the yolks. Soften 1 tablespoon plain gelatin in ¼ cup cold water. Add softened gelatin to hot custard mixture. Let mixture begin to congeal. Fold in stiffly beaten whites. Mold. Chill. Serve with whipped cream or fruit sauce.

Sweet Potato Pone

4 eggs	1 cup sugar
2 cups sweet milk	¼ cup butter
1 quart grated or ground	1 teaspoon nutmeg
sweet potato (raw)	1 teaspoon cinnamon

½ teaspoon salt

Beat the eggs, without separating, until well mixed; add the milk, and stir. Mix the spices and the sugar with the sweet potato, add the melted butter and mix the eggs and the milk. Butter the sides and bottom of pudding pan. Pour the pudding into it. Bake one hour in a moderate oven. Stir occasionally, as the mixture will brown on the sides and top quickly. The pudding should be grainy and nutty. Grated lemon rind and juice may be used for flavoring. The pudding may be served plain or with a sauce or whipped cream. If the potato is grated into the milk it will prevent its darkening.

Sweet Potato Custard

1 cup boiled, mashed sweet	3 eggs
potato pulp, packed down	6 tablespoons sugar
1 pint sweet milk	1 teaspoon vanilla

nutmeg

Heat the milk to almost boiling, being careful not to scorch it. (Rinse saucepan first in cold water—this helps.) Beat the eggs just enough to combine thoroughly, stir in sugar, sweet potato pulp, and vanilla. Stir into hot milk. Place mixture in casserole, sprinkle grated nutmeg on top. Put the casserole into a larger pan with 1 inch of hot water in it. Bake in slow oven, about 250 degrees until a silver knife run into middle of the custard comes out clean—about 45 minutes. Serve with cream.

MRS. G. O. WALLACE, McCormick County.

Fruit Whip

2/3 cup fruit pulp
2 egg whites
¼ teaspoon salt
3 tablespoons sugar
1 tablespoon lemon juice

For the fruit pulp, mash or put through a sieve cooked apricots, prunes, peaches or apples. Or use grated raw apples. Beat egg whites with salt until stiff. Add sugar gradually, beating constantly until glossy. Fold in fruit pulp and lemon juice. Chill. Serves 4.

Bread or Rice or Grits Pudding

2 cups milk
1½ cups soft bread crumbs or
   1 cup cooked rice or 1 cup
   cooked grits
1 tablespoon table fat
¼ cup sugar (increase to 1/3 cup
   when using rice)
¼ teaspoon salt
1/3 cup raisins or nuts
2 eggs, beaten

Heat milk; add bread crumbs or rice or grits and fat. Add sugar, salt and raisins or nuts to eggs, then slowly stir in the hot milk mixture. Pour into greased baking dish, set in pan of hot water. Bake at 350 degrees (moderate oven) 1 hour, or until set. Serves 4.

Berry Pudding

1 quart berries (washed)
1½ cups sugar
¼ cup butter
1 egg
¼ cup milk
1 cup flour
1 teaspoon baking powder

Cook in deep pan 1 quart berries and 1 cup sugar. While this is cooking, cream together ¼ cup butter and ½ cup sugar. Add 1 egg and continue to cream. Add ¼ cup milk, 1 cup flour, and 1 teaspoon baking powder. Drop by spoonfuls into boiling berries. Cook 12 or 15 minutes. Serve with whipped cream or butter sauce. Serves 6-8.

MRS. F. T. MURRAY, Calhoun County.

Berry Meringue Pudding

2 cups bread crumbs   ¾ cup sugar
2 cups milk   1 teaspoon vanilla
3 egg yolks   1 pint sweetened berries
(meringue for top)

Soak bread crumbs in milk until soft. Add beaten egg yolks and sugar. Vanilla can be added to milk. Bake in moderate oven (350 degrees) or until firm. Sprinkle one pint of berries with sugar and place on top of the baked pudding. Cover with meringue, made by using two tablespoons sugar to an egg white and vanilla to taste. Pile high and leave rough on pudding. Dot with berries and bake in moderate oven 12 to 15 minutes. Serve hot or cold.   Serves 8.

MRS. W. K. NELSON, SR., Calhoun County.

Cherry Pudding

1 cup flour   1 teaspoon baking powder
½ cup milk   1 teaspoon vanilla
½ teaspoon salt   1 can cherries
½ cup sugar   3 tablespoons butter
1 cup sugar

Mix flour, salt, sugar and baking powder. Add milk and vanilla. Mix and pour in pan. Drain juice off cherries and pour into boiler. Add 3 tablespoons butter and cup of sugar. Bring to boil. Put cherries on top of batter in pan and pour juice on this. Bake in oven 400-450 degrees until brown. Cut in squares and serve with whipped cream.

ELIZABETH H. WILKES, Fairfield County.

Lemon Cups

1 cup sugar   ⅛ teaspoon salt
2 tablespoons butter   1½ cups scalded milk
3 egg yolks, beaten   5 tablespoons lemon juice
¼ cup flour   3 egg whites, stiffly beaten

Cream together butter and sugar, add egg yolks, beat in flour and salt. Add milk, stir in lemon juice, fold in egg whites. Pour in custard cups. Place cups in boiling water and bake at 375 degrees for 10 minutes. Reduce heat to 350 degrees and bake 35 minutes longer or until toothpick thrust in center comes out dry. Chill, serve directly from custard cups with whipped cream, if desired. This is good if you substitute 5 tablespoons of juice from crushed pineapple and add about a tablespoon of crushed pineapple to each cup.

MRS. JOHN B. SCURRY, Newberry County.

Orange Pudding

3 tablespoons butter	2 cups flour
1 cup sugar	1 teaspoon soda
1 beaten egg	½ teaspoon salt
1 whole orange	1 cup buttermilk
1 cup raisins	½ cup orange juice
1 cup nut meats	½ cup sugar

Cream butter and sugar, add beaten egg. Grind orange and raisins in food chopper. Add to mixture. Sift flour, soda and salt, add alternately with milk to mixture. Cook in oven 325 degrees for 1 hour. When baked and still warm, pour over pudding ½ cup orange juice, ½ cup sugar, mixed together. Serve with whipped cream or used plain.

MRS. L. O. HUNNICUTT, Anderson County.

Rennet or Junket

2 cups milk	few grains salt
2 tablespoons sugar	1 teaspoon vanilla
1 teaspoon water	1 rennet or junket tablet

Heat milk until lukewarm. Add sugar. Dissolve rennet or junket in the water. Add warm milk, salt and vanilla. Turn into a glass dish, let stand in a warm place until set, then chill. Cover with whipped cream and sprinkle with nuts, if desired. Other flavors may be used in the same way.

Tapioca Cream

¼ cup minute tapioca	⅛ teaspoon salt
2 cups milk	2 eggs
¼ cup sugar	1 teaspoon vanilla

Scald the milk. Add tapioca to milk and cook in a double boiler until transparent. Beat egg yolks, add sugar, then hot mixture slowly. Return to double boiler and cook, stirring constantly, until creamy. Remove from heat and add vanilla and salt. Pour into serving dish. Beat whites until stiff, adding 3 tablespoons sugar gradually. Pile on top of pudding. Raisins and nuts may be added to pudding. If pearl tapioca is used, soak in 1 cup cold water an hour before cooking.

Cornstarch Pudding

1½ cups milk   2 egg whites
¾ cup sugar   4 tablespoons cornstarch
1 teaspoon vanilla

Scald the milk. Mix sugar and cornstarch, add hot milk, stirring constantly until mixture thickens. Stir constantly and cook over hot water for 20 minutes. When cooked, pour hot mixture slowly over beaten egg whites. Add flavoring, and pour into a mold which has been rinsed in cold water. Chill and serve with boiled custard or fruit juice.

Chocolate Cornstarch Pudding

Use recipe for Cornstarch Pudding, adding 2 squares of melted, unsweetened chocolate to the milk while heating. Follow general directions for Cornstarch Pudding.

Fruit Cornstarch Pudding

Use recipe for Cornstarch Pudding, reducing the milk to 1¼ cups and adding ½ cup fruit pulp and juice after the mixture has been mixed with the egg whites.

Date Pudding

½ pound dates   ½ cup sugar
1 cup nuts   1 tablespoon butter
2 eggs   1 teaspoon baking powder
1/3 cup flour

Mix and sift dry ingredients, mix with eggs, and add chopped dates and nuts. Pour in greased baking dish and bake until firm in a moderate oven. Serve with whipped cream.

Baked Indian Pudding

1 quart milk   ½ cup molasses
1/3 cup cornmeal   ½ to 1 teaspoon ginger
1 teaspoon salt

Cook the milk, cornmeal, and salt in a double boiler, for 20 minutes. Add molasses and ginger, pour into a greased baking dish, and bake in a very moderate oven (300 degrees) for 2 hours. Serve with hot or cold top milk or cream.

Coconut Pudding

3 eggs
½ cup sugar
3 cups milk

1 cup coconut
1 teaspoon lemon extract
⅛ teaspoon nutmeg

3 slices bread (broken)

Cut bread in inch strips and toast. Beat eggs, add sugar, milk, salt, lemon extract, coconut and mix well. Pour into a baking dish, add bread and nutmeg. Bake about one hour at 350 degrees. Serves 6 to 8. MRS. H. C. FURTICK, Calhoun County.

Chocolate Pudding

1 cup sugar
3 eggs (separated)
2 cups milk
1 tablespoon flour

3 tablespoons cocoa
3 tablespoons butter
¼ cup nuts
1 teaspoon vanilla

Mix sugar, egg yolks, milk, flour, cocoa and butter. Cook in saucepan or double boiler stirring all the time until thickened. Pour into baking dish. Sprinkle with chopped nuts, then top with stiffly beaten egg whites to which 3 tablespoons sugar have been added. Then brown in a slow oven (300-325 degrees) for 15 minutes. Serves 6.

MRS. EDWARD B. MARTIN, Richland County.

Steamed Chocolate Pudding

To be cooked in double boiler

2 tablespoons butter
1 cup sugar
2 squares chocolate, melted
2 eggs, beaten

1 cup flour
2 teaspoons baking powder
1 cup cream
1 teaspoon vanilla

Mix as you would for cake, in order as listed. Pour into top of double boiler and steam for two hours (it won't hurt to steam it longer). Never stir while cooking. When ready to serve, turn out on platter and serve with whipped cream.

KINNE ROWLAND STOUT, McCormick County.

Black Devils' Float

1 cup flour
¾ cup sugar
2 teaspoons baking powder
¼ teaspoon salt

1½ tablespoons cocoa
2 tablespoons melted butter
½ cup sweet milk
1 teaspoon vanilla

½ cup chopped nuts

Sift dry ingredients together. Add milk, butter, vanilla and nuts. Pour into greased square or oblong cake pan. Pour the following sauce over the raw batter.

½ cup white sugar   1 tablespoon cocoa
½ cup brown sugar   1 cup warm water
    Bake 40-50 minutes—350 degrees.

(This looks funny when you pour the watery sauce over the raw batter, but as it bakes the cake rises to the top and the sauce thickens up. It's really good, though rich.) Serve in small squares with spoonful of whipped cream, if desired. Leave in pan until ready to serve. Serves 6-8.   MARIE A. HAMILTON, Charleston County.

Plum Pudding

2 cups chopped suet   3 cups flour
1 cup chopped apple   ½ teaspoon salt
2 cups pecans (optional)   1 teaspoon soda
2 cups scedless raisins   2 teaspoons cinnamon
1 cup light molasses   ½ teaspoon cloves
1 cup cold water   ½ teaspoon allspice

Combine suet, fruits, molasses, and water. Add sifted dry ingredients and mix thoroughly. Fill greased molds 2/3 full; cover tightly and steam 3 hours on racks in covered container using small amount of boiling water (or may be steamed in pressure cooker for 1 hour; leave petcocks open for first 20 minutes). Serve hot with hard sauce, lemon sauce or whipped cream. A good Thanksgiving or Christmas dessert. Serves 10.

Refrigerator Cherry Pudding

½ pound graham crackers, rolled   1 can pie cherries (whole or
1½ cups cherry juice (if not   half)
    enough juice, make out   1 package cherry-flavored
    with water)   gelatin
1 egg white (well beaten)   1 cup chopped nuts
            1 cup sugar

Roll cracker crumbs, chop nuts. Combine sugar and cherry juice. Let come to a good boil and pour over gelatin and dissolve. Add well-beaten egg white, blend well. Add rolled cracker crumbs, cherries and nuts. Let stand in refrigerator until congealed. Use whipped cream over pudding if desired.

            MRS. MUSCO ALEWINE, Newberry County.

Refrigerator Lemon Dessert

1 cup sugar
3 eggs (separated)
2 lemons

1 large can evaporated milk
(chilled)
wafers

Mix sugar and egg yolks. Add lemon juice. Heat, but don't boil. Grate in lemon rind. Whip milk until stiff and add egg mixture. Whip egg whites, add. Line tray with crumbled wafers. Pour in mixture. Crumble wafers on top. Cover with wax paper, and place in refrigerator.

ANNA GUILDS GRIMBALL, Charleston County.

Ice Box Pineapple Pudding

1 egg, well beaten
2 cups crushed pineapple
3 tablespoons thin cream
1 cup chopped nuts

½ cup butter
1 cup sugar
½ pound vanilla wafers
⅛ teaspoon salt

Cream butter and sugar. Add egg, cream, nuts, pineapple and salt. Beat thoroughly. Fill mold with alternate layers of vanilla wafers and pineapple cream, having the top layer of pineapple and cream. Place in refrigerator over night. Serve with whipped cream. Garnish with sliced maraschino cherries.

MRS. D. K. RAY, Cherokee County.

Orange Bavarian Cream

1 tablespoon gelatin
¼ cup cold water
¾ cup unstrained orange juice
2 tablespoons lemon juice

½ teaspoon grated orange rind
1/3 cup sugar
¼ teaspoon salt
1 egg white

½ cup cream, whipped

Sprinkle gelatin on water; soak a few minutes. Heat fruit juices and rind with half of the sugar. Dissolve gelatin in hot juice. Chill until partly set. Add salt to egg white and beat until stiff. Add rest of sugar slowly, beating until glossy. Fold egg white mixture and cream into gelatin mixture. Pour into mold; chill until firm. Serves 4.

ICE CREAMS, ICES, SHERBETS, AND FROZEN DESSERTS

Ice cream, ices, and sherbets may be made in a freezer or in an automatic refrigerator. If a crank freezer is used, eight parts of ice and one part of salt is needed. Turn the crank slowly and evenly until the turning is difficult, indicating that the dessert is frozen. At this stage the dasher may be removed and the cream packed to ripen for

several hours. Ice cream made in the refrigerator has a tendency to be icy. This can be prevented to some extent by frequent stirring as the mixture freezes.

Vanilla Ice Cream

1 quart cream
1 cup sugar

1 tablespoon vanilla or 2 teaspoons vanilla and 1 teaspoon lemon extract

Scald ½ the cream and dissolve sugar in it. Add remaining cream and flavoring. Cool and freeze.

Junket Vanilla Ice Cream

1 junket or rennet tablet	½ cup sugar
1 tablespoon cold water	1½ teaspoons vanilla
2 cups light cream	1 egg

Dissolve the Junket or Rennet tablet in 1 tablespoon cold water. Mix 2 cups light cream and ½ cup sugar and heat slowly until just warm, not hot. Remove from heat and add vanilla and well-beaten egg. Add dissolved rennet tablet. Stir quickly and pour at once into refrigerator tray. Do not move until set, about 10 minutes. Then freeze until firm. Remove from tray to a bowl and beat until a thick mush. Finish freezing.

MRS. W. E. ROBINSON, McCormick County.

Vanilla Ice Cream Custard

1 quart milk	3 eggs
1 cup sugar	1 cup cream
⅛ teaspoon salt	1 tablespoon vanilla

Scald the milk. Beat the eggs in a bowl. Add sugar, salt and scalded milk and return to the double boiler. Cook over hot water, stirring constantly, for 3 minutes. Cool, strain, add cream and flavoring and pour into freezer can.

Fruit Ice Cream

1 cup fruit pulps (strawberries,	1 cup sugar
raspberries, peaches, apricots,	1 cup heavy cream
plums or prunes)	1 cup rich milk

1 tablespoon lemon juice

Put the fruit through a sieve. To the pulp, add the sugar and lemon juice. Stir until sugar is dissolved. Add the fruit mixture slowly to the milk and cream. Freeze.

Peach Ice Cream

2 cups peach pulp	½ pint cream
¼ cup sugar	2 whole eggs
juice of 1 lemon	2 tablespoons sugar
pinch of salt	½ teaspoon vanilla flavoring

Select soft peaches. Mash thoroughly. Add sugar and lemon juice and dissolve. When thoroughly dissolved pour into tray and freeze 45 minutes to 1 hour. Beat egg whites until stiff and add the 2 tablespoons sugar. Fold into beaten yolks. Whip cream to a thick custard consistency and combine with the beaten eggs. Add frozen peach pulp and mix lightly. Return to chilling unit to freeze.

Peach Mousse

2 cups fresh sliced peaches   3 or 4 drops almond extract
2/3 cup sugar   2 cups cream, whipped

Peel and slice peaches, cover with the sugar, and let stand 1 hour. Mash and rub through a sieve. Fold in cream, whipped until stiff, and add almond flavoring. Pour into refrigerator tray. Freeze without stirring. (Variations: use strawberries, apricots or apple sauce in place of peaches.)

Caramel Ice Cream

Follow recipe for standard Vanilla Ice Cream, using the custard type or plain. Add ½ cup strong caramel syrup made by melting ½ cup sugar in a saucepan. Stir constantly to prevent burning. Let it brown well then add a small amount of boiling water. Cook until thoroughly dissolved. Strain and add to ice cream mixture. Chopped almonds or other nut meats make an excellent addition.

Coffee Caramel Ice Cream

1 cup sugar   ¼ cup strong coffee
½ cups scalded milk   1 teaspoon vanilla
3 tablespoons flour   1 pint cream
3 egg yolks   pinch of salt

Caramelize the sugar. Add the caramelized sugar to the scalded milk, stirring constantly while adding the hot sugar. Beat egg yolks, add the flour, and mix well. Then add the coffee and pinch of salt. Add hot milk to beaten egg mixture and cook on low heat until thickened. Cool. Place in refrigerator to chill. Whip cream to a thick custard consistency. Add chilled mixture and vanilla. Mix well. Turn into tray and freeze. Requires no stirring.

Chocolate Ice Cream

2 squares bitter chocolate   1 tablespoon vanilla or
1 cup sugar   ½ teaspoon vanilla and
¼ teaspoon salt   1 teaspoon nutmeg
3 eggs   4 cups evaporated milk

Melt chocolate over hot water. Add sugar and salt and blend well. Add milk and heat mixture to scalding point. Pour over well-beaten eggs, stirring vigorously to keep smooth. Return to heat and cook 3 minutes over boiling water, stirring all the time. Cool, add flavoring, and freeze.

Raspberry or Strawberry Ice

1 quart water
1 1/3 cups sugar

2 cups raspberry or strawberry
    pulp

2 tablespoons lemon juice

Put raspberries or strawberries through a sieve. Make a syrup by boiling sugar and water together for 10 minutes. Cool. Add the fruit pulp and lemon juice. Pour into freezer and freeze.

Orange Ice

1 quart water
2 cups sugar

¼ cup lemon juice
grated rind of two oranges

2 cups orange juice

Boil sugar and water together for 10 minutes to make a syrup. Cool and add the grated rind and fruit juices. Strain and freeze.

Fruit Sherbet

To any of the recipes for ices given, fold in 2 stiffly beaten egg whites to which 2 tablespoons of confectioner's sugar have been added. Freeze.

Velvet Sherbet

1 quart milk
1½ cups sugar
juice of 2 oranges

juice of 2 lemons
2 tablespoons confectioner's
    sugar

2 egg whites

Scald the milk. Add 1½ cups of sugar and beat until well dissolved. Cool. Add the juices and pour into freezer can. Freeze until mushy. When frozen to mush, open the can and add the stiffly beaten egg whites mixed with the confectioner's sugar. Finish freezing. A rich sherbet may be made by substituting cream for a portion of the milk.

Lime Sherbet

1 quart whole milk
2 lemons
1 package lime-flavored gelatin

1 cup sugar
1 cup hot water
pinch salt

Dissolve gelatin in hot water. Let cool. Add juice and rind of 2 lemons. Add this to milk. Stir in sugar. Put in tray to freeze. A few drops of green coloring may be added if desired. Also ½ pint whipped cream may be added when freezing begins.

ANNIE CHILES, McCormick County.

Plain Orange Milk Sherbet

1 cup sugar   2 oranges
2 cups milk   1 lemon

Heat milk and sugar. Allow to cool. Place in tray and when it begins to harden, beat with rotary egg beater and add the fruit juice. Return to tray and freeze.

Mrs. R. W. Tisdale, Beaufort County.

Lemon Cream Sherbet

1 pint milk   ½ pint cream
1 cup sugar   2 egg whites
2 tablespoons sugar   grated rind, 1 lemon
juice of 2 lemons

Dissolve sugar in milk, add lemon rind and juice. Stir while adding juice. Turn into trays and freeze until firm (about 1 hour). Beat egg whites, adding 2 tablespoons sugar. Whip cream to a thick custard consistency. Combine with beaten egg whites, adding 2 tablespoons sugar. Whip cream to a thick custard consistency. Combine with beaten egg whites. Add frozen mixture and mix lightly. Return to freezing unit and freeze. Requires no stirring. May be served garnished with sprig of mint. Serves 6.

Mrs. J. D. Ruff, Newberry County.

Butterscotch Parfait

2/3 cup brown sugar   2 teaspoons vanilla
2 tablespoons butter   1 cup heavy cream
½ cup water   few grains salt
4 egg yolks

Melt sugar and butter in saucepan. Stir to prevent burning and boil 1 minute. Add water and cook until butterscotch is smooth and syrupy. Beat egg yolks, add butterscotch syrup slowly, and continue beating. Cook on low heat until light and fluffy. Chill. When thoroughly chilled, combine with the stiffly beaten cream and flavorings. Return to tray and freeze without stirring.

Apricot Banana Marlow, Frozen

16 marshmallows   ½ cup mashed bananas
¼ cup milk   2 tablespoons sugar
1 cup apricot puree   ¼ teaspoon salt
2 cups whipping cream

Melt marshmallows in milk in top of double boiler, stir in fruits, sugar and salt. Chill in refrigerator until mixture commences to congeal. Whip cream until stiff and fold into marshmallow mixture. Pour into trays and freeze without stirring.   Serves 6.

MRS. J. WHITMAN SMITH, Lee County.

Pineapple Torte, Frozen

3 egg yolks	2 tablespoons sugar
dash of salt	2 tablespoons lemon juice
½ cup sugar	3 egg whites
1 9-ounce can crushed pineapple	1 cup heavy cream, whipped
2 cups vanilla wafer crumbs	

Beat egg yolks, salt and ½ cup sugar. Add syrup from pineapple and lemon juice. Cook over hot, not boiling, water until mixture coats the spoon, stirring constantly. Add pineapple. Cool. Make meringue of egg whites and 2 tablespoons sugar. Fold in whipped cream and custard mixture. Coat sides of refrigerator tray with waxed paper. Cover bottom of tray with half of the wafer crumbs. Pour in custard mixture and cover with remaining crumbs. Freeze firm, about 3 to 4 hours. Can be made day before using.

MRS. MIRIAM BOBO TEMPLETON, Laurens County.

Five Threes

3 oranges	3 bananas
3 lemons	3 cups sugar
3 cups water	

Mash bananas, add juice of oranges and lemons. Make a syrup of sugar and water, add to fruit. Freeze. This freezes best in hand freezer.

Frozen Apple Sauce

Sweeten apple sauce to taste, flavor with nutmeg and vanilla also to taste. Put in ice trays of refrigerator and freeze. Cut in squares, serve with custard or whipped cream.

PASTRY

Good pie crust is flaky, rough, and blistered rather than smooth and firm. It is golden brown around the edge and lighter brown on the bottom. The crust should be crisp even though it contains a filling.

Method. Mix the fat carefully into the dry ingredients, either with fork, or pastry blender, or by cutting with two knives. Work quickly and only until the particles of fat are coated with flour. The exact amount of water needed cannot be given as the amount varies with many things, including temperature and fineness of ingredients and the rate at which water is added. The amount of water is less for cold materials, less for finely divided materials, and less when the water is added quickly. Keep the materials moderately cool, and work quickly.

If too much water is added it is necessary to work in more flour. This develops the glutin and makes a sticky dough and a tough baked crust. If too little water is added, there is not enough moisture to bind the particles of flour in baking, and the crust is crumbly rather than flaky. Also, there is not enough liquid to form the steam which, with the enclosed air, leavens the pastry.

The method of adding water, as well as the quantity, is important. Water should be added in such a way as to distribute it gradually and evenly over the particles of flour and fat.

Baking. Bake in a hot oven (425-450 degrees) for 12 minutes, or until the crust is delicately browned. Using a prebaked crust, custard-type pies are baked for 25 minutes in a moderate oven (350 degrees); fruit pies for 25 to 30 minutes in a moderately hot oven (375-400 degrees). Double crust fruit pies without a prebaked under crust are baked for 35 minutes in a hot oven (425 degrees).

What Does It Mean?

An Explanation of Some Terms Often Used in Pastry Recipes

Build up an Edge. A heavy rim of pastry is needed for any pie apt to cook over in baking. Roll pastry about 1½ inches larger than diameter of pan. Fold under surplus pastry all around edge so that pastry is double. Press folded edge between tips of fingers to make it stand up above pan. If you use a specially designed, deep pie pan made for fruit pies you do not need to build up an edge.

Flute. With thumb and forefinger of right hand close together inside edge of pastry, push pastry from outside between fingers of right hand, using forefinger of left hand. This makes a decorative flute or scallop. Many cooks have developed their own variations of this edge, using a slightly different crimp.

Pastry Mix

7 cups sifted flour   4 teaspoons salt
2 cups cold shortening

Mix and sift dry ingredients. Cut in shortening with pastry blender until mixture looks coarse and granular. Store in a covered container in the refrigerator.

Pastry Shell. Mix about 3 tablespoons water and 1¼ cups pastry mix. Roll on lightly floured board to ⅛ inch thickness. Bake in hot oven 450 degrees until brown.

Pie Crust

2 cups sifted flour   ¾ cup shortening
6 to 8 tablespoons ice water

Cut shortening into flour with knife. Add water and mix thoroughly. Roll on floured board to desired thickness.

Mrs. E. E. Wright, Sumter County.

Stir 'n' Roll Pie Shell

Preheat oven 475 degrees.

Mix together:
1¼ cups flour   ¾ teaspoon salt
Pour into measuring cup (but don't stir):
¼ cup salad oil   2 tablespoons cold milk

Pour all at once into flour. Stir lightly until mixed. Place between two sheets of waxed paper (12-inch square). Roll out gently until circle reaches edges of paper. If bottom paper begins to wrinkle, turn, roll on other side. Peel off top paper. Lift paper and pastry by top corners. Place paper side up in 8-inch or 9-inch pie pan. Carefully peel off paper. Gently fit pastry into pan. Build up fluted edge. Prick thoroughly with fork. Bake 8-10 minutes in very hot oven 475 degrees.

Mrs. Y. E. Seigler, McCormick County.

Boiling Water Pastry

½ cup lard   1½ cups sifted flour
¼ cup boiling water   ½ teaspoon baking powder
                  ½ teaspoon salt

Put lard in mixing bowl. Pour boiling water over it. Beat this until creamy and cold. Resift flour with baking powder and salt, and add to creamed lard and water. This forms a smooth ball. Cover and chill. This will keep for a week and can be used as needed. Makes 2 pie crusts.

Mrs. E. H. Ballentine, Anderson County.

Cream Puffs

1 cup hot water   1 cup sifted flour
½ cup butter (scant)   3 eggs

Boil water and butter together; while boiling, add flour dry. Take from stove and stir to smooth paste. Add eggs unbeaten, one at a time; beat mixture five minutes. Drop on buttered tin and bake thirty-five minutes in quick oven. This will make 12.

Cream Filling

1½ cups milk   ¾ cup sugar
1 egg   1 teaspoon vanilla
2 tablespoons cornstarch   pinch of salt

Let the milk come to a boil. Stir in cornstarch mixed with a little milk, beaten egg and salt. Take from stove, add sugar and vanilla.

Mrs. Carson Carmichael, Dillon County.

Old Fashioned Coconut Pie

3 eggs	1 tablespoon flour
2 cups water or milk	2 tablespoons butter
2 cups sugar	juices 2 lemons if desired

1 cup coconut

Beat eggs, add sugar, flour, butter and coconut. Beat and add water or milk, last add lemon juice. Bake in plain uncooked pie crust slowly, 250 degrees for one hour (add meringue of 2 egg whites beaten stiff and 2 tablespoons sugar, if liked). Or sprinkle top with nutmeg. Makes 2 8-inch pies.

"This is an old family recipe which has been used in the Page and Oliver families of Robeson County, N. C., for at least 5 generations and always wins very flattering compliments for the cook."

MRS. HAL D. WATSON, Dillon County.

Chocolate Pie

1½ cups sugar	2 cups sweet milk
4 tablespoons flour	3 eggs
4 tablespoons cocoa	1 teaspoon vanilla

2 tablespoons butter or margarine

Mix sugar, flour and cocoa. Beat egg yolks and add to mixture; continue beating until well blended. Slowly add milk, butter and vanilla. Cook in double boiler, stirring constantly, until very thick. Let cool and pour into a baked pie shell which is also very cool. Spread on meringue and return to 375-degree oven to brown, 12 to 15 minutes.

Meringue: To unbeaten egg whites add ⅛ teaspoon salt and beat rapidly until very stiff. Slowly add 3 tablespoons sugar and continue beating until well blended. Add vanilla and spread.

MRS. W. P. RUFF, Fairfield County.

CHIFFON PIES

Lemon Chiffon Pie

1½ teaspoons unflavored gelatin	¼ cup lemon juice
1/3 cup cold water	1 cup sugar
4 eggs separated	¼ teaspoon salt

½ cup heavy cream

Add gelatin to water, let soften. In double boiler top stir together beaten egg yolks, lemon juice, and ½ cup sugar. Stir constantly over boiling water until thickened. Add gelatin (that has been dissolved in water) stir 1 minute, remove from heat. Beat egg whites with salt until stiff, gradually beat in ½ cup sugar. Fold in hot lemon mixture, pour into vanilla wafer crumb crust. Chill 3 hours or longer. Spread with whipped cream before serving. Serves 6.

MRS. W. E. SENN, Newberry County.

Orange Chiffon Pie

1 tablespoon gelatin	4 eggs
¼ cup water	1 cup sugar
½ cup orange juice	½ teaspoon salt
1 teaspoon grated rind	

Soak gelatin in ¼ cup water. Separate eggs. Beat yolks and add fruit juice (orange), sugar and salt. Cook in double boiler until thick and add gelatin and grated rind. Cool. Add stiffly beaten egg whites to which ½ cup sugar has been added. Butter pie plate. Fill pie shell of rolled graham crackers. Put in refrigerator to cool. Decorate with whipped cream.

VIRGINIA BUSSEY, McCormick County.

Strawberry Chiffon Pie

1 envelope unflavored gelatin	½ teaspoon salt
¼ cup cold water	1 cup crushed strawberries
3 eggs	2 or 3 drops red coloring
¾ cup granulated sugar	½ pint heavy cream
1 tablespoon lemon juice	3 tablespoons granulated sugar

Soak gelatin in cold water about 5 minutes. Beat egg yolks slightly, and add ½ cup sugar, lemon juice and salt. Cook over boiling water until of custard consistency. Add this to softened gelatin, stirring thoroughly, then add strawberries and coloring. Cool and when mixture begins to congeal, fold in stiffly beaten egg whites to which has been added the remaining ¼ cup sugar. Fill baked pie shell and chill. Just before serving spread the pie with cream, whipped and sweetened with 3 tablespoons sugar. Garnish with strawberries if desired.

MRS. H. E. LINDSEY, McCormick County.

PECAN PIES

3 eggs
¼ pound butter
1 cup white sugar
1 cup brown sugar

¾ cup milk
2 tablespoons flour
1 teaspoon vanilla
1 cup nuts

Cream butter and sugar. Add flour, beat eggs together then add to mixture. Add milk, nuts and flavoring. Pour in unbaked pie shell and bake at 375 degrees for 20 minutes or until done.

PHYLLIS CHAMBERLAIN, McCormick County.

Pecan Pie

One eight-inch pie.
Prepare: A pie shell.
Cream: 1/3 cup butter, ¾ cup brown sugar (firmly packed).
Beat in one at a time: 3 eggs.
Stir in:

1 cup light corn syrup
2 cups broken pecans

1 teaspoon vanilla
¼ teaspoon salt

Fill the shell. Bake the pie in a moderate oven 325 degrees for ½ hour or until done.

MRS. OSSIE HARRELSON, Horry County.

CREAM PIES

Orange Pie

1 cup sugar
6 tablespoons flour
¼ teaspoon salt
grated rind of 1 orange

3 tablespoons sugar
1 cup orange juice
juice of ½ lemon
2 tablespoons butter

3 eggs

Combine flour, 1 cup sugar, salt and grated rind. Add fruit juices. Cook over hot water until thick and smooth. Stir constantly to prevent lumping. Add butter and slightly beaten egg yolks. Cook 2 minutes. Pour into baked pastry shell. Cover with meringue made of egg whites and 3 tablespoons sugar. Bake in slow oven 325 degrees, 20 minutes. Can serve with whipped cream.

MRS. J. D. WOODWARD, Aiken County.

Banana Cream Pie

½ cup sugar
1 teaspoon butter
2 egg yolks

1½ cups sweet milk
1½ tablespoons flour
1 teaspoon vanilla

2 bananas

Cream butter and sugar. Add egg yolks. Mix thoroughly. Add flour, milk and vanilla. Cook this mixture over low heat until thick. Place in unbaked pie crust (or graham cracker crust) with layer of bananas, sliced. Cover with meringue and bake 15 or 20 minutes in oven at 375 degrees.

MRS. LINDSEY WOOD, McCormick County.

Orange Pineapple Pie

½ cup sugar
1 egg

1 cup pineapple juice
½ box orange gelatin dessert

1 small can evaporated milk

Combine all ingredients, mix well, cook slowly until it begins to thicken. Cool, then pour into pie plate that has been lined with vanilla wafers. Then chill until firm.

MRS. G. W. DAVIS, JR., Sumter County.

Fresh Strawberry Pie

1 quart strawberries
1½ cups sugar
1 tablespoon gelatin
¼ cup cold water

2 tablespoons lemon juice
Red food coloring
1 cup cream, whipped
1 9-inch pie shell

Wash and cap strawberries. Sprinkle with 1 cup sugar. Let stand in refrigerator for several hours. Soften gelatin in cold water. Press half the berries and all the juice through a sieve to make 1½ cups of sieved berries and juice (if necessary, add water to make up the full amount). Add remaining ½ cup sugar and lemon juice. Heat to the boiling point. Dissolve gelatin in hot strawberry mixture. Add coloring to give a bright red color. Chill until mixture begins to thicken. Place remaining whole berries in pie shell. Cover with thickened gelatin mixture. Chill until firm. Top with sweetened whipped cream before serving. Yield: one 9-inch pie.

MRS. A. H. MAYBIN, Union County.

FRUIT PIES

Apple Pie

6 to 8 tart apples
1¼ cups sugar
1 tablespoon lemon juice

2 tablespoons flour
⅛ teaspoon salt
½ teaspoon cinnamon

1 tablespoon butter

Peel and thinly slice apples. Combine dry ingredients. Add to the apples and lemon juice. Mix well and let stand while preparing pastry. Line pie plate with pastry. Add filling, dot with butter. Cover with top crust and seal edges. Cut in a few places to allow escape of steam. Bake in preheated oven 425 degrees about 45 minutes or until crust is golden brown and apples are tender.

Pastry:

2½ cups sifted flour
1 teaspoon salt

¾ cup shortening
1/3 cup cold water

Sift together flour and salt. Add half of the shortening to flour. Blend in with fork or pastry blender until mixture is fine. Add remaining shortening and mix until particles are coarse. Sprinkle with water, one tablespoon at a time. Mix well with knife until moistened. Press into a ball and divide into two portions. Roll on floured board.

Mrs. Andrew Goodale, Kershaw County.

Deep Dish Apple Pie

3 or 4 apples cut in slices
    or No. 2 can of apples
1 cup flour
1 stick butter or ½ cup

½ cup brown sugar
½ cup white sugar
juice of ½ lemon
pinch of salt

Arrange apples in baking dish. Mix the remaining ingredients thoroughly and roll out and pat over top of apples. Bake slowly at 300 degrees for one hour or until done.

Florence County.

Apple Crumb Pie

4 large tart apples
½ recipe plain pastry
½ cup sugar

½ cup sugar
¾ cup flour
1/3 cup butter

1 teaspoon cinnamon

Pare apples; cut in eighths and arrange in 9-inch pastry-lined pie pan. Sprinkle with ½ cup sugar mixed with cinnamon. Sift remaining ½ cup sugar with flour; cut in butter until crumbly. Sprinkle over apples. Bake in hot oven 450 degrees 10 minutes, then in moderate oven 350 degrees about 40 minutes, or until apples are tender.

MRS. J. R. LEVER, Richland County.

Cherry Cobbler

1 can (No. 2) pitted sour red cherries	1½ teaspoons baking powder
2 tablespoons flour	⅛ teaspoon salt
½ cup sugar	3 tablespoons shortening
	1/3 cup milk

1 cup sifted all-purpose flour

Place cherries in greased pan. Sprinkle with 2 tablespoons flour, and sugar. Sift together remaining dry ingredients, cut in shortening, add milk to make soft dough. Roll out on lightly floured board to fit utensil and score in six squares. Place over cherries. Bake in 375 degree oven for 1 hour and a half. Serves 6.

MRS. STROM CULBREATH, McCormick County.

Deep Dish Cherry Pie

¼ cup butter	½ teaspoon vanilla
½ cup sugar	1 cup flour
1 egg	1 teaspoon baking powder
½ cup milk	½ teaspoon salt

Cream butter and sugar. Add egg and beat well. Add flour, baking powder, and salt, alternately with milk. Lastly vanilla. Pour batter in bottom of greased baking dish. Add 1½ cups canned sour cherries, drained, over top. Sprinkle 1 cup sugar over cherries and add 1 cup cherry juice (or add water to make 1 cup). Bake 45 minutes at 350 degrees or until brown. Batter will rise and cover cherries.

MRSS. ALFRED C. MARNE, McCormick County.

Date Nut Pie

4 egg whites beaten	1 package dates cut fine
16 saltines crushed	1 cup nuts cut fine
1 cup sugar	1 teaspoon vanilla

1 teaspoon baking powder

Mix all ingredients and bake in slow oven 30 minutes. Serve with whipped cream.

MRS. S. M. YOUNGBLOOD, Greenwood County.

Berry Pie

Line side of deep casserole with pastry.

Fill with 4 cups berries, 2 cups sugar and 4 tablespoons butter.

Cover with pastry. Prick with fork and bake in hot oven 450 degrees for 10 minutes, reduce heat to 375, bake for 35 minutes.

Serve hot.

Blackberries, strawberries or raspberries may be used.

Peach Pie with Never Fail Pie Crust

2 cups peaches	¼ cup lard
1 cup sugar	¼ cup water
¼ cup peanut butter	1½ cups flour
½ teaspoon salt	

Mix flour, salt, peanut butter and lard. Add water and mix to medium dough. Roll into two thin pie crusts. Place one into greased pie pan. Put peaches (sweetened) onto crust and place other crust over them. Bake until crust is brown at 375 degrees for 15 minutes.

Mrs. J. P. LaGroon, McCormick County.

One Crust Deep-Pan Peach Pie

3 cups flour, sifted (plain)
1 teaspoon salt
1 teaspoon baking powder

1 cup shortening
½ cup of ice water
more or less

Sift dry ingredients together and work in chilled shortening lightly. Add ice water slowly to form dough and knead.

Pie Ingredients:

1 quart canned peaches
2½ cups sugar

pinch salt
1¼ cups fresh cream

Dice peaches and pour back into juice in a saucepan. Add 2 cups of sugar and a pinch of salt. Bring to a boil and boil until all sugar is dissolved. Then take off heat and add 1 cup of cream. Pour into a deep pan or casserole dish, then roll out pie crust about ½-inch thick and cover. Prick holes in crust to let steam come out. When filling pan leave one inch from top. Bake in hot oven about 425 degrees or 450 degrees until crust is brown. Then cover with a topping made with ¼ cup cream and ½ cup sugar blended well. Glaze top of pie and cook until topping is caramelized. Serves 8–10.

Mrs. O. A. Troutman, Sr., Calhoun County.

Cherry Pie

2 pound can water pack red tart
cherries

1 cup sugar
2 tablespoons corn starch
pinch of salt

Drain cherries, stir corn starch in ⅛ cup of the drained juice. Add the sugar and salt to ½ of the remaining juice and bring to a rolling boil. Then pour in the starch and juice mixture and cook until thick and clear, stirring constantly. Add the thickened juice to the cherries. Cool this prepared filling before pouring into a pie tin lined with your favorite crust. Dot lightly with butter, and apply top crust. Bake approximately 40 minutes at 425 degrees.

Mrs. Monroe Saunders, Cherokee County.

Raisin Pie

2 cups seedless raisins	1 teaspoon cinnamon
2 cups water	⅛ teaspoon salt
½ cup brown sugar	1 tablespoon vinegar
(packed down)	1 tablespoon butter
2 tablespoons cornstarch	pastry for double 9-inch crusts

Boil raisins in 1¾ cups water 5 minutes. Combine brown sugar, cornstarch, cinnamon and salt; moisten with remaining ¼ cup cold water, and add to raisins, stirring until mixture boils. Remove from fire and add butter and vinegar. Pour into pastry-lined pie pan; cover top with pastry. Bake 25 minutes in hot oven 425 degrees.

MRS. MARY CHANDLER, Calhoun County.

Cherry Cream Pie

2 tablespoons butter	2 slightly beaten egg yolks
¾ cup sugar	2¼ teaspoons vanilla
¼ cup corn starch	2 cups pitted cherries
2 cups whole milk	2 egg whites
¼ cup sugar	½ teaspoon salt

Melt butter, blend in dry ingredients, stir in milk, place in top of double boiler and cook about 20 minutes. Then stir in beaten yolks of eggs and cook and stir 2 minutes longer. Cool, then add vanilla. Drain cherries and add to mixture. Put into cool baked pastry shell. Beat egg whites until stiff, gradually beating in the sugar. Then spread this over custard. The cherries can be placed in shell, then custard poured over them.

MRS. HARVEY YON, Anderson County.

Persimmon Pie

2 large Japanese persimmons
2 cups sugar
1 can evaporated milk
½ teaspoon salt
1 tablespoon cornstarch
3 eggs
1 teaspoon nutmeg

Peel persimmons and crush until smooth. Add sugar, beat. Add 3 egg yolks and one white. Add milk, nutmeg, and salt. Beat until smooth. Pour in a 9-inch pie shell and bake until done. Make meringue by beating whites of eggs until stiff. Add 4 tablespoons sugar. Put on top of pie and brown in moderate oven.

MISS JULIA B. KIRKLAND, Richland County.

LEMON PIES

Lemon Icebox Pie

1 small can evaporated milk
2 eggs
1 tablespoon grated lemon peel
1/3 cup fresh lemon juice
½ cup sugar
spiced crumbs

Pour milk into ice cube tray and chill until crystals start to form. Separate eggs. Mix yolk with sugar, lemon juice and grated peel. Beat egg whites stiff, then lightly mix in yolk mixture. Turn chilled milk into bowl, beat stiff and carefully fold into egg mixture. Pour into ice cube tray lined with spiced crumbs. Swirl top, decorate with lemon peel twists and freeze.   Serves 6–8.

Spiced Crumbs:

To ¾ cup crisp toast crumbs add ½ cup brown sugar, ½ teaspoon nutmeg, ¼ teaspoon allspice, 1 teaspoon cinnamon, ¼ teaspoon ground cloves, ¼ teaspoon ginger. Mix well. Work in 3 tablespoons melted butter. Line ice cube tray, pressing very firmly with spoon.

MRS. J. L. DICKEY, JR., Fairfield County.

Condensed Milk Lemon Pie

½ cup lemon juice
3 eggs
2 tablespoons butter

1 can sweet condensed milk
pinch of salt
12 graham crackers

Beat egg yolks—add milk—mix well—add juice and salt. Pour in pie crust made of crackers and butter.

For Crust:

Roll 12 graham crackers until fine. Mix with butter, until crust is formed in pie plate, pour in filling. Top with whipped cream. Place in refrigerator. If cream is not available, top with meringue and bake lightly.

Mrs. Houston Rogers, Marion County.

Lemon Meringue Pie

5 tablespoons cornstarch
2 cups water
1 cup sugar
¼ teaspoon salt

3 egg yolks
2 tablespoons butter
5 tablespoons lemon juice
2 teaspoons grated lemon rind

1 9-inch baked pastry shell

Mix cornstarch with ½ cup cold water in top of double boiler, blend sugar and salt. Add remainder of water and when well blended, stir constantly over low heat until mixture boils. Cover and cook over boiling water 10 minutes. Gradually pour hot mixture over beaten egg yolks, stirring constantly. Return to double boiler and cook 2 minutes longer. Remove from heat, add butter, lemon juice and rind. Mix well. Cool and pour into pie shell.

Meringue:

Beat 3 egg whites stiff, gradually beat in 6 tablespoons sugar. Pile on top of pie, bake in a slow oven 325 degrees 15 minutes. Serves 6.

Mrs. J. Frank Dillashaw, McCormick County.

Lemon Cheese Cake Pie

3 3-ounce packages cream
   cheese
2 tablespoons butter
½ cup sugar
1 whole egg

2 tablespoons flour
2/3 cup milk
¼ cup fresh lemon juice
2 tablespoons grated lemon peel
1 graham cracker crust

Cream the cheese and butter; add sugar and whole egg. Mix well. Add flour, milk, lemon juice and peel. Pour into unbaked graham cracker pie shell. Sprinkle with cracker crumbs and bake 35 minutes in moderate oven at 350 degrees. Chill and serve. Makes 6–8 servings.

Graham Cracker Crust:

Crush enough graham crackers to make 1¼ cups fine crumbs. Add 1/3 cup melted butter. Mix well. Reserve ¼ cup of mixture for topping. Press remainder on bottom and sides of 8-inch pie plate. Chill and set.

MRS. RAY P. HOOK, Fairfield County.

Emma's Lemon and Apple Pie

Grate rind one lemon	2 tablespoons flour
juice one lemon	½ cup hot water
1 cup sugar	2 apples pared and grated
1 egg yolk	1 egg white
1 tablespoon melted butter	pastry for 2-crust pie

Mix grated rind, lemon juice, sugar, egg yolk slightly beaten, melted butter, flour and hot water. Then add apples. When well mixed, fold in stiffly beaten egg white. Line pie plate with plain pastry, fill with lemon and apple mixture. Cover with pastry, bake.

Charleston County.

Lemon Fluff Pie

4 eggs	1 cup sugar
Juice and grated rind of 1½ lemons	3 tablespoons lemon gelatin
	1 cup whipping cream

Beat egg yolks, add ½ cup sugar, lemon juice and rind. Cook in double boiler till of custard consistency. Dissolve gelatin in ½ cup hot water and add to hot mixture. Let cool. Beat egg whites till stiff, add remaining ½ cup sugar. Fold into egg mixture. Whip the cream and fold into mixture. Pour in vanilla wafer pie shell and chill.

MRS. G. R. CHAPMAN, Kershaw County.

POTATO AND PUMPKIN PIES

Sweet Potato Pie

1 cup mashed potatoes	1 egg, separated
1 cup sugar	1½ cups milk
2 tablespoons butter	1 teaspoon vanilla

Combine all ingredients, adding stiffly beaten egg whites last. Bake in pie crust in a slow oven 250 degrees. Serves 6.

MRS. H. C. GOOD, Fairfield County.

Pumpkin Chiffon Pie

Beat three egg yolks with ½ cup sugar until thick. Add 1 1/3 cups mashed pumpkin, cooked or canned.

1/3 cup milk	½ teaspoon cinnamon
½ teaspoon salt	½ teaspoon nutmeg

¼ teaspoon ginger

Cook until thickened, stir constantly. Soften 1 tablespoon gelatin in ¼ cup cold water. Add to pumpkin mixture, stirring until dissolved. Cool. Beat 3 egg whites until stiff. Add ½ cup sugar gradually. Fold into cooled pumpkin. Fill baked, cooled pie shells. Chill. Top with sweetened whipped cream before serving.

MRS. W. D. BALLENTINE, Anderson County.

Pumpkin Pie

1½ cups cooked pumpkin fresh or canned	¼ teaspoon salt
	¼ teaspoon nutmeg
1 cup rich milk	¼ teaspoon cinnamon
1 cup sugar	2 eggs slightly beaten

1 teaspoon butter or substitute

Combine ingredients. Mix thoroughly pour into pastry-lined pan, bake in hot oven at 425 degrees about 25 minutes or until an inserted knife comes out clean. Serve with whipped cream if desired or serve while still warm.

LUCY K. HARTER, Allendale County.

MISCELLANEOUS

Buttermilk Pie

1 cup sugar
3 eggs
½ cup butter

2 tablespoons flour
1 cup buttermilk
1 teaspoon vanilla or lemon

Beat eggs slightly and add sugar and flour. Then add melted butter and mix well. Add buttermilk and flavoring and pour in unbaked pie shell. Bake at 325 degrees until custard is set.

MRS. HASTINGS WOODWARD, Aiken County.

Brown Sugar Pie

2 cups brown sugar
2 eggs
2 tablespoons flour

¾ cup milk
3 tablespoons butter
1 teaspoon vanilla

Mix sugar and flour, add milk, eggs and melted butter. Bake in uncooked pie shell.

MRS. EUGENE CRAWFORD, McCormick County.

Sugar Pie

½ cup butter
1 cup sugar

1 egg
3 tablespoons cold water

1 teaspoon flavoring

Cream butter and sugar, add egg and beat well, then stir in water. Pour into unbaked pie crust and bake it at moderate heat until done. It will have a delicate brown crust when done.

"This is an old heirloom recipe and is said to be the origin of the saying 'Sweet as sugar pie', the term used by old colored mammys to describe the white babies they nursed." Since this recipe is old it best fits a tin or enamel 8-inch pie plate such as was used before the days of more modern cookware.

MRS. D. H. LANGLEY, McCormick County.

Transparent Pie

An old family recipe.
Prepare pie crust for 8-inch crust and place in pan.

3 eggs
1 cup sugar

½ cup butter
1 teaspoon vanilla

Cream the butter and sugar, add eggs and beat well, add vanilla last. Pour into unbaked crust and bake in 350-degree oven until the filling is transparent and well browned.

Mrs. J. J. MINARIK, McCormick County.

Egg Custard Pie

3 cups milk   ¼ teaspoon salt
3 eggs   1 teaspoon vanilla
½ cup sugar   Nutmeg, few gratings if desired

Roll the pastry and place it on the pie dish. Be sure that it is flat to the dish so that no air bubbles are beneath. Scald milk. Beat eggs slightly, add sugar, salt and vanilla. Add scalded milk and pour this mixture into the crust. Bake at 350 degrees for about 30 minutes. Yield: one 9-inch pie.

Mrs. ROBERT L. LEMMON, Fairfield County.

Eggnog Pie

½ cup sugar   ⅛ teaspoon salt
3 beaten egg yolks   ⅛ teaspoon nutmeg
2 cups light cream   ½ teaspoon vanilla extract
           3 stiffly beaten egg whites

Beat sugar, egg yolks and cream. Add seasonings and vanilla extract. Fold in egg whites. Pour into pastry-lined 9-inch pan. Bake in hot oven (450 degrees) 10 minutes, then in moderate oven (325 degrees) until firm, about 25 minutes.

Charleston County.

Chess Pie

Yolks of 8 eggs   1 cup butter
2 cups sugar   2 tablespoons cream
           2 teaspoons vanilla

Cream sugar and butter thoroughly, add yolks and beat for several minutes. Add cream and vanilla. Bake in unbaked pie shells in moderate oven until jellied. Makes 2 pies.

Mrs. J. H. PROPST, Aiken County.

Molasses Pie

1 cup molasses   2 eggs
           2 tablespoons butter

Cook molasses until thick. Add two eggs well beaten. Add two tablespoons butter and mix thoroughly. Pour in uncooked pastry shell and bake in oven for 10 minutes at 450 degrees, then reduce to 375 degrees and bake until done.

MRS. S. S. McBRIDE, McCormick County.

Molasses Pie

¾ cup molasses	1 cup sour milk
½ cup brown sugar	1 teaspoon soda
2 tablespoons butter	½ teaspoon allspice
½ cup flour	½ teaspoon cinnamon
2 eggs	½ teaspoon salt

Sift all dry ingredients except soda. Dissolve soda in sour milk, mix in molasses. Add beaten eggs, then melted butter, and beat until smooth. Line a pie tin with flaky pastry, pour in filling. Bake at 375 degrees till pie begins to brown. Reduce heat to 350 degrees and bake until crust is brown and filling firm. Egg whites may be reserved for meringue or a lattice work of dough used.

MRS. WADE ERGLE, Aiken County.

Black Bottom Pie

16 graham crackers crushed   ½ stick melted butter
ginger snaps may be used

Mix and line pie plate (use at least 2-inch deep pie plate). Bake 10 minutes 310-degree oven.

Custard Filling:

2 teaspoons flour	1½ squares chocolate
4 egg yolks	1 teaspoon vanilla
½ cup sugar	1 tablespoon gelatin
2 cups milk	4 tablespoons cold water

Soak gelatin in water while making custard. Make a custard with first four ingredients. Melt chocolate over hot water. Add 1 cup of the custard to melted chocolate. Cool and add vanilla and pour into cool pie crust and set aside. Add gelatin to remainder of custard. Let cool but not until stiff. Cover with meringue.

Meringue:

4 egg whites   ½ cup sugar
¼ teaspoon cream of tartar

Beat whites and cream of tartar until very stiff. Add sugar a tablespoon at a time. Beat until thoroughly melted. While custard is smooth and soft fold in meringue and 1 teaspoon vanilla. When chocolate has set cover with fluffy custard. Chill until firm. When custard sets spread with: 1 cup cream whipped stiff; 3 tablespoons confectioner's sugar. Sprinkle grated chocolate over top of cream to decorate. Serves 6.

MRS. DUFFIE FREEMAN, Newberry County.

Strawberry Cream Cheese Pie
(Makes a 9-inch pie)

1 baked 9-inch pastry shell	2 eggs separated
1 1/3 cups (15 oz. can) sweetened condensed milk	1 cup sliced strawberries
¼ cup lemon juice	¼ teaspoon cream of tarter
1 package (3 ounce) cream cheese	4 tablespoons sugar

Blend together sweetened condensed milk and lemon juice. Beat cream cheese, softened at room temperature until smooth. Add one egg yolk at a time beating well after each addition. Add strawberries and mix thoroughly. Fold the cheese-strawberry mixture into sweetened condensed milk mixture. Put into cooled, baked pastry shell. Add cream of tartar to egg whites; beat until almost stiff enough to hold a peak. Add sugar gradually, beating until egg whites are stiff and dry. Pile egg whites lightly on pie filling. Bake in slow oven (325 degrees) 15 minutes or until lightly browned. Cool. Any of the following fruits may be used:

1 cup drained crushed pineapple	1½ cups (No. 2 can) red sour pitted cherries well drained
1 cup fresh raspberries	2 medium bananas sliced

MRS. HARVEY NEELY, Chester County.

Fried Pies

Cooked dried apples or peaches until tender. Mash and season with sugar. Make a paste about one half as rich as for ordinary pie dough. Roll out an ordinary size crust and spread one half of it with the fruit. Turn the other half over the fruit and pinch the edges together with a fork. Have enough hot fat in the skillet to cover them. Put in pie and fry to a rich brown, turning over once. Serve while warm.

MRS. D. L. HUTTO, Oconee County.

Cakes, Cookies and Icings.

Kind of Cakes

There are two distinct classes of cakes. These are butter cakes and sponge cakes. Butter cakes are made with butter or some other type of fat. True sponge cakes have no fat and no liquid or leavening except that furnished by the eggs.

Ingredients

Fat-tests show that butter gives a better grain and texture, as well as better flavor, to a cake than do other fats. If butter is substituted for other fats, 2 tablespoons more per cup should be used. Any fat used must be *sweet* and *free* from any rancid or undesirable flavors.

Sugar. A finely granulated sugar gives best results in cake making.

Eggs. The important thing in eggs is that they be fresh. An egg that is old and watery, even if not spoiled, will not make as good a cake. This is particularly true of angel food and other sponge cakes. Egg whites yield greater volume if they are as much as a day old and at room temperature.

Flour. A soft wheat flour should be used and a high patent flour will give best results. Soft wheat flour is also known as biscuit or pastry flour. If the flour you are using is not marked "hard" or "soft" wheat remember the flour that is grown in the Middlewest and South is chiefly soft wheat.

Liquid. Milk will give better texture and flavor to a cake and will add food value. Milk causes the cake to brown better. In certain cakes fruit juices may be used as part or all of the liquid and the milk from the coconut adds flavor when making a coconut cake.

Flavoring. Use good quality flavoring and above all avoid using too much. Nothing lowers the quality of a cake more than too much low-grade flavoring. A combination of flavors is often pleasing and a wider variety than is commonly used would be enjoyed by most

families. Spices, orange and lemon rind, or many other things which you have on hand might be used.

Leavening Agents. Baking powder is the most common of the leavening agents. Use whatever type you prefer but avoid using too much as it makes a coarse porous cake. Less baking powder of the sodium aluminum kind alone or with phosphate is required than of those made from tartrate or phosphate. (Read your label to see which you use.) One teaspoon of the first two named will be sufficient for one cup of flour. Use 1 to 1½ teaspoons of the tartrate or phosphate powders to 1 cup of flour. These proportions are for a plain cake. A cake with more eggs requires less baking powder. When you add eggs to a cake recipe reduce the baking powder ½ teaspoon for each egg white added.

Buttermilk, sour cream, molasses or lemon juice may be used with soda as the leavening agent.

Air is the leavening agent in sponge cakes and pound cakes.

Other ingredients. Cocoa and chocolate are the most common additions to cakes. For each ounce of chocolate added to a cake, decrease the fat by one tablespoonful and the flour by one tablespoonful. For each ¼ cup cocoa added to a cake, decrease the flour by one tablespoonful.

For each cup of nuts added to a cake, decrease the fat two tablespoons.

Spices, raisins, dates and other dried fruits may be added as desired.

A little salt should be added unless the cake is made with butter or other salted fat.

Baking

The baking of a cake can be checked by dividing the required baking time into fourths:

First quarter   —Cake should begin to rise (bubbles).

Second quarter—Cake should continue to rise and form a crust.

Third quarter —Cake should finish rising and begin to brown.

Fourth quarter—Cake should finish browning and shrink from sides of pan.

If the oven is too quick and cannot be regulated, place a pan of hot water above the cake and another below it. If no oven thermometer is available, watch the division of time very carefully and reduce the oven temperature if the cake is cooking too quickly.

Be careful not to move the cake during the second and third quarters. If the oven does not cook evenly, the cake may be moved in the first and fourth quarters.

Tests When Cake is Done:

    A. Cake leaves side of pan.

    B. Cake feels firm to touch of finger and will spring back into place.

    C. Put a toothpick or a fine knitting needle into cake. It will come out clean if cake is done.

LAYER CAKES

White Layer Cake

2 cups cake flour
2 teaspoons baking powder
¼ teaspoon salt
½ cup butter

½ teaspoon cream of tartar
1½ cups sugar
¼ cup milk
6 egg whites

1 teaspoon vanilla

Cream butter, adding the sugar gradually and working until the mass is entirely smooth. Sift flour, measure and add salt and baking powder, and sift twice more. Add flour and milk alternately to the creamed butter and sugar. Add the flavoring. Beat egg whites slightly, add cream of tartar, and continue beating until stiff. Cut and fold egg whites into the cake mixture. Pour into 8-inch layer pans and bake for 35 minutes at 350 degrees.

1 - 2 - 3 - 4 Cake

1 cup butter
2 cups sugar
4 eggs
1 teaspoon flavoring

3 cups flour
3 teaspoons baking powder
1 cup milk
¼ to ½ teaspoon salt

Cream fat until soft. Add flavoring and sugar, stirring until mixture is light and fluffy. Add eggs one at a time and beat well. Add the flour (which has been sifted with salt and baking powder) and milk alternately. Bake in two greased pans at 350°.

Layer Cake

(One bowl method)

2¼ cups cake flour
3 teaspoons baking powder
1 teaspoon salt
1½ cups granulated sugar

½ cup high grade vegetable
    shortening
1 teaspoon vanilla
1 cup milk

2 medium eggs, unbeaten

Sift flour, measure and add baking powder, salt and sugar. Sift into the mixing bowl. Add vegetable shortening. Add 2/3 of the cup of milk and flavoring. Beat for two minutes in cake mixer, or beat 200 strokes by hand with mixing spoon. Add unbeaten eggs and remainder of the milk. Beat for two minutes or 200 strokes. Divide batter evenly in two pans (9-inch) and place in preheated oven. Bake at 375 degrees for 25 to 30 minutes. After baking, let stand 5 minutes and then loosen from pan. This recipe can be used to make cup cakes.

Mrs. S. B. VASSEY, Cherokee County.

Coconut Mist Cake

3 cups sifted cake flour
2 teaspoons baking powder
¼ teaspoon salt
1 cup butter or other shortening
1 pound (3½ cups) confec-
tioner's sugar

4 egg yolks, well beaten
1 cup milk
1 teaspoon vanilla
1 cup shredded coconut
(optional)
4 egg whites, stiffly beaten

Sift flour once, measure, add baking powder and salt, and sift together three times. Cream butter thoroughly, add sugar gradually, and cream together until light and fluffy. Add egg yolks and beat well. Add flour, alternately with milk, a small amount at a time, beating after each addition until smooth. Add vanilla and coconut. Fold in egg whites quickly and thoroughly. Bake in three greased 9-inch layer pans in moderate oven 375 degrees for 25 to 30 minutes.

Mrs. M. C. WHITE, McCormick County.

Banana Cake

1½ cups sugar
½ cup butter or substitute
2 eggs
2¼ cups sifted flour

½ teaspoon salt
½ teaspoon soda
1 cup mashed banana (about 2)
1 teaspoon vanilla flavoring

¼ cup sour milk

Cream sugar and butter well, add 1 egg at a time and beat well. Add sifted ingredients alternately with banana and milk. Grease and flour two 9-inch cake pans well. Divide batter equally in pans and bake about 30 minutes at 350 degrees. Let cool.

FILLING

2 or 3 cups powdered sugar and ¼ pound of butter. Mix well until creamy. Add 3 tablespoons cream or top milk. 1 teaspoon vanilla flavoring. Add enough sugar until right consistency to spread.

Mrs. J. C. CRAPPS.

White Coconut Cake

2/3 cup butter	3 teaspoons baking powder
2 cups sugar	1 cup warm water
3 cups flour	1 tablespoon orange extract
½ teaspoon salt	8 egg whites, beaten

Put measured flour and eggs in refrigerator to chill. Cream butter and sugar 10 minutes. Begin to add warm water ¼ cup at a time. Alternate flour and egg whites. Add flavoring. Bake in two 9-inch pans in moderate oven. Frost with filling below.

FILLING

4 cups sugar	4 egg whites (beaten)
2 cups hot water	2 large or 3 small coconuts

1 tablespoon orange extract

Place sugar in pot and add hot water. Boil together very rapidly until it forms soft ball in cold water. Beat egg whites stiff; dip up ½ cup of hot syrup and pour over eggs, beating all the time. Let remainder of syrup cook until it spins a long thread. Pour over the other and beat until thick, then put coconut one inch thick. Top with a second layer of cake, cover with icing top and sides. Sprinkle coconut well over top and on sides.

MRS. T. C. McSWAIN, Dillon County.

Orange Chiffon Cake

Preheat oven to 325 degrees. Sift an ample amount of flour into square of paper.

STEP I. Measure and sift together into mixing bowl:

2¼ cups sifted flour (spoon lightly into cup, don't pack)	1½ cups sugar
	3 teaspoons baking powder

1 teaspoon salt

Make a well and add in order:

½ cup cooking salad oil	¼ cup cold water
5 unbeaten egg yolks	grated rind 2 oranges

STEP II. Measure into large mixing bowl:

1 cup egg whites (7 or 8)	½ teaspoon cream of tartar

Whip whites until form very stiff peaks. They should be much stiffer than for angel cake (do not underbeat).

STEP III. Pour egg yolks gradually over egg whites—gently folding with rubber scraper just until blended. Do not stir. Pour into ungreased pan immediately. 10-inch tube pan, 4 inches deep. Bake

325 degrees for 55 minutes then 350 degrees 10 to 15 minutes. Or bake in oblong pan 9 x 13 x 2 inches 350 degrees 40 to 50 minutes. Immediately turn pan upside down, placing the tube over neck of funnel or bottle or resting edges of square, oblong or loaf pans on 2 other pans. Let hang free of table until cold. Turn pan over and hit edge sharply on table to loosen. Ice with:

ORANGE BUTTER ICING

¼ cup butter or margarine (soft)   grated rind of one orange
2 cups confectioner's sugar   2 tablespoons orange juice
1/3 teaspoon salt

More juice or sugar may be added to give desired consistency.

MRS. C. R. WORKMAN, Laurens County.

Orange Filled Coconut Layer Cake

1 cup shortening   3 cups sifted cake flour
2 cups sugar   2¼ teaspoons double acting
½ teaspoon almond extract   baking powder
4 eggs   ¾ teaspoon salt
1 cup milk

(All ingredients should be at room temperature.) Cream shortening well. Add sugar gradually, beating until light and fluffy. Add flavoring then eggs, one at a time, beating well after each addition. Add sifted dry ingredients alternately with milk, beating until smooth. Pour batter into three round 9-inch layer pans 1 inch deep, lined on the bottom with paper, then greased. Bake in moderate oven, 375 degrees for about 25 minutes. Let stand for 5 minutes then turn out on racks to cool. Spread orange filling between layers and coconut frosting on top and sides of cake.

ORANGE FILLING

Mix ½ cup sifted cake flour, 1 cup sugar and ¼ teaspoon salt in heavy saucepan. Add ¼ cup water and mix well until there are no lumps. Add 1¼ cups orange juice, ¼ cup lemon juice, 2 tablespoons grated orange rind and grated rind of 1 lemon. Cook over low heat until mixture thickens and becomes almost transparent. Beat 4 egg yolks slightly; add hot mixture slowly, stirring constantly. Return to saucepan and, stirring constantly, cook slowly about 5 minutes or until sauce thickens again. Cool.

COCONUT FROSTING

1½ cups sugar
½ teaspoon cream of tartar
⅛ teaspoon salt
½ cup egg whites

¼ teaspoon almond extract
2 cups fresh grated or package coconut

Combine sugar, cream of tartar, salt and ½ cup hot water in saucepan. Cook without stirring 240 degrees on a candy thermometer or until a little of the mixture dropped in cold water will form a soft ball that holds its shape. Meanwhile beat egg whites until stiff but not dry. Add syrup slowly to egg whites beating constantly with rotary egg beater or electric mixer at high speed. Add flavoring, spread frosting on top and sides of cake. Sprinkle with coconut.

MRS. ARCHIE D. LEWIS.

Cherry Cake

2½ cups sifted flour
1½ cups sugar
½ cup shortening
¾ cup milk
¼ cup maraschino cherry juice
1 teaspoon vanilla
2 teaspoons baking powder

4 egg whites, unbeaten
18 maraschino cherries, well drained and very finely chopped
½ cup walnuts, very finely chopped
2 teaspoons almond extract

Sift flour and baking powder. Add sugar. Drop in shortening. Combine milk and cherry juice. Add ¾ cup of this liquid. Add flavoring extracts. Beat 200 strokes. Add remaining liquid and egg whites and beat 200 strokes. Add cherries and nuts and blend. Bake in two 9-inch pans that are greased in moderately hot oven until done. (Batter may be baked in two heart-shaped pans and decorated with Pink Valentine Frosting on Valentine's Day.)

MRS. R. H. HUGGINS, Dillon County.

Devil's Food Cake

2/3 cup butter or margarine
1½ cups sugar
3 eggs
2 cups cake flour
2¾ teaspoons baking powder

¼ teaspoon salt
¾ cup milk
2½ squares unsweetened chocolate
1 teaspoon vanilla

Cream butter, add sugar gradually and cream until light and fluffy. Add eggs and beat well. Add melted chocolate and blend. Sift flour once, measure, add baking powder and salt and sift again. Add flour mixture alternately with milk a little at a time, beating well after each addition. Add vanilla. Pour into two greased 9-inch layer cake pans and bake in moderate oven 350 degrees for 35 minutes. For filling use seven-minute frosting.

MRS. E. H. CHRISTIAN, McCormick County.

Devil's Food Cake

1 cup butter	3 cups flour
2¼ cups sugar	¼ teaspoon salt
4 eggs	4½ teaspoons baking powder
1½ cups milk	1½ teaspoons vanilla

¾ cup cocoa

Cream butter thoroughly. Add sugar and cream together, separate yolks and white of eggs. Add yolks to butter and sugar and beat well, add milk and the flour which has been sifted with the baking powder and salt and cocoa. Fold in stiffly beaten egg whites. Pour into three greased and floured cake pans and bake 25 to 30 minutes in a moderate oven at 350 degrees.

CHOCOLATE FUDGE FILLING

3 cups sugar	1 cup evaporated milk
3 tablespoons white syrup	3 blocks unsweetened chocolate

Butter size of an egg

Put all on together and cook until it forms a soft ball in water. Cool. Beat and spread on cake.

MRS. ELLEN ABRAMS, Newberry County.

Devil's Food Cake

½ cup shortening or butter	1 cup boiling water
1 cup brown sugar, firmly packed	2 teaspoons soda
1 cup thick sour milk or buttermilk	1 cup white sugar, sifted with brown
3 cups sifted flour	4 eggs, well beaten
1 teaspoon red vegetable coloring	2 teaspoons baking powder
	1 teaspoon salt
	2 teaspoons vanilla

4 squares unsweetened chocolate

Melt chocolate over hot water and add boiling water, mixing quickly. Add soda. Stir until mixture is thick. Set aside to cool while mixing cake. Cream butter or shortening. Add sifted sugars gradually.

Cream together until light and fluffy, the consistency of thick whipped cream. Add beaten eggs stirring until well mixed. Add flour, sifted with baking powder and salt, alternately with milk. Stir after each addition until smooth. Add chocolate mixture, vanilla and coloring. Mix thoroughly. Line three greased 8″ x 2″ cake pans with waxed paper. Pour in batter and bake in moderate oven 350 degrees for 25 minutes. Put together with fudge icing.

FUDGE ICING

3 cups sugar
1 cup milk

4 tablespoons butter
6 tablespoons cocoa or 4 squares chocolate

Let ingredients come to a boil slowly, stirring constantly; when boiling begins, do not stir. Let boil until soft ball forms when dropped from fork in cold water. Remove from heat, add vanilla and beat until stiff. Spread on cake. Makes enough for 3 layer cake.

MRS. CARSON CARMICHAEL, Dillon County.

Mayonnaise Cake

1 cup sugar
2 cups flour

2 tablespoons cocoa (level)
2 level teaspoons soda

pinch of salt

Sift all ingredients together then add 1 scant cup of mayonnaise dressing.

1 cup of water
1 teaspoon vanilla

Bake at 350 degrees until done.   Serves 6.

MRS. ROY N. JOLLEY, Newberry County.

Chocolate Nut Cake

½ cup butter
2 cups sugar
4 squares chocolate
2 eggs

1½ cups sweet milk
2 cups flour
2 teaspoons baking powder
¼ teaspoon soda

1 cup nuts

Cream butter and sugar. Add melted chocolate (melt over water) beat in eggs. Sift dry ingredients in mixture alternately. (Flour first and last). Add milk and vanilla. Add nuts. Bake in pan at 350 degrees for 45 minutes.

Note: Never substitute cocoa for chocolate squares. Be careful not to over-cook. Use favorite icing.

MRS. J. C. YOUNG, McCormick County.

Chocolate Marble Layer Cake

Melt 1 square unsweetened chocolate over hot water.
Sift together into a large bowl:

2¼ cups sifted cake flour	1 teaspoon salt
2½ teaspoons double acting bak- ing powder or	1½ cups sugar
3¼ teaspoons single acting	

Add:

½ cup vegetable shortening	¼ cup milk

Mix enough to dampen flour.
Add:

2 eggs	¼ cup milk
1 teaspoon vanilla	

Remove ½ of batter to another bowl and stir in melted chocolate. Turn white and chocolate batter alternately into 2 greased 8-inch layer pans. Bake in moderate oven 375 degrees about 25 minutes.

CHOCOLATE ICING

Heat together ½ cup water, 2 tablespoons butter and 1 tablespoon shortening. Add 3 squares unsweetened chocolate melted. Cool, then add 1 teaspoon vanilla and 3¾ cups sifted confectioner's sugar. Beat until creamy smooth. Frost cake.

MRS. LEE CLAYTON, Dorchester County.

Lady Baltimore Cake

½ cup butter	2 teaspoons baking powder
1 cup sugar	½ cup milk
1¾ cups pastry flour	1 teaspoon vanilla
⅛ teaspoon salt	3 egg whites

Cream butter. Add sugar and cream again thoroughly. Sift dry ingredients and add alternately with milk. Add extract and fold in stiffly beaten egg whites. Bake in two layers in moderate oven 350 degrees, for 25 minutes. Put layers together with Lady Baltimore filling.

LADY BALTIMORE ICING

2 cups sugar	candied cherries
2/3 cup water	2/3 cup raisins
2 egg whites	2/3 cup nut meats
	5 figs

Boil sugar and water to soft ball stage (238 degrees). Pour slowly on well-beaten egg whites, beating constantly. Set aside to cool. Put raisins, nuts and figs through chopper. Add to cooled boiled icing. Spread between layers and on top and sides of cake. Garnish with nut meats and halved candied cherries.

Mrs. E. W. Truluck, Sumter County.

Mocha Layer Cake

1¾ cups sifted flour
2¼ teaspoons baking powder
¾ teaspoon salt
1 cup plus 2 teaspoons sugar

½ cup shortening
2/3 cup milk
1 teaspoon vanilla
2 eggs, unbeaten

Sift flour once, measure into sifter, and add baking powder, salt and sugar. Set aside. Place shortening in mixing bowl and stir just to soften. Sift in dry ingredients. Add milk and vanilla and mix until all flour is moist. Then beat two minutes. Add eggs and beat one minute longer. Baking: Turn batter into pans. Bake in moderate oven, 375 degrees 25 minutes or until done.

Mix by hand or at low speed of electric mixer. Count only actual beating time or beating strokes. Allow about 150 full strokes per minute. Scrape bowl and spoon often.

Mocha Frosting

Sift together 2½ cups sifted confectioner's sugar, 3 tablespoons cocoa and dash salt. Cream 6 tablespoons butter, add part of sugar mixture gradually, blending after each addition until light and fluffy. Add remaining sugar alternately with about 4 tablespoons cold coffee until of right consistency to spread, beating well after each addition Add ¼ teaspoon vanilla.

Mrs. Garland Prevatte, Calhoun County.

POUND CAKES

Pound Cake

1 pound butter
9 large eggs
1 pound flour (4 cups)

½ teaspoon lemon extract or
1 teaspoon vanilla or
¼ teaspoon almond extract

1 pound sugar (2 cups)

Cream butter and sugar to consistency of whipped cream. Add one egg at a time until 5 have been added, beating each egg 2½ minutes.

Add others 2 at a time, beating 2½ minutes after each addition. **Add** flavoring. Fold in flour, in about 4 additions. Have cake pan lined with oil paper and buttered well. Bake 1½ hours at 300 degrees.

Mrs. W. H. Irby, Kershaw County.

FRUIT CAKES

Dark Fruit Cake

1 pound raisins
1 pound currants
1 pound figs
1 pound dates
1 pound cherries
1 cup molasses
1 pound butter
1 cup buttermilk

1 pound pineapple
1 pound citron
1 pound pecans
10 eggs
4 cups flour
2 cups brown sugar
¼ teaspoon each of cinnamon, nutmeg, allspice, cloves

½ teaspoon soda

Cut up fruit and nuts, then roll in 1 cup flour and spices. **Cream** butter and sugar, add beaten eggs and vanilla, blend well. Add molasses and mix well. Sift soda and flour together. Add dry ingredients and milk alternately to mixture. Add nut mixture and mix thoroughly. Pour into 2 greased stem cake pans. Bake in slow oven 250 degrees for 4 hours.

Mrs. S. B. Horton, Kershaw County.

White Fruit Cake

For the batter:

½ pound butter
1 cup sugar
6 eggs
4 cups flour

1 teaspoon salt
2 teaspoons baking powder
1 tablespoon vanilla
1 teaspoon almond extract

Fruits:

1 pound candied cherries
1 pound candied pineapple

½ pound white raisins
½ pound candied citron

1 pound shelled pecans

To make:

Cut fruits and nuts desired size. Using ½ cup flour, flour fruit and nuts.

Make batter by:

Creaming butter and sugar thoroughly. Add 3 eggs, one at a time. Sift salt, baking powder, and flour together. Add sifted mixture alternately with remaining three eggs. Add vanilla and almond extracts. Add fruit and nuts and mix thoroughly.

Place in paper lined tins and bake for 1 hour at 250 degrees. Then place a pan of water on the rack under the cake rack and steam in oven for one hour. Remove water and continue baking for one hour. Makes 6 pounds.

Mrs. H. F. Rush, Richland County.

White Fruit Cake

10 egg whites or 5 whole eggs
4 cups flour
1½ cups sugar
1 cup shortening (butter or lard)
2 teaspoons baking powder
1 cup white grape juice or wine
1 pound candied pineapple
1 pound candied cherries
½ pound citron
¼ pound each lemon and orange peel
1 pound white raisins
1 pound pecans
1 apple
1 teaspoon cinnamon
1 teaspoon cloves
¼ teaspoon salt
½ teaspoon soda

Prepare all fruits, peel nuts and citron, cutting into desired pieces with scissors. Flour, with 1 cup of flour reserved for this purpose. Add baking powder, soda, salt, cinnamon, cloves and sugar to 3 cups of flour and sift 3 times. Add this mixture to shortening and cream. Add wine and eggs and flour, mixing thoroughly (if only whites are used, the yolks of eggs are left until last). Add all ingredients, one at a time, mixing well. Add stiffly beaten egg whites. This makes 6 pounds. Bake in 275-degree oven 3 hours or until done.

Mrs. C. C. Sisk, McCormick County.

Ice Box Fruit Cake

1 box raisins
1 box currants
1 package figs
1½ large boxes marshmallows
¼ pound citron
½ pound cherries
1½ boxes graham crackers, crumbled
1 large can evaporated milk
1 cup nuts
½ pound pineapple

Heat milk, drop marshmallows in slowly until dissolved. Remove from heat, add all ingredients and work well together. Pour in pan, pack light. Set in ice box, do not cook.

MRS. ELLIOTT BERRY, Spartanburg County.

Fruit Cake—(for pressure cooker)

1 pound butter	¼ cup milk
1 pound light brown sugar	1 pound currants
9 eggs	1 pound seedless raisins
1 pound flour	1 pound almonds or pecans
¾ teaspoon cloves	½ pound citron
¾ teaspoon nutmeg	½ pound candied orange peel
¾ teaspoon mace	1 pound candied cherries
2 teaspoons cinnamon	1 pound candied pineapple
1 teaspoon soda	½ teaspoon salt

Wash raisins and currants. Blanch and shred almonds and brown in moderate oven. Cream butter and sugar, add beaten egg yolks. Beat egg whites stiff, and fold in. Cut fruit in pieces and dredge in half of the flour. Sift together the remaining flour, soda, spices and salt. Add milk and sifted dry ingredients alternately to cake batter. Add nuts and fruit and mix thoroughly. Line pans with waxed paper and fill with fruit cake batter. Tie three thicknesses of waxed paper over the pans to keep out moisture. Put 2½ cups of water in bottom of cooker. Put pans of fruit cake, one above the other on the rack. Cook 45 minutes at 10 pounds pressure and 30 minutes at 15 pounds pressure. When done place cake in slow oven for 12 minutes or longer to dry.

MINNIE TALBERT, McCormick County.

Old Fashioned Dark Fruit Cake

12 eggs	rind preserves
1 pound sugar	½ pound candied orange peel
1 pound butter	1 pound pineapple
1 pound flour	1 pound cherries
2 pounds raisins	2 cups nuts
1 pound currants	1 glass apple or grape jelly
1 package dates	1 cup wine or brandy
1 package figs	2 teaspoons baking powder
pinch of salt	spices to suit taste
½ pound citron or watermelon	vanilla flavoring

Cream sugar and butter, add the well-beaten yolks. Sift flour three times, adding baking powder and salt. Divide the flour, using half with spices (should be added a small amount at a time), next add wine, and the stiffly beaten whites, the remaining flour should be sifted over fruit and added last. Steam ¾ hour using tube pans for best results. Brown in oven ½ hour at 350 degrees.

MRS. J. S. J. SUBER, Newberry County.

NUT AND RAISIN CAKES

Raisin Pecan Ice Box Cake

1 cup milk
1 pound marshmallows

1 box seedless raisins
1 pound graham crackers

4 cups coarsely chopped pecans

Heat milk, then melt marshmallows in milk. Add raisins. Grind crackers to a fine texture and add to mixture. Add pecans. Stir well. Press into loaf pan and chill several hours and slice.

MRS. ANDREW GOODALE, Kershaw County.

Raisin Cake

1½ cups raisins
1 pint water
¾ cup plus 2 tablespoons sugar
¼ cup butter
½ cup black walnut meats
½ cup pecans
1 small bottle cherries (red)
1 egg

1½ cups flour (sifted)
1 teaspoon cinnamon
1 teaspoon nutmeg and cloves
(each)
½ cup juice from cooked
raisins
1 teaspoon soda
½ teaspoon salt

Boil the raisins 20 minutes in the pint of water with 2 tablespoons sugar. Let cool and drain off ½ cup juice to be used in the cake. Cream butter and sugar together. Add egg and beat well. Dissolve soda in the ½ cup of raisin juice and add to mixture. Sift salt and spices with flour and add the nut meats. Add gradually to cake mixture and lastly the drained raisins and cherries. Beat well and bake in greased lined tube pan in preheated 350-degree oven for 45 minutes.

MRS. DAN RUFF, Fairfield County.

Raisin Nut Cake

½ pound butter
2 cups sugar
6 eggs beaten light
1 cup whiskey
1 pound pecans chopped

2 pounds seedless white raisins
3 cups flour
2 teaspoons nutmeg
1 teaspoon soda dissolved in
½ cup molasses

Mix raisins and nuts in flour sifted with nutmeg. Cream butter and sugar. Add eggs, then whiskey, then flour mixture. Lastly, soda and molasses. Bake in pans lined with brown paper, greased well. 275 degrees for 2½ hours in two pans.

MRS. ALFRED C. MARANE, McCormick County.

Date Nut Cake

1 pound seeded dates
1 pound pecan halves (4 cups)
1 cup sugar

1 cup flour
1 teaspoon baking powder
4 eggs, well beaten

Cut dates into thirds and dredge in flour (extra). Mix evenly with pecan halves. Beat eggs, add sugar and beat longer. Add 1 cup flour which has been sifted with baking powder. Mix batter thoroughly with dates and nuts. Press down in greased papered loaf or tube pan and bake in very slow oven 275 degrees 2½ to 3 hours. Take one cup sugar, one cup orange juice, grated rind of one orange and heat until sugar dissolves. Then while cake is still warm, cover with above liquid. Eat while fresh. Does not keep well.

MRS. F. W. FACEY, McCormick County.

JAPANESE FRUIT CAKES

Japanese Fruit Cake

8 egg whites
2 cups sugar
1 cup butter

4 cups flour
½ cup milk
2 teaspoons baking powder

Cream butter, sugar, add flour (sifted with baking powder) and milk gradually, then fold in egg whites beaten stiff. Bake 3 layers, then add to remaining batter:

1 cup chopped raisins
1 cup chopped cherries
1 cup pecans
Bake two layers.

1 teaspoon spice
1 teaspoon cinnamon
1 teaspoon cloves, a little nutmeg

FILLING

2 cups sugar	1 can pineapple (No. 2 can
1 cup boiling water	crushed)
3 tablespoons cornstarch	juice and rinds of two lemons

2 cups coconut (fresh)

Cook until thick in double boiler.

Sprinkle cake with coconut.

MRS. ANNIE JOSEY, Lee County.

SPONGE CAKES

Sponge Cake

5 egg whites	5 egg yolks
¼ teaspoon cream of tartar	1 cup cake flour
½ teaspoon salt	½ teaspoon vanilla
1 cup sugar	½ teaspoon lemon

Beat egg whites until stiff but not dry. Add cream of tartar and salt. Beat until it stands in a peak. Add sugar gradually. Beat egg yolks until lemon color, cut and fold the two mixtures together with a spoon. Fold in flour with a spoon. Add extract. Put in a tube pan. Bake 325 degrees in a preheated oven for 40 to 45 minutes.

MISS VIRGINIA BUSSEY, McCormick County.

Four-Egg Sponge Cake

4 eggs	1 cup hot milk
2 cups sugar	2 cups cake flour
1 tablespoon lemon juice	2 teaspoons baking powder

½ teaspoon salt

Separate eggs and beat whites. Add ½ cup sugar; combine lemon juice and beaten egg yolks. Add remaining sugar to this mixture, also heated milk. Beat until foamy and add dry ingredients and beaten egg whites. Bake 50 minutes at 350 degrees.

MRS. W. A. HAMBRIGHT, Cherokee County.

Croton Sponge Cake

½ pound butter	1 pound sugar
6 eggs	1 teaspoon baking powder
1 pound flour	(rounded)

1 cup milk

Cream butter, add sugar, eggs (well beaten), milk and flour, sifted twice with baking powder. Start baking at 275 degrees, raise to 300 degrees, then to 350 degrees. Bake about 1 hour.

MISS KITTY GLENN, Fairfield County.

Sponge Cake

4 large or 5 small eggs
1 cup granulated sugar
1 cup flour measured after
  sifting once

juice of 1 lemon
1 teaspoon cream of tartar
⅛ teaspoon salt
grated rind of ½ lemon

Separate eggs. Beat yolks until light and creamy, add lemon juice and rind, beating well. Add sugar gradually, beating continuously. Beat egg whites until foamy, add salt and cream of tartar. Whip until stiff but not too dry. Fold whites gently into yolk and sugar mixture until completely blended. Sift flour over egg mixture and fold in. Bake in pan 9 x 9 x 2 inches, 50 minutes at 325 degrees. Makes 16 small squares.

EFFIE ALMEIDA, Charleston County.

Angel Food Cake

12 or 13 egg whites
1½ cups sugar
  (fine granulated)
1 cup plain flour

1 heaping teaspoonful cream
  of tartar
1 teaspoonful vanilla or
  almond extract

Beat whites until foamy and then add cream of tartar. Beat whites until very stiff, then add sugar, 3 tablespoonsful at a time, beating constantly; add flavoring and beat well. Fold in flour gradually and beat in well, but not long. Pour into ungreased pan and bake in quick oven. When done will rise to top of pan and fall slightly. Take up and cool on top of another pan.

MRS. ANSEL PRICE, Charleston County.

Angel Cake

1 cup egg whites
1 teaspoon cream of tartar
¼ teaspoon salt
1¼ cups sugar

½ teaspoon vanilla
½ teaspoon almond extract
1 cup sifted cake or
  pastry flour

Beat egg whites until frothy. Add cream of tartar and salt and continue beating until stiff. Add sugar, about 2 tablespoons at a time.

folding into whites and repeating until all sugar is added. Add flavoring with last sugar. Sift flour four times, and only add 2 tablespoons at a time folding into first mixture in same manner as sugar. Turn into an ungreased tube pan and bake in slow oven 325 degrees about one hour. Invert pan on wire rack and leave until cake is cold.

MRS. MONROE SANDERS, Cherokee County.

LEMON CAKES

Lemon Cake

2 cups sugar	3 cups flour
1 cup butter or shortening	1 teaspoon vanilla
6 eggs	1 teaspoon baking powder
1 cup milk	¼ teaspoon salt

Sift flour, baking powder, and salt together. Cream shortening, add sugar and cream until fluffy. Add eggs, then dry ingredients alternately with milk and vanilla, a small amount at a time. Beat after each addition. Pour into greased pans and bake in a moderate oven 350 degrees until done.

FILLING

grated rind and juice of 2 lemons	1 cup sugar
yolks of 3 eggs	½ cup hot water
2 tablespoons butter	1 tablespoon cornstarch

Mix together rind and juice of lemons, egg yolks, butter and sugar and after they have been mixed well add the ½ cup of hot water. Cook until thick and then add one tablespoon cornstarch that has been mixed smooth in a small amount of cold water. Cook until thick enough to spread on cake.

MRS. T. D. MOORE, Fairfield County.

Lemon Ice Box Cake

2 eggs	graham cracker crumbs
1 can evaporated milk	1 cup sugar
juice of 2 lemons	

Beat eggs, add sugar. Heat to just below boiling point. Chill milk, whip. Add lemon juice to eggs and sugar. When cool, mix all together and heat thoroughly. Line tray with cracker crumbs and pour mixture and freeze. Needs no stirring.

MRS. W. B. SHEALY, Newberry County.

Lightning Cake

½ cup butter	2 teaspoons baking powder
½ cup granulated sugar	1 cup sifted cake flour
4 eggs	5 tablespoons milk
½ teaspoon salt	1 teaspoon vanilla extract

Let shortening stand at room temperature until rather soft. Cream it in large bowl and beat a minute longer. Add egg yolks and beat 1 minute and add sifted dry ingredients alternately with milk to which vanilla has been added ½ of each at a time as quickly as possible. Pour into two greased layer-cake pans. Put meringue on top and bake in a slow oven, 325 degrees for 40 minutes. For meringue beat egg whites in small bowl of mixmaster with salt and baking powder until almost stiff using No. 7 or No. 8 speed. Add sugar gradually, using same speed until sugar is thoroughly combined with egg whites. Spread on top of lightning cake batter and sprinkle with nuts.

CUSTARD FILLING FOR LIGHTNING CAKE

2 tablespoons flour	1 cup scalded milk
3 tablespoons granulated sugar	2 egg yolks beaten
⅛ teaspoon salt	1 teaspoon vanilla

Combine flour, sugar and salt in top of double boiler. Add the milk gradually beating at No. 3 speed. Continue beating at same speed until smooth and thick then cook about 10 minutes. Pour slowly over the beaten egg yolks. Return to double boiler and cook for 2 minutes. Cool and add flavoring, and spread between layers of lightning cake, meringue side up. Two bananas cut in slices may be placed on top of custard.

MRS. BURNIE WHITE, Marion County.

Chris Lemon Cheese Cake

Have on hand the following items:

3 cups flour	7 eggs
1 teaspoon salt	4 cups sugar
3 teaspoons double acting	1 cup milk
baking powder	4 lemons
½ cup butter	2 tablespoons cornstarch

10 tablespoons water

Time—35 minutes—350 degrees.

STEP 1

3 cups sifted cake flour   3 teaspoons baking powder
1 teaspoon salt

Measure level, and sift together three times. Set aside.

STEP 2

½ cup butter or equivalent   1 1/3 cups sugar

Cream butter, add sugar gradually, creaming after each addition.

STEP 3

1 cup milk   1 lemon

Add ingredients from step 1 to step 2 alternately with step 3 beating after each addition until smooth.

STEP 4

5 egg whites   ½ cup sugar

Beat egg whites until foamy, then add sugar gradually, beating until whites stand in peaks. Add to batter folding in until smooth. Cook in 3 9-inch cake tins at 350 degrees for 35 minutes or until done. Cool.

FILLING

5 egg yolks   1 cup sugar
2 tablespoons cornstarch   5 tablespoons water
1 lemon, juice and rind

Mix cornstarch and sugar. Add water and beaten egg yolks and lemon. Cook, stirring in double boiler until thickened enough to spread. Spread between cake layers. Cover top and sides with lemon frosting.

LEMON FROSTING

2 egg whites   5 tablespoons water
1½ cups sugar   1 lemon, rind and juice

Combine whites, sugar and water in top of double boiler beating with rotary beater until thoroughly mixed. Place over rapidly boiling water. Continue to beat until thickened. Add lemon and continue beating until frosting stands in peaks. Remove—whip and cool to right consistency. Cover top and sides of cake.

MRS. ROBBIE BARNES, Hampton County.

Pecan Cake

1 pound flour	1 teaspoon nutmeg
6 eggs	1 cup wine or fruit juice
1 pound brown sugar	2 pounds seeded raisins
¾ pound butter	2 pounds (8 cups) pecans
2 teaspoons baking powder	1 grated orange peel
(sifted with flour)	1 cup sorghum

Cream butter and sugar and add sorghum. Add eggs one at a time, and beat vigorously one minute to each egg. Add fruit juice alternately with flour. Stir in orange peel, nutmeg and lastly add floured raisins and nuts. Bake at 325 degrees for 3 hours. This makes a large cake and is a delicious substitute for fruit cake.

MRS. G. E. LANGLEY, McCormick County.

Pineapple Cake

1 cup butter	3 cups flour
2 cups sugar	3 teaspoons baking powder
4 eggs	1 cup sweet milk
1 teaspoon flavoring	¼ teaspoon salt

Cream butter until soft. Add sugar and flavoring, stirring until mixture is light and fluffy. Add eggs, one at a time and beat well. Add flour which has been sifted with salt and baking powder and milk alternately. Add flour first and last to mixture. Bake in layers at 350 degrees.

PINEAPPLE FILLING

2 cups sugar	1 large can crushed pineapple
2 tablespoons butter	

Mix sugar and pineapple in saucepan. Cook over a low heat and stir regularly until sugar is dissolved. Then add butter and cook over moderate heat until right consistency. When cool, spread between layers. Ice top and sides with seven-minute icing or boiled icing.

MRS. WILLIE JOE RIDDLEHOOVER, McCormick County.

Never Fail Cake Recipe

1 cup sugar	½ cup butter
½ cup milk	1½ cups flour
1 teaspoon vanilla	2 eggs
2 teaspoons baking powder	

Cream butter, add sugar and mix well. Add beaten eggs and vanilla. Add milk, flour, and baking powder. Beat until smooth. Bake in moderate oven until done. Spread with favorite icing.

MRS. ROY HOUGH, Lancaster County.

Spice Cake

2 cups brown sugar
2 cups hot water
¾ cup butter

1 teaspoon cinnamon
1 teaspoon spice
1 teaspoon nutmeg

1 package seeded raisins

Mix all and boil 5 minutes. When cold, add 4 cups flour, 2 level teaspoons of soda dissolved in 4 tablespoons warm water. Beat hard and cook in layers.

FILLING FOR SPICE CAKE

2 cups brown sugar
1 cup white sugar

1 cup butter
¾ cup sweet milk

1 teaspoon vanilla

Burnt Sugar Cake With Caramel Frosting

½ cup sugar
½ cup boiling water
2/3 cup butter
1 cup sugar
1 teaspoon vanilla
2 eggs, separated

3 cups sifted cake flour
3 teaspoons double-acting
    baking powder
1 teaspoon salt
1 cup milk
pecan halves

All ingredients should be at room temperature. Heat ½ cup sugar slowly in small saucepan or skillet, stirring constantly. When sugar is melted and begins to smoke, add boiling water slowly and carefully, stirring constantly. Cook until sugar is dissolved. Set aside to cool. Meanwhile, cream butter well; add 1 cup sugar gradually, beating until light and fluffy. Add vanilla, then egg yolks one at a time, beating vigorously after each addition. Stir in cold caramel syrup. Add sifted dry ingredients alternately with milk, beating until smooth. Beat egg whites until stiff but not dry. Fold into flour mixture. Pour batter into three 9-inch pans, greased and floured. Bake in moderate oven, 375 degrees for about 20 minutes. Let stand for 5 minutes; turn out on racks to cool. Spread caramel frosting between layers and on top and sides of cake. Garnish with pecan halves.

CARAMEL FROSTING

2 tablespoons butter or margarine	1/3 cup heavy cream
2/3 cup brown sugar, firmly packed	⅛ teaspoon salt
	sifted confectioner's sugar (about 3 cups)

few drops vanilla

Mix butter, cream, brown sugar, and salt in saucepan. Bring to boil, stirring constantly. Remove from heat; add vanilla. Then add gradually enough sifted confectioner's sugar to make frosting of spreading consistency.

MRS. SAM YOUNGBLOOD.

UPSIDE DOWN CAKES

Pineapple Upside Down Cake

2/3 cup dark brown sugar	No. 2 can sliced pineapple
3 tablespoons butter	½ cup nuts

Drain pineapple. Melt butter in cake pan. Add brown sugar, blend and spread over bottom of pan. Arrange pineapple slices on sugar, add nuts in and between pineapple slices.

½ cup sugar	1 teaspoon salt
¼ cup shortening	2½ teaspoons baking powder
1 egg (well beaten)	1/3 cup milk
1½ cups cake flour	1 teaspoon vanilla

Cream shortening and sugar; add well-beaten egg. Sift dry ingredients, and add alternating with milk. Add vanilla. Pour batter over pineapple. Bake in moderate oven 350 degrees 35 minutes. Let cool slightly, then turn out on cake plate. Slice and serve plain or with whipped cream.

ANN HESTER, Pickens County.

Upside Down Cake

First Mixture:

3 tablespoons butter	1 cup diced pineapple
1 cup brown sugar	1 cup dates
1 cup nuts	1 cup cherries

Melt butter and blend well with brown sugar. Add nuts and fruit. Spread evenly in bottom of cake pan or iron skillet.

Second Mixture:

1 cup sugar	2 eggs
2 cups self-rising flour	¾ cup milk

½ cup butter

Make batter of second mixture and pour over fruit. Bake 25 minutes in oven at 350 degrees. Serve with whipped cream.

CUP CAKES

Apple Cup Cakes

½ cup butter or margarine	1 egg
1 cup sugar	1 cup fresh-chopped apples
½ cup raisins	½ cup nuts
½ teaspoon salt	½ teaspoon nutmeg
1 teaspoon soda	½ teaspoon cloves
½ cup cold coffee	1½ cups flour

Cream butter and sugar, add egg and mix well. Add other ingredients in order given and beat lightly. Bake in muffin tins 350 degrees for 25 to 30 minutes. These may be frosted or served warm with lemon sauce.

MRS. G. R. CHAPMAN, Kershaw County.

Cup Cakes

½ cup shortening	2 teaspoons baking powder
1 cup sugar	½ teaspoon salt
3 eggs	½ cup milk
1¾ cups flour	1 teaspoon vanilla

Cream shortening, sugar and eggs together until light and fluffy. Sift flour, baking powder and salt and add alternately with milk to creamed mixture. Add vanilla. Beat thoroughly. Turn into greased cup cake pans. Bake in moderately hot oven, 375 degrees, 15 to 20 minutes. Yield: 18 cup cakes.

ORANGE CUP CAKE SAUCE
(Prepare before making cup cakes)

Grate one orange rind. Add 1 cup sugar. Add juice of two oranges and mix well. Serve on cakes.

BETTY BIGGS, Jasper County.

Orange Cup Cakes

½ cup butter
1 cup sugar
2 eggs

½ cup milk
1½ cups flour
2 teaspoons baking powder

½ teaspoon vanilla

Cream butter and sugar. Add eggs well beaten, then milk and flour sifted with baking powder. Add vanilla. Bake in muffin tins. Make an orange sauce of juice and rind of 2 oranges and 1 cup of sugar. When done, remove from oven and immediately pour 1 tablespoon of orange sauce over each cake before removing from muffin tin and while still hot. As soon as sauce has soaked into the cakes, remove from muffin tin. These cakes are easy to make and are good served hot or cold. Yield 3 dozen.

Mrs. I. M. Smith, Jr., Newberry County.

One-Egg Cup Cakes

¼ cup of butter
1 cup sweet milk
2 cups flour

1 cup sugar
1 egg
2 teaspoons baking powder

1 teaspoon vanilla

Cream butter and sugar, add egg, then milk and flour alternately. Bake in greased muffin tins until a mild brown, in moderate oven. Serve plain or cover with your favorite frosting. Makes about 20 average size cup cakes.

Mrs. Clair Workman, Newberry County.

MISCELLANEOUS RECIPES

Short'nin' Bread

4 cups flour   1 pound butter
1 cup light brown sugar

Mix flour and sugar. Add butter. Place on floured surface and pat to ½-inch thickness. Cut into desired shapes and bake in moderate oven (325 to 350 degrees) for 25 or 30 minutes.

Mrs. David Ergle, Aiken County.

Scotch Shortbread

This sweet shortcake is delicious served with wine during the holidays and equally good with fruit or ice cream.

1 cup shortening   1¾ cups sugar
4 cups flour

Cream shortening, blend in sugar. Gradually work in flour with fingers or pastry blender. Turn on slightly floured board and knead until smooth. Pat or roll ½ inch thick. Shape and flute edges and prick all over with fork. Place on greased baking sheet and bake at 350 degrees for 15 minutes or until light brown.

MARGARET McKENZIE, Sumter County.

Sunshine Cake

2 cups cake flour   1 cup sugar
1 teaspoon soda   2 eggs
⅛ teaspoon salt   grated rind of 1 orange
½ cup butter or shortening   2/3 cup buttermilk or sour milk
1 teaspoon vanilla

Sift, then measure the flour. Sift three times with baking soda and salt. Cream butter until light and lemon colored. Gradually add the sugar, beating after each addition. Add grated orange rind, beaten egg yolks and vanilla. Blend well. Add sifted dry ingredients alternately with buttermilk or sour milk. Fold in beaten egg whites. Turn into greased, paper lined pan 10 inches by 10 inches. Bake at 350 degrees 45 minutes. When cool, frost with orange coconut frosting. Will yield 25 two inch blocks.

LIZZIE USHER, Dillon County.

Old Fashioned Johnnie Cake

1 cup sugar   1 teaspoon vanilla
1 egg   1 teaspoon baking powder
¾ cup butter   flour to stiffen
1/3 cup milk

Beat egg. Cream sugar and butter. Add egg and milk to butter and sugar mixture. Add enough flour to make stiff dough. Roll thin. Cut and bake as for biscuits.

MRS. THOMAS KEY COLLIER.

Jelly Cake

1 block butter	4 eggs
2 cups sugar	1 cup milk
3 cups sifted all purpose flour	2 glasses jelly

1 tablespoon vanilla

Cream butter and sugar; gradually add one egg at a time until thoroughly blended. Add one cup of sifted flour at a time and beat at least 2 minutes adding milk as needed. Add flavoring and beat 2 minutes more. Prepare cake pans as follows; grease pans with some good shortening on a small piece of waxed paper, then dust each pan with flour. This will keep layers from sticking. Dip four generous tablespoons of batter to each pan. Turn pan around in hand until batter covers the pan smoothly. Then bake in oven 375 degrees for 20 minutes. Take out, let cool on rack one minute. Then turn on a large sheet of waxed paper and spread generously each layer with jelly. There will be either 6 or 7 layers. This cake needs no icing.

MRS. RUBY C. BULTMAN, Beaufort County.

Gingerbread

½ cup sugar	1½ teaspoons soda
½ cup butter and lard mixed	1 teaspoon cinnamon
1 egg	1 teaspoon ginger
1 cup molasses	½ teaspoon cloves
2½ cups sifted flour	¾ teaspoon salt

1 cup hot water

Cream shortening and sugar, add beaten egg, molasses, then dry ingredients which have been sifted together. Add hot water last and beat until smooth. The batter is soft but it makes a fine cake. Bake in greased shallow pan 35 minutes in moderate oven 325 to 350 degrees. Makes 15 generous portions. Serve with whipped cream.

MRS. HOWARD LOCKE, Anderson County.

Old Fashioned Gingerbread

2 eggs	1 cup shortening
1 cup brown sugar	1 teaspoon baking soda
1 cup molasses	2 tablespoons ginger (ground)
2 cups flour (plain)	2 teaspoons cinnamon
1 cup milk	¾ teaspoons salt

Place all dry ingredients with shortening into large mixing bowl. Add milk and beat until smooth. Pour batter into deep baking tin, at least 4" x 10" or similar, bake in 350-degree oven for 30 minutes, reduce to 250 degrees and bake 10 or 15 minutes. Serve hot with butter sauce, lemon sauce or plain.

MRS. W. L. CURRIE, Sumter County.

Rum Cakes

2 eggs	1 teaspoon baking powder
1 cup sugar	⅛ teaspoon salt
1 cup flour	1 tablespoon butter

½ cup hot milk

Beat eggs and sugar very light. Fold in flour, baking powder, and salt. Melt butter in hot milk and fold quickly into mixture, beating as little as possible. Put in greased muffin tins and bake 20 minutes at 375 degrees.   Makes about 20.

RUM SAUCE

1 cup brown sugar	1 cup water
1 cup white sugar	1½ tablespoons butter

⅜ cup rum

Boil sugar, water and butter 5 minutes. When cool add rum. Spoon over cakes often.

MRS. D. G. F. BULTMAN, Sumter County.

Whipped Cream Cake

1 cup thick cream	1 teaspoon vanilla extract
2 eggs	1¾ cups cake flour
1 cup sugar	2½ teaspoons baking powder

¼ teaspoon salt

Whip cream until thick; add egg yolks and continue to beat until foamy. Add sugar gradually, add vanilla extract, beat well. Sift together flour, baking powder, and salt. Add alternately with stiffly beaten egg whites to first mixture. Bake in 10 by 10 inch loaf pan lined with oil paper in a moderate oven, 350 degrees, for about 1 hour. When cold, cover with butter cream icing. Cut into blocks and serve. Will make 25 two-inch blocks.

BUTTER CREAM ICING

½ cup butter	4 tablespoons cream
3 cups confectioner's sugar sifted	1 teaspoon vanilla

Cream butter. Add remaining ingredients and continue creaming until mixture is well blended and fluffy. Will cover tops and sides of two 8-inch layers.

LIZZIE USHER, Dillon County.

Snowflake Squares

1/3 cup shortening	¼ teaspoon salt
1 cup very fine sugar	½ cup milk
1 1/3 cups sifted cake flour	½ teaspoon almond extract
1½ teaspoons baking powder	3 egg whites

Cream shortening; add sugar slowly while creaming. Mix and sift flour, baking powder and salt. Combine milk and almond extract. Add flour and milk alternately to cream mixture. Beat egg whites stiff but not dry; fold in. Pour into 10-inch square shallow cake pan. Bake in moderate oven, 375 degrees, for 30 minutes. Cool, frost as desired. Cut into 9 squares.

MRS. CLAUDE PRICE, Newberry County.

Tea Cakes

3 eggs	1 cup ground pecans
7 tablespoons sugar	¼ cup lard or butter
Self-rising flour	1 teaspoon vanilla

Mix eggs, sugar and flavoring; add enough flour mixed with lard to form dough stiff enough to roll. Add pecans to dough. Sprinkle sugar over dough and cut with cooky cutter. Bake in moderate oven till brown.

MRS. HENRY P. NEWTON, Marlboro County.

Fruit Bars

1 15-ounce can condensed milk	1 cup broken pecans
1 pound chopped pitted dates	½ pound package coconut
1 teaspoon vanilla	

Combine all ingredients to make stiff paste. Line the bottom of large square cake pan with two layers of greased waxed paper and cook in moderate oven until golden brown. When cool, cut in squares.

MRS. C. C. WALLACE, Newberry County.

Praline Torte

6 eggs
Rind and juice of 1 lemon
1 cup sugar

16 lady fingers
1 cup finely chopped almonds
and pecans

6 eggs, beaten separately, very light

Add 1 cup sugar, 1 cup nuts, rind and juice of 1 lemon, and 16 lady fingers dried and rolled. Add egg whites last. Bake in 2 layers. Beat 1 pint cream until stiff. Flavor with sugar and vanilla and ice cake.

MRS. D. G. F. BULTMAN, Sumter County.

Blackberry Jam Cake

1 cup sugar
3 whole eggs
1 cup thick jam
1 teaspoon nutmeg
3 cups flour (all purpose)

2 teaspoons baking powder
¾ cup butter
1 cup sour milk
1 teaspoon soda
1 teaspoon cinnamon

1 teaspoon allspice

Cream butter, sugar together. Break eggs into this and beat again. Sift dry ingredients together three times, and add alternately with sour milk and last fold in jam. Pour into well greased pan. Bake in moderate oven about 45 minutes or until done in a 350-degree oven. Makes one large cake.

G. M. BARNETT, SR., Oconee County.

Jam Cake

6 eggs
½ pound butter
4 cups flour
2 teaspoons cinnamon

2 teaspoons cloves
½ cup sour milk
½ teaspoon soda
1 pint blackberry jam

½ cup sugar

Mix all ingredients together thoroughly as for any cake and bake in slow oven.

MRS. J. L. HIGGINS, Anderson County.

Ice Box Cake

1 pound graham crackers
1 pound marshmallows
1 cup milk

1 pound seedless raisins
3 cups chopped nuts
1 teaspoon allspice

1 teaspoon cinnamon

Roll graham crackers. Heat marshmallows in milk until creamy. Combine with graham crackers. Add raisins, chopped nuts and spices and mix thoroughly. Mold in desired vessel. Garnish with additional nuts and cherries. Chill in refrigerator about 24 hours.

MRS. EARL BERRY, Marion County.

Apple Sauce Cake

½ cup butter	1 cup sugar
1 egg	1 cup apple sauce, unsweetened
2 cups cake flour, sifted	½ teaspoon salt
½ teaspoon baking powder	1 teaspoon soda
½ teaspoon cloves	1 tablespoon each cinnamon and
1 cup raisins	allspice

¼ cup chopped nut meats

Cream the butter; add sugar, beat until light. Add egg and beat until fluffy; pour in the apple sauce and mix. Sift flour, salt, baking powder, soda, cloves, cinnamon and allspice together and add the chopped raisins and nuts. Combine the two mixtures. Pour into pans lined with greased waxed paper. Bake in a moderate oven, 325 to 375 degrees, for 25 to 45 minutes. This recipe fits an 8 x 8 x 2-inch square pan or a standard loaf pan.

MRS. E. M. JONES, Marion County.

Moravian Sugar Cake

1 cup hot mashed white potatoes	1 teaspoon salt
1 cup granulated sugar	2 eggs
1 yeast cake	4 cups flour (or enough to make
½ cup shortening—4 tablespoons	soft dough)
butter	

TOPPING FOR CAKE

2 cups brown sugar	4 to 6 tablespoons butter

cinnamon

Add sugar, butter, salt and shortening to hot potatoes. Dissolve yeast in ½ cup lukewarm water, then add to potato mixture and let rise until spongy. Add slightly beaten eggs and flour. Allow to rise about 5 hours or over night. Spread out on flat greased pan after kneading lightly. When light spread with brown sugar. Sprinkle liberally with cinnamon. Bake at 375 degrees for 20 minutes until golden brown.

MRS. W. M. PATRICK, Fairfield County.

Pineapple Refrigerator Cake

2 cups sifted flour
1¼ cups sugar
3½ teaspoons baking powder
1 teaspoon salt
1 teaspoon grated lemon rind

½ cup shortening
1 cup less 2 tablespoons canned
    pineapple juice
1 teaspoon vanilla
3 egg whites, unbeaten

Sift flour, sugar, baking powder and salt into mixing bowl. Add lemon rind. Drop in shortening. Add pineapple juice and beat 2 minutes. Add egg whites and beat 2 minutes. Bake in two square 8 x 8 x 2 inch greased pans in moderate oven, 360 degrees, for 25–30 minutes. Chill layers and split in half. Beat one cup heavy cream and sweeten with ¼ cup sugar. Spread layers of pineapple filling and whipped cream between layers and cover top with whipped cream. Store cake in refrigerator several hours before serving and keep refrigerated until all is served. Cut in slices about 1 inch thick. Serves about 16.

PINEAPPLE FILLING

Mix ¾ cup sugar, 2½ tablespoons cornstarch and ⅛ teaspoon salt thoroughly in top of double boiler. Add ¼ cup lemon juice and grated rind of 1 lemon and mix well. Add 3 egg yolks, beaten slightly, 1/3 cup canned pineapple juice and 2 tablespoons butter and blend. Place over boiling water and cook until smooth and thick, stirring constantly (about 15 minutes). Cool.

JULIENNE OXNER, Saluda County.

Strawberry Ice Box Cake

1 pound vanilla wafers or
    sponge cake
¼ pound butter or margarine

1½ cups confectioner's sugar
2 eggs
1 quart strawberries cut in half
½ pint cream—whipped stiff

Crush wafers fine or crumble cake and put more than half on bottom of pan (8 x 12 x 2 inches). Cream butter or margarine and mix with sugar. Add one egg at a time and beat well. Spread over crumbs in pan, then cover with sliced strawberries. Spread whipped cream over berries. Cover with remaining crumbs. Place in refrigerator and let remain over night. Slice and serve with or without spoonful of whipped cream and strawberry on top.

MRS. A. M. HUDSON, Aiken County.

Raspberry Ice Box Cake

1½ cups canned raspberries with juice
1½ tablespoons gelatin
2 tablespoons cold water
1 tablespoon lemon juice
1 cup heavy cream
2 dozen lady fingers
pinch salt

Put raspberries through a sieve and heat to boiling point. Add gelatin softened in cold water, stir until gelatin is dissolved. Cool and when it begins to harden, fold in the whipped cream. Stand split lady fingers around edge and on bottom of mold. Fill with alternate layers of raspberries and lady fingers. Set in refrigerator over night. Garnish with whipped cream and serve cold. Serves 6–8.

MRS. J. M. McCABE, Calhoun County.

Pink Party Cake

2½ cups sifted cake flour
1½ cups sugar
3½ teaspoons baking powder
1 teaspoon salt
½ cup shortening or butter
¾ cup milk
¼ cup cherry juice
1 teaspoon vanilla
2 teaspoons almond extract
4 egg whites unbeaten
18 cherries, well drained and finely chopped

½ cup walnut meats, finely chopped

Sift flour, sugar, baking powder and salt into bowl. Drop in shortening or butter. No creaming needed. Combine milk and juice. Add ¾ cup of this liquid. Add flavoring extracts. Beat 200 strokes or 2 minutes. Add cherries and nuts and blend. Bake at 375°.

FROSTING

2 tablespoons shortening
1 teaspoon vanilla
½ teaspoon almond extract
1 teaspoon salt
4 cups sifted confectioner's sugar
9 tablespoons scalded cream

red coloring

Combine shortening, vanilla, almond extract, salt and blend. Beat in ½ cup sugar. Add hot cream, alternately with remaining sugar. Beat well after each addition. Add only enough cream to make a nice spreading consistency. Finally add a few drops of red coloring to tint frosting delicate pink.

MRS. DAVID JORDAN, Darlington County.

Strawberry Shortcake

1 quart strawberries	2 teaspoons baking powder
sugar	2 tablespoons sugar
2 cups sifted all purpose flour	6 tablespoons shortening
1 teaspoon salt	2/3 cup milk

Hull, wash and drain the strawberries; cut into halves and mix with sugar to taste. Mix the flour, baking powder, sugar and salt and sift three times. Cut in the shortening. Add the milk. Turn out on a lightly floured board. Pat to uniform thickness in 2 8″ layer cake pans. Bake in a hot oven 450 degrees 15 or 20 minutes. Butter layers while hot. Spread the sweetened berries between the layers and over the top. Serve hot with whipped cream if desired.

MRS. M. G. HEMINGWAY, Clarendon County.

Strawberry Shortcake

2 cups sifted all purpose flour	¼ teaspoon salt
1 tablespoon baking powder	½ cup shortening
3 tablespoons sugar	½ cup milk
1 egg	butter
1 quart strawberries	whipped cream

While oven heats to 450 degrees, cut shortening into flour, sugar, baking powder, and salt mixture. Blend until slightly coarser than yellow cornmeal. Add slightly beaten egg and milk. Stir with fork until blended. Drop by tablespoonsful, two inches apart on cookie sheet. Makes 6 to 8. Bake 12 to 15 minutes. While cakes are hot, insert tines of fork around middle of each, lifting off top. Spread bottom half generously with butter, replace top. Place on dessert plate, remove top, put crushed berries on bottom half, replace top, put berries on top with "pour" or whipped cream.

MRS. BROOKIE A. ALLSBROOK, Horry County.

LOAF CAKES

Family's Favorite Plain Cake

2½ cups flour (plain)	1 cup butter
2 cups sugar	¾ cup milk
5 eggs	1 teaspoon vanilla or desired
1 teaspoon baking powder	flavoring

Cream butter and sugar thoroughly, add egg yolks one at a time, beating mixture all the while, add milk and flour alternately, beat egg whites till stiff, add to mixture, stir in lightly, pour in greased steeple or loaf pan and bake at 375 degrees one hour without opening oven.

MRS. STAFFORD ROGERS, Marion County.

Old Fashioned Plain Cake

Grease 5 x 10 tube pan and flour well. Set oven at 275 degrees. Sift flour before measuring. Measure accurately. Don't pack.

1 cup shortening	3 cups flour
2 cups sugar	3 teaspoons baking powder
6 eggs separated	½ teaspoon salt unless butter is
Flavor to taste	used for shortening

1 cup sweet milk

Cream shortening. Add the sugar gradually and mix until light and fluffy. Add egg yolks one at a time mixing well after each addition. Sift flour, measure, add baking powder and salt and sift again. Add flour a little at a time alternately with the milk. Commence and end with the flour. Add flavoring. Whip egg whites (4) until very stiff. Fold in the batter very gently. Pour in the greased and floured pan and bake at 275 degrees for one hour and 10 minutes. When removed from pan and cooled, ice with seven-minute icing made from the two whites saved out.

MRS. W. W. BEARDEN, Oconee County.

Silver and Gold Cakes

½ cup butter	⅛ teaspoon salt
1 cup sugar	½ teaspoon flavoring extract
1½ cups cake flour	4 egg whites (silver cake) or
1 teaspoon baking powder	4 egg yolks (gold cake)

½ cup milk

Cream the butter and sugar, mix the dry ingredients and add alternately with the milk. Last add the beaten yolks of the eggs if a gold cake is desired, or whip the whites stiff but not dry for the silver cake, and in the latter case, fold them in with a light hand. Bake in a loaf in a moderate oven 350 degrees for about 40 minutes. Half a teaspoon of almond for the white cake, and the same amount of orange, lemon, or vanilla for the gold cake. It is economical and handy to make the two cakes, using the separated whites and yolks.

No frosting is needed, but a plain boiled icing flavored with crushed fresh strawberries for the white cake and an orange frosting for the gold cake would be delicious.

MRS. A. B. ANDREWS, McCormick County.

Loaf or Layer

1¾ cups sugar
1 cup milk
3 teaspoons baking powder
2 teaspoons any extract

2/3 cup butter or other shortening
3 cups plain flour
7 egg whites

Cream the shortening, add sugar and cream together. Add dry ingredients which must be sifted 3 times. Add milk alternately. Fold egg whites which have been beaten to a stiff froth. Add extract. Use level measurements. If warm weather, chill shortening. Bake 45 minutes.

MRS. J. B. FOLK, Bamberg County.

INEXPENSIVE CAKES

One-Egg Cake

½ cup butter
1 cup sugar
1 egg

2 cups flour
1 cup sweet milk
2 teaspoons baking powder

Cream the butter and sugar; add egg and mix well. Then add milk and flour, sifted with baking powder. Add vanilla to suit taste. Bake in quick oven. This recipe is 60 years old.

MRS. SARAH D. DeLOACH, Laurens County.

Economy Cake

3 cups sifted plain flour
4 teaspoons baking powder
¼ teaspoon salt
½ cup softened shortening
(preferably butter)

1 2/3 cups sugar
3 eggs
1¼ cups milk
1 teaspoon vanilla or lemon
extract

Sift together flour, baking powder and salt. Cream shortening and sugar. Add eggs one at a time, beating after each addition. Add dry ingredients to creamed mixture alternately with the milk, using flour addition first and last. Can be baked in tube loaf pan one hour at

350 degrees or baked in layers at 350 degrees 25 to 30 minutes using any favorite filling.

Mrs. W. K. Nelson, Sr., Calhoun County.

Lazy Daisy Cake

Batter:

4 eggs	2 teaspoons baking powder
2 cups sugar	2 teaspoons vanilla
2 cups flour	Topping:
1 cup milk	6 tablespoons butter
3 heaping tablespoons butter	10 tablespoons light sugar
¼ teaspoon salt	5 tablespoons sweet milk

1 can coconut

Beat eggs until fluffy, add sugar gradually, then add flour. Beat well. Heat 1 cup milk and 3 tablespoons butter. Pour in small stream into cake mixture. Add vanilla. Bake in well greased and floured shallow pan, do not line with paper. Bake at 350 degrees for 30 or 35 minutes.

Add topping to cake while hot:

When cake is almost done bring mixture to boiling point but do not boil. Spread coconut on cake as soon as removed from oven. Then spoon hot mixture over coconut. Leave cake in pan, cutting and serving as needed.

Mrs. H. W. Rankin, Horry County.

ROLLED CAKES

Chocolate Roll

5 egg yolks	½ teaspoon salt
1½ cups confectioner's sugar	2 tablespoons cocoa
4 tablespoons flour	1 teaspoon vanilla extract

5 stiffly beaten egg whites

Beat egg yolks until thick and lemon colored, add sifted dry ingredients and beat until well blended. Fold in vanilla and egg white. Spread thinly in a greased 11 x 16 inch shallow pan lined with waxed paper. Bake in a moderately hot oven (400 degrees) from 15 to 20 minutes. Turn cake out on a damp towel. Remove paper, cut off crisp edges, roll up for 1 minute, unroll, cool and spread with sweetened whipped cream. Roll and ice with the following:

FROSTING FOR CHOCOLATE ROLL

1 cup confectioner's sugar	2 tablespoons butter
1½ squares unsweetened	½ tablespoon cream
chocolate	½ teaspoon vanilla

1/16 teaspoon salt

Melt butter and chocolate. Add sugar, salt and vanilla. Thin with cream until right consistency for spreading. After roll is iced, sprinkle it with crushed nut meats.

MRS. R. M. JENKINS, Lee County.

Jelly Roll

4 eggs, separated	¾ cup sifted flour
¼ cup sugar	¾ teaspoon baking powder
1 teaspoon vanilla	¼ teaspoon salt

Beat egg yolks until light. Add sugar gradually, then flavoring. When blended, add flour that has been sifted with baking powder and salt. Fold in egg whites that have been whipped until stiff, but not dry. Line a 15 x 10 inch pan with heavy buttered paper. Pour in batter and bake in moderate oven (375 degrees) for about 6 to 12 minutes. While cake is hot, trim hard edges. Spread cake with jelly, jam, or cake filling and roll it in waxed paper. Sprinkle with powdered sugar.

MRS. CONNOR POOLE, Aiken County.

Lemon Jelly Roll

4 eggs beaten until light   1 cup sugar

1 cup flour

JELLY

2 cups sugar	3 tablespoons flour
1 cup water	1 egg
1 lemon (juice and rind)	piece of butter

Beat eggs, add sugar and flour. Pour into buttered pan about 12 x 14 inches, which has been papered and cook about 10 minutes. Turn out on cloth, which has been sprinkled with sugar. Spread all the jelly over top and roll up immediately.

This recipe has been in the family of one of the members of Gaskin Club for many years, having been used by her mother and sisters.

Florence County.

Dried Apple Rolls

2 cans stewed apples
¼ cup white sugar

¼ pound butter
allspice and cinnamon

Use pie dough to make a roll 8 x 12. Spread apples mixed with sugar. Cut the butter over the apples, sprinkle with the spices, roll up and cut in 1½ inch lengths. Place in a buttered dish, cut end down, dot each roll with butter and sprinkle with brown sugar. Bake about 30 minutes. Add a few spoons of cream as the rolls come from the oven. Serve before they are real cold.

ANNIE MAE JOHNSTON, Newberry County.

ICINGS

Seven-Minute Frosting

1 egg white
⅞ cup granulated sugar

3 tablespoons cold water
½ teaspoon flavoring

Place the egg white, sugar and water in the top of double boiler. Place over bottom section of boiling water and beat with a rotary beater 7 minutes. Add flavoring during last 2 minutes of beating.

ALMA YOUNG, McCormick County.

Boiled Icing

2 cups sugar
pinch of salt

3 egg whites
8 tablespoons cold water

½ teaspoon cream of tartar

Bring sugar and water to a good boil, add gradually teaspoon at a time to the beaten egg whites. Keep sugar syrup boiling until all is used. Add cream of tartar and vanilla or almond; beat until very thick.

Charleston County.

Marshmallow Icing

2 2/3 cups sugar
½ cup white corn syrup
5 marshmallows

3 egg whites beaten stiff
2/3 cup water
1 teaspoon vanilla

Cook together sugar, water and corn syrup until it reaches 250 degrees to 275 degrees on a candy thermometer. Pour half of syrup mixture over egg whites and beat continuously. Add marshmallows to remaining half and stir until they have dissolved. Beat into other egg white mixture and mix well. Spread on cake. Note: this can be varied by adding pineapple, coconut, raisins, etc.

MRS. RALPH HAYES, Horry County.

Fancy Cake Frosting

2 cups sugar   1 cup water
⅛ teaspoon cream of tartar

Combine sugar, water and cream of tartar—stir only until the sugar is dissolved. Cook over direct heat to 226 degrees or a thin syrup. Remove from heat—pour into top of double boiler and cool to approximately 110 degrees. Add gradually 1-2 cups of confectioner's sugar until frosting is of consistency to pour. Add 2 teaspoons lemon juice or vanilla to flavor. Place a few cakes in rows on a wire rack over a cooky sheet, allowing considerable space between cakes. Pour frosting over cakes covering tops and sides, allowing frosting to drip onto cookie sheet. Scrape frosting from cookie sheet, reheat over boiling water and use for other cakes. Repeat the process until cakes are completely coated. Decorate with colored sugar, candied fruits, nuts or tinted confectioner's sugar icing.

MRS. W. H. IRBY, Kershaw County.

FILLINGS

Lady Baltimore Cake Filling

1 quart of pecans	1 package of raisins
1 grated coconut	2¼ cups sugar
4 tablespoons butter	3 tablespoons of flour
1½ cups of water and coconut milk	1 cup candied cherries

Grate coconut and cook in water until tender or done. Mix sugar and flour, put in cooked coconut. Let it cook slowly a few minutes then add pecans, raisins and butter. Then spread this between layers. The layers may be cooked as for any other cake. If layers are cooked in a long pan instead of a round pan, cake can be cut better.

MRS. HARRY W. HUGGINS, Williamsburg County.

Pineapple Filling

½ cup sifted flour (plain)
1 cup sugar
⅛ teaspoon salt
2 eggs

2 cups scalded milk
1 teaspoon vanilla or ½ teaspoon lemon
1 can No. 2 crushed pineapple

Mix dry ingredients, add eggs and milk. Stir until smooth. Cook in double boiler until thick, stirring constantly. When cool add flavoring. Spread this on each layer of cake then put pineapple on top of each layer as you stack. You can use 1, 2, 3, 4 cake recipe.

MRS. J. F. McKELLAR, McCormick County.

Lane Cake Filling

1 cup raisins
1 cup wine
6 egg yolks

1 cup nuts
1 cup sugar
butter size of walnut

Mix all together, cook up till thick. Remove from stove and beat till cool before spreading between layers.

MRS. A. B. ALLSBROOK, Horry County.

Lemon Cheese Filling

3 egg yolks
¾ cup sugar
⅛ teaspoon salt

2 teaspoons flour
1 cup water
juice and grated rind of one lemon

Mix flour, sugar and salt well, add water gradually, beat egg yolks and add the lemon juice and rind. Combine and cook over boiling water until as thick as you like it. This will ice a two-layer cake.

MRS. DAN WARREN, Allendale County.

Cream Filling

1 cup sugar
1/3 cup cornstarch
⅛ teaspoon salt

1 egg
2 cups scalded milk
1 teaspoon vanilla extract

Mix dry ingredients; add slightly beaten egg and stir into this gradually the scalded milk. Cook about 15 minutes in double boiler, stirring constantly until thickened. Cool slightly and flavor. Sweetened whipped cream may be used instead of this filling.

MRS. LEWIS DRIGGERS, Sumter County.

Lemon Filling

¾ package powdered XXXX
  sugar
2 tablespoons pure cream
2 tablespoons whole milk
2 tablespoons bottom milk

Let come to boil after mixing thoroughly. Grate rind of one lemon. Juice out of ½ lemon. Mix lemon and lemon juice with sugar, then stir into milk slowly. Add ½ teaspoon vanilla. Spread on cake.

MARIE SHARPTON, McCormick County

Lemon Filling for Cake

1 cup water
juice of 2 lemons
¼ cup cornstarch
2/3 cup sugar

Stir and cook until thick. Then add 2 well-beaten egg yolks to mixture. Also juice of 2 lemons and 1 teaspoon of grated rind. Add pinch of salt, and little butter. Will spread two layers.

MRS. LEE SHELLEY, Marion County.

Lemon Cheese Filling

This recipe was originally an old English one, brought over to America and guarded jealously by a few New England families. It was private property until recently.

Pour the juice of 6 lemons and the grated rind of 4 of them over 2 pounds of granulated sugar. Add ¼ pound butter and 6 slightly beaten whole eggs. Stir this mixture over a very low flame until it thickens. When sugar is dissolved and mixture begins to bubble the lemon cheese is done.

This recipe is a generous one, but it can be kept in the ice box in a tightly covered jar for several weeks, ready for the moment when you need a delicacy in a hurry. You can use lemon cheese as a filling for open pastries, or a spread for toast, or tea sandwiches.

MRS. J. H. RAST, SR., Charleston County.

Orange Filling

Mix ½ cup sifted cake flour, 1 cup sugar, and ¼ teaspoon salt in heavy saucepan. Add ¼ cup orange juice and mix well. Add 1¼ cups orange juice, ¼ cup lemon juice, 1 teaspoon lemon extract. Cook over low heat until mixture thickens. Beat 4 egg yolks slightly. Add hot mixture to them slowly, stirring constantly. Return to saucepan and cook slowly until sauce thickens again. Stir constantly until done. Cool and then spread between layers of cake.

Mrs. FRANK SENN, Newberry County.

FROSTINGS

Caramel Frosting

2 cups granulated sugar
1 cup thick cream
pinch of baking soda
1 cup ground raisins
1 tablespoon flavoring
2 tablespoons butter

Combine sugar and baking soda, add milk, cook until a soft ball forms in water. Add butter, flavoring and ground raisins. Whip thoroughly. Spread between layers of cake. Nuts added to this make a most delicious icing.

Mrs. WORTH ROGERS, Marion County.

Caramel Cake Frosting

3 cups dark brown sugar
1 cup white sugar
1 cup butter—not margarine
1 cup boiling water

Bring to boil. Then boil fast for 6 minutes without stirring. Add 1 teaspoon vanilla and set aside to cool. Beat until caramel will not run. Then spread between layers and on top of cake. Put pecans on layers and on top.

Mrs. B. P. McNEESE, Darlington County.

Caramel Icing

3 cups confectioner's sugar
1 cup brown sugar
1 stick butter
¼ cup hot water
1 teaspoon vanilla

Dissolve butter and brown sugar in hot water. Pour into sifted confectioner's sugar, add flavoring, beat until creamy and spread on layers at once.

Mrs. L. W. KING, Mrs. HARRY CHAMPY, Calhoun County.

Caramel Icing

2 cups light brown sugar
5 tablespoons milk or cream
½ cup butter or shortening
½ teaspoon baking powder
½ teaspoon vanilla

Mix sugar, cream, butter well. Bring to a boil. Cook 2 minutes. Take off fire and add baking powder and vanilla. Beat until smooth and creamy. Spread quickly.

MRS. C. D. WRIGHT, Lee County.

Chocolate Frosting

¼ pound margarine or butter   1 pound confectioner's sugar
2 egg whites   1 teaspoon vanilla
                  4 tablespoons cocoa

Whip egg whites until very stiff. Fold in 1 pound sifted powdered sugar. Melt margarine or butter and mix cocoa with it. Add this mixture to the whites and spread on cake. This makes enough for a three-layer cake.

MRS. J. N. GAINEY, Darlington County.

Butterfly Frosting

2 tablespoons butter   2 cups confectioner's sugar (for
2 tablespoons thick cream   special occasions add food
1 teaspoon vanilla   coloring)
                  1 egg white

Cream butter. Add part of sugar; add unbeaten egg whites and continue to cream; add more sugar and the cream. Add flavoring and all the sugar. Cream until smooth. Spread between layers. For special occasions add cake coloring.

MRS. WORTH ROGERS, Marion County.

Fresh Coconut Cream Frosting

1 cup heavy cream   3 tablespoons confectioner's
½ teaspoon vanilla   sugar, sifted
                  1 cup grated fresh coconut

Whip cream until stiff. Add vanilla and fold in sugar. Spread between layers and over top of cake. Sprinkle with coconut. Will frost two 8-inch layers.

MRS. HAROLD COLEMAN, Dillon County.

Coconut Icing

3 cups sugar   milk
1 tablespoon butter   1 grated coconut
                  1 teaspoon lemon flavoring

Mix sugar and milk, enough milk to dissolve sugar. Let mixture come to a boil. Add grated coconut. Cook until thick enough to spread. Remove from heat and add butter and flavoring. Enough for two small cakes.

MRS. M. R. STROM, Aiken County.

Orange Coconut Frosting

3 tablespoons butter
2 cups confectioner's sugar

¼ cup orange juice
¾ cup grated coconut

Cream butter until very soft. Add sugar gradually thinning with orange juice to spreading consistency. Beat until smooth. Beat coconut into frosting.   Yields 1½ cups.

MISS LIZZIE USHER, Dillon County.

Chocolate Fudge Filling

3 squares chocolate or
  4 tablespoons cocoa
3 cups sugar
1 cup cream

pinch of salt
¼ cup corn syrup
2 tablespoons butter
1 egg yolk

1 teaspoon vanilla

Mix cocoa, sugar, salt, add syrup and cream. Cook until forms soft ball in water or spins a thread; add butter and vanilla. Remove from heat and cool; then add egg yolk which has been thoroughly beaten. Whip also while adding egg yolk. Spread on cake. This filling does not get too hard and has a glossy appearance.

MRS. WORTH ROGERS, Marion County.

Minute Fudge Frosting

1 ounce chocolate
1 cup sugar
1/3 cup milk

¼ cup butter
¼ teaspoon salt
1 teaspoon vanilla

Place in saucepan chocolate finely cut, sugar, milk, butter and salt. Bring slowly to full rolling boil, stirring constantly and boil 1 minute. Add vanilla and beat until thick enough to spread. If frosting becomes too thick, add about one tablespoon cream. Double recipe to ice sides and top of cake.

NELL DOWTIN, McCormick County.

Fool Proof Icing

1 stick butter   1 pound powdered sugar
3 squares chocolate   1 egg
½ teaspoon vanilla

Melt butter and chocolate in double boiler. When they are melted add sugar and mix well. Add few drops of water if too thick. Break whole raw egg into mixture and mix well again. Add vanilla. Spread on cake. Try when you want a hurry-up icing.

MRS. S. J. BLAND, JR., Darlington County.
MRS. D. I. SENN, Newberry County.

Cookies

The difference in cookies and cakes is chiefly in size, shape, and the fact that cookies are made from stiff dough because of the use of more flour.

Recipes for cookies, must be followed accurately if you expect to have the finished product consistent.

Changes in ingredients and additions make *new* recipes.

If a thin cooky is desired, it should be baked in a moderate oven of 350 degrees. This will allow the cooky to spread before it bakes. Where it is desirable for a cooky to hold its shape, a hotter oven will be needed. Use 375 degrees to 425 degrees depending on the type of cooky.

For ice box cookies, have the dough as soft as it can be formed into a roll. Wrap the roll in waxed paper or a cloth and place in a cold place until chilled and stiff. Slice in thin slices and bake in moderately hot oven.

The recipes in this section are tested for quality and flavor. A crisp cooky must retain its crispness and a soft tender cooky, its tenderness.

Ice Box Cookies

¾ cup butter   ¾ teaspoon soda
1 cup brown sugar   ½ teaspoon vanilla
1 egg   ½ cup nut meats
¼ teaspoon salt   3 cups flour

Cream butter, adding sugar gradually, beat in egg, add flour, soda, flavoring and nuts. Form in rolls, chill (over night is best), slice, and bake in hot oven (400 degrees). For variety flavor with nutmeg or cinnamon, or use raisins or coconut instead of nut meats. A little more flour may be necessary to make a roll.

MRS. J. C. PEARCE, York County.

Nutty Fingers

¾ pound butter or oleo
1 egg
2 tablespoons sugar

3½ cups flour
1 cup nuts
1 teaspoon vanilla

Cream butter, add sugar and beaten egg. Add flour, nuts and vanilla and knead into dough. Put in refrigerator until chilled, roll in small finger cookies and bake at 275 degrees until golden brown.

MRS. W. H. IRBY, Kershaw County.

Chocolate Pinwheels

½ cup butter
½ cup sugar
1 egg
2 cups flour
½ teaspoon baking powder

¼ teaspoon salt
2 tablespoons milk
1 teaspoon vanilla
1 ounce melted chocolate
1 teaspoon cinnamon

Cream butter and add sugar. Add beaten egg. Sift dry ingredients and add with milk and vanilla. Divide the dough in two parts. To one part, add cinnamon. To other, add melted chocolate. Roll each ⅛-inch thick. Place chocolate on the cinnamon and roll like a jelly roll. Wrap in waxed paper and chill for several hours. Cut in thin slices and bake on slightly greased cooky sheet in a moderate oven (350 degrees) for 15–18 minutes.

MRS. W. H. IRBY, Kershaw County.

Crisp Cookies

1 cup fat
2 teaspoons **flavoring**
2 cups sugar
2 eggs

4 cups sifted soft wheat flour
4 teaspoons baking powder
½ teaspoon salt
¼ cup milk, or less

Mix the ingredients as for 1-2-3-4 Cake. Form the dough into a roll in waxed paper and chill thoroughly. Cut off thin slices from the roll and bake. For rolled cookies, cut off pieces of dough, roll on a lightly floured board to about one-fourth inch in thickness. Cut into desired shapes and bake the cookies on a greased baking sheet in a moderately hot oven (375 degrees to 400 degrees) for about 10 minutes.

MRS. G. K. LANEY, Chesterfield County.

ROLLED AND CUT COOKIES

Sand Tarts

½ cup shortening	1½ cups flour
1 cup sugar	½ teaspoon baking powder
1 egg	½ teaspoon salt
1 teaspoon vanilla	

Cream shortening, add sugar, add well-beaten egg. Sift the dry ingredients and add with the vanilla. Roll ⅛-inch thick on bread board lightly sprinkled with flour. Sprinkle sheet of dough generously with granulated sugar, rolling it lightly into the dough. Cut with cooky cutters and bake in moderate oven (350 degrees) for about 10 minutes.

MRS. W. H. IRBY, Kershaw County.

Benne Seed Cookies

¾ cup butter	1 cup flour
1½ cups brown sugar	¾ cup benne seed (toasted)
1 egg	¼ teaspoon salt
½ teaspoon baking powder	1 teaspoon vanilla

Cream butter and add sugar. Add beaten egg. Sift flour, salt and baking powder and add to butter mixture. Add vanilla and toasted benne seed. Drop with a teaspoon on cooky sheet—allow for spreading. Bake at 325° till a golden brown.

Caramel Cookies

2 cups brown sugar	½ teaspoon salt
½ cup melted butter	3 cups flour
2 beaten eggs	1 teaspoon baking powder

Cream sugar and butter, add beaten eggs, then add rest of ingredients which have been sifted together. Put through pastry tube or cooky press and bake in hot oven (425 degrees). Use more flour if necessary to keep cookies from losing their shape.

MRS. E. C. PEARCE, SR., Kershaw County.

Lemon Crisps

1 cup shortening	1 egg
½ cup granulated sugar	2½ cups sifted all purpose flour
½ cup brown sugar	1 teaspoon salt
2 tablespoons lemon juice	¼ teaspoon soda

1 teaspoon lemon rind

Cream shortening and sugars together. Add lemon juice and egg, and beat well. Sift flour, salt and soda together, and add to mixture. Add lemon rind. Put through a cooky press on ungreased cooky sheet. Bake at 400 degrees for 10–12 minutes.   Yield: 7 dozen.

MRS. E. C. PEARCE, SR., Kershaw County.

Pralines (Cookies)

½ cup butter	1 egg
1½ cups brown sugar	1½ cups sifted flour
½ teaspoon soda	1 teaspoon vanilla extract

Cream butter well. Add sugar and egg and beat until fluffy. Add flour into which the soda has been sifted, add vanilla. Drop by teaspoonfuls on cooky sheet, place a pecan half on each cooky and bake in moderate oven for 12 minutes or until nicely browned.

MRS. M. H. SMITH, Berkeley County.

Pecan Crispies

½ cup shortening	2 beaten eggs
½ cup butter	2½ cups flour
1 cup sugar	¼ teaspoon salt
1½ cups brown sugar	½ teaspoon soda

1 cup chopped nuts

Cream shortening and sugar, add eggs and beat well. Add sifted dry ingredients and nut meats. Drop from teaspoon about 2 inches apart onto greased baking sheet. Bake in moderate oven 350 degrees 12 to 15 minutes.   Makes 5 dozen cookies.

MRS. I. P. OWENS, Kershaw County.

Pecan Confections

1 egg white	pinch of salt
1 cup brown sugar	1 tablespoon flour (level)

1 cup chopped pecans

Beat egg white to froth, adding gradually while beating, sugar, salt and flour. Stir in 1 cup chopped nuts. Drop by small spoonfuls on greased tins. Bake in very slow (250-degree) oven for 20 minutes. Remove from tins when partly cold.　Makes about 2 dozen small cookies.

Mrs. W. B. Patrick, Fairfield County.

Date Nut Squares

3 eggs beaten separately	½ cup warm water
1 cup sugar	½ teaspoon vanilla
1½ cups flour	1 cup dates cut up
2 level teaspoons baking powder	½ cup nuts chopped

Sift flour once, then measure; add baking powder and sift three times. Beat egg whites stiff, fold in sugar, fold in well-beaten yolks. Add water. Mix in flour lightly, then add dates and nuts with as little mixing as possible. Pour in a shallow pan (10 x 15) lined with waxed paper. Bake at 350 degrees twenty to twenty-five minutes. Immediately turn out on board dusted with confectioner's sugar. Cut in small squares while warm and roll in sugar. Will keep well.

Mrs. L. A. Dantzler, Orangeburg County.

Butter Crisp

1 egg	1 teaspoon vanilla
1½ cups powdered sugar	1 cup chopped nuts
1¼ cups butter	3 cups cake flour
	¼ teaspoon salt

Cream butter and sugar together. Add 1 cup flour, then add the egg and beat well. Add the remaining flour and nuts. Shape into a roll and chill. Slice thin and bake, or you may drop them from a teaspoon on a buttered cooky sheet. Bake at 400 degrees for 10 to 12 minutes.　Makes 5 dozen.

Mrs. A. D. Woodham, Lee County.

Coconut Dainties

2 egg whites	½ cup white corn syrup
½ cup sugar	4 cups moist coconut
½ cup flour	1 cup chopped nuts

Beat egg whites until stiff. Add the sugar to them gradually folding it in so they will retain their fluffiness. Continue this folding while adding the flour, corn syrup and coconut. Drop by teaspoonfuls on well-greased baking sheet. Bake at 375 degrees from 10 to 12 minutes. Yields: 2 dozen cookies.

MRS. J. L. CARTER.

Peanut Macaroons

1 egg white
2/3 cup sugar
⅛ teaspoon salt
1/3 cup chopped peanuts
¼ teaspoon almond extract

Beat egg white stiff; add sugar and salt while beating. Fold in peanuts and almond extract. Drop by teaspoons on greased baking sheet. Bake in very moderate oven 325 degrees for 15 minutes. Makes 2 dozen.

MRS. CLARENCE HAZEL, Newberry County.

Brownies

¾ cup flour
½ teaspoon baking powder
½ teaspoon salt
2 squares chocolate or 4 tablespoons cocoa
1 cup sugar
2 eggs
1 teaspoon vanilla

1/3 cup shortening

Cream shortening, then add sugar. Melt chocolate over hot water and add to mixture. Add eggs one at a time and vanilla. Sift flour and salt and sift again. Fold in dry ingredients and mix only until blended. If you wish, add 2/3 cup of chopped dates or nuts. Bake 35 minutes at 350 degrees. Makes 2 dozen brownies.

MRS. DARRELL REYNOLDS, Darlington County.

Black Walnut Dream Bars

Cream ½ cup (scant) butter with ½ cup of brown sugar and work in one cup of flour until crumbly. Pat smoothly into a shallow 7 by 11 inch pan. Bake 10 minutes in a moderate oven.
Meanwhile, mix together:

1 cup brown sugar
2 beaten eggs
¼ teaspoon salt
1 teaspoon vanilla

Sift together 2 teaspoons flour with ½ teaspoon baking powder and mix with 1½ cups shredded coconut and 1 cup broken black walnut meats (or other nuts) and blend with egg mixture. Pour over the baked crust and return to oven 20 minutes longer. Cut in bars and remove to unglazed paper while still warm.

Christine A. Dukes, Charleston County.

Butter Horns

½ cup butter	1 cup scalded milk
½ cup sugar	3 eggs
1 teaspoon salt	1 cake yeast
	4 cups flour

Dissolve sugar, salt and butter in the milk. When cool add eggs and yeast mixed with a teaspoon of sugar. Beat in the flour. In winter, mix the night before, but in summer early in the morning. It should stand about 3 hours. Two hours before the meal, pour half the mixture on a floured board and roll to half inch thick, spread it with melted butter and cut in wedge shaped pieces like a pie. Roll up, beginning with the wide end and roll the buttered side out. Place in ungreased pans. Let rise about two hours and bake in moderate oven about ten minutes. Use remainder of dough when needed.

Mrs. E. McClellan, Charleston County.

Charleston Squares

¼ pound butter	½ teaspoon salt
1 cup sugar	1 teaspoon vanilla
2 eggs beaten	1 teaspoon almond
2 cups flour	1 teaspoon baking powder

Mix butter and sugar, add beaten eggs and other ingredients. Spread on cooky sheet and cover with the following:

1 egg white, beaten	1 teaspoon vanilla
½ cup brown sugar	½ cup nuts
	½ cup cherries

Cook in moderate oven and cut into squares while hot.

Mrs. H. M. McLaurin, Jr., Sumter County.

Chewies

¼ pound butter	1½ teaspoons baking powder
3 eggs	¼ teaspoon salt
1 package brown sugar	1 teaspoon vanilla
1½ cups plain flour	1 cup broken nut meats

Cream butter and sugar, add eggs (one at a time) then flour, baking powder, salt, vanilla and nuts. Bake ½ hour at 250 degrees.

MRS. WALTER MARTSCHINK, Charleston County.

Chinese Chews

1 cup chopped dates	½ cup flour
1 cup chopped nuts	2 eggs
1 cup sugar	½ teaspoon baking powder

¼ teaspoon salt

Beat eggs until light then add the sugar; when well blended add sifted dry ingredients. Add dates and nuts and pour into greased 9-inch square pan. Bake in a slow oven for about 20 minutes. Cut in small squares, roll in balls and dust with confectioner's sugar.

MRS. J. F. PHILLIPS, Aiken County.

Chocolate Nut Honeys

¾ cup cocoa	2 tablespoons honey
1¼ cups plain flour	½ teaspoon salt
½ cup brown sugar	1 teaspoon vanilla
1½ cups granulated sugar	3 teaspoons baking powder
1 cup butter	3 large eggs

1 cup chopped pecans

Place all ingredients in mixing bowl. Add eggs and mix thoroughly. Put batter in two well-greased and floured 6½- by 10½-inch cake pans. Bake for 15 minutes in 350-degree preheated oven. Reduce to 300 degrees and bake 5 to 10 minutes. Turn out on towel, cut in squares while warm.

MRS. W. L. CURRIE, Sumter County.

Date Swirls

½ pound dates, cut fine	1/3 cup water
½ teaspoon lemon juice	¼ cup sugar

In saucepan, cook together until thick. Remove from heat, add: ¼ cup nuts and let cool. Then take:

½ cup butter	1 egg
½ cup white sugar	½ teaspoon soda
½ cup brown sugar	¼ teaspoon salt

2 cups flour

Mix and roll into ¼-inch thickness. Spread with date mixture. Roll up like jelly roll. Wrap in waxed paper and chill. Slice and bake 12 minutes at 400 degrees.

MRS. P. B. MITCHELL, Laurens County.

Holiday Nuggets

½ cup shortening or margarine   1 tablespoon sugar
1 cup flour   ½ cup chopped pecans
1½ teaspoons vanilla   XXXX sugar

Mix butter and sugar. Flour nuts and mix together. Roll in small balls. Bake at 425 degrees for about 15 minutes. Roll in XXXX sugar while hot.

MRS. W. C. THOMAS, Charleston County.

Mincemeat Fruit Fingers

1¼ cups sifted flour   ⅛ teaspoon salt
1 teaspoon baking powder

Sift together. Beat 3 eggs until light and fluffy; then add gradually 1 cup sugar, beating well. Fold in dry ingredients, then add:

1 cup mincemeat   1 cup chopped nuts

Pour into greased shallow pan 14 x 9 inches and lined with waxed paper. Bake in a slow oven 300 degrees for 30 minutes. Cut while warm into narrow strips and roll in powdered sugar.

MRS. CHARLES DAVIS, Laurens County.

Pecan Rolls

1½ cups milk (scalded)

Pour hot milk over 1/3 cup shortening, 2 tablespoons sugar, 1 teaspoon salt. When lukewarm, add 2 yeast cakes dissolved in a little lukewarm water; add also 1 egg and flour to make soft dough (around 5½ to 6 cups). Let rise until double. While dough is rising prepare pans (pans with funnels are best). Grease pans generously, sprinkle a layer of brown sugar, put a layer of pecan halves, flat sides up, on sugar. Dot with lumps of butter. When dough is ready, roll out a half at a time on long narrow sheet. Spread with melted butter, sprinkle on brown sugar, roll up, cut into 3-inch rolls, put into pans. Let rise, cook, not too fast. Cover over if necessary for a while, when done turn into place upside down. This recipe will make 4 half-pound cake pans full, eight rolls to pan. It makes delicious plain rolls if you don't want to use it all for pecan rolls.

MRS. WILLIAM NICHOLSON.

Orange Bars

2 tablespoons butter, creamed
with 1 cup sugar
rind of 1 orange, grated
1½ cups flour

2 eggs, unbeaten
½ pound candy orange slices
(gum drops) diced
1 cup chopped nuts

2 tablespoons orange juice in batter

Bake in oblong cake pans at 350 degrees until done. Pour juice of 1 orange over cake while hot. Let remain in pan until thoroughly cold. Cut in bars, roll in granulated sugar. (This is better after several days. Keeps well. Tastes similar to white fruit cake.)

MRS. MARIE A. HAMILTON, Charleston County.

Marvels

¼ pound sugar   ¼ pound flour

¼ pound eggs

Mix thoroughly as for pound cake, adding a pinch of baking powder. Add sufficient flour to make soft dough. Roll out and cut in strips, about 3 inches long. Then twist or gash. Fry in hot deep fat until brown. Drain and roll in powdered sugar.

MRS. J. W. ENGLISH, Lee County.

Pineapple Squares

3 eggs
1 cup sugar

1 cup bread crumbs
2/3 cup chopped pecans

1 cup crushed pineapple

Beat egg yolks, add sugar, crumbs, pecans and pineapple. Fold in stiffly beaten egg whites and bake in a moderate oven 350 degrees for 20 to 25 minutes. Cut in squares.

MRS. J. R. WOODWARD, Aiken County.

Doughnuts

4 cups sifted flour
1 teaspoon salt
3 teaspoons baking powder
1 teaspoon grated nutmeg

1 cup sugar
1 egg
1¾ cups milk
2 tablespoons melted shortening

1 teaspoon vanilla

Sift together flour, salt, baking powder and nutmeg, add sugar and mix to a light soft dough with beaten egg, milk, melted shortening and vanilla. Turn onto well-floured board, roll half inch thick. Cut with doughnut cutter and cook about 3 minutes in deep hot fat, turning as they rise to the top of the fat. Drain on soft paper and sprinkle with powdered sugar. Yield 3 dozen.

MRS. CLYDE GAMBRELL, Anderson County.

Raised Doughnuts

Sponge: 1 package yeast, 2 cups lukewarm water, 4 scant cups sifted flour. Soak yeast 20 minutes in the lukewarm water. Mix with flour to a thick batter. Cover. Let rise in warm place until doubled.

Dough: Sponge as above.

½ cup shortening	2 eggs
⅜ cup sugar	½ teaspoon ground nutmeg
1½ teaspoons salt	about 5 cups or more of flour

Cream together the shortening, sugar and salt. Add this to the risen sponge, with the beaten eggs and spice. Stir in as much flour as mixture will take up readily, making a rather soft dough. Mix well. Let rise until doubled in bulk. If desired, stir down and let rise again until nearly doubled. Turn onto floured board, pat or roll until 1/3 inch thick and cut with doughnut cutter. Cover to prevent drying and let rise until doubled. Fry in about 1 pound of shortening, about 375 degrees. Immediately dip in hot syrup made of 1½ cups sugar, 1 cup water, and a lump of butter the size of an egg.

MRS. G. E. RABON, SR., Lee County.

Stickies

2/3 cup sugar	1 cup creamed butter

Use rich pastry, not too soft, roll thin, spread with creamed butter. Sprinkle sugar over pastry, roll lightly as jelly rolls. When you finish rolling, moisten the edge with water so it will stick together, cut in half-inch lengths, place in heavy skillet, with cut side down, not too close together. Bake in moderately hot oven until brown.

Sauce:

2/3 cup sugar	2/3 cup boiling water

two tablespoons white corn syrup

Boil to a rolling syrup, pour over hot stickies, turn pan from side to side until they are well glazed.

MRS. J. M. WILLIAMS, SR., York County.

Candy

The making of candies in the home is an art that is easily mastered and yet so few people ever put forth the time or the effort to make a really good candy at home.

Home made confections are wholesome and economical and can always fill the "sweet tooth" of children—and adults—that seems to have a bottomless cavity.

There are only a few fundamental rules that need to be mastered, then confections made at home can equal or surpass the quality, taste, and appearance of the finest candies made in the professional shops.

Briefly These Rules Are

1. Use only highest quality ingredients.
2. Follow standard tested recipes.
3. Use a candy thermometer. Most home made candies are hard and overcooked. A thermometer insures accurate cooking.
4. Use heavy, thick bottom, cooking pans, thus even distribution of heat and less scorched candy results.
5. Most candy may be stirred gently while cooking, but stirring or beating after cooking, before the syrup is cooled results in grainy coarse textured candy.
6. A very sharp and very thin bladed knife insures smooth uniform pieces of candy when cut.
7. Be careful in handling, storing, and packing candy. Store in airtight containers if candy is to be kept over a period of time.
8. Fudge of all kinds may be packaged in moisture-vapor proof wrappings and frozen. This may be kept 4 to 6 weeks.
9. When pecans are added to candy the flavor is improved if they are slightly toasted.

FUDGE

Basic Fudge Recipe

3 cups sugar	⅛ teaspoon salt
4 tablespoons corn syrup	3 tablespoons butter
1 cup milk, fresh or canned	vanilla
6 to 8 tablespoons cocoa	nuts, marshmallows, etc

Mix sugar, salt and cocoa, add corn syrup and milk. Cook until it forms a firm, soft ball when dropped in very cold water. If thermometer is used, cook to 232 degrees. Mixture can be stirred while cooking. Remove from fire, add butter and let stand without stirring until mixture is cool and begins to thicken, then beat until it is creamy and keeps its shape. Pour quickly on a sheet of waxed paper. Let stand until set, then cut with a thin bladed very sharp knife, wipe knife with a damp cloth after each cut. Add vanilla while beating, add nuts or marshmallows just before candy is poured out.

Variations: *Peanut Butter Fudge.* Omit cocoa and add ½ cup peanut butter while beating.

Caramel Fudge. Use brown sugar instead of white, omit syrup, add 1 cup pecans or black walnuts while beating.

White Fudge. Use water instead of milk; coconut, nuts, candied fruit, citron, dates, etc., may be added while beating.

Nuts, fruits, coconut, or various flavorings may be added to white fudge or brown sugar fudge to make any variety and flavor desired.

MISS MARGARET MARTIN, Extension Specialist.

Chocolate Fudge

¾ cup cocoa	1⅛ cups milk
3 cups sugar	6 tablespoons water
3 tablespoons corn syrup	⅛ teaspoon salt
1½ teaspoons vanilla	

Combine cocoa, sugar, syrup, milk and water in saucepan and stir over low heat until sugar dissolves. Boil slowly until few drops form ball in cold water. Cool. Add salt and vanilla. Beat until stiff. Pour in greased pan, put nuts on top, and cut when cold.

MRS. MAJOR BOLT, Anderson County.

Peanut Butter Fudge

2 cups sugar
¾ cup milk

4 teaspoons peanut butter
1 teaspoon vanilla

⅛ teaspoon salt

Boil sugar and milk to soft ball stage. Remove from fire and add peanut butter, vanilla and salt. Beat until creamy and then pour into buttered pan and cut into squares.

MRS. S. P. LEAZER, Cherokee County.

Double Fudge

FIRST PART

2 cups sugar
2 squares unsweetened
chocolate

1 cup milk
1 tablespoon butter
1 teaspoon vanilla

Cook ingredients together without stirring until they form a soft ball when dropped in cold water. Cool and beat until creamy. Add vanilla. Pour on buttered dish.

SECOND PART

2 cups sugar
1 cup milk

1 tablespoon butter
1 teaspoon vanilla

1 cup chopped nuts

Cook the sugar, milk and butter as above until soft ball stage. Cool and beat. Add vanilla and chopped nuts. Pour on top of first layer. Cut in squares when cool.

MRS. Y. E. SEIGLER, McCormick County.

MISCELLANEOUS CANDY

Mints

2 cups granulated sugar
¼ stick butter
2/3 cup water

1 tablespoon vinegar
4 or 5 drops of peppermint
vegetable coloring

Cook without stirring until syrup is thick enough to become brittle when held under cold water. Pour on buttered marble slab, add oil of peppermint and begin to pick up and pull. Pull until fluffy, then add desired color. Pull until mixture will hold its shape. Stretch out (on marble slab) in long shape, then cut mints the size desired. Makes from 60 to 75 mints.

MRS. HAL D. WATSON, Dillon County.

Mints (Uncooked)

¼ cup coffee cream
4 teaspoons butter or margarine
⅛ teaspoon salt

4 cups powdered sugar
vegetable coloring of desired
color and shade

6 to 8 drops of peppermint

Heat cream in top of double boiler, melt butter in cream, remove from heat, add salt and desired flavoring. Add sugar gradually, stirring until well blended. Place in bowl sprinkled with powdered sugar. Add coloring and knead until smooth and creamy and coloring thoroughly blended. Cut out very small portions, roll in balls between palms of hands, about the size of marbles. Place on well-oiled baking sheet or platter. Press flat with bottom of gelatin mold or stamp. This quantity makes approximately 60 mints about the size of a quarter.

MRS. JOHN H. BOOZER, Newberry County.

Coconut Patties

3 cups sugar
¼ cup sweetened condensed
milk
½ cup water
2 cups coconut, grated

1½ teaspoons vanilla flavoring
½ cup chopped nuts
1 tablespoon butter or butter
substitute
3 tablespoons cocoa

Combine sugar and cocoa. Add milk and water. Boil to soft ball stage (234 to 238 degrees). Cool to room temperature. Add coconut and nuts. Add butter and flavoring. Beat until mixture thickens. Drop on waxed paper in small pats.

MRS. C. S. NEWSOM, Lee County.

Molasses Balls

½ cup molasses
½ cup graham cracker crumbs
2/3 cup powdered milk

Mix and make into a roll and leave in refrigerator over night. Slice and roll into small candy balls.

MRS. G. E. PRICE, Kershaw County.

Caramel Nuggets

3 cups corn flakes
12 marshmallows (cut in halves)
2 cups sugar

2/3 cup evaporated milk
1 teaspoon butter
1 teaspoon vanilla

¼ teaspoon salt

Put 1 cup sugar, milk and butter on stove and bring to boil, stirring constantly. Add this gradually to the other cup of sugar, which has been melted to a golden brown. Then cook together slowly until mixture forms a soft ball when dropped in water. Fold in the corn flakes and marshmallows, adding vanilla and salt. Drop from teaspoon on wax paper. Cool until firm. Yield 3 dozen.

Mrs. Marie Powell, Fairfield County.

Popcorn Balls

½ pound popcorn	2 teaspoons cream of tartar
2/3 cup corn syrup	2 tablespoons vinegar
2 cups sugar	2 tablespoons melted butter
2/3 cup boiling water	2 teaspoons vanilla

⅛ teaspoon baking soda

Pop corn. Place in large pan. Combine syrup, sugar, water and vinegar. Heat to boiling. Add cream of tartar. Boil to soft crack stage (275 to 280 degrees). Remove from fire. Add butter, baking soda, and flavoring. Pour over pop corn. Form into balls.

Mrs. R. A. Newsom, Lee County.

Fruit Balls

½ cup dates, pitted	½ teaspoon lemon rind, grated
½ cup apricots, dried	⅛ teaspoon orange rind, grated
½ cup walnuts	½ cup raisins

Put dates, apricots, raisins and walnuts through food chopper, using medium-coarse cutter. Add lemon and orange rinds and blend thoroughly. Shape into small balls, coat with confectioner's sugar if you wish. Yield 2 dozen.

Annie Newsom, Lee County.

Lollipops

2 cups sugar	few drops any flavoring
2/3 cup light corn syrup	few drops any coloring

1 cup water

Cook sugar, corn syrup and water until a brittle ball forms when dropped in cold water. Add flavoring and coloring. Drop by teaspoons on toothpicks placed on greased waxed paper. Work fast so syrup doesn't harden on you.

Mrs. Ralph Epting, Newberry County.

White Taffy (Old Time)

2 cups granulated sugar	½ cup water
½ cup white vinegar	½ teaspoon salt
1 teaspoon vanilla	1 tablespoon butter

Boil together sugar, water, vinegar and salt. Boil until the mixture becomes brittle in water. Then add 1 tablespoon butter, remove from fire and add 1 teaspoon vanilla. Do not stir while cooking. Pour into a buttered pan and when cool enough to handle pull in fingers until white. Cut with scissors.

MRS. CARLISLE SULLIVAN, Abbeville County.

Chocolate on Cream Candy

2 cups sugar	1 cup chopped pecans
1 cup milk	1 teaspoon vanilla
½ teaspoon cream of tartar	2 tablespoons butter
½ teaspoon salt	4 squares cooking chocolate

Combine sugar, milk, cream of tartar and salt and cook over low heat, stirring constantly, until it has reached the soft ball stage. Add butter and cool. Add nuts and vanilla and beat until creamy. Pour on buttered platter. Have chocolate melted over hot water. Pour over top of first mixture, spreading evenly. Cut in squares when chocolate has hardened.　　　　MRS. M. W. PATRICK, Fairfield County.

Apricot Confection

1 pound dried apricots	juice of 1 large or 2 small
2 cups sugar	oranges

½ lemon

Wash apricots and dry with towel, put through finest grinder. Mix all ingredients and cook, stirring constantly about 12 or 15 minutes. Drop from teaspoon on wax paper. When cool roll in powdered sugar or ground nuts.　　　　Lexington County.

Marshmallow Squares

¼ pound butter or margarine	1 box rice crispies
2½ dozen marshmallows	1 teaspoon vanilla

Melt butter and marshmallows in double boiler. Add vanilla. Pour rice crispies slowly to mixture. Mix well and pour into buttered shallow dish and pack down. When cold, cut into squares.

MRS. H. D. MULLINS, Cherokee County.

Taffy Apples

6 medium-sized red apples   ½ cup light corn syrup
1 cup brown sugar   ¼ cup water
½ cup granulated sugar   1 tablespoon butter
1 teaspoon vanilla extract

Stick wooden skewer into stem end of apples. Place sugars, corn syrup, water, and butter in saucepan and stir over low heat until sugar is dissolved. Boil to medium-crack stage (272 degrees) without stirring; remove from heat and add vanilla. Dip apples one at a time into the syrup. Place upright on greased pan until cool or roll in finely chopped peanuts or other nut meats. Makes 6 candied apples. My favorite way is to use all granulated sugar and a few drops of red vegetable coloring and roll in shredded coconut.

MRS. JESSIE MACMILLAN, Hampton County.

Kisses

½ pound confectioner's sugar   1 cup broken nut meats
3 egg whites   ⅛ teaspoon salt
½ teaspoon vanilla   ¼ teaspoon cream of tartar

Beat egg whites until foamy, add cream of tartar and beat until it will stand in a peak. Add sugar gradually. Flavor with vanilla and fold in nut meats. Drop with a spoon on buttered tins. Bake for 20 minutes at 300 degrees.

MISS VIRGINIA WILKINS, McCormick County.

Sea Foam

2 cups sugar, brown   ½ cup Karo syrup
¼ cup water   1 cup chopped nuts
2 egg whites   1 teaspoon vanilla

Beat egg whites stiff. Mix sugar, syrup and water. Cook until threads or forms a hard ball in cold water. Pour slowly beating constantly, over stiffly beaten egg whites. Continue beating until mixture holds its shape when dropped from spoon. Add flavoring and nuts. Drop by teaspoonfuls on well-buttered pan.

MRS. A. H. HENDRIX, Aiken County.

Failure Proof Divinity

2 cups sugar

½ cup water

½ cup corn syrup

⅛ teaspoon salt

1 teaspoon vanilla

2 egg whites

Combine 2 cups sugar, corn syrup, water and salt. Stir until dissolved. Boil gently to soft ball stage. Beat egg whites until stiff but not dry. Gradually pour 1/3 of syrup mixture over egg whites, beating constantly. Cook remaining syrup to light-crack stage. Light-crack test by adding several drops of mixture to water. Mixture when done, will form thin, firm ribbon which will bend when lifted out of water. Beat remaining candy into syrup mixture. Continue beating. When mixture holds its shape when dropped from a spoon, add vanilla. Drop by spoonfuls on greased cooky sheet.

MRS. Y. E. SEIGLER, McCormick County.

PEANUT CANDY

Sugared Peanuts

2 cups raw peanuts

1 cup sugar

½ cup cold water

Put all ingredients in pan together, boil briskly until syrup is reduced to dry sugar. Reduce heat and let sugar slowly melt during which time peanuts will parch. As soon as all sugar melts pour up in ungreased platter.

Dr. A. B. Preacher, Allendale, S. C.

Peanut Brittle

2 cups sugar
¾ cup light corn syrup
2 cups raw peanuts
¼ cup water
⅛ teaspoon salt
3¼ teaspoons soda

Combine sugar, water, salt and corn syrup in a saucepan and when mixture is boiling, add raw peanuts. Cook until a little tried in cold water will be so brittle it strings as it strikes the water and hardens immediately. Remove from fire, quickly stir in the soda and as soon as the soda is mixed with candy, pour on a greased marble slab or porcelain table. As soon as mixture is cold enough to touch, stretch out as thin as possible. When cold break in pieces as desired and store in covered container.

Phyllis Chamberlain, McCormick County.

Molasses Peanut Candy

1 quart ribbon cane molasses   4 cups shelled raw peanuts
½ cup butter

Add peanuts to molasses and cook until a hard ball is formed in cold water. The peanuts will cook while molasses is boiling. Let cool, beat slightly, then pour in well-buttered square cake pan. When cool, mark in squares.

Low Country Recipe.

PECAN CANDY

Pecan Roll

1 cup light brown sugar
2 cups granulated sugar
½ cup white corn syrup
1 cup Pet milk
pecans shelled

Mix in saucepan. Cook slowly, stirring constantly to 234 degrees or until a few drops form a soft ball when dropped in cold water. Remove from heat. Cool at room temperature without stirring until lukewarm or until the hand can be held comfortably on the bottom of pan. Then beat until candy holds shape. Turn on board dusted with ⅛ cup powdered sugar. Knead until firm. Shape into long roll, about 2 inches in diameter and 16 inches long. Cover outside with 1½ cups broken pecans. Wrap in waxed paper and put in cool place to harden, then cut into ½-inch slices with a sharp knife. Makes 32 slices.

MRS. CARL KNIGHT, Kershaw County.

Spiced Nuts

1 cup granulated sugar	¼ cup boiling water
½ teaspoon cinnamon	2 cups nuts
½ teaspoon vanilla	

Mix sugar, cinnamon, cream of tartar, boiling water and boil to 246 degrees or until a little of this mixture forms a firm ball when dropped in cold water. Add the nut meats. Cool. Add vanilla and stir until mixture sugars, then turn out on flat surface and separate the nuts.

MRS. M. L. POWELL, Marlboro County.

Cream Nut Candy

1½ cups sugar	2/3 cup milk
1 tablespoon butter or butter substitute	½ cup chopped nuts
	½ cup chopped raisins
½ cup chopped marshmallows	1 teaspoon vanilla flavoring
⅛ teaspoon salt	

Boil sugar, milk, butter and salt to soft ball stage (234 degrees). Remove from fire, add marshmallows. Cook to room temperature. Beat until thick and creamy. Add nuts, raisins, and flavoring. Pour into well-buttered shallow pan. Cut in squares.

MRS. R. A. NEWSOM, Lee County.

Candy Coated Minted Nuts

1 cup sugar	⅛ teaspoon essence of peppermint (or 3 drops oil of peppermint)
½ cup water	
1 teaspoon light corn syrup	
⅛ teaspoon salt	6 marshmallows
3 cups nut halves	

Cook together slowly without stirring, water, sugar, syrup and salt. Remove from fire just before it forms a soft ball in water. Add marshmallows and stir until melted. Add peppermint, nuts and a few drops red or green coloring, if desired. Stir with circular motion until nuts are coated. Spread on unglazed paper to dry. Keep in tightly covered jar.

MRS. MARTHA SPEER MARJENHOFF, McCormick County.

Pralines

4 cups sugar   2 cups cream
1 teaspoon salt   3 cups pecan nut meats

Make a thin syrup with 3 cups of the sugar, the salt, and the cream. Melt the other cup of sugar slowly in a frying pan and stir constantly until caramelized. Into it pour all the syrup at one time, and stir constantly and rapidly. Boil the mixture without stirring to a temperature of 238 degrees, or to the soft ball stage. Pour into a flat pan and cool. Beat until it begins to be creamy, and add the nuts. Drop by spoonfuls onto waxed paper to form flat, round cakes. Makes about 2 lbs.

MRS. MARY CHANDLER, Calhoun County.

Sugared Pecans

1 cup sugar   ½ cup water
1 pint pecans

Boil sugar and water until a pecan will become coated if placed in a small amount of the syrup in a saucer. Then put pecans in boiling syrup and stir. Pour into buttered dish.

ANNA GUILDS GRIMBALL, Charleston County.

Benne Candy

2 cups granulated sugar   2 cups roasted benne (sesame) seed

Melt sugar in iron frying pan over slow heat, add benne seed and pour quickly in shallow greased pan. Break into pieces when cool.

Soft Benne Candy

3 cups light brown sugar   2 tablespoons butter
1 cup thin cream or top milk   1 cup roasted benne seed

Combine all ingredients except seed and butter. Cook to soft ball stage 232 degrees. Remove from fire, add butter, cool until thick and syrupy. Beat until creamy, add seed while beating. Drop by teaspoon on waxed paper.

MARGARET MARTIN, Extension Specialist.

Mother Walker's Method for Crystallizing Grapefruit Peel

1 pound grapefruit peel   1½ pounds sugar
6 ounces water

Preparation of Peel. Select bright fruit with a thick peel. Wash carefully. Grate lightly on an ordinary grater to break the oil cells. Cut the peel in quarters and remove from the fruit and weigh. Cut this peel into strips that are ¼ to ½ inch in width; or cut into small shapes. Place in a saucepan of water and for each quart of peel taken add 3 pints of cold water. Boil ten minutes and pour off the water. Repeat three times or until as much of the bitter flavor is removed as is desired. Dry the peels between folds of cloth, pressing gently.

Method. For each pound of peel used, add 1½ lbs. of sugar to 6 ounces of water. Bring to boil and cook until the sugar is dissolved.

Add the prepared peel and boil until the syrup is absorbed. Remove immediately from the fire and roll the fruit in granulated or powdered sugar.

Finishing Point. If cooking is continued for too long a period of time and evaporation carried too far, the product will be hard and unattractive. The point at which the product shall be finished may be determined by rolling a piece of the fruit when it has become transparent, in granulated sugar. If after a few minutes the fruit stiffens enough to retain its shape it is sufficiently cooked. A strip of the peel is preferred to the small shapes in making this test.

Pulled Molasses Taffy

2 cups molasses   1 cup sugar (optional)
¼ cup butter

Cook all ingredients slowly until hard ball is formed, 265 degrees. Pour on greased platter and let cool until a dent is left when pressed with finger. Gather it into a lump and pull with tips of fingers while very light and porous. Break into desired sized pieces. Nuts, benne seed or any flavoring may be added while pulling. A few drops of peppermint makes a pleasing flavor.

Low Country Recipe.

Turkey Stew

Turkey stew came into existence about four years ago when a group of hungry fox hunters had to have something to eat. Herman Wise, local Game Warden in Newberry County, served as cook for the occasion. Mr. Wise, quite expert at culinary methods, had been serving on such occasions stews made of fish, squirrel and chicken, all of which have now been replaced by turkey stew.

Since it was first served it has become popular at Parent-Teacher Association meetings; the Newberry County pasture tour, at which approximately 400 farmers were fed; twice a year at the Lions Club, who say it's a favorite; twice to the South Carolina Turkey Federation and to several other smaller groups.

Recipe for Turkey Stew

20 lbs. turkey	1½ lbs. fat back—diced
6 lbs. onion—diced	1 bottle Worcestershire sauce
6 lbs. potatoes—diced	1 quart tomato juice
1 No. 2 can corn	1½ jars mustard

1½ lbs. butter

Cook turkey in water until meat leaves the bone—about 3½ hours. Remove from water and cut in bite size pieces. Return to the turkey stock, add all other ingredients and cook till vegetables are tender. Salt to taste. This recipe serves 25 to 30 hungry people.

J. E. THAXTON, Extension Turkey Specialist.

Turkey Dressing

2 cups cold corn muffin crumbs	4 tablespoons butter
2 cups cold biscuit crumbs	2 teaspoons ground sage
8 small oysters drained, and	2 teaspoons finely chopped onion
seasoned with salt and pepper	½ teaspoon black pepper

1½ cups turkey broth

Cook corn muffin and biscuits day before making dressing to insure dry crumbs. To the crumbs add sage, onion, pepper and mix with fork. Melt butter and add to broth and heat to boiling.

Gradually mix broth and crumb mixture lightly with fork. The mixture should be damp enough to form into 4 moist balls. Place these balls in a greased biscuit pan. Open top of balls, place in the middle of each 2 oysters. Close openings and flatten balls slightly with fork. Bake in oven at 350 degrees for about 15 minutes and brown at 450 degrees for 3 minutes. Serve hot on plate with turkey.

JUANITA H. NEELY, Rock Hill, S. C.

Cottage Cheese Pie

¼ cup cottage cheese mashed very smooth
¼ cup sugar
2 level tablespoons flour
½ teaspoon salt
1 cup whole milk (or ¾ cup milk and ¼ cup cream)
1 egg well beaten
1 tablespoon melted butter
May add the juice and grated rind of ½ lemon

Mix sugar, flour, and salt and add to finely mashed cottage cheese. Add egg, milk, butter, and lemon juice. Bake in a pastry lined pie pan in a moderate oven (325 to 350 degrees) about 50 minutes until the center is no longer milky and the top is delicately browned. Serve while still slightly warm but not hot.

If the lemon juice is not used, sprinkle nutmeg or cinnamon lightly over the pie before putting into the oven.

ADA M. MOSER, Winthrop College.

Chicken Chantilly

1 tablespoon gelatine
¼ cup cold water
1 cup hot chicken stock
3 beaten egg yolks
1½ teaspoons salt
⅛ teaspoon pepper
dash cayenne
1 tablespoon lemon juice
½ teaspoon Worcestershire sauce
1 teaspoon onion juice
2 cups diced cooked chicken
2 teaspoons finely chopped pimento
1/3 cup finely chopped celery
½ cup heavy cream, whipped
⅛ teaspoon paprika

Soften gelatin in cold water. Stir a little of the hot chicken stock into the egg yolk; stir the mixture gradually into the remaining hot stock. Add seasonings, lemon juice, Worcestershire sauce and onion juice.

Cook over hot water, stirring constantly until the mixture thickens. Remove from hot water and add softened gelatine. Stir until the gelatine is dissolved. Chill until partially set.

Add chicken, pimentos and celery; fold in the whipped cream.

Turn into individual molds or a large mold or loaf pan first rinsed in cold water. Chill until firm.

Unmold on a bed of lettuce or water cress, garnish with large olives, cucumbers or tomatoes. Yield 6 servings.

HOME MANAGEMENT COTTAGE,
Winthrop College, Rock Hill, S. C.

Pecan Pie

3 eggs
½ cup granulated or brown sugar
1 cup pecan halves
1 cup light corn syrup

1 teaspoon vanilla extract
sufficient plain pastry for 1 crust
9-inch pan

Beat eggs and sugar until thick. Add corn syrup, nut meats and vanilla. Pour into 9-inch pastry-lined pie pan. Nut meats may be sprinkled over filling after pouring into crust, if desired. Bake in slow (300 degree) oven one hour. Serves 6.

MRS. CHRISTINE GEE, Greenwood, S. C.

Spoon Bread

1 cup meal
1 teaspoon salt
1 tablespoon shortening

2 cups water
2 eggs
1 cup milk

Place the meal, salt, shortening and water in a saucepan. Cook, stirring until smooth and thick. Allow to cool, add beaten eggs; finally thin down to a batter with one cup milk. Beat well. Pour into a pan or baking dish. Bake in a rather hot oven about thirty (30) minutes. Serve hot. Serves 6.

DIRECTOR AND MRS. D. W. WATKINS, Clemson College.

Orange Charlotte Russe

1 1/3 tablespoons granulated gelatin
1/3 cup cold water
1/3 cup boiling water
½ pint cream

1 cup sugar
3 tablespoons lemon juice
1 cup orange juice and pulp
3 egg whites

Soak gelatin in cold water, dissolve in boiling water, strain, and add sugar, lemon juice, orange juice and pulp. Chill in pan of ice water; when quite thick, beat with wire spoon or whisk until frothy, then add egg whites beaten stiff and fold in whipped cream. Line a mold with sections of oranges, turn in mixture, smooth evenly and chill.

LONNY I. LANDRUM, Atlanta, Georgia.

Artichoke Pickle

1 gallon green tomatoes	½ dozen red peppers
1 quart onions	½ dozen green peppers
1 head cabbage	2 quarts artichokes
1 stalk of celery	Substitute any desired vegetables

SAUCE

½ gallon vinegar	2 cups brown sugar
1 ounce celery seed	2 tablespoons tumeric
1 ounce white mustard seed	1 cup flour
10¢ box powdered mustard	½ cup salt

Mix vinegar and seasoning, and cook ten minutes. Stir. Add chopped vegetables and cook for five minutes. Seal in sterilized jars.

DR. AND MRS. FRANK POOLE, Clemson College.

She-Crab Soup

1 tablespoon butter	½ teaspoon Worcestershire sauce
1 quart milk	1 teaspoon flour
¼ pint cream (whipped)	2 cups white crabmeat and crab
few drops onion juice	eggs
⅛ teaspoon mace	½ teaspoon salt
⅛ teaspoon pepper	4 tablespoons dry sherry

Melt butter in top of double boiler and blend with flour until smooth. Add the milk gradually, stirring constantly. To this add crabmeat and eggs and all other seasonings except the sherry. Cook slowly over water for twenty minutes. To serve place one tablespoon sherry (warmed) in individual soup bowls, then add soup and top with whipped cream. Sprinkle with paprika or finely chopped parsley. Secret: if unable to obtain "she-crabs" crumble yolk of hard-boiled eggs in bottom of soup bowls. This serves 4–6.

This recipe is from "Charleston Recipes". This book is put out by the Junior League of Charleston, and this recipe was submitted by Mrs. Henry F. Church (Rhea Bryant).

GENERAL SUMMERALL, President, The Citadel.

Chicken Spaghetti

1 hen cooked
1 quart tomatoes
2 cans mushroom soup
3 large onions
2 packages of spaghetti
2 bell peppers

3 stalks celery (not bunches)
3 tablespoons Worcestershire
sauce
1 can tomato paste
salt, pepper and nearly 1 pound
cheese grated

Boil one large hen and cut in medium-sized pieces. Cook spaghetti. Cut up vegetables and cook. Divide the tomatoes and paste. Then into a large-sized roaster place a layer of chicken, a layer of cooked spaghetti, a layer of the cooked vegetables, mushroom soup and then the tomatoes. Continue layers until all is used. Add two cups of chicken stock. Cook in oven about 1½ hours slowly. The last 15 minutes sprinkle grated cheese on top. Serves 12 generously.

Dr. and Mrs. H. P. Cooper, Clemson College.

Sauce Recipe for Hot Dogs

1 pound of hamburger
4 medium-sized onions
4 tablespoons prepared mustard
3 teaspoons sugar

2 teaspoons vinegar
1 cup catsup
salt to season
½ teaspoon red pepper

2 teaspoons chili powder

Put hamburger meat on in enough hot water to make a thick mixture. Stir until all meat is smooth. Then add all other ingredients and cook slowly for an hour.

Dr. W. E. Barnette, Sr., Greenwood, S. C.

Riceburger Casserole

1 pound of ground beef
1 medium-sized onion

salt and pepper to taste
2 strips bacon

1 cup uncooked rice

Fry out bacon, place ground beef into grease, to which has been added onion (diced small) salt and pepper, and keep stirring until meat is done and well browned. While this is being prepared, cook the rice until done. When rice and meat have finished cooking put cooked rice in the frying pan with meat and mix thoroughly. This will serve from four to six, depending on other dishes served at the meal. Is delicious if served with tossed salad, sliced tomatoes and vegetables.

Mr. and Mrs. J. Roy Jones, Columbia, S. C.

Cold Asparagus Ring with Chicken Salad
(Suitable for a Guest Luncheon or Buffet Supper)

Drain 2 large cans of asparagus tips, reserving liquid. Cut stalks of asparagus the exact height of ring mold. Cook remaining asparagus in asparagus liquid 20 minutes, adding 2 whole cloves, 2 slices of onion, ½ teaspoon salt, ¼ teaspoon paprika, and 3 slices of carrot. The liquid should be almost evaporated. Press through a coarse sieve. There should be 2 cups of asparagus pulp and liquid. If there is more than this, cook slowly until evaporated to required amount. Soak 2 tablespoons granulated gelatin in ½ cup cold water. Soften the gelatin over hot water and add to the asparagus puree. Set aside to cool, stirring occasionally. When mixture begins to thicken, fold in 2 cups of whipped cream. Dip the ring mold in cold water. Place slices of hard-cooked egg close together on the bottom of the mold. Arrange the cut asparagus stalks around the outer edge, turning tips down. Pour the asparagus mixture into mold and set aside several hours, or until perfectly firm. Unmold on a serving plate on a circle of small lettuce leaves and fill the center with chicken salad.   Serves 8–10.

MRS. ANGUS MCCAULEY, Chester, S. C.

Special Luncheon Dish

I get a loaf of unsliced bread and cut slices thick—(cutting off rind). Toast on both sides and spread just a bit of anchovy paste on one side. Pile on this, soft scrambled eggs—(2 eggs for each 2 slices of bread). On top of scrambled eggs put a good slice of peeled tomato. On top of tomato put a slice of breakfast bacon cut in half and pierced through eggs with toothpick. Put all this under a low broiler until bacon and tomato are cooked.

MR. AND MRS. JIM SELF, Greenwood, S. C.

Brunswick Stew

3 lbs. pork
3 lbs. veal (must be veal, beef will not do)
3 lb. dressed hen
6 quarts tomatoes—or the equivalent of fresh tomatoes
2 lbs. onions

3 lbs. Irish potatoes
1 lb. dried butter beans (or 2 cans canned beans or 1 qt. fresh)
3 cans corn
2 lbs. butter
½ cup Worcestershire sauce

salt

Cook meat in pressure cooker until tender, save broth. Remove bones and shred meat with fingers, do not grind in meat chopper.

Place shredded meat in broth in large cooking pot or dish pan. Add tomatoes and *simmer* 2 *hrs.* Cook onions, potatoes, butter beans, mash or put through a sieve and add to meat and tomatoes. Then add corn, then butter, Worcestershire sauce, salt to taste. Cook slowly until mixture thickens, it must be stirred constantly to prevent scorching.

Recipe makes about 10-12 quarts. Will keep two weeks in refrigerator, or may be put into cans, jars, or other proper packaging material and frozen. Keeps very satisfactory frozen for 6 months.

When cold, the stew should be thick enough to spread, it makes excellent sandwiches.

May be served hot with a crisp salad (raw cabbage and onions) rolls or crackers and a simple dessert.

This is excellent for church suppers or other meetings where large numbers are to be served.

MARGARET MARTIN, Rock Hill, S. C.

Frankfurter-Spaghetti-Cheese Dinner

1 package spaghetti	1 can tomato sauce
1 dozen small carrots or	1 can tomato soup
6 large carrots quartered	½ pound sharp cheddar cheese
1 teaspoon salt	2 tablespoons butter

12 frankfurters

Cover carrots and spaghetti with water, add salt. Boil 15 minutes, drain; remove carrots from spaghetti. Pour the tomato sauce, tomato soup, and cheese, grated finely, over the spaghetti; mix well.

Melt butter in an iron or aluminum pot having a lid which can fit tightly. Place all frankfurters in a layer in the bottom of the pot. Place the carrots in a layer on top of the frankfurters. Pour the spaghetti mixture over this. Cover tightly. Cook for one hour either at low temperature on top of the stove or in the oven at 325° F.

Have ready a very large platter. At the end of the cooking period, lift the spaghetti and place in the center of the platter. Arrange the carrots on top of the spaghetti. Arrange frankfurters around the edge of the platter. Garnish with parsley. Serves 6.

This makes a fine one-dish meal. It is especially nice for a buffet supper in the fall. It has an unusual flavor imparted by the carrots during the cooking. To complete the meal, add a tossed salad, buttered biscuit, coffee or milk, and a dessert such as apple or cherry pie.

SARAH E. CRAGWALL, Winthrop College.

Lemon Ice Cream

1 quart milk	Juice 3 lemons (about ½ cup or
Few grains salt	to taste)

1½ cups sugar

Mix juice and sugar. Add gradually to milk. (Curdled appearance will disappear in freezing.) Freeze. Makes 1½ quarts. We usually serve warm spice cake with the lemon ice cream.

MRS. DONALD RUSSELL, University of South Carolina.

Herb Bread

1 pkg. yeast, compressed	3 tablespoons shortening
¼ cup luke warm water	1½ teaspoons pulverized sage
2 cups milk	1 teaspoon nutmeg
3 tablespoons sugar	1 tablespoon caraway seed
2 teaspoons salt	6 cups sifted enriched flour

Soften yeast in luke warm water. Scald milk. Add to milk all other ingredients except flour and yeast solution. Cool to luke warm (80 to 85 F.) and add 2 cups flour, stirring well. Add yeast, then more flour to make a moderately stiff dough.

Turn out on lightly floured board and knead until smooth and satiny (5 to 8 minutes). Shape into ball and place in a well-greased bowl. Grease surface of dough lightly. Cover and let rise in warm place (80 to 85 F.) until doubled in bulk. Turn out on board and knead again (5 to 8 minutes). Divide and make into two loaves. Place in greased bread pans. Let rise until doubled in bulk. Bake in oven at 400 F. 10 minutes. Reduce heat to 350 F. and bake 40 minutes longer. Turn loaves out on cooling rack. Brush surface of bread with melted butter to soften the crust.

MISS ALINE NEELY, Ebenezer Road, Rock Hill, S. C.

Macaroni and Cheese

½ box elbow macaroni	¼ lb. butter or margarine
4 eggs beaten	½ lb. aged cheese
3 cups sweet milk	½ teaspoon salt

Cook and drain macaroni according to directions on package. Mix milk and butter to beaten eggs and add salt. Place alternating layers of sliced cheese and macaroni in buttered baking dish. Pour milk and egg mixture over these. Bake in moderate oven 350° for 30 minutes or until milk and egg mixture is set.

MRS. JOHN HARGROVE, The Elks Club, Rock Hill.

HANDLING AND COOKING FROZEN FOODS

Handling

Frozen foods, whether coming from the home freezer, or the commercial locker plant, may be just as nutritious and palatable as fresh foods. However, since they are more perishable than fresh foods, they must be handled and prepared with utmost care if they retain their full food value and attractiveness.

Frozen foods are highly perishable when defrosted. They do not keep as well as fresh foods. Therefore, they should not be allowed to stand either at room temperature or in the refrigerator after they have thawed.

Once frozen foods are thawed, they should never be refrozen. After they are thawed fruits and vegetables become flabby and lose their shape. Meats when thawed become more susceptible to bacterial action and thus spoil easily.

Since all frozen foods are so perishable, much care should be taken in the thawing processes. Many frozen foods may be cooked in the frozen stage and need no thawing. Since unthawed foods require a longer cooking time, this must be considered in making plans.

Slow thawing is done in the refrigerator and is the best method. Spoilage is slowed down and natural food moisture is reabsorbed. If faster thawing is necessary, it may be done at room temperature or in front of an electric fan. In emergency the unopened package may be thawed in cool running water. Never use hot water and never put any food in water unless it is tightly sealed in the package.

Most fruits can be used in the frozen stage. If fruits are served as desserts or used in fruit pies, defrosting is not necessary.

[403]

If fruits must be thawed, leave in package and thaw in refrigerator or at room temperature or in a pan of cool or running water. Allow 6-8 hours on refrigerator shelf for thawing a one-pound package of fruit packed in syrup. Allow 2-4 hours for thawing a package of the same size at room temperature and ½ to 1 hour for thawing in cool water.

Fruit packed with dry sugar thaws slightly faster than that packed in syrup. Both sugar and syrup packs thaw faster than unsweetened packs.

Thaw only as much as you need at one time. If you have left-over thawed fruit it will keep better if you cook it.

All vegetables except corn on cob are better cooked without thawing.

Meats may be thawed or cooked in the frozen stage. It is more economical to thaw the larger cuts of meat because it takes longer time and more fuel to cook meat in the frozen stage. Poultry should be thawed quickly before cooking.

Ground meat should be packaged and frozen without seasoning. Therefore, it is necessary to completely thaw before cooking.

Generally the thawing time for meats is:

On refrigerator shelf....................... 5–10 hrs. per lb.
At room temperature....................... 2–½ hrs. per lb.

Cooking

Vegetables. Most vegetables are best if cooked while still frozen. To keep the fresh flavor and color and to retain food values, use only a small amount of water and cook until just tender. Use ¼ to ½ cup water and 1 teaspoon salt for a pint package of vegetables. Bring water to a boil, add vegetables and salt and cover tightly. When the vegetables begin to thaw, they may be broken apart with a fork. They must be watched carefully to avoid overcooking or boiling dry. Scalding and freezing vegetables tenderize them so they cook in about one-half to two-thirds the time required for fresh ones. The old fashioned method of cooking in a lot of water for a long time takes color, flavor, and food value from vegetables. They should be served immediately, and not allowed to stand. Left-over portions may be quickly frozen to be used later in soups or other dishes.

Greens, such as spinach, turnips, collards, etc., and also stalk vegetables as broccoli and asparagus, should be partially thawed before cooking. This prevents the overcooking of the outer leaves and the tender tops while the inside leaves and stalks are still frozen. Thaw about 4 hours in the refrigerator or one hour at room temperature.

Corn on the cob should be *completely* thawed before cooking. This will take about 6 hours in the refrigerator; 1½ to 2 hours at room temperature. Oven roasting is much better than boiling. Brush corn with butter, add salt, and roast 20 minutes at 400° F.

Cut corn may be pan fried, without first thawing, in butter in a skillet, then covered and simmered until tender. Or it may be heated in the top of a double boiler with no added water, or baked 30 minutes at 375° F.

Squash has better quality if cooked without water. Thaw, brush with butter, and bake until tender in a moderate oven. Or put frozen block in the top of a double boiler and heat. Season as desired with salt and pepper and butter or cream.

The time required to cook vegetables depends on their maturity. A timetable is only a guide; test vegetables with a fork during cooking for tenderness. Start timing when vegetables boil.

Oven cookery is good for some frozen vegetables. When baking other foods it is wise to cook them this way. Put the frozen or partly thawed vegetable in a buttered casserole. Season as desired. Add no water or just enough to prevent sticking. Cover tightly and bake in a moderate oven (350° to 375° F.) until tender.

Some approximate times for baking are:

Asparagus	30 minutes
Peas	14 minutes
Corn	30 minutes
Lima beans	45 minutes
Broccoli	35 minutes
Corn on the cob (thawed)	20 minutes

Regular standard recipes for preparing and cooking vegetables may be used for frozen vegetables. Salads, stews, and creamed dishes may be made from frozen vegetables.

Meat. There is no consistent difference, in losses of flavor or juiciness, between meat thawed before cooking and meat cooked while still frozen.

Use the method of preparation most suitable for the particular cut and kind of meat. Under usual conditions, freezing does not tenderize meat.

If the meat is to be thawed, leave it in the unopened container, or in one that will collect the drippings. To thaw: Leave at room temperature for 2 to 2½ hours. An electric fan may be used to speed up thawing. Or leave in the refrigerator, allowing about 5 hours per pound of meat. Thawing time will vary with weight and shape of the meat, thickness of wrapping, and room temperature. Do not thaw unwrapped meat in cold water.

Steaks and Chops. Thaw and cook according to directions for fresh meat, or cook without thawing. If you do not thaw the meat, allow it to cook slightly longer than you would fresh meat—about 8 minutes longer for 1-inch-thick pieces; 14 minutes longer for 1½-inch pieces.

Oven Roasts. Thaw and cook according to directions for fresh meat, or cook without thawing, or when partially thawed. If you do not thaw the meat, place it in the oven, which has been set for 275° to 300° F., with a meat thermometer. Insert the thermometer through a hole in the meat muscle so that the bulb is in the center of the roast but not against a bone. If the meat is frozen too hard to get the thermometer in, start the cooking and insert it after the roast thaws. Cook partially frozen meat about 10 minutes longer per pound than you would fresh meat. Cook completely frozen meat 20 to 25 minutes longer per pound.

Less Tender Cuts. Cook by moist heat, according to the usual directions. Allow a slightly longer time for large pieces of unthawed meat.

Poultry. Thaw fryers, broilers, or roasters in the refrigerator or at room temperature. Fricassee birds need not be thawed. Place them directly into the liquid in which they are to be cooked.

Cook all poultry according to directions for fresh birds.

Fruits. Most frozen fruits are served when they are still slightly icy, as fruit cup, fruit cocktail, or dessert.

For pies, cobblers, tarts or muffins, thaw only enough to spread.

FREEZING COOKED AND PRE-PREPARED FOODS

The field for freezing pre-cooked or prepared foods is wide open and the possibilities unlimited. With a few exceptions, almost any cooked food may be frozen, provided it is prepared and packaged properly. However, some freeze better than others and some recipes are more adaptable to freezing than others.

Much time and work can be saved by careful planning and preparation for a supply of frozen food for emergencies or special occasions. More food may be prepared than is needed for a meal and the surplus frozen. Often left-overs can be saved by freezing and then combining with fresh foods or with other frozen foods, thus eliminating needless waste. Baked beans, roasted meats, chop suey, soup, meat loaf and beef stew freeze well, as do homemade bread, rolls, pies, cakes, cookies and many other such foods.

The important thing to remember is that a good product must be prepared, handled, and frozen properly if a good product is to come out of the freezer. Freezing as a rule does not improve cooked food. Therefore, only top notch foods should be frozen, and only recommended moisture-vapor proof packaging materials should be used. Packaging materials generally are the same as for uncooked food— plastic, glass, celophane wraps, and ordinary locker paper make excellent packaging material. Special containers for pies or other baked products are available also. However, these must be properly wrapped before going into the freezer.

Breads, Rolls, Etc.

Any standard recipe for breads may be used for freezing. When yeast bread and rolls in the dough stage are to go into the freezer, it is well to increase 1/3 to ½ the amount of sugar except for ice box rolls which already have the extra sugar included in the recipe.

Yeast breads may be frozen in the dough stage or may be baked and then frozen. Freezing the baked product is usually more satisfactory. Baked frozen rolls may be kept longer than unbaked dough. Below are given recipes that have been used and tried out by the Extension Food Conservation Specialist at Winthrop College:

1 cup milk	1 tablespoon fat, melted
4 tablespoons sugar	1 teaspoon salt
1 package dry granulated yeast	soft wheat plain flour

Heat sugar and milk in double boiler to lukewarm temperature. Add yeast and let stand until yeast dissolves. Add 2 cups sifted flour, mix well, then add salt and fat. Then add enough flour to make a very soft dough. Knead very lightly, grease well, let rise until double in size. Work down lightly, shape into one loaf or make into rolls, grease well. If dough is to be frozen, place in proper package, wrap well and freeze immediately before bread is allowed to rise. When ready to bake, place in warm place and let rise until double in size.

If dough is to be baked, let rise until double in size. Bake in hot oven 375°-400°. Remove from pan, let cool thoroughly, then package and freeze.

The above recipe is a standard basic dough. It can be varied as follows:

For cheese rolls, add 1 cup grated sharp cheese to dough with the fat.

Whole wheat flour may be substituted ½ or full amount for whole wheat rolls.

The plain dough may be shaped into pinwheels, cinnamon buns, pecan rolls, date rolls, and any other plain or fancy roll.

If the dough is frozen, it should not be kept longer than two to three weeks. Baked bread may be kept from six to eight weeks.

Biscuit are more satisfactory frozen after baking. Mix and bake as usual; they must be thoroughly cold before wrapping.

Cake

Butter cakes may be frozen in the dough stage or after they are baked. Dough, when kept too long, often develops a bitter taste from the leavening and the shortening becomes rancid. Dough may be frozen in bulk or poured into individual paper forms for cup cakes or frozen in the cake pan in which it is to be baked.

Angel food cakes freeze well, as do sponge, devil food, and regular butter cakes.

Butter and uncooked icings freeze well. Boiled icings, or seven-minute icing freeze if cooked long enough for the mixture to become firm and not remain syrupy—in this case, a minimum amount of syrup should be used. Cream or custard-like fillings made with starch or flour thickening do not freeze well.

All cakes should be thoroughly cold before wrapping. Cakes with icing may be quickly frozen before wrapping. This prevents the icing from sticking to the wrapping. Cakes will keep well frozen from four to six months.

Below are recipes for cakes that have been tested by the staff members of the State Home Demonstration Dpartment, and have been found most satisfactory for freezing: :

Snow Cake (Two Nine-inch Layers)

1 cup butter	3 teaspoons baking powder
2 cups sugar	1 cup milk
3 cups sifted flour	1 teaspoon vanilla or other
½ teaspoon salt	flavoring extract

6 egg whites

Cream the butter thoroughly. Add sugar a little at a time and beat until well mixed and fluffy. Sift flour once before measuring, then resift three or four times with salt and baking powder. Add milk and flour alternately. Add flavoring. Fold in the stiffly beaten egg whites to which ½ cup of the sugar has been added and mix lightly until well blended. Pour the batter into two greased, wax paper lined 9-inch cake pans. Bake 35 minutes in a moderate oven, 350 degrees. Let layers stand in pans for five minutes on a cake rack, then turn out to cool.

Other Cakes and Cookies Recommended for Freezing

1-2-3-4 Cake—Page 326.

Chocolate Roll—Page 361.

Ice Box Cookies—Page 370.

Freeze the uncooked dough and bake when desired. Let dough thaw in refrigerator till it can be cut easily.

Chocolate Pinwheels—Page 371.

Proceed as for Ice Box Cookies.

Seven-Minute Icing

1½ cups sugar	2 egg whites
2 tablespoons light corn syrup	5 tablespoons water

¼ teaspoon vanilla

Put all ingredients except vanilla in top part of double boiler over boiling water. Stir mixture until the sugar is dissolved. Then beat with a rotary or electric beater. Remove from heat, add vanilla and spread on cake.

Chocolate Icing

3 cups sugar	1¼ cups milk
¾ cup cocoa	¼ cup butter
½ teaspoon salt	½ teaspoon vanilla

1 tablespoon Karo syrup

Mix sugar, salt and cocoa together thoroughly. Add milk and syrup and cook to a soft ball stage (232° F.). Remove from the fire and add butter and flavoring and let stand until almost cold. Beat and spread on cake.

Pound Cake

1 pound butter	1 pound sifted flour
1 pound sugar	4 tablespoons sherry or brandy
9 large eggs	2 tablespoons rose water

Cream butter, add sugar gradually and beat until sugar and butter are well mixed, an electric beater does this well. Add eggs unbeaten one at a time. Beat well after each egg, add sifted flour gradually, folding in well, then add flavoring. Line cake pan with brown paper, bake at 300°. After cake is thoroughly cooled, wrap and freeze (best not frosted).

Fruit cake may be made by adding fruit, nuts, etc., to this batter.

Pies

In certain sections of the country where the weather permits, the freezing of pies is an old practice. Housewives made up large batches and left the freezing to natural processes. Today, even in the South, with our modern freezing equipment, we do not have to depend on the fickleness of the weather for the success or failure of our frozen pies.

Most fruit pies freeze well. They may be baked and frozen, or prepared ready for baking before freezing. Pies that are frozen unbaked generally have a flakier, more tender crust, and a fresher flavor than those baked before freezing. When pies are baked and then frozen, they should be thawed and warmed in the oven.

Custard pies do not freeze well, either before or after baking. Meringue on cream pies often shrinks and becomes tough.

Pastry

3 cups pastry flour	¾ to 1 cup hydrogenated fat
1 to 1½ teaspoons salt	or lard
6 to 8 tablespoons water	

Sift the flour and the salt together. Cut in the fat. Add the water by tablespoonfuls; use only enough to hold the mixture together. Divide the crust in quarters. Roll one quarter for the bottom crust of a pie and fit it into a pie pan. Roll the second quarter for the top crust. Fill the pie shell with the filling, moisten the edges of pastry with cold water, put on the top crust, and seal the edges well. Do not cut vent holes. Package and freeze the pie.

The other two quarters of the dough will make another pie.

Peach Pie

pastry
3 cups sliced peaches
¾ cup sugar

1½ tablespoons cornstarch
2 to 4 tablespoons lemon juice
1½ tablespoons butter

Line the pie pan with pastry, have the top crust rolled out. Mix the sugar and the cornstarch. Scald the peaches about a minute, then remove to cold water and slip off the skins. Slice the peaches, and as each cupful is sliced, put it in the pie pan and sprinkle with some of the lemon juice. Sprinkle the peaches with sugar and cornstarch, and dot with butter. Cover the peaches with top crust and seal the edges well. Package and freeze the pie.   Yield: One 8-inch pie.

Apple Pie

3 cups thinly sliced apples
  (6 or 7 apples)
1½ tablespoons flour

2/3 to 1 cup sugar
1½ tablespoons butter

Steam apples for 2 minutes, cool them quickly, and put them in a pie shell. Sprinkle them with sugar and flour and dot them with butter. Cover the filling with top crust and seal the edges well. Package and freeze the pie.

SANDWICHES

Sandwiches may be frozen in advance in quantity and kept for school lunches, snacks or parties. Most sandwiches, especially those with fillings of cheese of all kinds, sliced or ground meat and poultry, fish and cooked egg yolk, freeze well. Those that do not freeze well are sandwiches containing raw vegetables, egg whites or jelly sandwiches. Also, if mayonnaise is used, use it sparingly, as mayonnaise does not freeze well. Butter as a spread is much more satisfactory.

Minced Meat Spread

Grind left-over cooked meat (smoked ham, roast chicken, beef, lamb, or pork) and add just enough mayonnaise to spread. Chopped pickle, stuffed olives, pimento, or relish may be added for seasoning.

Peanut Butter Spread

Add enough honey or marmalade to peanut butter so that it spreads easily.

Dried Beef and Cheese Spread

Chop or grind about 6 slices of dried beef and combine them with a 3-ounce package of cream cheese, 1 teaspoon grated horseradish, and a few grains of pepper.

Ham Salad Spread

3 cups ground cooked ham   1 cup pickle relish
½ cup salad dressing   2 teaspoons horseradish

Combine all the ingredients, mix them well, and chill.   Yield: 3½ cupfuls of filling for about 15 sandwiches.

Other Suggestions

Place a slice of processed American cheese on rye bread, spread with butter.

Place sliced Swiss cheese on rye bread, spread it with a mixture of mustard and butter.

Mix cream cheese with:

1. chopped nuts
2. honey and grated orange rind (1 tablespoonful each to a 3-ounce package of cream cheese)
3. finely chopped cooked chicken or ham
4. candied ginger, chopped
5. chopped olives with or without nuts

OTHER FROZEN FOODS

Below are given a few recipes for other types of food. All these recipes have been tested and frozen by the Food Conservation Specialist in the Home Demonstration Office at Winthrop College.

Frozen Fruit Salad

2 cakes Philadelphia cream   1 can crushed pineapple
  cheese   1 can fruit cocktail
            ¾ cup salad dressing (not mayonnaise)

Blend dressing with cream cheese, add fruits, freeze. To serve, cut in desired size pieces and place on lettuce leaf. No dressing is necessary. This should not be kept more than 4 weeks.

Chocolate Bread Pudding

4 cups toasted bread crumbs   1¼ cups sugar
3 cups milk   4 eggs
½ cup cocoa   ¼ cup butter
1 teaspoon vanilla

Soak bread in milk, mix sugar and cocoa, add to bread crumbs. Beat eggs well, add to above mixture. Add melted butter, and vanilla. Bake 1 hour or longer in very slow oven, 275°, until set. Serve hot with butterscotch hard sauce. This pudding may be baked and frozen or frozen in the raw stage. If frozen raw, it should be frozen in a container that can be placed in oven and used for baking. The hard sauce should be made fresh. It does not freeze too well.

Butterscotch Hard Sauce for Chocolate Pudding

Cream ½ cup butter in electric mixer if possible, add gradually 1 pound light brown sugar, 2 tablespoons cream or canned milk and 2 tablespoons vanilla. Beat until fluffy.

Ginger Muffins

1¼ cups sugar   1 cup Crisco
1 cup molasses   2 teaspoons soda
1 cup buttermilk   2 teaspoons ginger
4 cups flour   ¼ teaspoon cinnamon
1 teaspoon salt   ¼ teaspoon allspice
4 eggs

Cream fat and sugar, add eggs one at a time and beat. Add molasses and beat well. Add flour sifted with spices and soda and buttermilk alternately.

This is an exceptionally good recipe for freezing. The dough may be poured into paper baking cups, frozen and baked in cups, or it may be frozen in bulk and then thawed before it is poured into cups or baking sheet. Dough will keep 6 months.

Waffles

3 eggs	2 cups sweet milk
1 tablespoon sugar	3 to 3½ cups plain flour
1 teaspoon salt	¾ cup vegetable oil

6 teaspoons baking powder

Beat eggs, add sugar and salt, then flour and milk alternately. Add vegetable oil but do not mix in batter, leave to form a coat on top. Freeze. When ready to use, let thaw, add baking powder and mix in fat.

Ice Cream Snow Balls

Shape hard-frozen ice cream into balls, roll in freshly grated coconut. Place in freezing unit or freezer box. Serve with chocolate or strawberry sauce.

INDEX